Margaret Callahan

Mother Of Northwest Art

Brian T. Callahan

 **Trafford** PUBLISHING® **www.trafford.com**

North America & international
toll-free: 1 888 232 4444 (USA & Canada)
phone: 250 383 6864 ♦ fax:812 355 4082

For Ben, Rob, Jackie, Griffin, and
Jade Mikell who has inherited her great-grandfather's compulsion
to draw and her great-grandmother's love of the written word.

Preface

SOMETIME AFTER MY FATHER, Kenneth, died in 1986, my stepmother gave me several cardboard boxes with red lids. Inside each one was a jumble of notebooks, yellowed newspaper articles, unfinished manuscripts, and an enormous quantity of typed and handwritten daily journal entries: my mother's life story on paper. After a cursory examination of the contents, I stored the boxes in a safe place and resolved to go through them when time allowed. Our ranching life in northern British Columbia, Canada was a demanding one, and somehow the boxes rested undisturbed for several years. Another reason for my procrastination was a reluctance to revisit the time of Margaret's fatal illness in 1961.

Eventually, my wife and I semi-retired to a small island off the east coast of Vancouver Island, and one blustery winter morning in 2003, with some trepidation, I opened the first box and began an amazing journey. This book is the result.

Margaret Bundy's statistical biography is notable, if not exceptional. Born in Everett, Washington on January 24, 1904, she was the first of two children of Mabel and Edward Bundy, he a self-educated attorney and she with a degree in medicine from Northwestern University. Margaret lived all of her young life and most of her adult years in the Seattle area. After attending Greenwood Elementary School and Lincoln High School, she majored in journalism at the University of Washington, graduating with honors in 1924 at the age of 20. She worked as a 'sob sister' for the daily *Seattle Star*, writing human interest articles and exposés before landing a job with an arts and literary

v

weekly called *The Town Crier*. She worked first as a reporter and later became an editor. It was while on an assignment to cover the 1929 Northwest Annual art exhibit that she met Kenneth Callahan. They eloped in 1930, and she continued to write professionally and in her journals until her too-early death from cancer at 57.

What makes my mother's story exceptional was her ability and compulsion to record in detail and with sensitivity and humor the places she went, the people she encountered and her passion for nature, books, and ideas. Whereas my father was almost always in possession of a sketchbook and was constantly recording his visual impressions, Margaret was seldom without a notebook or her old Underwood portable typewriter.

When I lifted the lid of the first box, on top of the pile was a small blue spiral notepad. Inside and written in Margaret's typical, nearly unreadable scrawl was the following: "What do I really want to write? I don't want to just spin stories, but rather to set forth with depth and honesty the life of one human being in the round with all her experiences, associations, developments, etc. What am I afraid of? I don't know, but I am afraid to start in the same way I used to get stage fright as a child when I had to 'speak a piece'."

I spent much of 2003 and 2004 reading, deciphering, transcribing and chronologically arranging the contents of the boxes. It soon became evident that there was enough material to produce, almost entirely in her own words, a coherent account of the life of the woman Bill Cumming called his sensei and Mark Tobey described as the 'Mother' of the Northwest School of painters, a title with which she was not entirely comfortable.

In spite of her doubts, Margaret had unintentionally recorded her life story in her accumulated writings. I was struck by how contemporary were her observations on matters of the environment, urban living, politics, and life values in general.

The problem of compiling a narrative combining journal entries, some recorded as they unfolded and others written years later, was daunting. Incorporating, where pertinent, partial chapters from unfinished manuscripts and non-fiction stories and articles added to the complexity. Even so, I hope this book succeeds in "setting forth with depth and honesty the life of one human being in the round." I do think Margaret would have approved of the effort. Perhaps in some way she even anticipated the book. She wrote the following short journal entry on June 29, 1959, just two years before her fatal illness: "With whom am I communicating? I'm sure I don't know, but I feel a connection somehow, somewhere." BTC

1

THE NAME 'ROBE RANCH' had lured me from the start.
'Robe Ranch 1 Mi.' said the sign, pointing north toward a narrow
opening in the thick trees that lined the road up the valley. You'd
never think, looking in that direction that there could be anything but
wilderness behind that veil of trees. Whatever Robe Ranch was, it was
not visible from the two-lane gravel road.

On a summer afternoon in 1938 on our way back to Seattle from
a day in the mountains, Kenneth and I turned into a shady tunnel in
the trees, which the sign told us would lead to Robe Ranch. It was a
fateful turn. The day had been long, the air hot and dry, and we were
tired. We had climbed for the first time the trail to Barlow Point, a
Forest Service lookout station on a rocky ridge among a sea of mountain
peaks at the head of the valley. There, over a cup of tea brewed from
his precious supply of water, the forest guard, Everett Barrett, whom
we had met at a campground one year earlier, had talked of his wife,
two sons and baby daughter, who he said, were living at Robe Ranch.
And would we take down a gallon of blueberries he had picked from
the nearby Mount Dickerman meadows? "She'll put them up for future
pies," he'd said. I was delighted to have a reason to visit the ranch, for
otherwise Kenneth with his rigid abhorrence of any encroachment that
might be interpreted as trespassing, would have refused to go. Indeed,
he had been doing just that ever since I had been intrigued by the sign.

I've always loved to peer into vacant houses, investigate abandoned farms, and explore roads, regardless of whether or not they might be private. But Kenneth made it plain from the start that all such sorties were my own affair; that he would wait on legal territory for my return in case I were lucky enough not to be shot.

We'd been looking in vain for a rental cabin in the mountains since our first visit to the Stillaguamish River Valley in the North Cascades. Contact with nature was one of the primary sources for Kenneth's paintings, and it had become as necessary to our physical and mental well being as food and drink. Daytime trips were difficult with the baby, and childcare was a problem. A place to stay would solve that dilemma. The idea was ridiculous in a way, for we owned a house in Seattle, which needed a great many things done to it, and we had very little money. The Depression was on, and while Kenneth had managed to keep his job at the Seattle Art Museum and had sold an occasional canvas we were definitely not in the summer home bracket. But, we rationalized, we wanted not so much a place to play as a place to live and think and work. Somewhere in all of this beautiful vast Washington state wilderness, we told ourselves, there must be some little old deserted house we could afford to rent by doing our own repairs.

We decided that this particular valley was for us. We knew it in a mysterious, indisputable way. It seemed as remote as Shangri La, yet it was only fifty miles from our front door in Seattle, and it was part of the Mt. Baker National Forest, with its many miles of trails reaching into the innermost recesses of this frontier land. I was full of hope as we drove the rusty, green Model-A roadster into the tree-lined tunnel The light filtered dimly through the thick hemlock, fir, and cedar trees, their ghostly brown trunks bristling with dead limbs that had given up for want of sun. The green branches spread thirty feet above us, creating an eerie light. Here and there on rotting old growth stumps logged many years before, little gardens of huckleberry, fern and baby hemlock grew, the brilliant green of their foliage seeming to float like seaweed above an ocean floor.

The road through the dark, little forest stretched for about a mile; then the increasing light told us we were approaching a clearing. Suddenly, the trees ended and the road continued beside a split cedar fence that enclosed a pasture, which lay on our right like a green pool at the base of a steep hillside. Abruptly, the road took us up the side of the hill until we emerged on a ledge a few feet from the back door of a cedar shake-covered house. The view from the ledge was pure enchantment. The Monte Cristo Range, some peaks with glaciers nestling in their pockets, formed a jagged chalice in the distance. Mt. Pilchuck to the south rose alone above broad, timbered flanks. The top two thousand feet of the mountain, devoid of timber, was composed of billows of gray-white granite rock that sheltered lingering snow patches. In contrast to the rocky fastnesses of Mt. Pilchuck, the forest-covered flanks of Green Mountain to the North formed a long, undulating ridge stretching easterly as far as the eye could see. Nothing was visible but wilderness, save for the pasture, house, and outbuildings of Robe Ranch. I could feel the magic clear into the marrow of my bones. Gazing up the valley Kenneth mused, "this is the way it has always looked," and I knew he had caught the same feeling. The air was intoxicating. Pungent wood smoke mingled with the late-blooming honeysuckle that clambered over the woodshed, and the red rambler rose that twined along the cedar fence and the near-by evergreens.

A woman in a gingham dress with a baby on one hip came out the back door and approached the gate, dodging a pair of patched overalls that flapped from the line across the path. Her greeting was reserved, not particularly friendly, but not unfriendly. She had the same quiet dignity and shy reserve that characterized the lookout man. I asked if she were Mrs. Barrett. She answered, "yes" somewhat hesitantly and her gray eyes searched our faces apprehensively, as though fearing we might be about to impart bad news. Her brown hair, combed straight back, was flecked with silver. I gave her the berries and told her of our meeting with her husband. She became more friendly, but the shyness continued, the shyness of a small woods creature which would like to be trusting but isn't sure how safe it would be. She asked us into the house, and we followed her through the back door and the small kitchen that was dominated by an enormous old cast-iron wood range. The living room, unlike most rural parlors, was light and roomy with two large corner windows overlooking the sweep of the valley and mountains. An arched red brick fireplace had been sealed off and a more efficient drum heater placed before it. An old-fashioned walnut organ replete with carvings and curlicues, an ancient wooden rocker with its supports wired together, an old office chair that twirled on a spindle and an oak

Morris chair, its cushions covered with worn brown leather, comprised the furnishings.

So abruptly did the land fall away on the slope where the house was built that the front room rested on a six-foot-high foundation. Looking out the window you had the feeling of being suspended in space. When I exclaimed over the beauty of the view, Mrs. Barrett smiled and said yes, she enjoyed the view a whole lot whenever she had time to sit down and look out. She shifted the heavy, round-eyed baby to her other arm and said she expected she'd miss it, all right, when they went to California next month. I asked if she knew of any cabin at Robe Ranch that might be for rent at present. She thought a moment and said there were two empty now, and that when they left for California the Lewises would be moving from their cabin into this house, which would leave another available. Holding my breath, I asked how much the rent was. "Now, you'd have to talk to old Mr. Robe about that," she said, "but I think the Lewises are paying two dollars a month for theirs, and I guess the others are the same. We pay four dollars a month here because the house is bigger and has running water inside. "When the pump works," she added wryly. "Just now it's broke down and the storage tank is empty."

"Where do you get your water when the pump breaks down?" Kenneth asked. "Carry it from the creek, down in those woods there," she replied, pointing to the dark trees beyond the pasture at the base of the hill. "Water for all that big washing?" I gasped. She nodded and smiled. "The boys help me, Herbert and John. They're down at the pond fishing now. As long as I let them stay and fish awhile they don't mind going for water." She glanced at a clock on the mantle below a .30-.30 rifle and a 12-gauge shotgun and said, "I'd have time before starting dinner to walk up the hill to where the vacant cabin is if you'd like to see it. Kind of a climb, though. It's clear to the top of the hill." By this time I could see that Kenneth was as excited as I was, but he started to say we'd better wait until another time. I interrupted, thanked Mrs. Barrett heartily, and said I'd dearly love to see the place if she really wouldn't mind.

Kenneth carried the chubby, passive baby, and we started off. We soon passed two cabins, one of logs with the bark still on them, the other covered with shakes. The first one, Mrs. Barrett said, was occupied by two men who'd been cutting pulp and were moving out

4

in a few days. The second one was rented by the Lewis family. "The Lewises are going to be real glad when we move out," Mrs. Barrett said. "They're crowded something awful in that small cabin. The three boys are all growing big, and Mrs. Lewis is a great big woman. It's a good thing Mr. Lewis is skinny. They don't hardly have room to breathe."

The climb was steep through bracken and logging slash, and we paused now and then to catch our breaths. At the top of the gravelly hill, where the land leveled off to a wide shelf, we struggled through a dense growth of bracken higher than our heads. We emerged into a small thicket of trees where stood what might have been a model for a Hansel and Gretel hut. It was made from shaggy, bark-covered logs and had a huge cobblestone fireplace, small, cross-paned windows, a Dutch door with upper and lower divisions hinged separately, and a narrow front porch perched on the very edge of a cliff like an eagle's aerie. "There're John and Herbert," Mrs. Barrett said, pointing to a glassy pool of water among the trees far below in the valley. "Still sittin' on the beaver dam fishing. My! Don't they look little, though. Where I come from in Arkansas they'd call this hill a mountain."

Broken glass and empty liquor bottles littered the floor of the cabin. Mrs. Barrett looked at the mess and shook her head. "A man and his wife lived here last spring--- used to drink quite a lot. They got to owing Mr. Robe so much money for rent and groceries he asked them for a payment. It made them sore, and they moved out, but before they left they broke up the place, just out of spite. I can't imagine people acting so mean." She added, as though the thought hurt her, "Mr. Robe's a nice old man, an awful nice old man."

On the way down the hill, Mrs. Barrett suggested that if we wouldn't mind the crowded state of the Lewis's cabin, we might as well take a look at that one, too. She was sure Mrs. Lewis wouldn't mind. "She always likes a chance to talk, especially to new folks," she said. As we scrambled up the steep little side path, the door of the cabin opened wide and a massive woman in men's overalls and work shirt, called in a rich Texan drawl, "come in, come in......that is if you kin git in. Hit's so terrible crowded, we're like to be drove crazy." The inside of the cabin was almost solid with objects, the only clear space being a passage about two feet wide from the side door to the front door, which opened onto a porch or balcony. This cabin, too, was perched on the steep hillside like a mussel on a piling. A partition shut off just enough of the back of the hut to hold a bed and cot. The main room contained a cook stove, heavy table, double bed, cupboards and a few straight wooden chairs. Empty jugs and jars were piled over every square inch of flat space, and the walls were entirely concealed beneath a jumble of beat-up clothes hung from nails.

Smells of old clothes, unwashed bodies, stale bedding, strong coffee, and day-old beef stew mingled. But from the high porch, hugged at one end by the sprawling tendrils of a lush hop vine, you looked out over the branches of a cherry tree to that far-reaching vista of valley and mountains, the forms blending into the early evening shadows. "It's a real nice little cabin," Mrs. Lewis said as we were leaving, "but as fur as I'm concerned hit's beginnin' to seem littler than nice. I just thenk sometimes I'll climb up in one of them trees out thar and roost for the night like the birds do. Hit's going to a real pleasure to git into a dwelling where a body can stretch out and yawn without fearin' to knock out a wall." As she talked she mauled the stew with a large wooden spoon. She used her big hands with an airy daintiness. Her bulk and stance made me think of a magnificent Percheron. She stood in the doorway smoothing back wisps of her straight brown hair with the back of her hand and bade us good-bye with hearty cordiality in a voice that stirred up an echo in the evening quiet.

I asked Mrs. Barrett how soon they planned to leave for California. She hesitated, as she frequently did before answering a question, as though she were not used to making direct statements. "Well, I think Everett will want to get started as soon as his government check comes through. Sometimes the Forest Service checks are slow. He'd ought to be getting laid off any day now. I know this much, we can't leave 'til his check comes because we wouldn't have enough money to buy a day's supply of gas." When we reached the car she said, "if you'd like, you could talk to Mr. Robe before you go. He might know something definite about when the men in the first cabin are leaving, and you could find out if he's promised the cabins to anybody else. I think he's over in his store now....well, it's really his house and his store both."

"Good idea," I agreed. "Where is his store?" "Why," she said, pointing, "it's right there, just beyond the woodshed." I looked where she pointed. The only apparent structure was a hut not much bigger than a large dog kennel. It was covered with mossy boards and had one small pane of glass set high on the side, about eye level for a tall man.

"That's the place," she said, adding apologetically, "it's not much of a store. He just sells a few supplies to the folks that cut pulp for him." Ignoring Kenneth's fidgeting, I approached the little shack and knocked on the battered door, and a deep, gruff voice said, "come in." The interior was semi-dark, the only light dim through the cob-webby, fly-specked pane of glass. A pot of something simmered on the stove. Shelves built from floor to ceiling held an array of canned goods. Gunny sacks full of potatoes, beans and other staples were stacked about the floor. In the light from the doorway, I saw a mouse scoot across the rumpled cot in the corner. From the bowels of a great leather-covered chair leaking horsehair stuffing from its ancient seams a tall, lanky man arose and looked at us in mild surprise. "Oh, I thought you was one of my tenants wanting some groceries," he said, shoving an old gray hat back from his forehead and puffing hard on his corncob pipe. His face and hands were grimy and so was the underwear protruding from the sleeves of his shirt and hugging his neck where the shirt opened in front. His hair stuck out from under the faded gray hat like hay from under a tarp.

He put down his magazine and removed his bifocals. He smiled and, growing accustomed to the dim light, I saw that his right eye was pulled badly out of shape by a long scar, but his left eye was alive and radiant. His nose was a mass of scars; the side of one nostril was red and sore looking. The smile and the clear light blue eye brimming with life queried us with a lively curiosity that came through the dirt and scars like sun through an autumn haze. I immediately sensed about the man an indefinable quality of goodness. "Oh, I dunno," he said in response to our questions. "Looks like there ought to be two or three empty cabins around here before long. I've just about finished cutting that twenty acres of pulp up there. I haven't got much more work for 'em. Guess it depends on whether the Turner brothers start logging over there on Canyon Creek. If that outfit gets going over there, the two fellers in the lower cabin may stay on. Oh, I dunno. I'd say if you called around about a month from now we ought to have a place for you. Thought I'd rent these two lower cabins for $25 a year and the one on top for $15. You could have that one any time, but there's no water up there except from a rain barrel. Of course, it isn't often you have empty rain barrel trouble around here. Started a well once, fellow went around with one of them forked stick water finders, swore up and down there was water here. I went around with him and that stick pointed right straight down, I swear I saw it with my own eyes. Said we'd strike water 25 feet down, but we dug eighty feet and not a sign of it. Pure gravel, not a drop of water....". He cleared his throat, spat ten feet out the door and was about to continue, but I seized the pause and said we'd be back in a short time, and please not to rent the first vacancy to anyone else because we wanted it. I said I loved the cabin at the top of the hill, but I thought the water problem might be too troublesome.

Kenneth had a way of inhaling in short rapid sniffs when he was thinking hard about something, so I wasn't surprised, as soon as we were underway, to hear him exclaim, "lord, that's really a beautiful place. Any of those cabins would be fine to have, but I think we ought to take one of the lower ones, as they have water ----- considering the baby and all. If it were just the two of us, it wouldn't matter. You know, we could spend week-ends up here all year around, and I might be able to get off long enough in the summer so we could have a month or six weeks. I could learn a lot about painting in a place like this!"

It was my turn to brag. "Now *see*, if you just let me follow my big nose once in awhile, what nice things I find for you? *Now* aren't you sorry you were nasty?" "That cabin the Lewises are in," he went on, ignoring the prod, "it wouldn't take long to make it pleasant, just a lot of soap and water and some paint...." "Clean oil cloth on the shelves," I added. "And we could burn some sulfur candles. I remember they used to do that when I was a kid in Montana...." I knew what he meant. I'd had the same dark suspicions. We'd moved many times during our eight years of marriage without encountering anything worse than houseflies, but still, you never knew.

The world had suddenly become a place with limitless possibilities. I had a vague, rather unsettling emotion, too; that we were turning the first pages of a fascinating, fateful book, a volume we would read and re-read and which would set the pattern of our lives. That strange web of causal encounters, their import unrecognizable at the time, in retrospect became a pattern accented with crucial moments or turning points like junctions on a map. Does each of us draw our own map or do we traverse an already prepared route like rats in a maze? Had we declined to take the two quarts of berries to Mrs. Barrett we might never have gone into Robe Ranch. How many times in life might we approach a side road or a turn-off with our initials on it but be going so fast or inattentively that we miss it?

As we bumped and joggled along on our way back to Seattle, Kenneth humming and deep in thought, I reflected on how the mountains had become such an integral part of our lives. What brought it all about in a convoluted way was a cold drink of clear water from the side of the Nisqually Glacier .

It was 1932, and we were in one of those charming small pueblos an hour's ride out of Mexico City. Dust blew from the cobbled streets into our smarting eyes and was gritty between our teeth. We hadn't had un-boiled water to drink for two months. We sat on the stone bench in the plaza, mesmerized by the noonday glare and chewed on the giant red bananas we had bought for lunch. The pulp was mealy, like potatoes, and when mixed with the yellow dust that swirled in frantic little eddies all about, stuck gluily in our dry throats. "What'll we get, beer or bottled water?" Kenneth asked. It was then, as the Mexican dust settled on me, that I remembered a pool of water at the foot of the Nisqually Glacier where, some five years before, I had knelt and drunk, siphoning crystalline water through pushed-out lips. A vision of sweetly moist Puget Sound mist floated before my burning eyes. "Gosh," I said, "imagine a spring of ice-cold water, pure as pure, coming right out of the rocks. You can drink out of it without even thinking about contamination. You can drink out of any stream you find, and you can't go five steps without coming to water, running water. Did I ever tell you about those college vacations on Mount Rainier?"

"I know an even better place," Kenneth answered. "It's a place in the Stillaguamish Valley of the North Cascades called Silverton, and one can get there on a crazy little gas car that runs on a narrow gauge railroad: narrow valley, rushing river, mountains straight up on all sides." "The air," I mused, still following my own trails, "out on the Nisqually Glacier has the strangest quality, sort of metallic perfume. Old ice has a smell. It's a peculiar clinging…" "There was a girl in one of my art classes," Kenneth interrupted, who had a summer place at Silverton. Her father was a musician. We used to hike around all day....seemed like all the trails went straight up."

"I went to the summit of Rainier once," I said, tacking back to my train of thought. "You just keep putting one foot ahead of the other....." and as Kenneth and I sat on the bench in far away Mexico, he sketching the local scene, my mind wandered back to that summer of 1924. The alpine meadows on the slopes of Mt. Rainier held enormous appeal during the summers of my college years. A rough road led to the lodge, which was built on Paradise Meadows in the national park. Knowing several of the summer workers and meeting the interesting visitors who were often about the place were additional attractions. By sleeping in a small tent away from the lodge and helping Jessie, the cook's assistant, in exchange for leftover lodge food, I was able to spend time there at little cost. Mary or Betty Bard, Claribel Colby or other college friends sometimes came, too. I loved everything about the mountains: the flowers, birds, and animals; views of the majestic snowy slopes above; and especially the meandering trails through the meadows near timberline. Visitors to the lodge were seldom adventuresome. A half-mile hike away from the lodge provided solitude even at the busiest times.

The idea of climbing to the top of the mountain was in equal parts fascinating and frightening. I knew I would one day make the trip, but until this time I had not gone beyond the imagining stage. At the end of the summer season of 1924, my friend Edie Porter had booked a climb with some of the summer employees we knew, but she was beginning to get cold feet, complaining that she was the only female climber. She decided I should come, too. Now I had an excuse to take the next step. So I got all the necessary gear from another acquaintance: woolen shirt, tin pants, slicker with a hood, caulked boots, and a walking stick. We started up to Camp Muir, the staging area for the next day's climb, in the hot afternoon sun and, after we ate dinner and watched a glorious sunset, tucked ourselves into sleeping bags and prepared for the 3:30 AM awakening. We all fairly fell out of bed at the witching hour, all exclaiming about how much we did or did not sleep and everyone shivering so that their teeth chattered. As we began to climb, a tiny slit of crescent moon hung in the sky among stars that had never seemed so brilliant.

My memories of the climb are of crevasses, giant boulders, ledges of melting snow, drops of thousands of feet, terrifying to look down into, legs I wasn't sure would carry me to the top but did. I watched Edie sink to her knees from fatigue at one point only to be helped to her feet and propelled to the top by two other climbers. A sense of serenity, of immense tranquility, pervaded me as I looked out into space from the top; looked down on everything surrounding us, on peaks that to persons below seemed lofty, but which to us were piles of rubble. All around us were giant boulders interspersed with countless crevasses.

I felt unutterably superior to the humans who were swarming the crowded habitats below, living stunted, prosaic lives, people who had never felt the exaltation of attaining the highest peak around. The thin air somehow invigorated us, and pretty soon even Edie, who had immediately gone to sleep, began to show signs of life. I contemplated pleasantly on what a huge share of all that nature had to offer was mine at that moment, the very purest air, the most astounding view, everything around us breathtakingly huge.

It's a queer thing, but nobody who went to the summit that day, except myself, ever wanted to talk about it during the trip. No one was enthusiastic or even commented on the scenery. Outside of a few remarks about feeling insignificant, I didn't hear anyone voice any opinion on our surroundings. But it made a huge impression on me, which has stayed with me to this day.

Interrupting my Mt. Rainier reverie, Kenneth said, "that kind of mountaineering doesn't interest me, the kind where you're killing yourself trying to make it to the top of something, or chopping steps in ice and packing a lot of ropes and axes and what not. I like to just go along a trail until I find a place where I want to sit down and draw or just stretch out against a mossy tree and have a smoke." Resisting an urge to defend my brief mountaineering career, I replied, "I know, and a big, fat lunch and a drink from a little brook which is running along over the rocks." I ran my tongue around my mouth, and it was like licking the chalk trough of a well-used blackboard. The Mexican beer tasted flat, but at least the table was in the shade. We sat for quite awhile, smoking our Mexican cigarettes, which smelled like a ripe old barnyard, and talked about what it was like in the Cascades. The image of cold glacier water prompted the following turn in our discussion .

"I don't know why we keep thinking we have to move to New York City," I exclaimed, for it had long been a thing in our lives we had accepted as inevitable, as soon as we could make the break. It was generally assumed, and often correctly, that the artist and the hometown were incompatible, one's life culminating only in frustration and defeat. "Not getting homesick, are you?" Kenneth muttered, manipulating his cigarette to one corner of his mouth. He was drawing hastily with a thick black charcoal pencil on a page of his dog-earred sketchbook the passing figures of a white, cotton-clad Indian and a loaded burro. *"Buenos dias,"* the Indian said in passing, smiling with his wide mouth and black, far-apart eyes from the shade created by his big straw hat. His small feet were as leathery as his donkey's hide and padded softly over the hot paving stones. "I wonder if he knows he loves his land, or if one always has to go away to find out what it means," I pondered.

"You know what I think we ought to do," Kenneth said after a moment, "is forget about moving to New York for awhile anyway and try to get enough money to buy some kind of an old Ford. There are all kinds of wonderful places we could get to, right around Seattle." I thought about how fast our money was dwindling and wondered. We had received a windfall of $500 from picture sales, which, combined with the $300 I had saved from my salary on the weekly *Town Crier* newspaper, had made our Mexican trip possible. Kenneth had become very interested in mural painting, and we had wanted to see the walls done by the Mexican group under the leadership of Rivera and Orozco. We had our $25-a-month flat, which we had sublet, awaiting our return, and also I had my job. Less concrete, but also reassuring, were the murals Kenneth could hardly wait to start painting. He didn't know where he'd do them or for whom, but his imagination was fired with them. Discovery of our mutual nostalgia for the Northwest made our Mexican summer all the richer, for we didn't have to be sad about its wonders coming to an end.

2

WE DROVE HOME IN a euphoric state and creaked to a stop on the hill in front of our house in Seattle. I looked for the babysitter, Katie, to open the door as she always did to greet us, but the door remained closed. The house was dark. I hurried into the front hall; still no Katie. There were two large puddles on the hall floor. Tobey came toddling from the kitchen shouting "hi, Baga, hi, Kensus!" He added "widey-widey-waaa!" which covered anything in the way of exciting reportage. "Darling, are you all right? Where is Katie?" We found her asleep on the couch. I shook her and she muttered thickly. "Kenneth!" I exclaimed. "She's drunk, passed out."

Kenneth shook her and shouted to her and finally she sat up, bleary-eyed and flushed. "Oh, I'm terrible sorry," she said with a burp. "I got a little sleepy, I guess." She looked about wildly. "Where's Tobey for the lova God? Oh, goodness-gracious-me. Thank heaven he's all right. I don't know what happened to me, Marrgarret," she wailed. "I'll get Tobey to bed and Kenneth will take you home," I returned. "We can talk about what happened later."

Tobey gobbled his dinner and was asleep before Kenneth returned. He had apparently enjoyed his interlude, for there were no tear streaks in the dirt on his face. I found three puddles on the floor, which meant he had been untended for at least four hours. The door to the basement was open. I shuddered, thinking of that steep stairway and the concrete floor below. The world of magic gave way to a depressing sense of guilt

I couldn't shake off the flood of conjectures about what might have happened. "Don't forget to be thankful we got off so lucky," Kenneth said, "and that we may soon have a place we can stay overnight so we can always take him with us."

November was beating its brains out; wind and rain howled and ranted and threw themselves about the city streets like a legion of furies loosed from hell. It was Monday evening and Kenneth was at the museum sketch class, which he conducted once a week, arranging for a model, posing her, calling the rest periods, and collecting the fees (only enough to pay the model). He would come home with numerous drawings---sometimes in delicate thin ink lines, sometimes in heavy lithograph or charcoal, sometimes full figures, sometimes just feet or hands or head and shoulders or torsos.

Before Tobey came along, I had attended a few of the classes, mainly because I didn't want to stay home alone, and had learned to really see the beauty of certain little lines bodies have---the joining of the neck and shoulder, the wonderful under-arm concavity, the curve of a breast, the subtle planes at the base of the spine, the strong straight line behind the knee.

Drawing is something people and artists are often confused about. "I couldn't draw a straight line," people are fond of saying in a rather self-congratulatory tone. It's the same way amateurs in the kitchen say "I couldn't boil water without burning it." I watched the artists in the class and marveled at how many would look closely at the model, measuring on their brushes and squinting quite professionally, and then do the same characterless nude they had been doing since the class began, or the same wooden charcoal drawing or tight little oil.

Other artists sneer at the whole idea of drawing from life as archaic and entirely unrelated to the doings of the "*avant garde.*" These artists could draw a straight line and did so and felt their work to be superior because the lines weren't put together to resemble anything except lines and the colors didn't resemble anything except colors. I wonder why more artists don't want to draw from nature's marvels of construction and form and then use the skill they develop, not as a virtuoso accomplishment, but to create a unique thing out of themselves. This is the long, hard way, of course. Short cuts are tempting, but too often lead to dead ends.

From the kitchen came the raucous ticking of our cheap alarm clock, and from the rug before the fireplace arose our wire-haired terrier Mike's rumbling inhalations. Wind and rain without, rhythmic sounds from within, and the fire dying to coals. I was rereading D.H. Lawrence's *Lost Girl*, impressed anew by the insight he had into character and the way he caught people's manners of speech. The Alps, as Lawrence wrote of them, have somewhat the mood of our beautiful Cascades, which we had not seen since that Indian summer day. Life had simply bogged us down again. We'd had colds and the Ford had been laid up and the budget crippled. I had written a note urging Mr. Robe to let us know when a vacancy occurred, but had not had a reply.

I had just returned to my book after checking Tobey when the phone rang. There was a pregnant pause after I said hello, and I thought I heard labored breathing. Then, "Is that you, Marragrret?" I sensed trouble. "Well then, I tell you Marrgarret," the voice went on, obviously under strain. "Would Kenneth be able to come down here to the police station right away? I'll explain all about it when I see you, Marragarret."

Since the day we found her drunk on the couch, Katie had become a major problem in our lives. I felt her tragedy keenly, as the picture became clearer. I found, upon talking to her husband, Maxie, she had been drinking heavily for years. He had hoped the experience with us would give her sufficient reason to stop, and indeed it seemed to have worked out that way, but of late she had begun again.

"She's worried about her health," I had told him. "Don't you think it would help her to see a good doctor?" He responded at length, "I told her if she stops drinkin' long enough, I'll let her go to a doctor. The whole thing is, she worries too much, worries about the kids, worries about me not getting enough work, worries about everything. After all, we ain't so bad off, Mrs. Callahan. Our kids is good kids, stays home, helps around the house. Our rent is low, and we get enough to eat. Things will pick up pretty soon. Jobs in my line are already beginning to show up, because people are going back to work in the factories.

Soon as we get caught up on our debts we'll think about having our roof fixed." I don't worry about things----hell, what's the use?"

"Kenneth's not home, he's working tonight, Katie. Besides, I think it would be wrong to keep this from your husband. I think you'd better call him. He'll have to know sooner or later." I felt terribly guilty. I knew I should fly to her rescue, but I feared entering a dark forest of predictable disasters. "Oh, so that's the way it is, Marrgarret," said the injured voice, and the phone clicked.

Kenneth looked so tired when he came home, I hesitated to tell him, but I knew I must. He called the police station reluctantly, saying he didn't know what good it would do or what help we could be. Bail had been arranged, they said, and Mrs. Koslowski had left. "There are a lot of things in life that don't seem to make sense," Kenneth said when I expressed my bitterness, "but you have to keep on believing."

"You think you had an evening," he said when we'd got to bed. "I certainly had a situation. This model---I've always felt sort of sorry for her anyway---she's that heavy, sort of homely one with the beautiful big breasts and the luminous skin. Well, I guess I must have posed her in a sort of a strained position because she broke wind---not quietly and inconspicuously, and not once, but in rapid succession. There was the most awful frozen moment. Every hand stopped moving, the sound of every pencil stopped dead. I didn't know what to do, whether to call a rest or pretend to ignore it or what. The poor girl started to blush and kept getting redder from her feet to her head. I could have died for her. And then to make it even worse she came up to me after the class and apologized. God, I didn't know what to say, and we were both blushing---oh, it was awful." "What *did* you say," I asked, appalled. "I said not to feel badly, that she showed signs of becoming a critic," he said. "The trouble is, she didn't laugh."

Six months later we were to read in the evening paper of the death in a cell of the city jail of a middle-aged Seattle mother, Mrs. Katherine Koslowski, who had been arrested on a charge of drunkenness and disorderly conduct. A childhood of poverty in Belfast, hired out as a domestic when she was old enough to scrub a floor, shipped out to Canada as a bonded servant at sixteen. She met Maxie and moved to Seattle. Then there was more hard work and poverty, the undying twinkle of merriment in the blue eyes, the rough and reddened hands, the clean, starched aprons, the countless washings hung on the line when "there ain't no dryin' though, Marrgarret." And there were her pitiful moments of cheer in the dreary murk of a neighborhood tavern and the effort to try again.

3

IN MAY OF 1932, Kenneth and I booked passage from San Francisco to Acapulco on a rusty old freighter called the Charcas. We boarded the ship after a few days visiting old friends in San Francisco. I found that city to be breathtakingly beautiful. From the moment we started hiking those gold and brown hills outside the Golden Gate I experienced a delight that didn't let down all the time we were there. I saw Edie, my college chum, and met Jack Finn, Kenneth's friend who had traveled with him to San Francisco in the mid-1920s. He liked it so well he stayed. Jack turned out to be even more of a darling than I suspected from hearing Kenneth talk.

Our friends Tom and Frances Toomey joined us at the dock. Unfortunately, it soon became apparent that a friendship based on occasional social contacts can wear thin with too much familiarity. An urbane wit, while amusing in small doses, can become a disagreeable whine in larger portions and Frances began to annoy me soon after we sailed. Their constant complaining detracted from the adventure of the voyage.

Adding to the tension was the discovery that the ultimate destination of the ship was South America and the delivery of her cargo of dynamite and gasoline. So other than becoming accustomed to cockroaches and the fear of fire and explosion, highlights of the trip were sightings of sharks, devilfish, and flying fish glowing with phosphorous at night, plus getting to know some of the crew.

But Manzanillo was an unforgettable experience that nothing could spoil. We got there late in the afternoon. I was trying to sleep

18

in the stateroom with the ceiling fan going, but the heat kept me awake. Kenneth came in to tell me we were getting close, and I looked out the porthole. The sight of the red rock slopes, banana plantations and little houses on the hill had me out on the deck in a few moments. This was my first glimpse of another civilization.

The Charcas dropped anchor noisily and Mexican authorities soon came aboard. Kenneth and I and Cadet Seaman Davis went ashore that night by small boat. I bought sandals in the cute, crowded and smelly market place for two and a half pesos. We stopped at a cervezaria for beer and I danced with Davis and the homesick engineer from the Charcas. The latter was a swell dancer and I had fun. A young Mexican cranked the phonograph but didn't have much to choose from except "Ramona". The engineer and I danced many times but I could see Kenneth getting annoyed so I stopped. I don't know why I like to dance so much. I guess it's a disease.

On Sunday Kenneth, Davis and I walked up the hill through town. We passed endless open yards with pigs, chickens, etc. underfoot. From the top we looked down at the crazy composition of the village below. On the way down we joined the First Mate who was drinking with some Mexican pals. As we pulled up chairs an obliging waiter stomped, with bare feet, a giant cockroach right before my eyes. What a squash that was!

After two days we sailed to Acapulco. It appeared a little bigger than Manzanillo and not as interesting, although the enclosed harbor is unique. The trip on the *turismo* bus from Acapulco was a strenuous one. We bounced and rattled along from eleven A.M. until midnight. From coastal valleys with temperatures of 120 degrees, we climbed to over 10,000 feet with snow on the ground between Cuernavaca and Mexico City (called just Mexico). The hot stuffy bus in the low lands became an icebox in the mountains.

We were two cold, exhausted travelers when we finally arrived in the city. We were also ravenous having eaten very little since breakfast. The bus had stopped once at a town called Chilpancinqo but we had been warned to avoid fresh fruit and vegetables on the road and the cooked food didn't look too good. Shortly after midnight we coaxed our long-since-paralyzed legs into activity and crawled out of the bus in front of the Hotel Tacuba. Baggage was unstrapped from the roof of the small bus and carried into a dimly lit lobby. With our faces frozen by masks of dust we sat on uncomfortably stiff chairs breathing the thin air and waiting for a receptionist as the bus drove off into the night.

Then from a door at the rear of the lobby, an eerie figure with hollow black eyes came flitting forward like a character in a bad horror film. His faded black cape swung back and forth as he led the way upstairs. We learned that the bath was at the other end of an interior courtyard but the water was shut off at nine p.m. as it was in most of the city. After showing us to our room, the man in the black cape gave us directions to the Tacuba restaurant, which was open at that hour. The thought of bacon and eggs and coffee was overwhelming. We ordered number 28, *huevos fritos con tocino* (fried eggs with bacon) but the black-eyed waitress with spit curls misunderstood. She brought number 26, a mixture of pickled pork, green olives, peppers and various unknowns. Rather than wait another half-hour we dabbed at number 26 and went to bed hungry.

In spite of the shaky start, Mexico soon captured our hearts. We became used to the elevation and bright sunlight. The food began to taste good and we adjusted our eating schedule to dinner at two p.m. and supper no earlier than eight p.m. Once we could walk around without getting heart flutters from the altitude we discovered that Mexico holds an unlimited store of delights. In the first letter we received from my parents, they asked if we had been able to get out into the real Indian towns. We certainly did, almost every day. All the pueblos in the valley surrounding the city are as primitive as though there was no such thing as Mexico City nearby. Even in the city, the Indians live in their original state. We went to a few places out of the valley. The country you go through on the way to Michaocan is untouched by modern culture. Farmers plowed with oxen and hand-carved wooden plows. A toilet was wherever the urge was felt. One sight that never failed to amaze me was to see the Indians squatting in broad daylight, even in the city.

We went to the museum a couple of times. The newly excavated Monte Alban artifacts, Aztec carvings such as the huge stone calendar, and the Mayan objects from the Yucatan were all impressive. The Aztec items were the most interesting. They are very Egyptian looking. I wondered if there was an influence or if it was just coincidence. At Chapingo in the agricultural college there are some murals by Diego

Rivera. These are the finest things we've seen of his; very beautiful and deserving of being called great art.

One of the most interesting places we went was a wonderful walk down a dirt road and then off on a narrow trail between farmers' fields. It was very rural and pastoral. Mexicans passed us carrying water cans and leading loaded burros. Chickens strayed everywhere. Crickets chirped and the air smelled of pepper trees which were shading the road. Beautiful brown hills rose close by. We rested at a small white church on a hill, enjoying the shade and a cool breeze. Kenneth sketched and I just sat and enjoyed a fine view of the valley below.

Later we returned to the village and visited a state sponsored art school operated by a Japanese-Mexican named Kitigawa. He is a very intelligent guy, a painter-teacher who coaxed excellent work from his students. We talked a long time and he gave us the low-down on the art scene here. He was open, not so reticent as the other artists we'd met. He suggested we return the next day to do some more hiking with one of his students named Pena and receive some wood block prints he generously offered us.

We had quite an adventure while walking into the hills with Pena. As we approached a tiny village along a dusty trail, two horsemen appeared from a small wood and stood in our way. One looked for all the world like Pancho Villa with a huge sombrero, grand mustachio, and crossed bandilleros. A rifle was slung over his shoulder. His saddle and bridle gleamed with silver. The manner of the two bordered on threatening as they asked where we were going and why. When Pena told them Kenneth was an artist who was going into the hills to paint and see Mexican village art, the leader's demeanor totally changed, and he smiled a huge smile and nodded with many *muy biens*. Kenneth in a fit of relief heaped praise on the Indian's horse, his *caballo bonita*. To our surprise, the fellow quickly dismounted and gestured for Kenneth to have a ride. The short Mexican horseman tried to hand Kenneth the reins. At first Kenneth attempted to reject the offer, but Pena muttered that it would be better form to accept and take a short ride. I held my breath as Kenneth climbed aboard. As far as I knew, he hadn't ridden since childhood, but he looked O.K. in the saddle. Bandito laughed heartily, and saying *arriba* he whacked the horse on the rump.

Kenneth trotted up to a bend in the road, turned around and trotted back, much to the amusement and delight of our new friends.

Pena told us later that they were indeed bandits and probably intended to rob us or worse. But even the bandits of Mexico have great respect for artists, as they do for teachers and priests. They also realize how poor most artists are, so decided to treat us as amigos instead of targets. But I must admit, I spent the rest of the day looking over my shoulder in case they changed their minds.

We met a swell Mexican couple at a friend's house party soon after we arrived in Mexico. Francis Toor, who was working on a tour book, called <u>Francis Toor's Guide to Mexico</u>, invited us and the Toomeys, a young musician named Soliz, Rufino Tamayo, a serious painter, his lovely wife Maria Izquierda, and others. Soliz played the guitar and sang Mexican folk songs. Tamayo played *St. Louis Blues* on the piano. There was dancing and good Mexican food.

Not long after that evening we went to Tamayo's newly decorated studio. Maria was gorgeous in a white evening dress with her hair Indian fashion twined with colored cloth. *Muy bonita*! The cocktails were good and there was dancing *con mucho gusto*! We became good friends with Tamayo and Maria. Subsequently, they spent a lot of time showing us the sights of Mexico.

A trip to the Pyramid of the Sun was a memorable one for more than one reason. We went by touring car with Tamayo and Maria. The pyramid was incredibly impressive, as was the temple of Quetzlcotyl. The steep climb to the top was worth the sweat. On the trip back early in the evening as we entered a large village, we noticed considerable numbers of people, brightly dressed, walking in the same direction as our car was going. The driver began honking to clear the way. We told him to just go slowly while we enjoyed the sights. Riding in the back with Kenneth and Tamayo, I noticed an unusual amount of waving and smiling aimed in our direction. As we entered the brightly lit town square, music burst forth from a mariachi band and a cheer went up from the festive crowd. At that point, Tamayo figured out what was happening and clambered over to tell the driver to get out of the square as quickly as possible. He told Kenneth to smile and wave his hat. So as the fireworks began in earnest and music blared and people cheered, we wove our way through the crowd and out of the town. Once the coast was clear, Tamayo didn't seem to know whether to laugh or cry. It seemed we were mistaken for some local big shots that were expected to arrive by car and their grand celebration had been wasted on us. He thought they would not be amused by their mistake and felt it best to be far away when they realized what had happened.

On another occasion we were invited to Francis Toor's to meet Martha Graham. Unfortunately the Toomeys monopolized her all night. But I talked to her companion Greta Heilbreth at great length and think she's swell. Speaking of the Toomey's, they told us they were disgusted with Mexico. So they planned to go home on the train or the boat. We silently gave 'three cheers'. The last straw for us was the night Tom got very drunk. He called our landlord at about ten P.M. and said soldiers had beaten him up and were holding him for ten dollars American and for Frances to leave that amount immediately at the Western Union office. He didn't know where he was. We all suspected that he was drunk and wanted more money to get drunker. But Frances went into hysterics. So Kenneth and I, the landlord, his friend and his friend's friend, an interpreter, went down to the Western Union office to wait. I was already tired from lack of sleep due to recent earthquakes and the anticipation of more predicted. At Midnight Kenneth started back to the apartment and saw Tom stagger out of a cantina across the street. When he came back to the Western Union office Kenneth was so mad he wanted to murder Frances. She later told us she had wanted to leave Tom but didn't think he could survive without her.

Another highlight of our Mexican trip was our time in San Angel. One day in the middle of July we met Francis Toor and went to San Angel to visit the H.L. Davises, who were acquaintances of ours from Bainbridge Island. Marion and Harold were living for a year in San Angel on Harold's Guggenhein Fellowship, which had been awarded, primarily, for his book *Honey in the Horn*.

The Davises lived next door to Diego Rivera's home and studio. There was a group of three very modern houses designed by young Juan O'Gorman, a government architect and follower of the Bauhaus School in Germany. They were the only modern German style houses in

Mexico. One was bright blue (Rivera's house); one bright red (his studio); and the third, yellow, was the Davises'. We were asked to tea at the O'Gorman's, so Kenneth could meet Juan, who was also studying mural painting. He was doing some at the time for a new government building. Their tea hour was from six p.m. to midnight. The O'Gormans were aristocratic Mexicans, old family stuff and all that. He was descended, of course, from Irish settlers way back. So we had a chance to meet the moneyed class and it was interesting, but I decided I much preferred the artist-intellectual type we had been associating with. We liked the Davises however, and they insisted we move in with them for a couple of weeks. We were delighted, as there were fine places to walk around San Angel, such as the El Pedregal lava flow, where remnants of the oldest civilization yet discovered in Mexico were being excavated. Rivera's studio was almost all glass so when he came back Kenneth could sit in Davises' garden and watch him work.

I wrote the following letter to my parents on July 17:

Dear family:

We have moved to San Angel and are now living in luxury in a lovely bright room with a bath of our own. It is good being in the country, hearing birds instead of trucks and breathing fresh air. We are very grateful for the windows because the last place in Mexico was very cold and dark.

This morning we had a lovely and creepy time going through the old Carmelite monastery here in San Angel. It was built in 1628 and has some remnants of frescoes, paintings, furniture, etc. But, best of all, down many dark stairways in a dim musty smelling little chamber underground are ten mummified remains of church dignitaries, resting nicely upright in their own coffins. Garbed in their ecclesiastical robes are three women and seven men. Their hair streams down and their robes are crumbling with age. One of the women was buried alive, we were told. She has her arms in front of her as they were when she died, pushing, trying to get out. Her tongue hangs out and her eyes protrude. In a nearby crypt are the skulls and bones of others who were not accorded the dignity of clothes, but merely tossed into a corner and left. It is all very morbid and interesting.

One big relief about going to San Angel was that we could avoid the Toomeys who had decided to "stay a little longer." Mark Tobey arrived one day with the famous New York personage Romany-Marie of Romany-Marie's Tavern in Greenwich Village. The tavern is one of the old-time Greenwich Village restaurants and Romany-Marie knew hosts of famous people. She's a swell old girl and I liked her very much. She said when we came to New York she was going to have a reception for us. She went nuts over Mexico and said it was like going home to Romania. Mark Tobey said he was planning to do a portrait of Martha Graham.

One day we went to Teuazaca, a small pyramid with a stone serpent curving around the base.. Subtle remnants of blue and red paint were still visible in spots. A beautiful child took us under her wing while we hunted artifacts in a newly ploughed field of maguey cactus. We found a few. She was most patient with our lack of understanding of Spanish, and was very eager to direct us or be of any assistance. We went there again with Romany-Marie and Francis Toor. We found that she had two grown brothers and four younger sisters. She lived in a small stone house near a big hill across the railroad tracks. When we got there the next morning, she was making tortillas. She is utterly charming, bright, and courteous. Everywhere we went, she would call *"Quiere munecas?"* and all the little kids would come tearing toward us with handfuls of little stone carvings. *Muneca*, we found, means puppet or doll head. We bought a number of good ones; at least we think they are good.

Love, Maggie

The remainder of our time in Mexico sped by. After a mix-up in a scheduled passage we coincidentally were able to book space on the northbound Charcas. We were glad to see our friends on the crew and to learn the ship was scheduled to land in Seattle on this trip.

Mexico cannot be reduced to a formula. It is not a dreadful sandy expanse filled with grim desperados, as portrayed by Hollywood, nor is it a modern Eden. Mexico is a strenuous experience and a bewildering one until you learn to accept it dispassionately. The longer you experience the country, the stronger its hold on you. Martha Graham, who was affected violently by the altitude and change of food during her first weeks there, had the foresight to comment one day that the person who got nothing out of Mexico had only themselves to blame.

4

W HEN WE RETURNED TO Seattle in the Fall of 1932, we found our three-room flat in the attic of the apartment block under an overhanging roof just as we had left it and our lean, fierce, gray cat, too. September was at its very best, bracingly foggy in the early mornings and lazily sunny during the day. Everyone was complaining about the worst summer in years and telling us that we should feel darn lucky to have escaped. As routine elbowed the Mexican experience ever further into the background, many memories of the trip became increasingly dear, and we clung tightly to them.

Although we talked a lot about getting a car, as the Depression sank its teeth deeper into our hides, we found it necessary to prune expenses. Staff salaries at the *Crier* were cut in half. Spasmodic publicity jobs, an occasional article, and irregular commercial art assignments for Kenneth from a loyal friend employed in an advertising agency served as too few aces in too many holes. Our landlady, a charming, white-haired grandmother of kindly disposition cut our rent to $15 per month, but shortly afterwards the bank foreclosed her mortgage and she told us with tears in her nice blue eyes that she would have to relinquish ownership and go to live with her daughter. The bank people curtly informed us the flat was no longer available due to insurance complications.

Luckily, I like trying on living places as well as trying on hats so the days spent peering into vacancies weren't drudgery. We poked about old houses with old smells and rheumatic custodians in carpet slippers. We explored attic apartments, basement quarters, and share-the-kitchen deals. One gloomy, old three-story house we investigated had a printed sign in its hallway, replete with lilies and curlicues that urged "TRUMPET NOT LOUD ON THE SABBATH MORN". The motto has haunted me ever since, and sometimes I put myself to sleep on restless nights building verses on it that start.......

The sign in the hallway, dark and forlorn, read 'trumpet not loud on the Sabbath morn".....

We finally found half a house, including a fireplace and view of the Cascades for $12.50 per month with no objection to our cat. Mr. and Mrs. Gustafson lived in the other half of the house. Ole Gustafson was a carpenter, friendly and garrulous, who had lost an eye in a logging accident. Mrs. Gustafson was a tall, statuesque Swede with straight black hair, dark, forbidding eyes and a temperament right out of Strindberg. Her hair, which hung to her waist, she wore unconfined, and she went barefoot about the house and yard the year around. Our cat, which was usually savage toward strangers, took to her immediately, and she reciprocated in a cold, unsmiling way that Pancho seemed to understand and appreciate. The next job was to arrange to move our belongings, such as they were.

We walked down to Ninth Avenue and Pine Street one morning to ferret out our favorite expressman. Freddie operated his business with a minimum of overhead by parking his sole asset, a Model T Ford truck, just off the alley and maintaining office quarters in the back end of it. Snugly bedded down in the gray blankets he used for padding when occasion demanded, he would hold forth on topics of the day with passers-by, who included the cop on the beat and the proprietor of the hamburger stand a few feet away.

Moving at that time was a simple process, as we had accumulated few belongings. There were, however, about two hundred paintings and drawings in various stages of completion, and as many assorted frames, none of them fitting any of the paintings. Kenneth was in a spell of making dry points and had a stack of copper plates he could hardly lift. These items, together with the Navajo rugs from Mexico, the oak Morris chair, the work table, our clothes and bedding, and a few other odd items, were sufficient to tax the capacity of Freddie's Model T.

Knowing the steepness of the grade to our new quarters, Kenneth offered suggestions about the loading process, but Freddie brushed them aside with the air of a man who knew his business. When the job was completed, the load swathed in blankets and tied in a maze of frayed rope, Kenneth mounted the rickety seat beside the driver and they were off, down the hill. As the truck lurched forward down the steep grade, I held my breath, for the whole load shifted until it was balanced uneasily on the backs of the two in the front seat. Kenneth leaned far forward and the load did, too. "Just sit tight, boy, she'll hold, she'll hold!" Freddie shouted as they creaked faster and faster down the hill. Freddie was right, 'she held' and we moved into the Gustafson house that day.

In spite of fringed lamps and the pink and blue water paint spattered on plaster we were happy, for it was the first fireplace we'd ever had. We put the nicest of the Mexican rugs before it, and evenings, when the dishes were finished, we would both crowd into the Morris chair and bask in our luxury.

As autumn progressed, however, and the days became noticeably shorter, we discovered the Gustafsons shortened their day, too. They didn't want any noise after they retired, which got to be around eight o'clock. Unfortunately, as their bedroom was directly above the fireplace room, our lives became severely restricted. The matter of how often one could turn on the gas for a hot bath soon became another issue. Mr. Gustafson would come to us with complaints, awkwardly apologetic and obviously reluctant, while Mrs. Gustafson listened, breathing heavily, just behind a slightly opened door. Before long it was obvious that we would have to move again, the beginning of a series of moves over the next few years.

Always in sight from our various abodes, the Cascades leaned against the eastern sky and beckoned to us. Yet it seemed impossible to get to them; they might as well have been the Himalayas. Rent, groceries, and the necessary clothing were all we could manage. We still dreamed of the time when we could own something on wheels, and in the meantime life in the city absorbed us. The *Town Crier* continued to appear each Friday in nice, smooth stacks, smelling beautifully of fresh ink; Kenneth edited the art page, reviewing exhibitions and commenting on various matters, including his ideas as to what an art museum in Seattle should and should not be.

(Should be alive, functional, accessible to the public; should not be a mausoleum, nor a palace.) Seattle as yet had no art museum. The only public collection of art was still housed in the Henry Mansion on Capital Hill, the place where Kenneth and I had met three years earlier.

5

IT WAS A FATEFUL day, October 29, 1929. I was in my little Town Crier office on Fifth Avenue. The stock market was in the news, but we had other concerns. "There's an art exhibit up on the hill, Maggie, at the old Henry residence. You know, the Fine Arts Society took it over. Take a run up there and see what you think of it and do a little review, will you?" Chauncy Rathburn's kindly old eyes crinkled into an amused smile as he add the "will you?" so it wouldn't seem like an order. I quit typing and looked up, startled and plainly scared. "Art?" I asked. "Gosh, I don't know anything about it." "Doesn't matter," Mr. Rathburn said. "Just write what you think. Nobody will know the difference. I'd like to have it for this week," he added as he left my cubicle with its plywood walls, window looking out on the tarpaper roof of the print shop, and its dusty desk littered with papers. "If you go up this afternoon, there's plenty of time."

"Art! What have I descended to?" I asked myself as I slung a short red velveteen jacket over my shoulders, tucked my battered purse under my arm, and clattered down the stairs to the street. At the foot of the stairs I turned into the print shop to leave a few sheets of copy with my foreman. Green eyeshade over green eyes, standing at his tall desk, checking over figures, always frowning in concentration, Mac was a top craftsman, fiery-tempered, perfectionist, and temperamental. "Now what have you got there, Maggie?" he said crossly in his Scottish burr. "Nothing to lose any sleep over," I said. "But wait 'til you get my art criticism." A little further along the catwalk I hear, "Wait a minute,

Margaret." The heavy figure of the proofreader motioned me into her work area, removed her spectacles from tired eyes, and ran a worn hand through sandy, frizzy hair.

"I want to ask you about this paragraph." Ma was rummaging through long galleys of type, marked in the margins with the hieroglyphics of a proofreader's sign language. "Reads kind of mixed up to me,' she drawled. I quelled my annoyance and read it through. It *was* mixed up. Ma was always right. "There," she said, inserting a phrase and rearranging a sentence. "That's better." As I watched Ma return to work, I thought how lucky I was to have this job. The comforting sound of the presses, the friendly smell of printer's ink, fresh on paper, all part of the indefinable charm of everything about a print shop. I had a first inkling of my love affair with journalism back at Lincoln High School when I had worked on the staff of the school paper. I continued past the two linotype machines, which were clickety-clacking. The fingers of the operators touched the keys so delicately it was like a caress.

The door into the outer office, the business office, shut out everything about the print shop, the rhythmic sounds, the comfortable smells, the peopled murkiness. In stark contrast, the business office was light, ordered, and dotted with clean desks. The switchboard and Lucy occupied one corner. "Which boyfriend are you going to meet today?" Lucy asked sardonically, neatly manipulating the switchboard cords with long white fingers. "Oh, I've got them planted on every street corner between Times Square and the Post Office," I smiled as the heavy door to the street checked its own slam and eased itself shut.

The October fog, which had hovered over the city since early morning, filling the downtown streets with salty-fishy smells from the waterfront, was dispersing before the rays of a tired autumn sun. Always fond of walking, I rarely took the streetcars unless time demanded; the Henry residence was about two miles away, uphill for the most part, but having been raised on Seattle's billowing contours, I found walking up hill more invigorating than tiring. I turned east toward Capital Hill, the great mound lying like a sleeping camel between Lake Union and Lake Washington. On Denny Hill at the northern fringe of the business section the sagging frame houses with their narrow windows and gingerbread trimmings were already being torn down preparatory to the great re-grade job which would in time level the rise to a flat little prairie.

The spacious grounds of the old Henry mansion were bathed in pale sunlight, filtered through yellow leaves. A watering system whirled iridescent droplets over a rich carpeting of green lawn. An imposing, three-story building of dark red brick and heavy plate glass stood before me. Before the H.C. Henry mansion was given to the city as an abode for the visual arts there existed a Fine Arts Society, which was housed in several downtown office buildings over a period of years. Carl Gould, a successful architect, was its president. Mr. Gould and the Fine Arts Society moved to the comparative magnificence of the Henry mansion, and the society was reorganized as the Seattle Art Institute. Mr. Gould later designed the Seattle Art Museum building, which would be located in Volunteer Park.

In the hallway, just inside a heavy door, a delicate blonde girl sat at a desk, typing. My footsteps echoed as I walked over the polished hardwood floors. As I went I noticed the high ceilings, dark, mahogany woodwork, and a central hall with rooms opening off either side. The hushed, vacuous atmosphere was heightened by the many shade trees outside the windows. It seemed appropriate to speak in subdued tones. "Oh, yes," the pretty girl at the desk said pleasantly. "I'll call Mr. Hatch. He's down below in his office, I believe. Or perhaps you would like to go to his office. I'll show you the way." I marveled at the slim delicacy of this perfect little creature with her air of quiet efficiency. Around that sort of femininity I felt myself growing larger and clumsier by the minute, like Alice after swallowing the 'Drink Me' potion.

Paintings were leaning against the walls in stacks. "They haven't finished hanging the exhibition yet," the secretary explained with a tiny smile. Mr. Hatch finished a telephone conversation and replaced the mouthpiece on its wall hook as I entered the office. The desk was stacked with books and papers and several paintings hung on the walls. Mr. Hatch was at once suave and nervous, self-confident to the point of arrogance, and yet with a basic uncertainty. I had talked with him on the phone, taking announcements of Art Circle activities, and I had thought his tone patronizing and artificial. I found I liked him better in person than I thought I would. He always introduced himself using his full name, John David Hatch III, for example but his eager responsiveness to my questions seemed real. At any rate, I felt comfortable being open with him, and soon we were on a firm footing. David Hatch had graduated in architecture from the University of California and had migrated to the Pacific Northwest, hoping to become established as a landscape architect. Working as a beginner in that field, trimming borders and spreading fertilizer, he had been 'discovered' by Mr. Gould. Gould recognized certain talents in the young man and before you could say "onward and upward with the arts" he stepped into the directorship of the organization.

"I know so little about art that it's pathetic," I explained as we walked upstairs to the galleries. "My background is strictly newspaper, except for a few months on a financial weekly." "How, then, do you happen to be writing art reviews?" Hatch asked, surveying me quizzically and tapping a pencil against his teeth, one of his many nervous mannerisms, along with frequently running his fingers over his faint mustache or through his sparse sandy hair, blinking his eyes spasmodically in rapid succession, and laughing abruptly and inappropriately. "That's what I've been asking myself," I said. "My boss at the *Town Crier* looked me up one dull afternoon when I was busily banging up a fascinating item about building permits and said he'd read some of my editorials, liked my style, and offered me more money than I was getting. I figured nothing could be deadlier than what I was doing, so I took a chance on it. I warned him I was pretty ignorant, but he said he could tell by my writing that I would adjust. So here I am, assistant editor of an arts and literature publication."

"You've never tried to paint, I take it." "Not since I was in grammar school and the teacher used to put up a daffodil or a tulip or a leaf and have us copy it. Daffodils were the easiest." Mine were always messy, I remembered to myself. But for me the fun was in looking for things to take to the teacher for models: the branch of dogwood blossoms in May, perfect dogwood leaves, too, searched for assiduously among the blown heaps along the gutters and board sidewalks. Maple leaves were wonderful for drawing. I could almost do one from memory still. "Some of the public schools teach art a little more intelligently now," Hatch offered. "You know, letting the child express him or herself freely. One method is patterned after the Viennese theory of creative approach. We may get an exhibition of Viennese children's paintings soon. They're quite amazing."

I liked Dave Hatch more all the time. We had reached the main gallery, the former living room of the old residence with its ample fireplace taking up a good part of one wall. An assistant was hanging pictures. A man in his early twenties, carrying a soiled trench coat and wearing ripply gray trousers, a spotted white sweater, a wilted shirt, and a saggy tweed jacket roamed about the room. As he teetered about before various of the pictures, which were in the process of being hung, he slapped a gray felt, snap brim hat with a stained band and a hole in the front of the creased crown against his side and repeatedly ran the other hand over his forehead and back over his receding somewhat curly hair as though removing perspiration.

Observing an assistant carefully straightening a large watercolor of boats on Lake Union, he said, "It still lists a little to starboard. Maybe you should hang everything slightly crooked so we could get a cheap jag." "Pretty disrespectful attitude for a painter to have toward art, don't you think, Miss Bundy?" Hatch joked, his bushy eyebrows in constant up and down motion, his small mustache twitching nervously. "I like your picture this year, Kenneth," he added more seriously, pausing before a strongly painted watercolor of a merry-go-round.

"You two should meet," he went on. "Margaret Bundy---Kenneth Callahan. Ken has just come back from Honolulu. You ought to write him up." Kenneth smiled and shyly shook my hand before turning back to Hatch. "It isn't much of a painting, but I sort of like it. To be honest, I was surprised when your jury didn't throw it out. It seems like they must have rejected a lot of the old standbys. "Well, it's about time, don't you think?" Hatch said. "Sure I do," Kenneth said, laughing, "but I think you're going to have a lot of mad artists on your hands." His body shook as he laughed, standing, as he was, with his right arm across his chest, his left elbow leaning on his right arm, and his left hand cupping his chin. "Dave," he added, "I wouldn't want to be in your shoes."

"It's none of my doing," Hatch said, his tone a little on the defensive. "The jury selected the show and awarded the prizes." "You don't have to convince me," Kenneth said. "They accepted my picture. I'm just saying you'd better wear a pie tin in the seat of your pants until local blood pressures go back to normal." Hatch turned and, noticing my look of puzzlement, said, "you see, for the first time in Seattle an art jury has gone modern. Not only did they not give prizes to any of the five or six masters who have customarily won them, but a good many other established favorites were thrown out of the show as well. There isn't a single familiar name on the list of awards. Personally, I think it's swell---like a fresh breeze."

None of it made sense to me at the time, but I detected an art community dispute, had found two people I liked, and my curiosity was aroused. I looked around at the room full of paintings and sensed a vitality that comes from human beings creating something they truly believe in. "What makes art modern?" I asked, looking helplessly at a swirling mass of brilliant color, which leaped at me from the south wall. "When you're through answering that one, Dave," Kenneth put in, "explain what makes art art!" "Modern art is free expression, and conservative art is representation." Hatch offered. And turning to Kenneth he asked, "how is that for a sort of hasty pudding definition?" "You get an A for effort, anyway," Kenneth smiled.

"Let's have a look at the first prize winner," Hatch suggested. "This one over here, the boats on the beach. It's by a Portland artist named C.S. Price. Do you like it, Miss Bundy?" I studied the painting before answering, although my first reaction was to say yes. The paint was applied in bold, flat strokes; the colors strong reds, greens and blues. After looking awhile, I made out the forms of three rowboats upturned on what might be sand. Everything in the painting worked together toward a harmonious whole; what was important was not that here were three rowboats on a beach, but that here was color and form and design and an intangible quality of excitement that made the painting alive. "Yes," I said with enthusiasm, "I like it very much. It's not like any painting I've ever seen. But then, I haven't seen very many. I think I'm beginning to understand what you meant by modern art being free expression."

Hatch continued, "We discovered, when we looked him up, that Price has been turned down fairly consistently by juries that only want pictures of recognizable objects. Pretty objects, mind you, not just any old thing. Mountain landscapes, marine landscapes, flowers, brass and copper pots, and well---there you have it. If you venture out of these categories, you are a radical." "And you probably live in squalor and eat your young!" Callahan added. His green eyes crinkled in amusement. "And that's only half true!" I noted his unusually high forehead, still tanned from his recent travels, his peculiarly shaped eyebrows, which

35

ran to a point at their outer edges, then made a brief, sudden descent. I again noted the very frayed collar of his shirt and the badly tied bow tie, which stuck out and tipped to one side. The seat of his gray tweed trousers sagged as though the pockets had carried too many heavy objects, and his jacket sagged in front from a habit of thrusting his hands deep into the pockets. His brown shoes had been polished, but the laces were knotted, the toes turned up, and the soles worn paper thin.

"What made this jury so different from other juries?" I asked. "Mainly an artist named Mark Tobey. He came to Seattle from New York not many years ago, and in the eyes of the local realist painters he's a dangerous revolutionary. I thought it would be fun to see what he'd do on a Northwest jury. The other members were Tucker Palmquist from Southern California and Miss Lydia Cotterill from Portland. The three seemed to be soul mates, hardly disagreeing at all."

Callahan said he had to leave. He said his good-byes diffidently, holding his limp gray felt hat at his chest and looking at the floor. "Will we see you at the preview?" Hatch called. "I doubt it, I've outgrown my party clothes." "No one will care, Kenneth, you should come," Hatch said. I surprised myself by quickly adding that I would come if he would. I had no inkling that this was the beginning of a life-long relationship. "We'll see," said Kenneth as he turned away. I watched his purposeful walk, almost comical, as he moved to the front door. He seemed to put an extra spring into each step, sort of bounding from the ball of one foot onto the other, the whole effect bouncy and jerky but somehow extremely determined.

Hatch was called to the telephone, returning soon to say he had to leave for a short while. Would I excuse him, take my time looking at the paintings, and ask his assistant, John Moore, any questions that I might have. I returned to the small watercolor of a carnival scene that was Callahan's contribution to the exhibition. My untrained eye caught a vitality and a direct, bold style. The little merry-go-round seemed to rotate, and I could almost hear a calliope.

I was still looking at paintings, jotting down titles and names of artists, making notes on my opinions when the delicate blonde appeared at my elbow and apologetically said, "I'm sorry, but we close at five and it's already a quarter past." Suddenly, I had my first taste of museum fatigue: tired all over, aching feet, and the start of a headache. "Thank you," I sighed, "I have more notes than I can possibly use. If I find I need further information, I'll call." Weary as I was, I decided to walk down the hill to the office. I felt, through my physical exhaustion, strangely stimulated, and I knew intuitively that my horizon had altered, my point of view had shifted, whether for better or worse didn't concern me at all.

A red sun was sinking behind long streaky abstract fish forms in a fiery sea. I watched the last flaming crescent disappear as I walked rapidly down the west side of Capital Hill. By the time I reached the printing company, the first pale glow of Venus was visible, and I repeated to myself, "I wish I may, I wish I might---" but I couldn't think of anything to wish for. Always before there had been something specific---that I would get a date for a certain dance or that some male or other would return my ardor. I couldn't remember a time when I wasn't in love with somebody. I certainly didn't fall in love with Kenneth at first sight. It took a long time, and sometimes I wonder if I ever did.

One spring morning in 1930 I left the following penciled note on the front porch of my parents house at 2262 23rd North in Ravenna:

Dear Family.

We came out to see you, but on account of not wanting to wake you up we didn't. Anyway, it's because Kenneth and I got married today. I know you are shocked, but it really isn't as bad as it might be. And I couldn't let brother Bob get ahead of me. The reason I didn't tell you today (I decided quite suddenly), was that I wanted everything to be brief and get it over with, and I was afraid Mabel might cry or something and make me cry and all that. Don't think it was because I don't love you both more than ever. I'll call tomorrow. We have a lovely, big studio apartment at 623 23rd North.

Love, Mag

P.S. (Judge) William Hoar married us and wanted to know if I was any relation to Attorney Bundy. Barney and Marjory were witnesses.

6

NOT HAVING A CAR, we took long walks in and about the city, finding people and places for Kenneth to sketch and me to write about. Among them were: a Jamaican tattoo artist named Julius down on skid road; an old Irish sea captain, Johnny O-Brian, who had known Soapy Smith, the bandit, in early Alaskan days and who was ending his career by piloting ocean-going ships through the straits into and out of Puget Sound ports; a whaling man named Captain Mogg, who had guided Wilkins and Stefanson in the Arctic and who was apt, while crossing a downtown street to clutch my arm and say "gad, a frozen fish would taste good right now!" Other subjects for stories and sketches were friendly hobos in the jungles between the railroad tracks south of town, vaudeville personalities caught back-stage, beachcombers, and hermits. We spent much of our time with individuals who had succeeded in escaping the humdrum. Seattle has always been rich in such personalities.

We nearly always walked to work, three miles up, over, and down Capital Hill, and home again three miles up and over the hump to the east side. Then we'd walk at night again just for fun because walking under the stars or in the soft, enveloping mists of evening was something else again.

Some have suggested that there are only four cities in the world: San Francisco, New Orleans, New York, and Paris. At the risk of being called a 'home town booster,' I am asserting that Seattle should be included in that select group, because I think Seattle has an atmosphere that cannot be duplicated anywhere. And much of this atmosphere comes from the character of its streets. A city's streets are like the wrinkles on an old face. They depict the comedy and tragedy of the life that has passed there. That is why cities that are too ordered and new do not appeal to me. It isn't always the pretty features on a face that make you love that face. It can be the frown line between the eyebrows or the smile gashes down from the sides of the nose or the puzzled horizontal lines that affect the smoothness of a forehead. Sometimes these are dearer than a Cupid's bow mouth or long curling lashes. And so it is with a city. It's not the crisp storefronts, nor rows of brand new houses, nor even the beautiful, wooded boulevards and parks that make Seattle a fine city; for me it is the character streets I love.

In every kind of weather our walks included the waterfront where Puget Sound's waters, iridescent with oil, lapped against the rotting piers. And there was Yesler Way, the border of respectability, with its of Greek restaurants, smelly drugstores, and diminutive, open-air Japanese markets. The streets below Yesler were lined with drab, leaning houses, punctuated now and then by a meaningful red glow oozing from a curtained window. Farther down Seattle's Harlem merged into an area of Kosher markets. Old women in shawls, men in skullcaps and children with the look of age in their big, dark eyes occupied the streets and doorways.

The beaches of Harbor Island also attracted us. As far as the eye could see stretched groups of tumbled, weather-beaten shanties. We wandered on slabs of boardwalk, among huts built of wood washed ashore by the waves. Harbor Island offered a sort of last frontier for beaten old men who were pushed out of the way by a world that was in a hurry and was no longer interested in them.

At least once a week we visited the Pike Place Market. From the conglomeration of farmers' booths under striped parasols up on Western Avenue down through the rows of stalls to the vortex at Pike Street, all is a moil of reaching, craning, shouting humanity. Visitors from the East and Mid-west go into ecstasies over the "the market." It is one of the greatest open-air shrines to the human appetite ever conceived. But return in the evening, and the market place is as quiet as a corpse. Rows of empty stalls and bare metal tables exist in the silence where during the day the sweating vitality of buying and selling permeated the scene. The pigeons that strut confidently in and out of traffic and flay the air with iridescent wings have vanished to wherever city pigeons go at night. There is life only in the figure of an old woman who paws delicately through the refuse in the gutter. Her red hands protruding from her worn black sleeves pick over the coarse outer leaves of lettuce and cabbage, the carrot tops, the husks and cores. She seems always to be searching for some tidbit, some mouth-watering morsel which this time might be there.

We knew of all sorts of unusual places to eat, where we could quiet our enormous appetites for fifteen to thirty-five cents. The Japanese grill on Jackson served Irish stew that was a joy to taste; the Swedish cafe on Howell Street, had a lunch of rye crisp, yellow cheese, and a big pitcher of hot milky chocolate; the Kosher restaurant did sour cream dishes, gefilte fish, and crisp, chewy apple strudel; Rafferty's Table Board on First Avenue served meals logging camp style; and the Open Kitchen, across Joe Desimone's arched bridge in the Pike Place Public Market, served a full course dinner for sixteen cents, and a mountainous breakfast was eleven cents.

Outside the Open Kitchen, though, you passed the bread line, and the Great Depression closed in on you. Gray figures, hunched in wrinkled old clothes, so worn they seemed a part of the listless bodies, were always there, like a sculpture against the dark red brick wall. Then you could see the seeds of the future being sown in this poor, rejected soil, and the vision of a nightmare harvest became a haunting menace.

Kenneth's painting from its earliest stages had been concerned with men functioning in their worlds: stevedores, merchant sailors, market vendors, forest workers. His figures were vigorous and engrossed in their activities. Since our return from Mexico he had been working on a logging mural, not with a specific wall in mind, but in response to some inner challenge. Now for the first time, he began to paint abstracted figures in groups that were regimented into geometric patterns. It was the time when American artists were delving self-consciously into the American scene; it was the time when the movie newsreels ended with threatening shots of uniformed men marching.

Many artists, city-bound, hemmed in by their own poverty, confronted daily by the unhappy shadows waiting in the long lines, consoled themselves with the hotly stoked fires of their own hatred.

Some painted "propaganda" paintings; some stopped painting altogether; others sought solution in the refuge of dogma, political or religious; still others climbed an ivory tower, locked the door and tossed the key out the window. We had many heated arguments, as cups of dinner coffee grew cold and flecked with ashes from gesticulating cigarettes. Those evenings sometimes broke up with disagreements more firmly lodged and friendships tottering. Ideas were attacked and defended with equal vehemence. Easel painting was doodling, artists were escapists, great art had died with the Renaissance, what was needed was a "whole new set of symbols." Sometimes Kenneth and I would continue the argument as we walked home. "What's going to be the new symbolism?" I goaded him on a homeward stroll one spring midnight. "Not the clenched fist or the raised night stick," he said. "There are plenty of symbols; life is full of symbols. What is lacking is belief!"

We came to a vacant lot where Balm of Gilead trees were in bud, their branches spreading outward and upward like the fingers of a gently open palm. We stood there, sniffing their fragrance. Balm of Gilead leaves on a wet spring night will cure a headache, if inhaled deeply. An old Alaskan we knew always said what brought him back to the Puget Sound country was the smell of the "Ba'm o' Gilly" trees near the lakes. A small Chinook breeze stirred the wet leaves, which glistened in the light from a street lamp. "It's a pretty swell place to live, my friend," Kenneth said in a tone as reverent as a prayer.

7

LOGGING AS A SUBJECT for Kenneth's murals such as the Weyerhauser mural in Everett and paintings like the large one in Seattle's Rainier Club were in large part inspired by a mid-thirties visit we made to a logging camp near Pysht on the Olympic Peninsula. Through a family connection with Prentice Bloedel, we had arranged a visit to the Merrill-Ring camp. The Merrill family was interested in art, and I think J.D. Merrill had been impressed with Kenneth's Marine Hospital mural.   As usual, I kept notes of my impressions while Kenneth did prolific sketching. From my notes, the following unpublished article emerged

.Far back in the mountains of the Olympic Peninsula – even the veteran loggers called it rough country – a small gasoline speeder slid along railway tracks from a logging camp six miles into the hills to where crews were at work getting out huge old-growth trees. The grade wasn't steep, but the climb was steady and slow. Fifteen minutes out from camp, the speeder's only occupant could have looked behind him and viewed repetitive ranges of mountains being swallowed by the rolling clouds of mist that were moving in from the ocean. He didn't look, though; he'd seen it all too many times.

At nine o-clock the speeder was to pick us up from where we had been watching a huge steam donkey being moved to a place where piled logs would be loaded onto a train. As we waited we sat on an enormous cedar stump, Kenneth sketching and I scribbling.

Margaret Callahan

Nobody but loggers get to see shows like this anymore because the activity is so far back in the hills. First you have to negotiate very rough mountain roads. Then you have to ride the logging trains or the speeders before you can watch a spar tree being rigged or old veteran trees crashing out from their birthplaces. And in five years or maybe ten, according to the crew, you won't find this kind of logging going on in the backwoods because there won't be any forests like these left. Not for another fifty years, when the second growth matures, will there be anything called woods here at all. By that time maybe they'll know enough not to mow down the forests like hayfields. Maybe selective logging will be the rule.

I had worried that the loggers would resent our presence, but the crew figured that as long as the big boss sent us up, everybody had to be pretty nice to us. So it was quite comfortable staying there at the camp, eating more kinds of food from one table than we'd ever seen before and getting a feeling for it all. Morning began early, waiting by the tracks in the thin gray light. Breakfast is over by 6:30 a.m. The men stand by themselves or in small clusters, their thick caulked (they say "corked") boots crushing the April dew into the soil. They hold lunch boxes in one hand and usually a cigarette in the other, as they wait while the locomotive snorts about its business down the tracks. It chugged up and down picking up cars and doing all the things a locomotive seems to have to do before departure. All the men have a padded look from plenty of wool underclothing and wool shirts and sweaters. The beauty and dignity of outdoor workingmen in their clothes is unequalled. Being in a group of them and not dressed as they are exaggerates your isolation from them.

The superintendent said to the foreman as he gestured toward us, "the Callahans want to see what logging is all about: just what happens up there in the woods and how it is all done." And with that he turned us over to the foreman, Pete Johnson, a powerful looking man with a barrel chest and hardly any neck. He displayed a simple dignity in his manner toward us, and, we noticed later, toward his men as well. "I take you first," he said, "to where we're moving one of the donkeys You can ride in the cab."

Pete Johnson is a French Canadian, and his real name is Pete Jean. To loggers, however, there isn't any such thing as a last name of "Jean", so they kept calling him Johnson, and he let it go at that. He left his

43

home in Quebec when he was fifteen, and when he was sixteen he was greasing the skids in British Columbia logging camps. They used oxen then to draw the logs over the skid roads. He remembered how they all shook their heads as they squinted over the peaks that fell back like regiments from the Pacific coast. They told each other that nobody would ever cut that timber; they'd never be able to get it out, let alone get to it.

We rode in the cab behind the two engineers, and for the first time I was at the source of those long haunting train whistles, right there where I could watch the hands that control them. We leaned from the doors of the cab as the engine rocked on the tracks like a ship on a rough sea, and we breathed the oily, sooty smell from the stack. After about half an hour we came to a stop. "You can walk along down there," Johnson told us, indicating where we would be out of the way. "That's the one we're going to move," he said, pointing to a huge donkey in the distance. "You got the time?" Ours checked with his and he said, "that's all right then. I told Jack to pick you up at nine o'clock. In case I get to working and forget…" "We'll keep track," we told him.

From our perch on the tall cedar stump we could see that they had already hauled the donkey down the far bank of a great ravine and up a five hundred foot hill on the other side to the top where it now rested. It is one of those things you can't imagine until you have seen it done. That twenty-ton donkey on its great sled looked bogged down in the mud for good, but by eight o'clock the men had strung cables, and secured them around tree trunks in strategic places so that when the signal was finally given and the donkey puncher put the steam on, the giant drum wound in the cable and the thing skimmed right over that wreckage strewn course like a child's sled on ice. Talk about Paul Bunyan – the modern donkey with its steel arms makes the old legends pale.

Soon it was nine o'clock, and we heard the speeder coming up the track, adding one more sound to the chorus of shrieks and chuggings made by the donkey. Once aboard, friendly but shy, Jack Olsen began immediately tampering with the engine of the speeder. "You are going to watch some loading now, aye?" He peered into the gas tank and measured it with a stick. "Well," he speculated, "if we're lucky, it'll just about get us there… just about, and none to spare." He was a short, heavy man in the customary brown oiled canvas pants and coat with the pants cut off at his boot tops. On his head was the ubiquitous round, brown cloth hat. He had pink, almost florid cheeks, a white mustache, slightly yellow around the edges and needing trimming, and white hair showing under the shapeless, little hat. We smiled at him and when he smiled back, I noticed that one of his very blue eyes had been injured and failed to focus properly.

There was no more talk on the short ride down the tracks, and when we stopped once more, he was again busy about the engine. "It's funny," he muttered, "they can't fix this damn thing in camp. I like to tell them that if they can't fix it here, they should take it to the Weyerhauser boys," he winked. "I'll have to give them hell again." And he started off into the woods along a narrow trail. Looking over his shoulder at us, he said, "Just kidding, you know. We have a lot of fun."

There were deer tracks on the trail. "We see them all the time in the summer; bear too, little black fellers. They won't hurt you none. We might see one today, if we look out. But I think it's still too early in the season though."

The trail ended at another railway track and there before us was a crew of men loading logs. The scene included another donkey, a long train of flat cars, and a spar tree like a great May pole with its steel cabling rigged at the top, reaching in all directions and secured to the bases of stumps. We scrambled up a wreckage-strewn bank and again found stumps to perch on. Jack, after going away for a time, came back to where I was sitting. Again, the sweet smile came shyly from under the brim of the shapeless cloth hat. I noticed in him, as with other men in the woods, a strength that is not unlike the trees they spend so much of their lives with.

As we talked there in the sun and the wind with the fast-moving clouds above us and the peaks of the hills rising against the sky, the air was full of the donkey's shrieks and the shouts of the men. The singing steel cable was tested to the very limit of its endurance. Overall was the wonderful smell of great cedars and hemlocks, of spruce and fir with the sap oozing from them. It was a smell so solid that it gets into the back of your mouth and you feel you could almost chew it.

The whistle punk's short sharp bark signaled the go-ahead and was followed by the clatter and fury of the donkey, the cable winding on the spool, and the spar tree quivering in long undulating waves as its inner strength was put to the test. The logs come, the chokers about them in a death grip; all before them is crushed to earth. As they near the loading area, more signals in short, shrill succession are heard. The various toots can mean: stop, slack away, go easy, and go ahead full. As soon as the logs come to rest on the ground, the loaders are in action; one releases the chokers and others are ready with the tongs. The loaders run with their hands grasping the great steel hooks, toss them just at the right moment and in just the right manner, so that they bite into the log at a point of perfect balance for lifting onto the flat car.

While watching all this, we talked, and Jack poked the pitchy part of the stump with a little stick. He said that forty years ago he was logging out around the north end of Lake Union in Seattle. "Lake Union, forty years ago; just think of it. And now it's all settled and built up like it hadn't ever grown anything bigger than a thistle." But before that he had started way back in Wisconsin. He got married in Spring Valley, and he and his wife came west. He'd worked in the woods the whole time, and after their family was raised, his wife had come and lived in the camps with him.

That was when he had been taken off the heavy work and put on the fire patrol. "They don't make me work very hard around here anymore. They give me lots of leeway." His wife went on all his fire patrol trips with him, and they were real companions. "It's all different now, since she died last year. A stroke, she had. She'd had one before, but she was just about all cured from that one. Well, those things have a nasty habit of repeating... I don't know... since then I have been restless. It seems like I can't feel right anywhere. I go to town and visit the children and grandchildren for a few days. Then I get restless for the woods. I come back here and get restless again!"

The rigged spar tree, like a great octopus with its steel arms tightly gripping the anchoring stumps, swayed slightly as another bunch of logs skidded down to where the loaders were waiting. Off in the distance other spar trees stood deserted among the littered hills where the loaders had come and gone. Nothing was left but wreckage and the hills and the old spar trees still standing against the sky. "Don't they blow down?" I asked Jack. "No, they never blow over," he said. "Once they're topped and the branches taken off, there's nothing for the wind to catch in."

As he spoke, a bunch of logs with the chokers about them, still suspended from the cables, lurched to the side, knocked against some loose logs and started them sliding toward the area where the loader men were waiting, relaxed, for the sign for action. As instinctively and swiftly as a deer leaps a hedge, the men sprang to their feet, arms over their heads in a protective gesture, and scrambled from the path of the threatening logs. One of those logs could roll a man flat.

I asked Jack if they had many accidents in the woods these days. "Hardly any, anymore," he said. "Oh, last year a man was killed. Crushed by a falling tree. He lived quite awhile in the hospital before he died." I told Jack about Earl Fields whose brother was cut in two by a swinging choker, and whose brother-in-law, a high rigger, fell 200 feet when he chopped his rope in two. "There used to be many more accidents," Jack said.

"It used to be that the crazier the men worked, the better the company liked it – anything for speed. Now, because of the union, it costs the companies too much money when a man gets killed. So everybody has orders to work as careful as possible. These men are all specialists; they know exactly what they're doing. Take a whistle punk – a whistle punk used to be just a green kid. Now he has to be an experienced man. There are so many signals to remember, and if he gets one wrong, anything might happen.

Riggers get top pay, and sometimes buckers and fallers do too, depending on how fast they work (they still work on a sliding scale based on production.) On down the line you have head loaders, then second loaders, and then choker setters, and lastly whistle punks. Jack had been a rigger. He'd done pretty much everything in his day, but mostly rigging. Wasn't it pretty dangerous, rigging? No – not so much dangerous as plain hard work, hard work in an unnatural position. He commented that swinging the axe and pushing the saw while belted in and hanging from the top of a tree makes your back and shoulders and legs "awful tired."

I scaled the height of the spar tree before us. "It must be pretty exciting to see someone rigging a tree that high," I said. "I've climbed 'em a lot higher than that," Jack offered. He stopped poking with the little stick, hitched his trousers, switched his weight to the other foot and back again as he looked at me from under bushy, white brows, "lots higher'n that."

Nobody wasted any time when the donkey blew the signal for the lunch hour. Jack had built a fire down by the tracks and a few of us squatted there with our "nosebags" full of thick sandwiches, cake, pie, cookies, a hard-boiled egg, and fruit. Everything was neatly wrapped in waxed paper. A thermos held a pint of coffee.

Tuesday evening, and our last. It has grown dark and the frogs croak in the outer blackness where we know the rusty old donkeys, the little gas car, the coils of cable, and the heaps of rusty spikes wait to be animated again tomorrow. It has only been a few days, but I feel nostalgic about leaving all this and about the men waiting in the early morning without us while the locomotive puffs white steam and stomps about getting ready to go. We watched as they raised a portable spar tree this morning. There was a whole day, yesterday, spent in preparation, as well as another half hour or so this morning. The raising was gradual, a little lift, then more adjusting of lines, etc., and it was nearly lunchtime when it stood straight at last. One of the men said tonight that they still have more work tomorrow fastening it securely. You would never believe how much of logging activity is the stringing of endless lengths of great steel cables.

Going back down the tracks to the spot where they were loading, we met Pete, and he said they had broken a main pinion gear on the donkey, and he told Kenneth not to draw any pictures of that to show Mr. Merrill because he would come up and can the whole bunch of them. Every time I see Pete Jean, I realize more keenly the beauty in that great bull-like figure and flat broad face with the high cheekbones, high color, and small, very intelligent brown eyes. We talked with him for an hour yesterday afternoon, he on a pile of logs on one side of the track, we on the other, shouting to each other, but that was the way it happened, and it seemed natural that way.

We talked about the war, and he said it didn't make sense to spend $65 million building a battleship and then blow it up with $20 worth of bombs. "Doesn't that seem silly? When you think of it, isn't it silly?" he said. He's for the New Deal and Roosevelt, because he thinks he's seriously tried to do something to help, and it hurts him to have the business men malign him the way they do. The unions, he says, have done a lot, but they are going too far. The time was, he remembers, back in the early thirties, he had to turn his head away when he gave his men their checks, as it was so embarrassing. They received $2.50 a day, and by the time they bought their supplies (a logger's boots cost $18 and lasted six months), there would be only about $20 left to last until the end of the month. "And you know, you can't buy much with $20." But now, he feels, they are going too far in the other direction, and the result is that lumber is so high-priced nobody can afford to build a house.

We had a long talk after lunch with the donkey puncher on the duplex machine. He's been in logging for twenty-three years and in various camps. He has an active mind and is a supporter of the union. At first I thought perhaps he was a communist, but he turned out not to be. He thinks the radicals are bad for the unions. He says most of the men aren't interested in union activities and that only about 20 or 30 out of the 250 men in camp attend meetings regularly. He says the unions no longer get opposition from the employers. The controversy now is over the production wage scale versus standard daily pay for the fallers and buckers. The unions are working to change the present system to standard pay for safety reasons.

We ate lunch in the same place as yesterday, by a fire in a little hollow by the tracks with the silent little Swedish rigging slinger for company. Seagulls and crows waited for scraps, the gulls swooping about overhead, alighting wherever they spied a crust, and the crows hunkering in nearby trees. There have been showers, then sun, then showers this afternoon. Most of our time has been spent watching the skyline yarding, the most fascinating of all the activities. We watched from below, where we could see the trees come looming over the top of the hill, with the chokers about them. They dangle from the yarding block, great, helpless, inert forms, crashing over the course to where the donkeys wait, noisy and impatient.

Jack came and before we left on the speeder we talked awhile. He has a bad cold in his chest but won't do anything about it. He won't even button his shirt over his chest. He says many a snowflake has fallen in there and never did any harm. But he says that if the missus were still around, he'd be home with mustard plasters and steam clothes and hot baths, and oh lord, anything is better than all that. The missus was a graduate nurse and apparently lavished the family with care when they were ailing. "Well, I guess it's time for you to go," he said, and we made our way down the trail for the last time.

8

ALTHOUGH KENNETH AND I never lost our love of walking, a chance meeting provided an opportunity to buy a Model A Ford roadster for $150, requiring only $50 down. It had belonged to a Japanese salesman, we were told, and who had given it loving care. Good rubber, no immediate repairs necessary. The next day we were steering along the by-roads on the outskirts of town, quarreling over whose turn it was to drive.

During the ensuing years most of our leisure was spent rattling over every conceivable kind of road, exploring the vast backcountry of the Pacific Northwest. We ambled through rural villages and mining towns, farmlands, logged-off foothills, and rolling wheat country. We navigated all the Cascade passes and rambled along ocean shores and river valleys.

Summers we drove with the top down and the hot sun and dry winds burning our faces, the dust of country roads whirling up through the floor boards and over the windshield. In the winter we traveled with the rain pelting hard against the car, splashing over the glass and under the canvas onto our knees and toes. During autumn and spring months, gales threatened to shove the small green car into the ditch.

There were day-long trips and longer ones, with nights spent in dreary auto cabins of the depression period, with their thin-mattressed beds, cold water only taps, and always the lone bare light globe hanging from the center of the ceiling.

On one memorable trip to Oregon, we had visited Charles Heaney, C.S. Price, Louis Bunce and other Portland area artists. We also spent three days with Kenneth's friend and fellow museum employee Earl Field and his Finnish family in Woodland, Washington. There is something about the high flat country above the Columbia River that could capture one, but I am too much born into the misty, green, rank and rainy country nearer the coast. When I am away from it for long I thirst for it. Kenneth felt the same way, and we had come to know, through all our senses---the look, the feel, the smell--- that this small wild part of the earth's surface was home, and it would always be an inseparable part of ourselves.

From my journal, July 21, 1935: we arrived today on the Oregon coast at Port Orford after an easy drive from Woodland. I'm propped up here on the rocks out of the wind and most of the blowing sand, and before me is a glittering world of tumbling and roaring sea. The ocean varies from turquoise to green-blue. The sun's shimmering reflection glistening from the breakers that pile up one after another, then tumble themselves into a white maelstrom of froth and foam. The land curves in a dark crescent and is topped with a heavy growth of evergreens that juts from the sea. Black rocks look as though a giant had playfully tossed them from the shore.

I have let my bathing suit slip down to my stomach, and the feeling of warmth is wonderful. What a shame so much of one never tastes the sun and the wind. Day before yesterday we went farther up the beach behind some sheltering rocks and I went naked for awhile. My breasts and stomach drank in the warmth of the sun and the movement of the air. I can see a reason for nudism. It's ridiculous we can't have that pleasure whenever we care to.

I have been in the ocean every day. It's very cold, so I stay only for a few moments, just to let a breaker or two crash over me. It's enough to provide that exhilaration, which is inevitably followed by an increased appetite for food and sleep. One does become aware, too, of D. H. Lawrence's dark gods when the sun and the wind play on one's bare breast and belly. I'm enjoying keenly his letters and read them aloud to Kenneth for a long time yesterday and this morning.

I've also been reading *Lost Girl*. I love escaping with that nice respectable English girl from her nice respectable English environment into the mountainous wilderness of north Italy where she comes up against that elemental male-ness and female-ness of the people in their isolated villages. When joined together, these opposites become a whole like the Chinese yin-and-yang. Many men today seem to have lost that basic male-ness, no longer conscious of their power. I don't mean the maleness that goes about flexing its muscles nor the femaleness that quivers in boudoir whimsies, but the quiet inner power that simply is. I wondered if nature really does create this sort of thing, or if writers like Lawrence and philosophers like the Chinese just dreamed it up. It does seem such an order might eventually become tiresome. Shades and variations of male and female are probably desirable, although sometimes they become tiresome, also.

Port Orford has three hundred people and one main street with a few stores, a beer joint and an enclosed space with a big sign which reads: "Teddy The Singing Lumber Jack Evangelist Every Night." But I guess Teddy has gone. Our auto camp faces one end of the main street. The Lone Café, where we eat along with the workmen, is up on a little rise at the other end. How we relish those meals, and with what anticipation we walk twice a day up the street, fighting against the wind, to the Lone.

This morning we spent a couple of hours out at Battle Rock, a monolith jutting into the sea. We watched diving bell divers and then a tiny lizard, which crawled onto my arm to bask in the sun. I'd like a hot shower this afternoon, but the old lady only heats water on Saturday for the tourists in the place. But it's nice to have so fine a place all to ourselves. Nice? It's just plain paradise. I hate to pull my wet, sandy suit up over my skin that thirsts for sun and air. Let's not forget to live! The great new things that need our doing must not dry up our thirst to feel. Life is the first great wonder; just life itself and all that makes up living. This song that my skin sings, drinking in the sun and wind, lungs filled to bursting with salt air off the sea; these and a million other joys we must cherish. True, we must search for answers and in finding them we must do. But in the stress of doing, let's not forget to live. This, then, is my prayer. Let's not forget to live!

July 26, 1935. We reached Newport after a day's driving from Port Orford, interrupted every few minutes by free ferry rides across small inlets, five of them, the last one landing us on Newport's waterfront. It is a bustling, small place: just one street against a high cliff that offers protection from the wind, which do be a blowin' and a blowin' most all the time. We ascended a hill and came to an auto camp, The Roosevelt. One dollar and fifty cents got us a noble cabin with a tiny stairway going up to two bedrooms. We had a private shower and a stove that heated water immediately. What a luxury! I had two showers and a hair wash and I also washed clothes. I hate to get home with dirty laundry.

On this trip to Oregon my biological clock has begun to tick loudly. In the winter I want to get started on something. Whether or not to have a child is one question. Somehow, I can't see ahead clearly enough to answer the question satisfactorily one-way or the other. I think my wanting one is mostly curiosity, a vanity. My not wanting one is probably fear of it's effect on Kenneth and on the life we have, of the stress of a lack of adequate finances, and of the unknowns of a potential war. The papers are full of the possibility of a war. England is maneuvering in the Mediterranean. Italy is bombing Ethiopia now that the Ethiopian rainy season is over. It's all such insanity. It seems impossible that because a few individuals are insane, the whole race of men will allow themselves to be used as pawns. When I ask Kenneth what he thinks of having a child, he says, "I think it's a good idea," which means nothing.

Yesterday, at the end of our trip, we went through Raymond, Washington, because Kenneth wanted to see where he used to live. The whole town is very different, he says, with new buildings and only a few houses left on stilts. The streets are all torn up, and Kenneth's old house is gone. He felt quite empty for a minute, I think. But then we found the bakery where he used to work and the mill where he was a water boy, which brightened him up.

As it turned out, we had less to say about when to start a family than I thought. It was to be almost two years before a successful pregnancy decided the next phase of our lives.

9

For two footloose people to have become prospective parents AND homeowners in the same year was an acid test of our marriage. It worried me considerably and while we didn't discuss it, we were both aware of the subterranean alarms that rippled about from time to time.

I kept in mind D.H. Lawrence's tirade against bourgeois smugness concerning permanent homes; his feeling that homes should always have a transient character, as though the occupants could clear out at any time without any major upheaval. One should, he says, avoid any heavy, anchored quality and emphasize light, space and simplicity. Those ideas had also vaguely defined what we had looked for in our various rentals. We had lived like gypsies since our marriage in 1930. If we wanted to go to Mexico and we could scrape up the fare, all we had to do was pack up some boxes to store in somebody's basement. Now our lives were to be quite different and we wondered how it might change us.

The house was dilapidated when I found it in the early spring of 1937. The catalpa trees on the curb still looked dead with leafless bare boughs, but I could see from its view, its fireplace and its solid construction that a little fixing would make it a pleasant place and the price was only $1700: $200 down and $20 a month. What interested us more than the concrete basement or the hardwood floors was the way it rested its elbow, so to speak, on the steep side hill with the great expanse of Lake Washington and the Cascades in the distance and a varied hillside of trees and modest roofs in the foreground.

Influencing our decision to buy this place was Mrs. Bruce, who lived across the street, and kept a key for prospective buyers. "It's an awful good house," she said when she handed me the key. "It's a good-built house. You couldn't find no better – and a nice neighborhood. They're all nice people and mind their own business. Nobody'll bother you around here."

Mrs. Bruce's bosom stuck out like a shelf. From her expansive hips, her legs slimmed down to very slender ankles. She had small, good-natured blue eyes, framed by puckers, in a broad sympathetic face. And, with her short bobbed hair parted on the side, she looked oddly like a little girl.

I knew why she was so anxious to get the house sold. The neighborhood was just a few blocks removed from the East Madison "colored" center and there was always the dreaded possibility that vacancies would be filled by darker folks. Actually, the district was a shorter distance from the east capital hill area of large elegant homes with their extensively landscaped grounds.

This contrast was emphasized in the immediate vicinity of the house we were considering. Up the hill were two blocks of comparatively large and well cared for homes along 24th Avenue. Across the street and down the hill to the north were humble dwellings, some hardly more than shacks. We had rented one recently ourselves. The one "colored" family in the immediate neighborhood lived about a block down the hill.

Mrs. Bruce's attitude was a common one among whites. "We don't mind the Harrises," she said. "They're as nice people as you'd want. Nice as white people -- nicer than some -- but we don't want no more movin' in."

We finally bought the house and I did feel some pleasurable anticipation about living in the first house of our own. But still something unpleasant permeated my perception of a homeowner, a solid member of the community with the interest in the well being of the neighborhood. It was against my principles and all my inclinations to care whether colored people moved in or who my neighbors were, or what they did.

By October the house was ready for us. A builder friend had completed some necessary repairs. Of the jobs he had done, the most important to us was the cutting of a large window in the living/dining room on the view side looking east to the mountains. We could see Mt. Baker on the North, Mt. Rainier on the South and the long, irregular line of the Cascade peaks in between. Our neighbors were convinced, however, that we had invested in the window in order to better keep track of the community's goings-on and envied us our choice position in this regard. With its new coat of paint, inside and out, its concrete bulkhead and steps 2407 Ward St. was an alarmingly respectable house, we thought.

Each time we had moved we found our worldly goods increasing a little, and we eventually reached the limit of what Freddie's model T could carry. The last three times we'd used the Tokyo Express from Jackson Street. In the 1930's, Seattleites of lean income looked to the Japanese for inexpensive and well-done businesses. We had come to know several. There was Mr. Tokita, the pleasant suave artist who had run a cleaning establishment downtown, and another artist, Mr. Nomura, from whom we had bought flowers. We patronized several small, cheap-but-good Japanese restaurants and of course, the truck farmers selling their succulent and gorgeously arranged produce in the public market. The Japanese in the Pacific Northwest were admired and respected citizens for many years.

At that time just about the only painters we knew with families were the young Japanese. They had all received a good deal of recognition in local exhibitions. I remember the last time they paid us one of their evening calls. Mr. Tokita, Mr. Fuji, and Mr. Nomura had bowed, smiled their greetings with typical formality. They sat stiffly on the edges of their chairs while we discussed the health of their wives and children, and the prosperity of their sign shop by which Nomura and Tokita now earned their living.

"You promised you would bring your wives next time you came to see us," I said reproachfully. "Our wives are pretty busy," said Mr. Nomura, who was usually the spokesman, as his English was most fluent. "Mr. Tokita now has seven children. He has just had another son last week." "And how do you find time to paint, Mr. Tokita?" I asked. They exchanged glances and laughed again. Mr. Nomura said, "The two paintings which were in the Northwest Annual exhibition are the only two pictures Mr. Tokita has made in the past year."

There was an extended pause while Kenneth put the kettle on the gas hot plate for tea. While he was in the kitchen, the three had suddenly begun talking to each other rapidly and explosively in Japanese. They had talked at length, gesticulating very seriously, their dark eyes intent. Then just as suddenly they had ceased; each had turned a deadpan face toward me, and Mr. Nomura, after a preliminary polite chuckle, had announced, "Mr. Tokita, Mr. Fuji and I have decided you and Mr. Callahan should have only one child. It is a very easy matter to teach one child. You keep your paint things where you want them to be – you make it plain they are not to be touched." The implications were obvious, especially in Tokita's case. Perhaps Mr. Nomura, Mr. Tokita and Mr. Fuji would have been pleased to learn their advice was followed, if unintentionally, seven months after that evening tea, when Tobey was born.

Several Ito brothers operated Tokyo Express. Each brother was equipped with a pair of shoulders like a prizefighter and an unfailing conviction that life was a funny, funny business. This was particularly true when an old oak Morris chair dropped on one's toe or when one was trying all by one's self to juggle a 300-lb. box of books down a flight of stairs or when one was wrestling with a hundred picture frames of varying size and decrepitude.

"Well," the boss brother said, as he pocketed the pay and mopped his smooth brow, "you have good house now. You better not move any more. Anyway, I think next time you have too much furniture for our truck." Before there was a next time, the world itself moved from the domain of peace into the realm of war and the Ito boys of the Tokyo Express as well as the other Japanese in Seattle were sent over the mountains to an internment camp.

10

THE FALL OF 1937 was warm and lovely. I can remember sitting out on the grass at the side of the house in November writing a letter to California boasting that the sun was actually too warm for comfort. I was getting more and more pregnant, feeling wonderful, sewing no little garments, but being overcome, occasionally, with awe and disbelief over the event that was to take place the latter part of January. I would look at the empty bassinet and try to digest the miraculous idea that there would be a face there, a now non-existent face that would come into being – and, when I think about it now, the whole thing is just as crazy and inconceivable as it was then.

I wasn't minding a thing about being pregnant, except for the on-going vague worry about being tied down and wondering what it would do to a marriage that had been childless and independent for seven years, with its cornerstone of mutual interest in painting and its framework being the free, unconventional habits common to artists everywhere. We'd never had more than enough money for rent and hamburgers except on three occasions when picture sales or grants for government murals provided small windfalls. Each time we had spent it as rapidly as possible on travel – Mexico in 1932, New York in 1934, and Europe in 1936.

Neighbors, to us, had never existed at all, except as vague some bodies who might have to be coped with if records were played too late or too loud or parties broke up too noisily. . So it was a startling experience to receive a visit one afternoon from a trim little old lady in white gloves and severe black with white touches at the neckline. Mrs. Lownes was the neighbor who lived in the gracious colonial house with the super-duper view a block south on the corner of 24th. I had long coveted this house, with its simple, well-proportioned lines, its fireplace at each end, and its sun porch with windows and potted plants all along the eastern view exposure. I had seen Victorian furniture through the window and had allowed the unholy thought to flit through my mind that maybe the occupants were elderly. And that in not too long a time, there might appear a 'For Sale' sign on the premises. Further, perhaps the heirs would live far away and be eager to clear up the estate at a fabulously low sum.

I told her of my warm feelings for her house and apologized for always staring when I passed. "I love the house too, and my daughter – she lives with me, you know –feels the same way about it," she said. My hopes faded. "We have lived there for forty years. Both my children were born there, you know," she lowered her voice. "Some of our friends advise us to sell out because the colored people have moved up so close, but my brother always says, 'Broadmoor is just as close to them, and they don't even have a view'."

True, our hillside looked across of woods of Washington Park, to Broadmoor, down in the hollow toward the lake. There people paid a fancy price for the privilege of building an expensive house behind a high fence which excluded certain races. The gatekeeper greeted all visitors with "Where away?" Within the walls existed a welter of bastardized English, Spanish, Italian homes and fake "modernistic" architecture such as you've never seen outside a Hollywood set. It is a pathetic thing, this seeking of a man to isolate himself from his fellow men and to be as close to the 'cream' of society as possible. Those who are not admitted to the reservations of the elite make for themselves close replicas and keep out the next lower income group and of course all the races they regard as inferior.

Perhaps there are good motives at the root of this sort of thing: the desire to protect one's family, to further the welfare of one's children or to advance in some concrete way through achievement. But why must the way be so far from any commonly professed values? Maybe, living on a side-hill with the roofs of so many little houses, each with it's squared chimney and its floating column of smoke, all nestling close to the earth under the great sweep of the sky, made us more conscious of this sort of question. Certainly, the relationships of people to one another and to nature has been of consuming interest to Kenneth in his painting and to me in my thoughts during this last tumultuous decade.

I never returned Mrs. Lowne's friendly call and it weighed on my conscience all the time we lived at 2407. I always intended to, but there was some sort of hesitation. We did get to be friends through casual encounters, and years later when she had a broken leg I took over the fruits of a baking venture.

Kitty corner from us was the small square house of the MacLeod's and in their tiny back yard they kept a large police dog on a six-foot chain. In all the time we lived there I never saw the dog as there was a high fence about the back yard and he was never taken out for a walk for fear he might break away – he had grown extremely vicious from the constant confinement, and part of every night was made horrible for me by the dog's incessant barking, which continued at exactly the same pitch at intervals of five seconds for two hours at a time.

Other than barking dogs, the neighborhood was a beautifully quiet one, with only a few soothing sounds such as the patter of rain on the catalpa leaves just outside our north window, the seasonal rhythmic chorus of frogs from the Washington Park swamps and maybe an occasional raucous old tree toad. An exception was when some misguided car would think to escape the traffic on the long Montlake hill by driving up 25th Avenue. Coming to the dead end at Ward Street, it would attempt the steep short climb up past our house. This sort of intermittent, comparatively brief bedlam could be endured.

Kenneth's occupation as an artist provoked a great deal of interest among our daily acquaintances. Some were quick to assume the role of critics. One was old Chaldo, a swarthy Italian in his late 50's who lived in the next block with his enormous coach dog, Dixie. He would go by the house dragging a pile of empty boxes with one hand and holding Dixie's leash with the other. Chaldo occasionally made a little money doing jobs of metal fabrication for the Catholic Church. He was a skilled artisan but usually unemployed. One day I heard his steps coming up the porch and I opened the door. "Just a minute lady," he shouted, "I'll tie up Dixie to this post. Down, down Dixie… there now cara mia, there now. I'll be out in a minute only." He removed the broad-brimmed black fedora he always wore and from under his long black overcoat drew a large paper sack. "I got some more stuff here, some rice, some barley, some sugar," he said. "I thought maybe you could use them. You got a family, I got none and I get more of that stuff than I need." Chaldo, had taken to raising a bit of cash selling government relief food and I was getting overloaded with dried staples what with his and Katie's surplus, but I couldn't say no although I knew every cent went for a friendly jug.

Chaldo always examined Kenneth's paintings with the eye of an expert. He squinted at a figure composition over the mantle, a group of semiabstract nudes. "Did your husband do that?" he asked with a sly grin. "It's one that he's been working on lately," I said. Chaldo nudged me and, grinning like a satyr, said, "the little devil." Dixie began to howl and Mike to bark and I hurried Chaldo out. And a new milkman got the wrong directions and left four homogenized instead of three pasteurized and on the wrong porch. While waiting for me to get the empty bottles, he studied Kenneth's paintings, which were stacked about the hallway. "I wonder how much he'd want for one of these – they look like real class to me. I'd like to have something like this hanging over my mantle so that people coming in would say, 'What in God's name is that?' Then after looking at it awhile they'd get to liking it better. No fooling, you ask him how much he'd want for one." Then the Sears repair man: "I can really see something in these. I can't understand some of those dumb things they had at the Puyallup Fair."

Regularly on my daily walks with our wirehaired terrier Mike, a young fox terrier would come and meet us, always at the corner of 25th and Helen Street, where he and Mike would go through a stately ceremonial, each with his stub tail quivering and erect and a few back hairs on end. Then the meeting would resolve into the usual leg-lifting pantomime, and we would go on, the fox terrier following us back up the block before deserting us for other interests. One morning a nondescript little boy standing on the curb said, "Don't go near that dog. He got the mange."

Instant horror on my part. Mike already had eczema, and I didn't want to cope with mange. After this I would scold the little dog and send him away, tossing rocks and sounding as ferocious as possible, as he was for his part determined that our pleasant little meetings should continue. A short time later I saw Mrs. Bruce come out of her gate across the street with a snowy little dog on a leash. He was so clean and stepped so proudly I could hardly recognize him for mangy little mutt of our street encounters. From then on he was Spot, and if not the most cherished dog in the neighborhood, certainly a close competitor for that position.

We saw few of our friends during that period, the painters we knew being for the most part unattached and childless, and definitely repulsed at the idea of embarking on such a project. Among the first to whom we had broken the news were Malcom Roberts and George Mantor, and the look of unadulterated dismay that spread over their faces is still etched in my mind. "The predicted date is January? But our New Year's party! Ruined!"

Ah, that New Year's party. We could never understand why to Malcom and George it had been such crowning success. I wasn't inclined toward nausea during pregnancy, but mere mention of that New Year's party nearly brought it on. Our customary quiet evening at home (we planned it that way always) was interrupted by the arrival of George and Malcom laden with mysterious packages, including bottled goods of assorted kinds. We shared our whiskey and water with them during the early evening, which was pleasant enough with games and rising spirits, and all the time George was making trips to the kitchen where the evening's glory was being concocted.

By midnight we were all as gay as grasshoppers, Kenneth having reached the height of feeling good, which he always manifested by leaping into the air and clicking his heels together with more enthusiasm than grace. When the booming and banging began, we burst out onto our little balcony, and I remember experiencing that feeling of excruciating good will toward the world in general, compounded by the anticipation of an ultimate food experience. We threw miles of colored tape up into the night; a seemingly important ceremony, that tossing of the serpentine, and it took quite a while, for George had brought lots.

In the midst of all this hilarity, we were served the evening's glory. It was in a bowl with pineapple floating about and to me tasted heavenly. Kenneth had better sense. He sniffed it, set it down, and decided he was tired and was going to bed. But the rest of us drank it, and started casting about for new fields of activity. To go forth and to see people, that was it. And who better than dear old Barney and

Marj Nestor? I called them, they were having a party, and over the telephone it sounded like fun.

One of my weaknesses has always been the strong desire to mix oil and water in the way of people dissimilar in every way, but of whom I am fond for varying reasons. My inaccurate formula seems to go like this, that if C likes A and C likes B, then obviously B and A are bound to like each other. Needless to say, this is hardly ever the case. If George and Malcom were A, then Barney and Marj were B.

I realized we were on foreign territory the minute we stepped through the door and should have followed the impulse to back out and run in the opposite direction. The small frame house was full to bursting with a stationary population sitting about on the floor and a floating element drifting from room to room. Marj didn't get up off the floor and waved an indefinite greeting. I could feel hostile eyes boring into us from all sides, as we were "the turncoat stinkers, the ivory-tower aesthetes, the spineless liberals," and they were the fighting vanguard of the proletariat. I hadn't seen any of them for months and hadn't quite realized how bewitched they were with their fine new philosophies, which they wore like coats of armor, hiding all sorts of frustrations and blockages, laziness and fears. As was always the case with these gatherings, a few poor tired children lay about in chairs or on cushions on the floor sleeping restlessly, their faces flushed from the heat and smoke of the overcrowded rooms. My New Year's glow faded like a coat of old paint. Here were faces which once had meant the warm exchange of comradeship, and which now shone with a hostile fanaticism.

A specific reason for the hostility I met with that night was Kenneth's and my trip to Europe in 1936. Our destination was Spain to see the works of El Greco and Goya at the Prado and also to visit Mark Tobey in England. Our radical friends thought we should donate any extra money to the cause or at the very least to travel to Russia and see the 'workers paradise.' Ironically, the Spanish Civil War began as we were crossing the Atlantic and we were unable to travel to Spain.

As we were leaving, a burst of song set off by some silent signal fairly blew us out the door. With clenched fists beating time, their eyes hard and mocking, they were really giving it -- a bouncing refrain -- "The Soviets are Marching." Oh god, I thought, how can they be like that -- the clenched fists, the spilled drinks, the neglected children and all that hostile bravado in the stuffy rooms behind the drawn and cracked blinds.

"Do you know what that simple-minded individual said to me?" demanded Malcom when we were again in the freshness of the night. "Of all the rude bastards! He came up to me and said, 'What the hell do you think you're doing with a Hitler hair-cut?'" Malcom had had an extremely short haircut, practically a pig shave, and in growing out it had reached the upright brush stage. "He must have got the Hitler and Prussian military cuts mixed up," I explained. George and I laughed it off, but Malcom continued to be deeply disturbed by this deliberate, in-the-face rudeness, for no reason but the sheer pleasure of being offensive. If it had happened to George, the thrust would have been parried, for George could be rude himself, but Malcom's always impeccable manners were part of his nature, and the stab seemed to have hit some deep sensitivity.

Kenneth had been sound asleep for an hour or two when I returned home and coldness had settled inside the house, our only heat being the drum stove in the living room. I finally drifted off to sleep stiff with cold and my head whirling in a dreadful nightmare in which pieces of pineapple floated about a stuffy room crowded with clenched fists. I woke to the shouts of delighted kids in the frozen gray dawn. They had found and were collecting the serpentine from our joyous midnight revelry.

While still buried in the pit of our decrepitude the next afternoon, we were amazed to receive calls from two unbelievably chipper individuals – George and Malcom, who were still exulting over the success of the New Year's party and had declared it an Annual Institution. The looks on their faces when I had later informed them of my 'condition' almost convinced me that I had betrayed some vital trust in not timing things more considerately.

One break from the monotony of that pregnant winter happened on a mild, sunny December Sunday. It was one of those out-of-season days that can occur any time in a Puget Sound winter. Early in the morning we heard the familiar squeaking and creaking of Morris

Graves' Model A pickup parking at the curb of our steep hill. We greeted each other with our usual ecstasies over the state of the weather. Morris was always completely satisfactory in that way and was the only person I had known who was as responsive to rain, wind, sun or fog as I, none of this stuff ever getting to be an old story, and rarely being anything to complain about.

Morris was acquiring some cheap property -- a 40-acre tract near Index in the Cascades and how about the three of us going up to take a look at it? Kenneth was willing to quit painting for the day, as he was in one of his 'limbering up' periods, doing relaxed, fanciful compositions of semi-abstracted figures. To me they carried a symbolic suggestion of the regimentation of people throughout the world during the 30's, the de-humanized nudes grouped in patterns suggesting a grotesque dance of destruction.

As I was feeling healthy as a bird, it was without a qualm that I crowded into the single seat of our airy little roadster. We set out filled with high spirits on one of those unplanned expeditions that were a symbol of freedom from the restraints the world seemed constantly trying to impose. As we drove east, the mountains seemed particularly lofty, and the thin coating of snow accentuated the rich brackish colors of the foothills.

I was moved to try to repeat, stumblingly, the Biblical chant that I believe goes: "I will lift up mine eyes unto the hills, whence cometh my strength." I have looked in vain for it, but I know it is there somewhere. Nowhere, incidentally, are the mountains treated with such beauty and sonority of phrase as in the Old Testament. As I said the words, Morris's sidelong glance gauged my seriousness. He seemed about to add something, but apparently thought better of it. We knew only a few of the many facets of this complex personality at that time, all of them in the good companion and creative artist department. His only pronounced eccentricity was his avowed devotion to Father Divine. The Peace Mission Movement and its founder, Father Divine, were generally dismissed as an eccentric, dangerous cult with a power-mad charismatic leader. The sober look in Morris's large round, slightly protuberant, brown eyes were like a closed curtain on the acts to come. The magician, the comedian, the tragedian, and the mystic would emerge later.

We parked the Ford and walked across a small footbridge to the other side of a creek. The beaten path ended abruptly, and we faced a thick growth of sapling firs, hemlock, vine maple and huckleberry under which grew in profusion the usual sturdy assortment of Oregon grape, salal, sword fern, and the multiple small plants that hug the soil in this juicy Puget Sound country. Morris's long legs plunged into the thicket as though it were so much meadow grass, and I floundered along behind. It was every man for himself, over and under logs, through thorny underbrush, and every step up a rather a steep grade. If a log was too high for me to get over under my own steam, Kenneth would shove and Morris would pull, and I'd suddenly find myself on the other side. It scares me now to think of what might have happened, but at the time I had not a qualm.

We finally reached a wide ledge that curved around the mountain. The high point of the shelf was rocky and sparse of growth. We looked out over the tops of the trees to the town of Index and the river, and at our backs arose magnificent granite cliffs. Here, Morris had decided, he would like to build. Elation shone from his eyes and his voice quivered with excitement as he told us of his plans.

"Where would you get your water?" was my first question. I could see that such a practical consideration was repellent to Morris. "Oh," he said as though that were the last thing to be concerned about, "I'm sure there must be a trickle coming from these rocks somewhere. Somewhere along this ledge there's bound to be a spring." I asked also about a road, and that too was a simple matter to arrange. He indicated with a sweep of his long arm where the road would cut through the trees. It looked a staggering project to me, but I controlled any disparaging thoughts that I had. The whole idea of wrestling nature with one's bare hands was completely foreign to us; we loved the wilds, but as something to accept as is, for pilgrimages, not to possess and subdue. Morris attitude was mighty intriguing however, and proved contagious.

There was one thing that seemed to be bothering him about the rock ledge as a home site. "Guy Anderson says that he wouldn't take a chance on building here, because pieces might drop loose from those cliffs and roll down on you." He sounded a little scornful of Guy's trepidations, and to me they sounded ridiculous. Those monumental walls looked much too permanent to worry about. "Still," Morris ruminated, "they have broken off in the past." True, great slabs of rock

66

lay all about, with small leaves of shale plentiful throughout the green carpet of moss.

"But think of the wonderful building rock," Morris exclaimed, exulting again. "Everything you'd need right here at hand for a complete rock house." It all sounded wonderful and impossible. Again Morris eyed the towering precipices. "To have that to look out on when you get up in the mornings," he breathed ecstatically. "But then Guy insists that we could have a severe earthquake that would dislodge tons of it."

The early winter dusk was gathering as we started back. Fortunately, we were going downhill; it still makes me weary to think of heaving that load up and over those fallen logs. And, in view of what has happened to me since (a miscarriage that shelved me for six months), I marvel that all hell didn't break loose right there on the spot.

As it turned out, Morris did not build on the mountain after all, and his focus soon turned to the La Connor area where he eventually built his famous place called 'The Rock.' The great tonic about that whole day was that it was a link with the non-domestic world, that too familiar world in which regular trips to the doctor with little bottles of urine tucked away in the deepest recesses of one's purse, opinions as to whether Vanta baby garments were worth the extra money, and radical culinary experiments such as hot water pie crust were completely forgotten.

11

THE NEW MOON WAS just getting under way, a curved white blade in the daytime sky, when my long period of waiting came to an abrupt end. The doctor, upon hearing that January 24th was my birthday, decided we might as well make it a 2-in-1 affair, and issued orders for all sorts of activity starting early that morning. I was appalled at the number of enemas and doses of castor oil on the program, but pitched in with cooperative spirit. Between these charming divertissements, I cleaned house in the morning, went for a long walk up and down hill with Mike in the afternoon and cooked dinner – answered the phone – doctor's office calling, any symptoms? – Not a symp, and the nurse and I exchanged condolences. I was really pretty discouraged; it had been a hard day's work.

Kenneth and I decided to go to the library after dinner, both of us feeling as restless as sand fleas, and we parked the car far up on the Madison hill, which meant another climb when we returned to it. We stopped on the way home and bought a sack of candy, a chewy kind with ground nuts in it. In my nervousness, I ate too much of it and I could feel it settling down into a leaden ball in my insides. Before going to bed, I talked again with the doctor, who was in a surly frame of mind; but he had nothing on me. I was so tired I was nearly unconscious and I had no sooner hit the pillow than sleep washed over me like a tidal wave.

The stab that rent the thick veil of my exhausted slumber was so vicious that I was wide awake instantly. "Here we go," I said to Kenneth. "And I'm so tired." Fortunately, the Model A got us to the hospital without a flat tire or motor trouble. The pains had me almost doubled up so that the formalities at the desk seemed a heartless delay. From that time on everything assumed a dreamlike quality. You no longer have an identity. You are simply an implement being used by mysterious forces over which you have no control. You acquiesce to whatever it is that is happening to you. With the initial preparations over I seem to remember climbing with difficulty on to a hard table with lots of fresh linen around and a nurse appearing and disappearing. Kenneth was admitted to the small room, where he sat looking helpless and anxious. He had brought a book we had picked up at the library that evening, *Army Without Banners*, an account of the doings of the Irish republicans. This he proceeded to read aloud, but I found it difficult to keep my mind on the Irish.

Dr. Paul Rollins arrived shortly, exuding a feeling of comfort and confidence. "Say," I complained, "I thought there was supposed to be some peace and quiet in between these things." "That's just what I'm going to arrange," he said, "but first I want to watch you have a pain." It was no trouble at all accommodating this request. These pains are really indescribable. They take possession and they own you for the time being. But the strange thing is how nature erases the memory of them. You have no precise account of the pain left in your mind. It's a neat trick of mother nature aimed at the old perpetuation business.

I remember grabbing hold of the bar at the end of the bed and gripping it with all my strength while I breathed in deep gasps. I guess some women yell, but this I had no inclination to do. I needed all the air I could crowd into my lungs. "I guess that'll do," Dr. Rollins said nonchalantly. "It seems to be the real thing."

Kenneth was told to wait below. The doctor fiddled around with a hypo. I knew I was to have skaplomine, which is the truth serum they use on criminals to make them tell all. Its virtue in maternity cases is that you do not lose consciousness completely; you respond to instructions and thus are not inert and are able to assist nature in the job at hand. I must say I had a few qualms over the thought of what I might give forth under the influence of this drug's peculiar properties. I gave my conscience a thorough overhauling, looking in all the dark corners for any dire little matter that might be lurking there ready to disclose itself when the guards were asleep.

I said good-night to Kenneth and watched him go out the door feeling as though we were two lost figures in a vast unfriendly cell. The first hypo, Dr. R explained, was a preliminary and in a half-hour, at 1:30 he would administer the skaplomine. In the meantime I was to be quiet, and try to go to sleep.

"Margaret!" The voice came from far, far away, and kept repeating endlessly, "Margaret! Wake up! It's 7:30! Margaret!" Strange that somebody should be calling my name and saying the time, from far, far away. It was irritating, with sleep so compelling. Again from the echoing void, "Margaret! Wake up!" But I have no desire to wake up, even when my eyes open slightly and there is Kenneth's face bending over, smiling and misty and soft with a new tenderness. His hand is on my shoulder and he saying something. "Wake up, it's a boy. It's all over, and it's a boy." All over? Ridiculous! Let me go back to sleep. All over? How could it be? "Don't you believe me? Feel your flat stomach. I tell you it's all over, and it's a boy."

As consciousness returned, it was uncanny how wonderful I felt. No nausea, but a terrific hunger, and consumed with the desire to see my child. Not knowing hospital routine, and the inviolability of schedules, I began to wonder whether there was something wrong. Perhaps there was some reason why they were hiding him from me – not enough legs, or too many hands. I called the nurse and protested. After all, I remonstrated to Kenneth, the little guy was getting older by the minute and his own mother was not allowed to set eyes on him. The nurses apparently grew sick and tired of all this insistence, and finally one appeared, looking pretty surly about the whole thing, with a bundle in her arms. Masks were adjusted, and the blanket lifted. Crumpled pink face, like a poppy petal just unfolding, a mere suggestion of a nose, tiniest mouth but so perfect; then the eyes flew open and such a battery of blue light! I knew he would be a reasonable soul for the most part when I saw into his opened eyes. Just to be thorough, I made them show me both hands and feet. The feet seemed too long and mature-looking, and the fingers, I noticed with satisfaction, were shaped like Kenneth's – the same spatula nail formation. I had hoped for this, about the only physical specification that entered my mind.

This is undoubtedly one of the great privileges life can offer; no one can understand who has not produced a child. There is an unspeakable delight when one first lays eyes on one's infant. The artist appraising a finished product does not have the same satisfaction, a critical sense always underlying the appraising eye or ear. But the mother, gazing upon the tiny form, is not critical; all judgment is suspended, leaving the certainty that here, at last, is perfection.

It was difficult to say good-bye to Kenneth, for in all the years of our marriage we had never been separated over night, and a good part of our days had been spent together, in travel, in work, in long walks. I watched him go with a pang; he looked so tired, his always thin face seemed thinner, and his always wrinkled clothes more wrinkled than ever. What a strange thing, this linking of two individuals through love, and the creation of new life through shared sacrifice.

Years later, when the war had gone into its full and dreadful swing, I was to read Lewis Mumford's powerful work, *Faith for Living.* And those moments of realization in the hospital that morning came again to life with new meaning as I read: "from love spring all the special Christian virtues -- mercy, charity, peace -- and, above all, the capacity for sacrifice. There is no creation without this sacrifice. The parent knows it. But so does the poet who turns his back upon an easy job and dedicates himself to lonely days, days of poverty, in order that he may have that abundance of spirit out of which his poems can grow..."

There has been a constant interlocking between my reading experiences and my life. Sometimes the reading pioneers and sometimes the life experience, but inevitably the two inter-relate, which makes living a doubly rich affair. It's what the Chinese philosopher meant when he said, "you look at the painting to see the mountain, and you look at the mountain to see the painting."

Hospital routine swallows you up like a revolving door, and strangely enough, the time passes quickly. The most exciting events were Kenneth's visits, the moments when the baby was brought in, and the arrival of the flowers and gifts. The number of these astonished me, coming from people I hadn't heard from in years. I felt guilty, thinking of all the blessed events I had ignored, never realizing how important to the morale of the mother is the thought that those on the outside remember her.

On the third day, I got the greatly anticipated tabulation of weight gained by Brian Tobey (Brian for the great king, who drove the Scandinavians out of Ireland, and Tobey, of course, for Mark, the painter, whose friendship and counseling was something of first importance in our lives). A half-pound a day was the average gain.

Every evening when Kenneth left, I was homesick and couldn't keep back a short spell of tears. At night the hush of the impersonal hospital closed in on me. Everything became depressing and dreary, and I yearned for the time Kenneth, the baby, our dog Mike and I could be home together, really living once more.

"I've found a new place for us to explore. As soon as you are navigating again we'll bundle up the baby and start off some morning early. It's really a wonderful place." Kenneth looked down at me from the bedside, and I thought his smile looked a little pleading. I had worn off that walloping maternity jag, which comes from the first sight of the newborn, and was undergoing the gestation jitters, full of apprehensions and ready to weep for anyone. Out of the hospital window, the January sun was feebly lapping at patches of sooty snow on gray rooftops, visible through the winter-bare branches of a rangy old maple. I had never before been confined in a hospital, and the impersonal square room with its blank white walls were making me stir crazy. "Tell me what you found," I begged.

"Well, Morris and I started out about 6:30 this morning and stopped at a little place by the railroad tracks at Woodinville for breakfast. A nice old Alaskan runs it, and he makes swell hotcakes. Remember how I used to talk about a place along the narrow-gauge railway called Silverton? Well, the railroad has been abandoned for years. The government sold the rails to the Japanese for scrap iron. Slides have washed out the bed, but now there's a gravel road up the Stillaguamish River valley. The road starts out from Hartford and goes past Granite Falls and about twenty-five miles farther up the valley to Silverton." I recalled a day at the river at Hartford with Kenneth. "I remember how swift the river was through there. We waded around in some of the pools at the edge."

"Too much snow to get to Silverton today," Kenneth went on, "so we stopped at a campground just beyond a place called Robe. It used to be a mill town, but there isn't anything left of it now, except a few of the early settlers, a café, and a post office."

There was a swish of starched skirts causing a slight breeze as a nurse whipped a thermometer into my mouth, and was gone again. I indicated through shut lips for Kenneth to continue. "There's a certain spot, shortly after you leave Granite Falls where you seem to pass into a different world; meadows, wide valleys – then all of a sudden the whole character of the place changes and you're in the mountains. From then on you're not conscious of the world of people – it's pure wilderness." He looked out the window a moment where dusk had swallowed the last of the afternoon twilight. "Then there's Susie's Place where we had dinner. Susie runs it logging camp style. She has mostly loggers and road-workers for customers. Not many outsiders go into the valley because it's a dead end road. It was just extended to Silverton a year or so ago."

Again, there was the airy presence of the temperature-taking nurse. She frowned a little as she concentrated on reading the instrument, jotted something on the pad of paper, flashed us a cool, professional smile, and was gone. "They fill me with terror," I said, "but I wish I had a little of their efficiency." I was beginning to worry about how it would be at home. Never in my thirty-four years had I taken care of an infant. Other people's babies always cried when I picked them up. I was relying on nature to supply me with that mysterious know-how that is supposed to come with maternity.

"Did you do any sketching?" I asked. "We both made a few drawings on the river bank. The camp ground where we stopped is called Gold Basin and it has some very high, eroded sand bluffs -- beautiful mottling where they've been worn away." His hands were drawing the sandbanks in the air.

"I'm sorry to have to mention these things," I said, looking him over critically, "but you need a haircut badly. You also need your tie straightened. Yours pants need pressing, and that shirt had better go to the Goodwill." "I shaved, though, after I got home," Kenneth said in a pleased tone. Visiting hours were over and there were noises of the bedpan cart wheeling down the hall. "I guess I'll get along," he said, folding his old rain coat over his arm. He had been teetering on his heels and toes and flapping his hat against his legs as he did when restless. "I might do a little painting before I go to bed. I was up at 5:30 this morning."

· Every time after he left, I felt sad and deserted, but when the nurse brought in the baby I cheered up. He was always sound asleep when he arrived and asleep when he left. "Doesn't he ever cry?" I asked the nurse through my gauze mask. "You'll find out," she said. "Is this your first?" "Yes," I said. "It took us a long time to get around to it. We've been married for seven years. So many people told me it was dangerous for a woman to have her first baby after the age of thirty I pretty nearly got scared out altogether." "That's what they used to think," the nurse scoffed. "Now lots of women don't have their first until they're forty and they get along just fine. It's bound to make quite a change in your life though. By the time you're thirty you get in the habit of doing what you want to do when you want to. A baby soon changes that." "Hmmm," I said, "so I've been told. We've always been pretty independent you know, doing things on the spur of the moment." "Are you going to continue nursing the baby?" "For a couple of months anyway." "You'll be tied down all right," she called over her shoulder as she left the room with the blanketed bundle. "But I imagine you'll think it's worth it."

Hardest were the long hours before dawn, tooth brushing over, face washed, baby fed and whisked back into his stall. I would lie wide-awake in the darkness, hearing the murmur of hospital sounds from the hall through the half-opened door. A stifled exclamation, tense tones of a murmured dialogue, a low laugh, the squeak of the bedpan cart, and always the soft rapid pad, pad of rubber soles going and coming down the long corridors blended to form the music of the hospital. I thought how strange it was to be a part of this world within a world: all the people lying on beds under one roof, hearts beating in the darkness, lungs filling and emptying, eyes staring at the dark ceilings, umbilical cords being cut and souls being severed. Thinking of pain, wondering what it is and why. Wondering if the whole thing were part of one very big organism, if all the pulsing hearts were part of one big rhythm, if all the inhaling and exhaling lungs were actually integral parts of one universal tidal breathing. I fell asleep trying to imagine Robe, Gold Basin and Susie's Place.

After ten days in the hospital, going home time finally arrived. But the moment for which I'd been yearning with such ardor suddenly terrified me to my very bones. Now that it was about to be abandoned, the hated routine took on a halo of security. I was full of doubts and fears about the incredible difficulties I could foresee. My milk would probably give out and the poor little thing would starve. He'd cry all night, and we'd be wrecks by morning. I'd never be able to bathe the slippery little tadpole, and that frightening thing on his stomach would probably burst wide open. But I pulled on my clothes, which were too small, watched my mother dress the baby in clothes which were too large, quivered over the germs to which he was being exposed, and wobbled forth into the world again.

I had rebelled mentally when told to stay upstairs for three weeks, but I soon discovered that after ten days in bed my two perfectly good legs had been mysteriously supplanted by a couple of deflated inner tubes. Our small staircase assumed the proportions of the Matterhorn, and I was glad enough to consider the upper floor of our house my quarters at least for the time being. When we arrived, Mikey was in the hall going through his greeting routine with frantic intensity. We paused while I explained about the baby, showing him the contents of the basket, which he sniffed thoroughly and with apparent approval. "It's your baby, Mikey," I told him, "isn't it wonderful? Mikey's got a baby." He entered into the spirit of the whole thing right from the start, never showing any jealousy or resentment. We had been cautioned with stories of the tragic results of canine jealousy. In fact, there had just been a story in the papers about a baby being killed by a jealous bulldog. My reasoning told me the way to forestall jealousy was to make the dog an intimate part of the activity and be careful never to deprive him of any of the attentions he was used to getting. It worked beautifully with Mikey.

The impact of color on eyes grown used to blank white walls for ten days was an experience I'll never forget. Paintings and Navajo rugs glowed, and the thought flashed through my addled mind that I would never take the world of color for granted again. Hospitals should hang paintings to relieve the austerity of their rooms and halls. The world of art can offer new horizons for all who are physically confined. Come to think of it, paintings in prison might do more to rehabilitate prisoners than do some of the uninspired sermons they are constantly getting.

The best thing about going home from the hospital, aside from going home from the hospital was having Katie Koslowski to help grease the skids. I had never felt so totally incompetent, even at my first day at the newspaper job. "Ah, goodness-gracious-me, Margaret," she trilled in her high Belfast singsong, when I had wobbled into the house on the shaky inner tubes I had mistaken for legs. "Ain't he the cutest little bugger? Well, I guess between us we can get his pants changed and his stomach filled." The baby cried too, the first time we'd heard him do so. "It's two hours yet before he gets fed," I bawled. "What in the world shall we do?" The hospital, the beautiful, orderly hospital was the only place to be!

"Katie's had two children," Kenneth reminded me, "She ought to know a little something about what to do." He stuck a cigarette into my mouth, lit it, and fluttered a paper before my swollen eyes. "Read this," he suggested. "Maybe it will make you feel better. I saved it for a surprise." The letter was from the U.S. Treasury Department, and Kenneth's sketches had won the Centralia post office mural contest. "It will pay the doctor and something on the house, too," he said. "Nothing like being married to a good provider, I always say."

I groped for a handkerchief . "Maybe you're right," I sniffled, hating myself for being such a sissy. "Maybe I did get in on the ground floor of a good thing." The crying had stopped. "He's all dry and comfortable now," Katie said. "I think he'll sleep till his ten o'clock feeding." I composed myself for a wakeful night, worrying about whether he might starve before the schedule permitted me to feed him. Kenneth drove Katie home, and I was asleep before he returned. The next thing I knew I was jolted awake as though I'd been goosed with a live wire. The baby was crying. "Must be almost ten o'clock," I thought wildly, reaching for the bedside lamp. It was 5:30 in the morning.

12

WITH THE INVALUABLE HELP of Katie, my mothering skills slowly emerged and my body eventually regained its former vitality. But it was some months before an opportunity to escape from the city came to pass. Our chance came one day in April. Squalls of rain pattered on the budding leaves just outside our bedroom window. Katie stood in the doorway, her starched white apron standing out where the iron had creased it, watching with an amused smile my frenzied preparations for our first day's outing since Tobey's birth. "Look at his eyes followin' yez, Marrgarret," she laughed. "He ain't missin' a thing. For only three months old, he's an awful smart kid." "Too smart this morning," I retorted. "He should still be sleeping. He doesn't usually wake up for another hour."

"Well, he probably knew there was something unusual going on. You know, Marrgarret, I think the little rascal can hear the grass a' growin'." She picked him up from the bed to return him to his crib, automatically feeling his diapers. I said, "I've got his washing done and plenty of dry dipes. Formula is in the bottles. He gets vitamins and orange juice and bath at ten, pablum and formula after bath, cottage cheese and formula at two..." "I know, Marrgarret, I know, dear," Katie protested. "You don't have to keep tellin' me. Just you get along now and enjoy yourselves. Have a good time and don't worry none about us. And don't hurry back."

I clumped downstairs and she followed. Kenneth had gone to get the car out of the garage we rented from a neighbor. While I pawed through the hall table's accumulation for my gloves and beret, Katie picked up a dust cloth and began whisking about the living room. She circled the small table on which moped the wilty still life Kenneth had been painting; a segment of squash, a purple cabbage and a few green pears. She started to whisk at it with the dust cloth, then paused, hands on hips. "Marrgarret," she began in an unusually high tone, "when is Kenneth goin' to be through" (her voice gliding lower and finishing in a growled) "with this goddamn thing?" "I have no idea, Katie," I said. "He wouldn't know if I asked him. Just pretend it isn't there." "And these paintings stacked against the wall? I guess there's not much use tryin' to dust around them," she said querulously. I told her not to bother. This five-room house had no possibility of a studio room. Kenneth painted either in the dining room or the living room, which opened into each other with a wide arch. Works in progress were always lined up three-deep against the walls. In dusting the floors, if the mops happened to knock against one painting, dislodging it, the others would all start to slide too. You just waited and stacked them back again.

"When he's through with that there paintin', if you're goin' to just throw out the cabbage and the squash I could use them at home if you wouldn't mind," Katie suggested. As I was going out the door, she said hesitantly, as if it were an after thought, "And say, Marrgarret, I brought with me a five-pound sack of sugar and a few pounds of barley in case you'd be going to buy them anyway. We get more of that stuff than we can use." I told her to remind us when we returned. Her family was still on relief, as there wasn't much call yet for her husband's job as a hod-carrier. To get a little extra cash Katie would bring over an occasional surplus of government-issued dried foods and staples. We didn't suspect what she was spending the money for. I had offered her a glass of wine with lunch one of my first days downstairs and she had declined, shaking her head vehemently, her eyes brimming with amusement. "Maxie wouldn't like it," she had explained, "if I took a drink, even one. He'd smell it on me sure when I got home." Then looking at me quizzically she had asked, "Do you think there's anything so terrible wrong with takin' one little drink now and then, Marrgarret? I think myself sometimes that Maxie's just talkin' a lot of hooey." Katie dismissed a good many aspects of life as a lot of hooey, always pronouncing it 'hughie'.

Kenneth and the green roadster were waiting, the front tires braked against the curb on the steep hill. Mikey dashed out ahead of me and into the car, where he stood on the seat quivering, his spike tail stiff as a handle, the pink tongue flapping in his panting mouth. Anxieties swarmed in on me like moths around a street light as we started off, and they almost turned me back home. The normal mother deserves no praise for devoted or even heroic attention to her infant. She can't help herself.

Kenneth looked sideways at me and took one hand off the wheel to pat mine. Mike licked both our hands, opened his mouth wide, said, "yeeeouw," and panted deliriously. "We're lucky we can get Katie to baby-sit," he said, and I knew he'd been reading my mind. "You can be darn sure she'll look after him more closely than you would yourself." As we rattled down the Montlake hill, a patch of sunshine splashed the Laurelhurst area across the ship canal. "This is the life of Riley," Kenneth said, laughing. He began singing the Irish Washerwoman, "Oh-dee-deeedley-deedley-deedley-dee." "You sound like a carefree artist," I said. "The artist is a happy chap. He's free the whole daylong. His nights are full of revelry, women, wine and song," Kenneth recited.

The familiar squeaks and rattles of the old car, the feel of the April-balmy air and the fine look of the countryside as we moved through it loosened our thoughts and our tongues. There were so many things to talk about. It seemed we hadn't had time to talk without interruption for ages. We talked about painting, about the news, about our friends, about attitudes towards life and how many different ones there were, and which were right, what made people get old, and why some old people did not seem old at all. "It's not closing your mind that's most important," Kenneth said. "Once you nail up the shutters you're through having fun. You start settling into the grave right then."

"What makes people close up," I wondered. "I don't know," Kenneth answered. "Fears, mostly, I suppose, but maybe something to do with ideals, too. Young people start out with ideals, but the ideals are so tender that they bruise easily, and the more bruises they get, the thicker the bandage. Then the bandage gets mistaken for the ideals. And they're afraid to take off the bandage and finally the ideals get buried so deeply that they can't find them any more. But they go on cherishing the bandage."

"Of course," I suggested, "if you have standards at all you have closed your mind to some extent." "Yes, you can't be just a piece of blotting paper," Kenneth smiled. "But how do you know when your standards are intolerance?" I inquired. "You mean where is the fine line that turns principle into blind dogma?" he asked. "Well, what confuses me sometimes," I said, "is that so many people are thinking so many different things, and every damn one of them is sure they have the answer. Maybe Wordsworth had something when he wrote that verse about 'one impulse in a vernal wood can teach you more of man, of moral evil and of good, than all the sages can'. Trouble is we're cutting our vernal woods down so fast that there aren't hardly any left to get any impulse from."

On the road to Bothell, we passed the abandoned brick works with its broken walls, rubble, and chalky, earthy colors. Young green shoots were pushing through the ruins. "If you were an artist wouldn't you like to paint that?" I kidded. Kenneth said, "Hmmm." He was interested in the big, overall landscapes. I was always seeing specific small patterns of design or color: a clothesline strung between a barn and a house; a pile of brown manure against a faded red barn; the sun on a flowering orchard against cloud-darkened evergreens or a thundery sky. He saw the rising lines of the hills against sky, the spread of the broad meadows with structures, animals and men always a part of an enveloping whole.

We passed through the broad Snohomish valley, along the narrow blacktop road between cabbage and lettuce gardens and pastures emerald with new spring grass. The sky was a bowl of moving clouds, and the sun, like a giant searchlight, caught now a cluster of farm buildings, now a plumy line of poplars, now a pair of frisking horses and the small figure of a man driving a tractor.

A long line of freight cars prevented us from crossing the bridge at the entrance to the pioneer town of Snohomish. The Snohomish River flowed full, wide and gray-green, against the heavy piling and plank bulkhead that prevented the fringe of buildings along the town's main street from falling into the current.

Leaving Snohomish, the road wound along the side of a high bluff, overlooking the peaceful Pilchuck River Valley, an area more like northern Europe than the Pacific Northwest. The houses, dating from the 1880s, wore little gingerbread collars around their eaves and porches: their paint had faded to mellow shades of yellow, ochre and green, harmonious with the maples, dogwood and alder The tumbling warble of a western meadowlark sang in our ears from the roadside grasses. Just before we reached Granite Falls a break in the clouds revealed a peak, formed like the crest of a breaking wave. White with snow, it loomed surprisingly near. "That's Mount Pilchuck," Kenneth said excitedly, "that's what we're heading for. The Robe Valley's on the other side."

At Granite Falls, the blacktop road became gravel. The remains of a burned out mill, with a nest of unpainted cabins around it, near the Falls bridge over the Stillaguamish River, defined the boundary of civilization. Beyond lay only a rhythmic expanse of rolling foothills. Over the hills to the North a triple-spired, glacier-capped peak spoke of the proximity of the high Cascades. Kenneth said it was named 'Three Fingers.'

The road, just wide enough for two cars to pass, wound its twisted course through the hills, generally following the swift, boulder-strewn Stillaguamish River. It plunged through tangled salmonberry brush and feathery young hemlocks one minute and dipped into the shady recesses of old forest growth the next, now climbing, now descending. It was a leisurely road, following nature's contours. It went over or around obstacles, rather than cutting through. Other roads might go farther in a shorter time, but this road partook of many small delights. We hit a stretch where the road straightened out for several miles along a flat, cleared terrain. A few farm buildings sprouted like little islands in a green pasture sea. Mount Pilchuck was now entirely visible on our right, white nearly to its base, its peak narrowing to a rocky point against the sky. It was so near that we seemed to be within its shadow.

Just ahead, plodding slowly at the side of the road was a slim figure in a red jacket, bowed beneath a packsack. I said I could hold Mike on my lap, and we could give him a lift. The figure turned as we approached, giving us the familiar thumbing gesture of the hitchhiker, and we saw it was a white-haired woman, certainly no younger than sixty. She smiled broadly as we stopped, the smile ending in a slight grimace as she worked her false teeth more securely into place. "We aren't going far," Kenneth said, "but we'd be glad to give you a lift."

"Thanks," she said, climbing in briskly. She settled her pack between her thin legs, clad in red flannel trousers, wound in army puttees to the knees. "I'll go as far as you're going anyhow." Her eyes were bright, pale blue, and her white hair was tightly curled. Her cheeks were rouged and powdered, and her lipstick was bright and unsmeared as though she had just stepped from her boudoir. Under the make-up her skin was thin, and a mesh of tiny wrinkles stretched taut over her jaw and cheekbones. Her stooped, spare figure gave an impression of frailty, but her movements were vigorous, without any hint of tremor. She fished out cigarettes and a lighter and offered them to us, then lighting hers and mine with her strong, bony hand cupped about the flame. Then she searched our faces piercingly, flashed us another grin, and said, "whew, it's warm for this time of year. I wore my long johns and heavy boots, because I thought I might run into snow by the time I got this far."

She introduced herself as Kate Knowlton. She lived, she said, at Alderwood Manor (near Seattle) in the winter months and at Monte Cristo from thaw to snow fall. Had several mining claims in there she had to keep up. Had to work them a little every year or she lost her claim to them. She'd started from home about seven that morning and had been fairly lucky about rides. "I don't expect I'll get clear into Monte today but I'll get as far as Silverton as least. I can stay over with friends there. Hasn't been near as much snow as usual this year. The trail into Monte should be open in another week or so."

Elderly people who live alone are apt to either clam up completely or talk a blue streak. Kate Knowlton was the latter type. We learned in the next few miles that she had been a nurse in World War I, had suffered a breakdown from overwork, had been ordered by the doctors to live an outdoor life, and had liked it so well she had stuck with it. She'd never owned a car and always hitchhiked the distance between her Alderwood home and the cabin at Monte. "Monte's due to boom again," she said decisively. "They took a lot of gold out in the '90s, but they didn't get all that's there. We just got to hang on a little while longer. I know of several parties getting mighty interested." She looked sidelong at us, twisted the corner of her mouth, and said in a low, suspicious tone, "there's been some peculiar parties in there lately too, mighty peculiar. I'm keeping my eye on them, you bet. I don't know what they're up to, but they act peculiar. I was down to the Chamber of Commerce meeting in Seattle last Monday, and I heard it said they may even put a road into Monte before long. All this war talk. Certain minerals are wanted bad. Moly (Molybdenum) is one of them. Well, I've hung on for fifteen years. Yes, sir, Monte's going to boom again, don't let anybody tell you different." She tightened her lips and the blue eyes snapped behind the bifocals.

"Here we are at Gold Basin," Kenneth said. Several miles back we had passed a sign marking the entrance to Mount Baker National Forest. Through an opening in the trees we could see the river. "We were going to stop here for awhile." "That's fine, that's just fine," Kate Knowlton said heartily, "I'll walk awhile; somebody's bound to come along." "How much further do you have to go?" I asked. "Oh, about fifteen miles," she said indifferently. "Pretty near there. I feel rested up again now." She swung her pack over her back. "It looks too heavy for you," I protested. "T'aint so heavy as you might think," she said, grinning. "When I have my pick and shovels with me, then it's really a load. Well, I sure thank you folks, hope we meet up again some time." She trudged off, waving back over her shoulder.

The day that Kate Knowlton hitched a ride a long friendship began. Later, during the war years, Kenneth worked near Monte Cristo as a forest guard for the U.S. Forest Service. His patrols often took him to Monte. Kate was one of a very few residents of the 'ghost' town in those days, and she was always happy to talk to visitors. I found Kate's personality and connection to the mining town fascinating. Following are excerpts from an August 19, 1945 Seattle Times article I wrote:

Monte Cristo is located in the heart of the Cascades. After nearly half a century as a ghost town, it is as charming a spot as anyone could ever hope to see; its beautiful silvered buildings snug in the basin where the Sauk River has its source. The walls of Wilmon Peak, Silver Tip Mountain and Monte Cristo Peak rise to 7000 feet on three sides.

It was the Fourth of July 1889, the story goes, when Frank A. Peabody and Joseph Pearsall first looked from Silver Lake to the mineral-streaked crags across the valley. Pearsall exclaimed, "why, Peabody, it's as rich as Monte Cristo!" "Then," said Peabody, "we shall name it Monte Cristo." About three years later, Rockefeller money took over the two leading mines,

Pride and Mystery, paying $300,000 and taking out $2,700,000 in gold and silver alone, according to Whitfield's History of Snohomish County.

One of the most active and picturesque persons who still maintains a claim at Monte, tirelessly hoping for better days, is Miss Katherine Knowlton, Kate to all who know her. Other titles bestowed upon her have been "The Belle of Monte Cristo" or "The White-Haired Lady of Monte Cristo." Kate Knowlton can keep a pace on the trail carrying a pack that would wear out many a husky male.

The Frank Peabodys were neighbors of Miss Knowlton in Edmonds -- the same Frank Peabody who had discovered Monte Cristo's mineral riches. Upon his death, Mr. Peabody turned over some of his claims to Miss Knowlton, who had nursed him during his final illness. To keep the claims meant to do the required work of maintenance, which involved lots of hiking and digging. Though frail at the time, her spirit was strong, and since taking up the claims, Miss Knowlton has hitchhiked the 75 miles from Edmonds at regular intervals. Kate became so accustomed to the weight of her backpack she often carried a few river rocks for a sort of ballast when she hitchhiked back to Seattle at the beginning of the winter.

Shortly after her husband's death, Mrs. Peabody became convinced that his spirit could never be happy as long as his mortal remains were confined to an urn, and Kate promised she would remove and scatter the ashes on the rocky slopes of the Monte Cristo he loved so much. According to Kate, she carried out her mission at sunset one sunny July day. As the ashes left the urn, out of the blue, a great bolt of lightning split the air, followed immediately by a terrifying crack of thunder that echoed back and forth from peak to peak.

We turned into Gold Basin, driving through a grassy, brush-grown old orchard. Near the river the road turned again, leading through a hemlock and vine-maple forest. Within the shelter of the grove were picnic tables and benches, hewn from great slabs of trees, and crude stoves built of cemented river rocks, all built by Roosevelt's Civilian Conservation Corps, the C.C.C. The vine maples were the biggest I'd ever seen. They grew in great clusters, their graceful boughs some fifty or sixty feet high meeting overhead in a series of arches. They reminded me of the trees in Cézanne's watercolors of the bathers. The new leaves were bright green, still crinkly, with waxy red stems; the trunks gray-green and pocketed with lichen. We parked the car and walked along the road under the arched boughs. Mike raced about in circles, trying to follow every enticing scent. The sound of axe blows drifted to us from somewhere up the path. I mentioned roasting hot dogs on sticks and making coffee. "Hard to find dry wood this time of year," Kenneth said. "Besides, you have to have one of Susie's dinners this trip. Next time we can bring picnic food if we feel like it." We admired everything about the campground. The amenities were all fitted into the surroundings with as little disruption as possible. Even the garbage disposals were made of hollow stumps and covered with mossy lids. At the end of the camping area was an open-air kitchen of peeled fir logs and a cedar-shaked roof. It contained a table and benches, a water faucet and a big stove with an oven.

Just outside the shelter, a man was chopping logs into stove size pieces. He stopped working as we approached, greeted us quietly and with a certain stiff formality. Mike jumped all over him and he responded with a few restrained pats. I was full of questions. Who was responsible for such an attractive campground? How long had it been in existence? Why hadn't we ever heard of it? Did many people make use of it? We told him our names and he said his was Barrett, and that he and his family had come west from Indiana. He had black eyes and hair, high cheekbones, and spoke slowly in a soft, rather hesitant voice.

"I understand this site used to be a homestead along in the '80s, quite a big farm. They did a good deal of placer mining in here, too, I guess. The Forest Service bought the whole 160 acres because it seemed like an ideal spot for a recreational area. The C.C.C. boys helped build the equipment."

I knew there were such things as forest rangers, and I was familiar with the National Park set-up on Mount Rainier, and I knew there was a state forestry department, but I was completely unfamiliar with that branch of the Department of Agriculture called the U.S. Forest Service. The man before us, leaning on his double-bitted axe in the subdued forest light, began to assume heroic proportions in my eyes: a sort of combined Daniel Boone, Ezra Meeker and Chief Seattle. One who knew 'Secrets of the Woods.' I asked the names of the trees and plants about us, and if he didn't know them he made them up, to my complete satisfaction.

"Just what are the duties of a forest ranger?" I asked. "I'm not a forest ranger," Mr. Barrett said patiently. "I'm a forest guard. The District Ranger is the headman of each district. It takes a long time to work up to a ranger's job. I do all different kinds of jobs. I've been helping build the new station at Verlot. Pretty soon now we start trail work: clearing old trails, building new ones. Then there's the look-out work in the fire season and fire fighting, if we get unlucky."

"To say nothing of answering questions," Kenneth said, "I'd like to ask you one myself, though, if you don't mind. About the trails you spoke of, are there many around here?" "We're trying to maintain about 150 miles of trails in the Monte Cristo district," Mr. Barrett said. "We can't really keep them up like we should on the amount of money we are allotted. Every year a certain percentage of trails is abandoned, but we do the best we can." Kenneth asked which trails were best for one-day trips. "Well, now, there's a good many beautiful trips under five miles. I'd suggest the lakes on Mount Pilchuck -- Heather Lake and Lake 22 and Pinnacle. Then there's Canyon Lake on Green Mountain. The Canyon Creek trail is very nice and there is pretty good fishing in the creek. The Pilchuck Mountain summit is only five miles from the river to the top. It's kind of strenuous, but not bad if you're in condition."

A shower began to spatter through the trees. Kenneth apologized to Mr. Barrett for taking so much of his time. "I've been swinging this axe pretty steady since early morning," he said. "I'm glad to get a rest." As we turned toward the river he called after us, "If you'd want to see a relief map of the Monte Cristo district you might stop at the ranger station. The trails are all marked with mileage and elevation."

The river, though high with April's thaw, skirted a wide gravel bar, apparently covered only at extreme flood. Rocks of all sizes from pebbles to huge boulders were strewn where the rushing waters had left them. Tough clumps of willows and alders pushed up out of the gravel. Many of the rocks wore bonnets of moss, dark purple-brown and bright yellow-green. We roamed over the gravel bar selecting rocks we thought would look fine in our garden. The pile quickly grew too big, for each rock when examined closely had some unique beauty or distinction. There were pink ones, green ones, salt and pepper ones shiny with mica flakes. All were water sculpted, and many appeared to be marked with cloud and mountain forms. Some had delicate lines of white, like Chinese landscaping drawings. Mike devoted himself to fishing thrown rocks and sticks out of the river, exploding in sneezes and snorts when the water went up his nose.

By the time we had lugged our rocks to the car, we were ready for supper. On our way to Susie's Place we talked about all the trails we were going to explore. "I can make a pack sack," Kenneth said, "and carry Tobey on my back. We can go anywhere." Under his breath he hummed the Irish Washerwoman.

Susie's Place was a green, cottage-like structure, with vines and shutters and a thin trail of blue smoke drifting from the chimney. No indication of being a restaurant, save for a small sign saying Susie's. Within were three narrow tables about eight or nine feet long covered with immaculate white oilcloth, set with silverware and heavy white crockery. In the center of each table were a sugar bowl, salt and pepper shakers, a can of evaporated milk, a bottle of ketchup, and a glass filled with paper napkins folded cornerwise. An archway at the back of the room opened to the kitchen, where a blond, heavy woman was peeling potatoes and another with dark hair and eyes was washing dishes. An infant slept in a crib at the far corner of the dining room. A heavy round cast-iron heater occupied another corner.

Roast meat and coffee smells mingled. The blond woman put down her pan of potatoes, wiped her hands on a towel and came forward to meet us. Her white apron and gingham dress was tightly starched and fresh from the iron. Her hair, light and silky as a child's, was bobbed, parted on the side, neatly in place. Her skin was pink and white and she wore glasses. She called us 'folks' and was friendly in a direct, sincere way. To Kenneth she said with a twinkle in her eye, "I was beginning to wonder if you were ever going to keep your promise about bringing the rest of the family up this way. What have you done with the baby?"

"This is my escape," I said. "But maybe next time we'll bring him, too. If you don't mind warming bottles and baby food."

"Well, there's quite a bit of that sort of thing goes on around here already. Patsy here must be about the same age as your boy. She's three months." I exchanged a few words on weight and feeding accomplishments with the mother, whose name was Mrs. Kennedy. To my surprise, along with a first baby comes a curiosity, tiresome to all but the new mother, about how it compares with others its age.

Golden rolls and crusty loaves of bread on a table by the window smelled heavenly. A ray of sun slanted briefly through the white-curtained window, filling the room with soft, golden light. "The weather is certainly acting like a woman today," Susie said, ladling soup from a great kettle. "Like a woman is supposed to act anyway, according to the men. I don't know how many times it's changed its mind since I got up this morning." The soup was a full-bodied meat broth with finely cut vegetables and rice. Soup was followed by a succulent pot roast of beef, browned potatoes, rich dark gravy, and green beans flavored with bacon and onion. Everything was placed on the table in bowls and on platters, family style. There was even a bowl of chopped carrot pickles and a clear, dark red jelly, which, Susie said, was a mixture of Oregon grape, salal berry, and wild blackberry. "Now if there's anything I've forgotten or if you want more of anything, just holler," Susie said. "Will you have raisin custard pie, apple pie, or stewed fruit and cookies for dessert?" We had to linger with coffee and cigarettes quite a while before we could move. In the interval Susie's husband, whom she introduced to us as Bob Buchanan, came in the back door with a big sack of greens and a hat full of mushrooms.

"Here's those nettle tops I promised you, honey," he said. "And, by God, look at the mushrooms I found over in the apple orchard. Morels, you call 'em? Wouldn't touch 'em myself, but I know you think they're a treat." Bob Buchanan was tall, lean, and leathery of skin, with small, gray eyes encased in wrinkles. He wore a mackinaw and black, battered fedora shoved far back on his shiny bald head. He had a breezy, profane way of talking and sort of a rakish charm. He left, saying he was going out to "get them pole beans planted".

"You know," Susie said apologetically, "I hate to do it, but except for my regular boarders, I've had to raise the price of my dinners from 35 cents to 45 cents. Prices have gone up for so many things. Bob blames the administration for ploughing under crops, destroying potatoes and hogs and such. I suppose they've got a good reason for it, but it doesn't seem right, as long as there's hungry people in the world. Of course, Bob takes every chance he gets to put me on the spot for voting Democrat."

On our way out of the valley Kenneth pulled over on a small rise and we plunged through the brush to climb a tall cedar stump for a farewell view. The mountaintops were bright salmon-pink from the setting sun; the sky behind them cobalt blue. We lit cigarettes and watched the shadows swallow the valley. The peaks lost their brief flame, turning coldly dark, the sky's blue soon deepening and intensifying. Kenneth was drawing with quick, nervous hand and wrists movements, the pencil sometimes not touching the paper, like a dog turning in circles before settling. His eyes blinking rapidly between scene and paper were squinted almost shut to avoid the smoke from the forgotten cigarette in one corner of his mouth. To remember the color he scrawled a few key words on the sketch. Frogs and robins chanted their evening calls. From the darkness of the woods came the occasional long, haunting note of the varied thrush's evening song. The sustained, trailing minor note, vibrant with overtones, is nostalgic for anyone who has known and loved the deep woods of the Northwest coast. "Gee," I said, "it would be nice to own some kind of little shack out here, someplace where we could build a fire and cook and sleep. Sunrises must be wonderful. And moonlight." No sooner having said it I chided myself. Always wanting to own something, to plan, to look ahead. What the hell's the matter with the way things are now?

"You know, I think I can do some good paintings some day," Kenneth said as we climbed into the car again. "Maybe this summer." I hadn't heard him say that since before I went to the hospital.

13

TRAILS HAVE HELD A fascination for me ever since, at the age of nine, I was lucky enough to be allowed to walk back from Portage to Ellisport on Vashon Island with the men. The women boarded a small Puget Sound steamer for an easy ride to the next landing. The fact that bedtime, rigidly enforced in our family, was being evaded added to the excitement. But there was also something special about walking single file in the company of others, but under my own steam. Once in the dark I blundered into some bushes. Before I realized I was off the trail my father's hand was in mine guiding me back. "When it's too dark to use your eyes," he explained, "let your feet do the thinking. If you are sensitive to the feel of the trail, you know immediately when you've lost it." I then felt as one of the initiated. I thought through my feet, and not again did I lose the beaten path. If only life could be that simple.

But my love of mountain hiking really began with my introduction to the Robe Valley, the mountains and the trails that would come to play such a great role in our lives. Kenneth's description of his trip to Silverton while I was in the hospital had intrigued me and it was not long after that day at Gold Basin that we took our first hike in the valley. Susie said we could leave Tobey with her for the day. Eventually, Kenneth constructed a baby carrier by cutting two legs holes in a canvas packsack and on those occasions when we didn't leave Tobey with Katie in Seattle or with my parents, we explored the high meadows, alpine lakes and ridges with Tobey on Kenneth's back.

We selected Heather Lake on Mount Pilchuck for our first exploration. It was a good selection. The trail, only a little over two miles with an elevation gain of about 2500 feet, began in a virgin rainforest and ended in the alpine.

The rain-fed trees of the 'asbestos valley' are enormous. (The average rainfall in the valley of the south fork of the Stillaguamish is over 130 inches a year). Only because they are in the National Forest do the trees still exist, and I'm afraid that with the present cutting program, they will not exist for long. But at that time the logging hadn't started.

The towering forest through which our trail wound its steady uphill course from the river bottom was populated with hemlock, silver fir, a few Douglas fir, red cedar and Engleman spruce, all varying from saplings to old veterans eight feet in diameter. A shrub layer of devil's club, vine maple and huckleberry covered a carpet of Canadian dogwood, twinflower, saxifrage, trailing blackberry and countless ferns and mosses.

Moss, fern and giant cedar are all close cousins. Indeed, the more I examined closely the forms of growing things the more convinced I became that all things did originate from one source, one great parental cell. The same is true of inanimate objects. The patterns in rocks are reflections of cloud and water movements; a rock is a mountain in miniature; its growth of moss, a belt of trees. The feeling of the interrelationship of all life became, through the trips begun that day at Heather Lake, the dominant theme of our philosophies of life. This awareness doesn't explain all the mysteries of existence, but it comes the closest for me. It occurs to me that anyone holding this view cannot help but see the utter folly of war, because the destruction that man justifies in war is so obviously destroying himself.

The remainder of the climb consisted of steep switchbacks, and with every turn the surroundings became more exciting. Alaska cedar, tough and gray of bark, replaced the pinky-brown trunks of the mammoth western red cedar. The latter has my vote for the most extravagantly beautiful of all low-elevation trees. The massive strength of its great up-sweeping trunk, the trailing grace of its down-swept branches, the close neat pattern of its leaves, and the fragrance of its wood and foliage deserve a greater reverence than the cedar shake industry acknowledges. And, added to this, the bark plays host to miniature lichens that form a lovely gray-green sort of film which blossoms with round pink spores in the summer. The trail leveled out on a boggy Alaska cedar flat. Soon we heard running water, the sound of Heather Lake's outlet creek tumbling away into the forest. We were in a garden of the gods, huge slabs of fallen rock rising like monuments, each with its own miniature garden of dwarf trees and wild flowers. Perhaps it was from such terrain that the Japanese evolved their idea of gardening with rocks. Tough, twining roots of trees spread over the trail in a mat.

Alone at the very edge of the lake we sat on fallen mossy logs under boughs of Alaska cedar. Our eyes roamed over the smooth crystalline waters that reflected the rock cliffs and snow patches at the enclosed end. Weather beaten trees clung to the rocky precipices except where a slide had dashed everything before it to bits. A mass of vegetation crowded about the lakeshore with blue huckleberry bushes the most plentiful. Large trout swam lazily by, surfacing occasionally for a fat fly or an ant.

We returned to the car that night as giddy about our discovery as any fortune hunter uncovering a chest of gold. And we became seriously committed to finding a way of having a base of some kind in the area. But over a year would pass before our fateful re-acquaintance with Everett Barret.

Betty Bard and Margaret on Paradise Meadows at Mount
Rainier

Mexican Family, 1932

Mexican Landscape, 1932

Reporter Margaret (on right) prior to stunt plane flight

Captain Mogg

Harbor Island

Loggers waiting for the morning train at Pysht

Field sketch of donkey engine

Loading log train at Pysht

Loader man with 'nose bag'

Margaret and Tobey at the Ward Street house

Callahans' Model A Ford on Ward Street

Gold Basin

Kenneth with ever-present sketching supplies

14

BACK IN SEATTLE I'VE been taking advantage of Tobey's naps to read over my jottings from 1935 and 1936, years of social awakening. There were so many meetings and great expectations. What a lot has been blasted away since then, hopes and illusions, actually delusions in a way, not to mention the human flesh blasted all to hell and gone. While embarrassed at the naiveté that some of my writings reveal, I find that revisiting those passionate and confusing times helps me understand who I am today.

I don't suppose even the American Civil War period caused more bitter personal animosities than did that period in the 1930s when those who thought at all were deeply disturbed over the unemployment and the bread lines. Some of us felt a solution to be a quick switch to a communist doctrine, while others wanted to preserve the fundamental freedoms and bring about a more democratic and workable economic set-up. And some of us were to change our points of view as world events evolved and we became more knowledgeable.

The first entry I happened to read was a Monday morning recollection of a Sunday evening get-together. Young artists, writers and political types comprised the bulk of our circle of friends. We often combined our meager food, money, and records on Sundays. These informal affairs were often held wherever Kenneth and I lived at the time. Their main function was to exchange ideas, books recently read, and phonograph records. I refer to the following jumbled dialogue as three-dot conversation.

November 10, 1934. All morning long, black smoke has pawed the air outside my window, with a strangely disturbing effect. I can't see the ground where the bonfire is, and I can't see where the smoke ends. I only see great swirls and puffs and volleys of black smoke going up and up. And looking into the black smoke gives me the odd feeling that I am falling and falling endlessly, so I could swear at this moment I am miles down in a bottomless abyss, making rapidly for hell, China, and all points south. The smoke echoes the confusion and turmoil that romp around in my brain this Monday morning, registering only a blur of impressions from last night.

This apartment is too small for the noise and smoke and people who mill about, and I envy the fly aloof on the ceiling. There are so many cigarettes; the ashtrays won't hold the stubs. Too many records on too loud a phonograph – "Diga-diga-doo-digga-do-do" and the long sobbing wail of the blues from Gershwin's American in Paris. Voices mouthing words – the troubles of younger generation literati, too much confusion, no aim, no fixity of purpose – but life hasn't any fixity of purpose. Books must have form even if life hasn't or because life hasn't. Young writers don't have convictions. They just record experiences, and experiences are not enough. They must be molded. The young generation lives to taste, but there are too many tastes in the mouth and not enough substance under the hat: everyone to his prejudices. How does anyone know that tasting isn't the best system? Taste a lot but swallow very little. Botticelli and Goya are the only artists who count. As for music, it's Bach and Bix and the cornet in Willard Robinson's recordings. Prejudices! It's every man to his own prejudices. It's not a dry point; it's an etching. Ethel Waters' recordings, there are dozens of them. Ethel Waters, always urgent. "He shakes my ashes, he greases my griddle – aw, give it a rest." – "Singing in the rain, just Singin' " – Change the needle, somebody. Hemmingway is all right, but he's just entertainment, nothing that will stick; he records his experiences, no interpretation. Why bother with interpretation? And she filled the tub with water and put the baby in it, and set the whole business on the stove. "Listen to the Rhythm Kings." Play the other side!

Cigarette conversation is a three-dot conversation, silly stuff. A jumble of black smoke pelting upwards, and I am falling faster and faster, and the black smoke makes me dizzy, 'formless and multi-form' – no more looking out the window.

November 23, 1934. We are moving to our little shack down the hill in a few days and our apartment is being shown. "Nice light rooms and bed comes down. Convenient," the ad reads. One of the prospective renters was smoking a smelly old cigar that has stunk up the whole place. I'll be glad to be out of here.

I was reading the *New York Times* this morning and the effect was depressing. So depressing. Roosevelt is edging around to the right. "Business is raring to go," he says. Why is everything sane stifled? Thank god for the *New Republic* magazine. It is my greatest salvation these days.

The John Reed Club is doing a bit of nonsense tomorrow night at a Mrs. Gunnell's house, where Earl Fields rents his studio. Paul Ashford is organizing the event. The local revolutionaries, a bunch of skim milks like Paul, are doing a revolutionary drama and charging admission to raise money to start a newspaper. For refreshments they are serving sandwiches and a whiskey sour. That typifies Paul.

It's turning nice. I think I'll go out for some air. I need a jolt to wake me up! Kenneth is absorbed with the idea that maybe he can get a Guggenheim Fellowship to study mural painting in Mexico. He should get one on the basis of merit alone. His panel of the two hands on the crosscut saw is beautiful and significant.

November 27, 1934. Yesterday we were off to the Marine Hospital to see a fellow's drawings that an acquaintance, Emerson Daggett, had mentioned to Kenneth. The artist is a tuberculosis patient, and his kidneys are failing. The condition is incurable. He been there now for four years, a nice-looking person. He has taken to writing and drawing as a means of release. He has none of his work on hand, other than a few poems he had made into a booklet. The cover was copied from something and painted in watercolor. An introduction to "dear reader" was too self-conscious and elaborately worded, but the verses themselves were rather nice, wistful things about good things he remembered which are now forever denied him.

They have no books to read up there, so we're going to take some books and magazines to them. Daggett works on the *Voice of Action*, the local communist weekly. Just how sincere he is, I don't know, but I respect him and like him for what he's doing anyway. I feel strong warmth for anyone who acts altruistically for the benefit of mankind. I would do anything I could to help them out on the paper if it weren't for Kenneth's job. As it is, he thinks we don't dare even subscribe to it. Certainly things seem to be edging nearer and nearer to a crisis of some kind. Mr. Hearst writes horrible editorials about fascism and communism, painting fascism as the favorable alternative in case communism becomes too threatening.

We had a pleasant evening Saturday with Mark, the Ivar Haglunds, Joe Cohen and Earl and Gladys. There was much talk about Gertrude Stein with Mark supporting the old gal. The quotes from her new book are the same old thing. Mark says she expresses the subconscious, perhaps. Well, perhaps! At dinner Kenneth and Mark discussed Mark's Bahai religion. It apparently desires the same ends as communism, but wants to bring them about without hate or violence. And the Bahai believe there are divinities. Mark is all for it. He needs something to bolster him. I suspect he has a strong sexual urge toward Negroes, and this 'brotherhood of man' religion justifies it to him.

I grow more rational in my philosophy as I see more. There is a great unknown which is mystical, but my belief is that man must sense and accept and not dabble with it. We are given enough. At any rate, let us first solve the problems before us. We are going to a Bahai meeting tomorrow night at Mark's studio. I am curious.

November 28, 1934. Tomorrow is Thanksgiving, and I still love the holiday. It's a hangover from childhood, no doubt. Holidays mean nothing to Kenneth, probably also a hangover from childhood! I hope we move Friday, although it might have to be Saturday A.M. due to wet paint. I am sorry in a way to leave this place, but I have less attachment than I had to either of our other places. What I like here are the big rooms and high ceilings, the little desk where I write, the nice warm bath and hot water, the poplar trees across the street, and the washing machine. What I'll be glad to get away from is the girl who plays a diddy-bum piano above, the baby that cries in the night, the landlady who won't take phone calls, and the dark kitchen being right off the street. We're moving to a quiet street. It's more private and has a little garden between the street and the front door. It's quite an isolated little house.

Kenneth and I walked to the library last night, our first long walk in months. It was a good brisk evening that made walking fun, but we were both exhausted when we got back home after walking up that hill – those hills. We both like the old library. I have known it off and on since I was old enough to read. And Kenneth would go there when he was broke. One never quite exhausts its possibilities, although, god knows, the stock is pitifully limited. There are always the shabby, earnest people there. Every seat at every table is filled with people reading. Reading, then prowling, cat-like, to shelves, searching, snatching, then creeping back to a table and reading again greedily. The smell of the place is unique. It's a smell of very used books, of thumbed paper, and faintly of the lavatories below. There is the quiet hum of subdued talking. Overall, it is an atmosphere I could never forget.

December 5, 1934. It is quite still in the little house where we live now. I can hear only the crackling of the fire in the kitchen range, a real wood fire, and the steaming of the kettle of water and the occasional rustling and gnawing of our white mouse, which has not yet been named. We found him yesterday morning when eating breakfast at the Club Café. He was shivering and cowering in the dirt at the base of a potted shrub – probably a runaway or a castaway. We took him home in a little mayonnaise carton with a hole cut in the top, which the Club Café man gave us for the purpose, he being very relieved that the mouse was going to be taken care of. He is an amazing creature, our mouse. Yesterday when he got warmed and fed, he scampered about and did tricks. Today he has crawled into the mayonnaise container inside his wooden box that is actually a drawer from an old bureau. He has buried himself beneath the cloth we gave him for warmth. He has the most amazing delicate, transparent ears and tiny, perfectly formed paws with microscopic fingernails. I have to hide him quickly when old Pancho the cat comes stalking in. The old devil adopted us again immediately after Mrs. Anderson, our previous landlady, brought him over. He is huge and wild and still as temperamental as ever.

I build fires in the little stove and never hear anyone, except the sound of an occasional car going past. It's like I crawled out of the world into a cave somewhere and am living an existence apart. It doesn't bother me or depress me, but I know I must keep contact with people, because that's a part of me that I mustn't let die.

December 13, 1934. Two things happened last night: Viola Patterson's one 'man' show and *Alien Corn* at the Studio Playhouse. On account of colds, we did neither, but after dinner, Kenneth grew restless and started looking at the neighborhood movie ads. There were two unrecognizable things at the Broadway Theater dime night, so we went, and one turned out to be *All Men are Enemies*, the adaptation by Samuel Hoffenstein of Richard Aldington's book, which I read last summer in Panama. The movie was a poor and futile thing, but it brought back vividly my feeling while reading the book. I have a keen feeling for Aldington. I'll never forget reading *All Men are Enemies*, the love story of Kathy and Tory at Capri, when we were in hot, humid Panama waiting for the ship that would take us through the Panama Canal. Our hotel had a big, brown bedroom with double beds and lattice work doors opening onto a balcony. Sadly, they only occasionally let in anything resembling fresh air. There is something about reading very potent books in strange cities, such as in Victoria where I read Peter Ibbetson and Christina Alberta's *Father* and in Mexico where I devoured *The Good Earth*.

I would like to feel Christmasy, but Kenneth can't abide the thought. Mark and Ted Abrams are coming over tonight after the show. I'll try to remember some of the talk. I miss Joe Cohen. He hasn't been around for about three weeks. I am missing my *New Republic* on account of the post office not getting our change of address. Mark says he's leaving for the east in January. He can't make enough money from his classes. It's a crime that Cornish school won't make him head of their art department.

December 28, 1934. Once more we're settling down to peace and order. First there was the confusion of moving and getting settled. Then there was Kenneth's cold, and then there was my cold. Then came Christmas, and, as it happened, a considerable spate of seeing people, which always ruins Kenneth for a time. But now the house is straightened up, my clothes are washed, and we're in running order again.

The building of fires got to be too much for Kenneth in the morning, so now we have hired a nice, earnest schoolboy to come in at 7:30 each morning and build the fires and chop wood for $5 per month. I hate to spend it, but I guess it's worth it to keep Kenneth on an even keel. We are invited to a party at Roy Kennedy's on Saturday night, and I accepted, but Kenneth said he couldn't bear it. Hell! I enjoy it out there because it's always a party with drinking and milling about. But to Kenneth that's devastating, so it's out, I guess.

Mark Tobey told us one evening here at dinner about his marriage, a most unhappy affair. I never knew of it before. It was in New York. She was a fascinating neurotic, and because Mark is somewhat neurotic himself, the inevitable happened. She and her mother became demanding and began to stifle him. He, in trying to escape them, developed fear complexes and escape complexes and what not, and he's got them still. I knew he was tortured by these feelings, but I didn't know what caused them. He has a great insecurity, but if he were offered security he would probably grow restless and have to go off seeking again. That's the trouble with his work. He's always trying to dissolve everything of reality into an 'art form'. Reality distresses him. We have seen a great deal of him, and we will miss him keenly when he goes. He is vital.

The world outside is gray. The streets are covered in slush. I remember how it was, sloshing through it as a kid and hating to have it melt; praying it would snow some more. I must get started on my book again, but I lose faith in it periodically. I'm reading H.G. Well's autobiography. He thinks Marx a resentful, hating egocentric. How can he? He has a vague sort of socialism of his own. He's not a clear-thinker in any one field. He is the egocentric.

Our white mouse is still with us, and so is the cat, although the horror of having a strange person coming in to build the fires almost shocked him fatally. I love my house. Our mysterious neighbor has a fire going, as there is smoke coming from the chimney, but other than there are no signs of life. I wonder if he is hiding out.

Kenneth and I were lying in bed last night wondering what makes warmth in bodies. Perhaps it is the motion of blood in the veins. Perhaps it's a chemical thing. And from that we got to marveling about life, how mysterious it is and how there may be infinitely more varieties of life than we know of. And that made me think of my old mental game: wondering whether there might not be some race of giant things we know nothing of that would be in proportion to us as we are to microbes. Perhaps we infest some giant form of life. Perhaps nature herself is as much superior to us as we are to microbes, and we're just a pain in her neck. Maybe nature has a mind and wills such things as earthquakes, typhoons, lightening, and all the violence.

We saw Hepburn in *Little Minister* last night and liked it or, rather, thought <u>she</u> was wonderful There is a rare quality about her that gets me completely. The tears poured down my cheeks and drizzled off my chin most uncomfortably. I wonder why I always feel furtive and embarrassed about crying in movies.

January 3, 1935. It's snowing again for the third day in a row. I seem to always want to start out with the weather report as though I were writing a ship's log or something. The weather is pretty close to me and I know all about it, due to having to get up before seven to see about the fires. Our friend, the fire builder, comes at six these mornings on account of having to be at school at eight. Sunrises are fine things. It's too bad I'm asleep when they happen. They're far superior to sunsets or moonlight or any of the other phenomena that poets praise.

Ted dropped in and stayed for lunch with me today, and it seems Kenneth has offended Mark by appearing indifferent about one of Mark's pictures that got misplaced at the museum. It's a good thing Ted mentioned it, because I wouldn't like to have Mark's feelings hurt or have him offended.

January 19, 1935. It is ironic that last winter, when we lived in a heated apartment, we had the warmest winter ever recorded, and this winter, the first time we've lived in a house relying altogether on our own heat, we get the coldest winter since we've been married. The last week and a half it's been freezing with much snow, such as is seldom seen hereabouts. Icicles as big as machine guns are hanging in a fringe all about our shanty, and I look out of the window over a perfect snow scene.

Joe Cohen dropped in last night, the first time since before Christmas, and we talked over the revolution again as always. I must read *Coming Struggle for Power and Fascism* and *The Social Revolution*. My family seems concerned lately over our political ideas. My father sticks to liberalism (Mabel just leaves the room when a discussion comes up). Dad is afraid of the communists, because they endorse violence. "Civil war, you know what that means," he said. "Brother fighting brother. It would mean Kenneth fighting Bob. That is what civil war means." And I said, "But history ignores such sentiment," which may or may not mean anything.

My mother comes through with a gem from her work at the Seattle Children's Home every once in awhile. A girl with two babies and one on the way wanted a place to leave the first two while having a third. When questioned as to whom the father was, she said she didn't know.

There was a different one for each child. "Are you in the habit of having relations with men you scarcely know?" asks Mabel. "Oh he was no relation to me." "I mean, are you in the habit of going to bed with every man you meet?" "Oh, no! Not every man." Mabel, horrified, "But, don't you know nice girls don't do such things?" "Well, here's one who does!"

I should be out be playing in the snow. I wish we could get a bobsled with the Fields and the Nestors and have some fun. Mark and Richard Bennett are coming for dinner tonight. What to have?

January 28, 1935. For four days now I've been thirty-one years old, and that goddam novel is still half-finished. I've been sitting here for an hour trying to get going. I'm too damn hazy about the business end of the ranch that the Bard's lost due to financial problems.

October 24, 1935. We've moved form 448 24th N. to 440 25th N., one more block down the hill. My desk faces a big window overlooking the hollow with East Madison running slantwise through it, over the Madrona hill and onto the lake and mountains, a splendid lot of space. Again we have a stove, and friendly creatures they are. With radiators you could get terribly lonesome, but not with a stove. Maggie, our little Wirehaired terrier, stands under my chair with her rear end sticking out and mopes. She is miserable until I let her out to run up to the Nestors. I try to keep her in until noon anyway, just to cut down the chances of her being run over or making a pest of herself at the Nestors. She loves it there because of their dog Sandra and the kids and all the activity.

We also have Bonzo now, who has turned out to be Bonzita, much to my chagrin. But I got an idea this morning and called Dr. Flynn at Seeley's Animal Hospital and suggested he let us take out the $5.00 credit we have coming for the loss of Pancho in an operation, and he agreed to spay the cat.

Kenneth has nearly finished his sketches for the Marine Hospital mural, and I have high hopes for the job. I think he gets, without any artificiality, the latent power of the workers. To me, his work has more significance from a proletarian standpoint than any of the moralist paintings the young leftists are doing now in New York. But how I would like to get to this artist's congress that's coming up. Such a lot of fine names they have sponsoring it...including Cook Glassgold and Lewis Mumford.

Our lives go on in a routine sort of way, particularly mine, but seething all through it these days is the class struggle. There's still a lot of confusion, in my mind. I know there must be an overthrow and a building of a new order so that life may be lived with joy, but only for that purpose. There must be no overthrow for the sake of overthrow or for the sake of vengeance or to build anything so grim as I know a lot of young revolutionaries have in mind. Just how much grimness will be necessary while the struggle goes on is the question; not so much in this country as in Russia, I hope.

I have just read Anna Louise Strong's *I Change Worlds*, in which she vindicates all the policies and mistakes of the of Soviet Union and wants to convince us that Stalin is the real thing. And I'm willing to accept most of it. But then I go and get old counter revolutionary Max Eastmen's *Artists in Uniform,* and I think there is much in what he says, also. I do think the Soviet Union has taken a stupid attitude towards art, if what he says is true. He says Lenin's idea was that proletarian art meant the education of the masses to an appreciation of art, and not the use of art for propaganda purposes. Of course, real art must always be deeply felt, and there really isn't such a thing as meaningful propaganda art that is coerced. If there is propaganda art, it must come naturally from the core of the artist's being, and anything else will only be propaganda, valuable in a way, perhaps, but not art.

What I feel about artists today is that any sensitive person must feel the tremendous forces at work in the world, and that, therefore, no artist who is really worth anything can help but get something of these things into what he's doing. Any artist who can still retreat from the world and do still life and toy with the technique of painting as an end in itself these days is decadent and not a vital person, and it will show in his work. But just telling him to go out and paint the class struggle isn't going to bring forth anything important. He's got to find out for himself.

We just received a letter from Mark from England saying, "New York is a Mecca for communism, and if it's a force you want, it's all right, but it's not what I want or want to be near." I think, though, that in spite of himself, Mark isn't going to be able to escape conflict. Bahaism isn't going to go on filling him indefinitely, I am sure. I don't think it does now. He may hate the turmoil, but being conscious of it, he can't, by his very nature, dodge it completely.

Kenneth's been trading some pictures lately, and has made a good haul. We have a swell one of Tokita's, a Margaret Camfferman, a Viola Patterson, an Ambrose Patterson of course, some good ones of Mark and Morris, the one that Bunce gave us, a couple of Earl's, the portraits Barney did of Kenneth and of me, and we'll get one of Nomura's. It's fine to have them. It's like having a piece of the person about. Or doesn't that sound so desirable? I can't see how people can get so worked up over the mechanics of a home, the end tables and such, and not even be conscious of the need for paintings for the walls. If I had money, I would buy contemporary paintings. It could be the most absorbing game. What a richness it could add to lives afflicted with the poverty of nice rugs, a framed flower print or two, the right drapes, and the right cocktail service. Just these and nothing more represent a kind of poverty and coldness to me. I would always want my home to have lots of windows to let in light, open space for many growing plants, and paintings on the walls. I hope this does not stamp me as hopelessly bourgeoisie in the eyes of the class strugglers.

November 19, 1935. We had a fine long walk on Sunday near Enumclaw. Walking is the thing we both love to do. And we like to do it often. It makes me feel prayerful and solemn about this country that I love so much. It makes me feel happy and at peace with things.

Sunday morning we had a pancake, little pigs, and fried egg breakfast with the Fields. It was supposed to be at the Nestor's, but Barney was not agreeable. Marj has to do something about her life pretty soon, or it will be too late. Me too, as far as that goes: some writing or a child. But now Kenneth says we should go to Spain next summer to see the El Grecos, which would be pretty fine, too. We both agree on El Greco and Peter Breughel, and Daumier. They are my three best loves in art, I think.

Saturday night we parked the Ford downtown and walked the length of First Avenue, early in the evening. I like to do this, but often Kenneth does not. He thinks he does, but he often won't actually do it. I wanted to go down below to the real skid road, where I could see dimly from a block or two away great throngs of men gathered, listening, I suppose to the soap boxers. I can hardly get myself away from activity of this kind. I wish I could just become one of them in appearance, could mingle and not be stared at or cause self-consciousness. I am fascinated by all this waste, all this latent power rotting away. Kenneth isn't comfortable among them. He feels they resent our presence.

From where the lights begin on First Avenue, it's like a cheap down-at-the-heels New York Broadway. Everywhere are the girly shows and horse operas, the trick stores and pawns shops. We watch a cowpuncher just in from the range in a ten-gallon hat and rolled up pants. He is sharing the street with a red-suspendered logger in from the woods. Then there is the tall, rangy youth, all alone, looking in the pawn shop windows at the banjos and knives, the field glasses and the clocks and rings. Two very young girls with two very young sailors, their arms all entwined, are prancing and happy. And then I see an incredible face on a young woman coming out of a hotel with two men. (I was in it once for some reason I can't remember, probably when I worked for the *Star*). Her face was lined with disgust, as if she had experienced every conceivable ugliness. The skin of her face seemed to be pulling away from her eyes, a complete corruption of the flesh.

November 20, 1935. Ted and Jo were here last evening. Talk was very pleasant, the subject being the decentralization and building up of regional cultures that would take place under socialism. Kenneth and Ted were arguing the opposite; that it would more likely lead to standardization all over the world.

A man called Bayer is here to organize the Friends of the Soviet Union. We've had two interesting evenings, the last one being at the Haglund's. Mr. Bayer is a keen, sharp, analytical fellow with three years' experience on the Soviet planning council. He's able to state things in clear, understandable terms. Why are so few willing to listen, even members of our small groups who heard him and might be expected to be among the sympathetic?

December 17, 1935. One dark afternoon at Nestor's last week, the Haglunds came over. They sat about brooding and flush-faced, and then began to push us into taking a more active part in things. That led to an attack on me for even thinking of going to Spain next summer instead of Russia, then an attack on Kenneth for not painting propaganda. It was all very silly. According to Marj, after I left they said they were going to ask me why I didn't give money to the movement rather than go to Spain. Joe Cohen came over the next evening, and he said they had been after him, too, in that same hysterical manner, and he is such a consoling and sane person. I was quite upset for a time.

All those thoughts had occurred to me, as anybody with a perception would have known they had, but I know the important thing now is to develop Kenneth's painting. It's the one thing that something might come of and far more important than any gestures we might make at this time, except studying, which we are doing extensively. A group of us, including the Pattersons, the Fields, the Nestors, and us with Joe as leader, meets every second Sunday night for discussion and study. Six of us were at the Nestor's last night for dinner and got to talking about dreams. Kenneth has the most and the longest and the clearest. He loves them.

We've been making up limericks these winter evenings at Nestor's, quite a tax on our mental equipment. Some aren't bad; some are very bad. Earl reveals the funniest quirk in his. His vulgarity is earthy and kind of weird. Marj had a swell catty one the other night; and Elsie Matthews, a funny one. Paul Ashford and Jean were there, too. Paul felt he was wasting time not to be talking about the movement. He tried to turn the limericks political without much success. The exception was one on Hearst, whose balls burst on the last line.

January 2, 1936. It was a warm rainy New Year's, and as usual, no celebration for us. Weenies and sauerkraut at the Nestor's, with whom we have spent every New Year's since being married, as far as I can remember. And Kenneth got an upset stomach (presumably, the weenies).

Kenneth and I have decided to spend $5.00 a month on books. I'd like to spend the first fiver today. Also, we're going to start a regular payment of money to the party, the same as if we were members, only very much under the hat. We'll pay it to Jo Norrie and she'll send it on. She's also doing so. I'm glad to have our convictions crystallized into some form of useful action, however small. And there's no going back, only forward. They want me to do book reviews for the Voice of Action, which I am going to do, but under another name. First I want to do a review of Gerstle Mack's *Cezanne,* which I've been reading aloud to Kenneth. If I do these reviews, I'm going to save them. I haven't saved a damn thing from all the *Town Crier* days, and some of it I'd like to have saved.

Cezanne had the same fear of what he called the 'Grapplin', or grappling hooks, as Kenneth has. That is, he feared getting hooked by other interests than painting. But he didn't shun what was the revolutionary struggle of that day. It was the side things, the little divergences, people, social occasions, etc. that he shunned, but not the main struggle.

January 10, 1936. It is very hard not to feel sad about Maggie. Two weeks ago today was the first morning without her. This is one of the few days since the accident happened that I have stayed at home all day. If she were here she would be running from me to the front room and back, every once in awhile, voicing a little cry to please take her out for a walk, her toes going click click clickety click on the kitchen linoleum. Then later I would take her to the store and stop in at Nestors on the way, and she and Sandra would have a romp. When I started for a walk with her she was beside herself and ran and leapt along the way, racing back to me, panting with mouth open and laughing, and her eyes shining. This may all be very silly, but I'll never forget her like that. She was nearly as dear as a child, I imagine.

It happened Sunday afternoon, two weeks ago, when Kenneth and I had gone to breakfast and left her at the Nestors. Marj went for a walk with the dogs and kids, and it happened so quickly, she didn't see or know what happened until she turned around and saw Maggie struggling to get up. She picked her up in her arms, and Maggie relaxed and died in a very few minutes. The first few days without her were unbearable. Real grief is incomprehensible until you have tasted it yourself. I am afraid, when I think about it, that I have only skimmed the surface. I hadn't realized until this happened how important Kenneth is to me, and how very much I love him. With death so actual and so near, I got an inkling of the abyss there would be if I weren't to have him. How closely the human creature twines itself about the life it has known and loved. To be torn up by the roots would bring me very near to death. Some take to transplanting better than others. The ones who take root deeply are the ones who suffer.

How shallow are these squirrels that take so lightly to the thought of revolution, myself a short time ago among them. Of course, I still have no idea what it would mean. Abstract ideas don't mean much compared with the real thing. I know it must come, but it may be unbearable for many of us who have had no preparation. It is strange that the death of a dog should bring such thoughts. But I really loved Maggie. It is curious, too, how my mind reacts to shock. It at first refuses to hold the thing. It throws it out, but the thing comes back. Slowly, it begins to taste it, to lick it a little on this side then that. Then a violent convulsion and the thing is thrown out again. But like a ball on rubber string it bounces right back. These feelings went on for days. Slowly the mind gets around the thing. Kenneth says, "try not to think about it, just forget it, think about something else." It's impossible to think of anything else until the mind has digested the reality. Even the horrible aspects must be thoroughly dwelt upon, until they are no longer appalling, until they have become familiar and can fit into some obscure corner, taking their place in memory, inconspicuously. Slowly the wound heals, but there is always the scar.

February 20, 1936. Our group has been meeting about a month now, every Sunday night: Joe, the Pattersons, Art and Sophie Weinstein, Earl and Gladys, and the Nestors. Earl and Gladys must be dropped, however, because Gladys can't get the need for secrecy through her head. Next week I report on Lewis Coorey's *Crisis of the Middle Class*. It is too bad about Earl, but last week, without asking anyone, Gladys brought her younger brother, the pseudo-sophisticated and so-callow Kenny. Gladys has no clue about confidentiality. The Haglunds we see no more; not since the hectic session when she lit into us for not giving our 'all'. Again, it's too bad.

Dr. Fuller is back from his three or four months' trip. Kenneth expects to find out more today about Fuller's reaction to the Maynard Walker Gallery's letter to Kenneth. Walker is interested in representing Kenneth in New York. Kenneth is restless in his job and would like to have all his time for painting, or so he thinks. He is tempted to go to New York and see what we could do. By summer we'd have enough to live for a year. I am skeptical; not only about our chances there, but also about whether we'd want to stay.

March 1, 1936. I feel I should blush as I read this over. I haven't got started on anything useful, but the problem is Kenneth. Should I be trying to make life easier for him and his painting or to follow along my own path? On the whole, I'm sure his work is more important than anything I could accomplish in the way of meetings, committees and organizing. I am sure of his painting, and he can't do it, apparently, under just any old conditions. Most people we know misunderstand him. That's not a whine, just a fact. We can be blamed for some attitudes and especially Kenneth's intolerance of certain people, I suppose. But it comes from real concern and conviction and not from his desire to knock individuals. As for our inactivity, if he's to keep his job, he can't do political things publicly. Kenneth is working on plans for a panel, Justice toward Labor, for the Justice Building competition in Washington, D.C. I have my fingers crossed.

15

THAT WAS A WONDERFUL spring, in 1936, looking forward to Spain, and we made the most of it, in spite of being bitterly criticized by some of our newly proletarian friends, who passed the word about that we were a couple of "goddamn shitheels" for not putting the funds to better use. I don't suppose the American Civil War period had more bitter personal animosities caused by political friction that that period in the 1930's when those who thought at all were deeply disturbed over unemployment and bread lines. Some felt the solution to be a complete switch to a communist doctrine, while others wanted to preserve the fundamental freedoms while bringing about a more democratic and workable economic set-up. There is something almost psychopathic in the way the communists hate the liberals.

We boarded the American Merchant in New York's July heat. Spain was the goal by way of England, France and Italy. Soon after departing New York reports were posted on the ship's bulletin board of the trouble in Spain, and before we docked in England, the Spanish Civil War was going full blast. Spain and the El Grecos were to remain part of the future. We were afraid we would never find the Spain we'd hope to see. But the Goyas and El Grecos would be there. As Longfellow pointed out, art is long-lived.

Before we embarked, we took the subway down to 14th Street and ate lunch at Luchows, the old rendezvous of the J.G. Huneker, H.L. Mencken, crowd. The atmosphere was interesting. The room is the same as it was in 1862. It's a large space with high ceilings, brown paneled walls, and a dark interior with greenery. There's a gentleman's grill in a separate room. I had fishcakes and Kenneth had a salad and beer, and it all tasted wonderful. New Yorkers demand and get a higher standard of service than do people anywhere else I've been. Smartness is the keynote of everything. There is the nonchalant earnestness of people getting on and off the subway. Just having to be physically quick all the time seems to have given them a different air. You don't get the feeling of defeat that people in other parts of the country have now. In N.Y. there is a belligerent aggressiveness I haven't seen anywhere else.

Through the intense heat by cab on the way to the boat, we passed a horse that had collapsed and lay gasping, running with sweat, on the hot pavement. A group of kids, a cop, and stragglers were looking on while the poor thing died. I can't get the picture out of my mind. I dreamed about it last night.

July 18, 1936. At Sea. The deck chairs are mathematically laid out on a broad deck. There is a high hum from the ventilators. Ho hum for the way I feel this A.M. I got no sleep until after daybreak. In our little stateroom it was hot and air circulation was zero. The wind was from the other side of the ship. There is a nice scarcity of passengers, the boat carrying only eighty at most. There are more women than men and more old than young, and I'd describe them generally as uninteresting. But I would like to talk with the 'slightly past young' woman who has made movies in Mexico. She's on the make for an Englishman or almost anyone else, I think. Also noteworthy is a homely blonde woman in thick glasses who plays games too cutely with her three tow-headed kids. We eat with a nice gentle, little schoolteacher and a funny scrawny little hen from Chicago whose brother works in the steel mills.

The ocean is glassy-smooth and there are big swells. We rolled a good deal in the night. It's a good sensation but it keeps me awake until I get used to it. The decks are dirty and littered on this boat and it needs a coat of paint. Today they are shoveling manure off the stern. There must have been livestock on the last trip over. A woman with one short leg gets around nimbly with two canes. Her cheerfulness does not seem to be put on and is perhaps nature's compensation for her infirmity.

All the obnoxious people on board play decks games passionately. Just now the awful little white-headed boys are doing so. Earlier it was the two well-bred Eastern college boys in their very college boy clothes. But there was no rah-rah stuff there. It was all refinement and smugness. A large drunk man sleeps with his mouth hanging open and hands limply crossed over belly expanse. In the chair next to me a girl in a hand-knit green dress rapidly knits a little number from the pattern book in her lap. The envelope reads "Lustre Crepe Dress, No. 3645."

The sun creeps out warmly from white misty clouds. It's nearly lunchtime, and I am hungry, but the food on the boat is pretty dull so far. A pot-bellied, middle-aged man with a hearing aid has watched the shuffleboard games assiduously all morning, running over ponderously to examine the exact positions of the little slabs on the numbers. Watching the crew going about their business and then looking over the passengers prostrate in deck chairs always makes me ashamed of being a passenger. It is much more comfortable to take freighters whenever possible. Now a wispy-haired man in knickers and specs plays shuffleboard with the boys. His wife looks peeved.

And then there is Harry, and he's a retired sea-going man. He's been in the same degree of stewed since we started. Apparently it's a fine art with him. He takes a few drinks, feels high, sleeps a time, wakes up still feeling high, and takes a few more. He never gets ahead or behind himself. Often when I am sitting in a deck chair over the rail will appear, coming up from below, the round, red, beaming face of Harry. He's bald on top with a tuft in front and a fringe all around. His face is the color of the raw purplish-pink behind of a baboon. His eyes have nearly disappeared into the flesh about them, which has grown over like the folds of bark around the scars on a tree. He laughs boomingly about everything and nothing. He walks with unnecessarily high steps, swaying slightly -- in case the deck comes up unexpectedly, I suppose. He knows whom he can approach without getting snubbed and talks to them in a whiskey-sour voice. He could be a nuisance, perhaps, so we haven't responded except to smile in passing, but I like him. He has a bigness about him, a certain loftiness. Today in the bar, I suddenly felt very sorry for him. He looked depressed sitting silently in the corner, with chin in hand. People should always be kind to him.

We asked our little Scottish waiter about the eastern strike. He was on the California when they held up the sailing for four days in

Pedro. "It's not very easy to go on strike for three or four weeks, to see somebody else getting your bread and butter. They got a $5 raise." Then he added, a little defiantly, "We should get a raise, you know; we only get $62 a month."

I finished Huxley's *Eyeless in Gaza* , loaned to us by Miss Lent at our table (her name, Marietta Lent, couldn't be better). It's an absorbing, deftly handled tome. He's an essayist trying hard to "come to terms with reality," but the nearest he can get is positive pacifism. He says Communism is "the wrong means to a doubtful end." The Communists might do well to consider what he says, about organized hate particularly. There must be some realistic approach that would eschew hate. That word liquidate, for example, is a very unfortunate one. There should be a thorough renovation of all Communist terminology. I'm definitely convinced of that.

I played a game of shuffleboard tonight. It's not such a bad game after all. It's nice to use unaccustomed muscles. The phonograph is playing an awful sentimental thing on the chimes. Harry likes it, and says, "...nice, soft music...no jazz...just nice, soft music."

The loading rigging in the stern makes a fine pattern against the sky: verticals, horizontals and diagonals. The sea was really rough for a time today. There was a strong south wind, which whistled and whined in the rigging, a fine sound. The ocean was a moiling, seething maelstrom, swept by spray, the waves breaking, clawing, and spewing from its heaving bosom. Spray went flying over the deck, and a group of the crew who was washing paint aft got soaked. The sailors were working with a hose and the deck was swimming with water. The passengers were leaping from hatch to hatch like Eliza on the ice, and the sailors were enjoying it thoroughly. And there was gossip about two passengers, a man and a girl, caught back in the crew's section. England tomorrow!

August 3, 1936, England. He was riding his bicycle down the hill from Dartington Hall as we were returning from a walk to lunch this afternoon. When he saw us he dismounted rather hastily, asked us for directions, if it was a private road, and said the hill was a little steep for riding. Really, he just wanted to talk, and I'm certainly glad he did. It was the most delightful incident since we landed in England. He was rather short and sturdy with a tanned, leathery face and deep furrows down his cheeks. He had shaggy eyebrows and very keen bright eyes peering out from under them; eyes that were sly and shy. "I've been to America, aye, clear through it: through New York and Pennsylvania, clear through it to Wyoming, Nebraska, aye, clear through to Seattle." His eyes challenged us to doubt him. We said we were from Seattle. He said he'd got his engineer's papers in New Westminister, B.C.

"I've 'ad some lovely jobs in America, aye, I'ave. I've 'ad pockets full of dollars, aye, pocketsful, pocketsful, I'ave. I've 'ad it hard in America, and I'ave 'ad it good." He rode a boxcar over the line into Canada. "I was supposed to 'ave twenty-five dollars, and I didn't 'ave a cent. Aye, you meet some chaps traveling that way, aye you do," shaking his head reminiscently and stroking his chin with a rough, brown hand. "And the booze, the lager and the beer." A swift, sly smile appeared from under his brows. He said he could drink barrels of beer. Money was to be had in America in those days (circa 1910). England is very bad now. He knows a chap who hasn't worked for two years. It's best to stay off the dole, he offered. It's bad, and it's not enough to live on anyway. And the means test, it's wicked and cruel. They take your furniture away from you and sell it.

He said we must go to Buckfastleigh to see the abbey that the monks are building there. "It's something wonderful, aye. "I can't explain it," he said. "I wish I could. But, oh it's a wonderful sturdy thing to see. It did my eyes good to look at it. I said to a chap standing there, I guess that'll take a bit o beatin', and he said, 'aye, that's right.' There's no two ways about it. When you see it you'll say, aye, that bloke told us the truth."

"And Princeton where the prison is, oh, the poor devils, they suffer there. I don't like to think of how they suffer. Oh, the poor devils." And on and on. "I could have held the jobs I had all right. There was no trouble about that, aye. It was easy going for me, but for the travel and the booze. And it's better to see the world. A bloke in Canada, who worked in the log booms, said, 'I've traveled more before breakfast than you've traveled in your whole life.' I said, 'Oh, you 'ave, 'ave you?' 'Aye, I did,' he said. 'But 'ave you ever been to Whitehall?' I asked. He said, 'No,' and 'e 'adn't, you see, 'e 'adn't done it." A sly smile came swiftly, as he climbed back on his bike and waved goodbye.

Tomorrow we leave for the continent after a pleasant if uninspiring visit with Mark at Dartington Hall.

August 13, 1936, Italy. What a jump from England to Florence. Here the sun shines, the air is warm, the earth is warm, and the pavements are too warm for my feet (which behaved beautifully in England, but are now asserting themselves). The Italian language flows like the river Arno below our window. There is wine instead of tea, fruit instead of puddings, and fresh, green salads everywhere. The buildings are mellow rather than grim with age. The colors are richly pastel and the past overshadows everything. Everywhere there is beauty: the old doors carved with ancient patterns, the old stone churches, and the castles topping the hills. These things still live. People scurry like insects in their shadows. There is no feeling of gloom among these people. They are riding high just now. The streets, the trains, and the stations are all patrolled by solid, well-fed fascist men in drab uniforms with fat pistol holsters. You see so many different kinds of uniforms everywhere.

At Modane station customs men came on board. The train was suddenly swarming with officials, mostly in black shirts. The police had gaily feathered hats. There was a terrible storm beating on the metal roof of the station building, a long, high affair with lots of signs in Italian on one side and French on the other. A small, insistent boy crying "buffet, buffet" wheeled a two-story cart of biscuits, fruit, wines, and mineral waters. There was a blast of thunder that at first I thought was dynamite, and the rain came down all the harder.

At Florence, we searched for the Pension Godkin, but the address the Caffermans gave us turned out to be an old one. What a time we had making the taxi driver understand we wanted to go to it at its new address. But we're glad we found it. It's real luxury, by god: two beds, a private bath, and enormous rooms. French doors open onto a balcony overlooking the River Arno and the hills beyond with their cypress and old castles. The food is acceptable and is served by a most polite, doll-like waiter. The proprietress is an intelligent young woman with protruding front teeth.

Today Kenneth woke me from a wonderful dream. I was making up a song called "I'm Just a Ripe Peach Left Hanging on the Tree." Another line went, "I'm just a watermelon that's been growing on the vine." This was written for a girl who thought that men didn't like her. I was getting her together with Joe Cohen. Hmmm. I wonder what all that means. We had breakfast of rolls, butter, preserves, and café latte, and then went to the bank to change money. I don't like the faces of bankers anywhere in the world. Then we walked down narrow, very old, very clean swept streets and over that wonderful thing, the Ponte Vecchio, to the Uffizi Gallery. I can't believe how beautiful Florence is. It is overwhelming. The early primitives in the Uffizi are marvelous: Fra Filippo Lippi, Filippino Sizzii, Bronzino, Botticelli, and others. There are room after room of them. What wonderful centuries for art were the fourteenth and fifteenth.

We were in the Pitti Palace this afternoon, both of us being very tired. We saw some fine Titians, Tintorettos, and del Santos, many of them very large. Ledoc and the Swan is a beauty. There were some swell Ruebens, but also some lousy stuff by later artists. There is too much on the walls, and the walls are very high. It's terribly tiring trying to distinguish the real quality of a work, especially with the spouting guides with their entourages on every side. A guide or attendant who took his work very seriously insisted on our seeing Maria Lousa's private bath, and it was even more elegant than our pink, black, blue and gold affair at Pension Godkin. It's a wonder that I can get Kenneth to leave the tub and come to bed.

August 17, 1936. There is a very Sunday-like feeling in Florence this morning. We started early when there weren't so many horses' hooves clacking on the pavement. After breakfast we started to 'polish off' the Uffizi. Aside from a magnificent Ruebens of a battle with horses and men and a huge, very swell triptych of Hugo van der Goes, there wasn't much we hadn't seen. Then it was through the gallery, over the Ponte Vecchio, and to the Pitti Palace again. It was lined solidly with lousy portraits of priests, royalty, etc. However, among them there were some terrific faces.

The heat really mounts in the afternoon and I'm happy to read and relax but Kenneth is dissatisfied with inactivity and wants to leave tomorrow. After lunch we started out in a horse taxi for the Piazza Michelangelo across the river, but we didn't have the heart to make the poor, tired animal go to work. So it was back to the hotel, I to reading an absorbing and appealing, but sentimental, tome. Later, when a breeze started, we made another attempt. We got the same taxi we had looked at before; the horse, a poor, thin, gray creature, needing better care.

It was a beautiful ride up the hill across the river with vistas of Florence in panorama. We exited through the old city gates, built by the Romans, and visited the public garden, which covered much of the hill along with a number of great, rich villas. My enjoyment was compromised because I was so sorry for the poor horse pulling us up the hill, the bells tinkling rather pathetically and the funny, red-faced driver constantly coaxing and commanding the horse, clicking and muttering. When flicking the whip, he let out a queer little moany sound that had us giggling every time. But the agony I felt for the poor animal is a different feeling than I have for humans. I put my hand on his throat and head when we got out and he was hot and damp.

We stopped at a very interesting monastery, and went in just by chance, me quietly and warily because of my prohibited bare arms. We found in the back room the most marvelous frescoes by a painter I've never heard of called Artemos Pinello. They were covering four quite large walls. In the outer church there were some fourteenth century fresco panels by an unknown. They were simple and flat, but they had wonderful color. Then we went on the Piazza Michelangelo, which has a wonderful sweeping view of the city, river, and distant hills; then down the hill and home. Kenneth was in a better mood by that point. We will see more churches tomorrow, I hope. Kenneth's been reading D.H. Lawrence's *The Rainbow* to me, more of his and Frieda's conflicts and love. Lawrence never wearies me, though.

A good morning: first to the Annunziatta, then to San Marco Church and Museum. The San Marco has wiped the Annunziatta out of mind. The Fra Angelicos in the monestary, a small fresco in each cell and about 20 cells at least, were most exquisite and pure in their simple beauty of line and design. They have a certain pristine, fresh quality.

At lunch, the American from California brought out her day's purchases, including some Majolica, the "best" wine to be had, she said. We then got to talking, and the fellow who sits alone and reads a book (we have referred to him as 'that German') joined in a little. He was amazed at her purchases. He would never buy such things, he said. She told us later that he is a violent communist. We learned that Dr. Blei's a Rumanian doctor of law from Bucharest and is here teaching languages. I'd like to have a talk with him, but don't suppose we'll have time now. He is blonde with a big head, a bit arrogant, but with a face full of life. In manner he's exaggeratedly polite, and yet rude at the same time, intolerant of any but his own beliefs. "But all these churches, this art," he says. "I have no interest in them." He also said, "People in Italy are slaves now and happy to be so."

We found *Hiawatha* in the parlor today, and I guess we'll read it tonight. I have always loved it, really. It seems a bit strange to be reading it in Florence. We were the only ones in the dining room tonight. It was nice, except for a strange half-pint fellow who came in late and guzzled spaghetti louder and longer than any I have yet heard. We got to giggling uncontrollably, like back in high school, over Kenneth's crack about his celluloid collar. After dinner, Kenneth went out to get the Paris *Herald Tribune* so that we can find out about what's happening in Spain. I hate to think what it may be.

August 27, 1936. Letter to Ed and Mabel Bundy.

Dear family,

Sorry my letters have been slow in arriving. I've been trying to write at least once a week, but I lose track of time, what with batting around so much. There has been such a confusion of things and so much to absorb that it's very hard to single things out to write about. As far as getting any lowdown on the situation over here, it all has to come from what we can sense really, not being able to speak enough to converse.

It was obvious that Italy is just bound, hand and foot, body and soul. The whole country is seething with uniforms. Every train is guarded by several black-shirts, and a black-shirt always follows at the elbow of the conductor as he checks up on tickets, etc. The station is full of men in uniform, and the trains pass by innumerable camps of young soldiers all through northern Italy. Immediately when you get into a hotel, the police collect your passport, disappear with it, and you get it back in the morning, in spite of the fact that instructions on the passport say that it's not to leave your sight.

The streets in Italy are constantly policed by the fascists, and you get the feeling that everyone is living in fear of something. As far as we can tell, many people seem to be happy enough now with the recent action in Ethiopia and all. Surface indications are that much improvement has been made, which fools a lot of tourists: that is, trains are fast, electrified, and keep perfect schedules. There are a lot of new, very modern stations. Streets are clean and free from beggars. There seems to be quite a bit of building and remodeling going on.

We noticed an acute difference crossing the border into France. No more snatching of passports, no more prowling police, and everyone saying and thinking as they please. It really is an entirely different atmosphere and like fresh air after a dungeon. We have enjoyed Paris more than anything else. It's impossible to say what's so grand about it. There is a feeling of being perfectly at ease and being free to do as we like; and everyone else seems to feel the same. I think it is probably the most civilized city in the world.

We live just a block from the river at the Hotel du Seine on the Rue du Seine. Florence has great beauty of the past but no living present, while Paris has the past and is at the same time very alive and stimulating. I think most people here believe that the Spanish affair was instigated from outside, and that Germany and Italy and sympathizers in other countries have been helping it along. The labor movements in both England and France want to help Spain, but the governments of both countries are playing it safe.

I could go on and on, but will stop for the present. We go to Chartres tomorrow for the day. We're very glad your vacation was successful. I'm pulling for you to buy the farm, and so is Kenneth. It won't be long before we see you.

Love Maggie

August 28, 1936. I am sitting in our room of the Hotel du Seine. It is a small, high ceilinged and has two French windows over-looking the street three floors below. The interiors include red carpets, red plush drapes, a thick, red comforter on the bed, many mirrors and lace curtains over the windows. There is a screen encircling the washbasin in the corner, and a sign warns not to let the water run and to always use the stopper. The lights are arranged so only one will go on at once. There are three: one over the washstand, one hanging in the middle of the room, and one over the bed. But you can use only one at a time. Also, in the toilet room the light only goes on when the door is latched. French thrift is no mere myth. When handles break off cups they contrive handles of bent wire. So anyway, I am sitting in the half-dark, waiting for Kenneth to come from the toilet so we can start out.

We had breakfast as usual in our room on the table with the yellow peasant cloth. We buy fruit across the street, and a maid brings at 9:00 a.m. a tray with bread, butter, marmalade, coffee, and hot milk. It's very pleasant. We bought some honey in the market one day.

We took the 1:30 river boat from the Louvre Port and rode to St. Claude, then took the bus to the Bois de Boulogna, and here we are in the sunshine with the blue sky above. The grass seems especially green; the trees filter the sunlight, letting it fall gently in patinas over the earth. All about us is a labyrinth in trees: small graceful ones with brown trunks swaying upward and lacey leaves making tracings; trees whose sole mission is to live happily and to make life more pleasant for those who stroll beneath them.

From the paper today, it seems the Spanish business is reaching a climax with the Spanish storming Guernica and, I gather, being defeated. The situation is one of the mercenaries fighting men with a principle behind them and a real goal ahead.

We've been here a week tomorrow. Everyday it's a matter of starting out in the morning feeling good after solid sleep, wandering by the river, pawing through things at old book and print stalls, seeing galleries, walking from one part of town to another, eating at sidewalk cafes, and crawling back to our hotel at night so tired that the three flights of circular stairs are almost too much to make. We found some swell Daumier lithographs and a numbered Renoir print.

The Cezanne exhibition convinces me that he is a great master, one of the very greatest. Reproductions can't give an adequate idea of the quality of his work: the glow of color, the careful analysis of everything, the taking apart and reassembling with real feeling. Every work is a serious thing. The woman in blue seated by a table, the large one of two men playing cards, and the landscape of St. Victorie stand out most to me.

We've been in the Louvre only one day so far and seen some magnificent big Courbets and the lovely one of the deer in the forest. He is a fine painter and a communist, too. There are some swell Delacroix. They are sometimes overly dramatic for me, but they have real power. We looked at some interesting French primitives, which are cold and not with the beauty of those of the Italians. Nonetheless, they've a strange, grotesque beauty. There are some fine big Ruebens and some awful big Ruebens. But how he adored painting the magnificent breasts and rump of Helen Fromant. And there was a beautiful small work of a peasant festival.

We've had one or two days of showers, and the rest of the time it's been crystal clear with evening fading blue and pink, the trees and buildings along the Seine magical in the evening light. Towers and turrets break the skyline; the warm tones of gray and brown in the old stone buildings contrast with the greens of the trees and the accents of color in the river. We are mesmerized by the easygoing life along the river: the boats lazing by and men along the banks shaving each other, urinating, fishing, playing with their dogs, or eating little lunches wrapped in newspaper.

August 30, 1936. Yesterday we went to Chartres early in the morning. We took the autobus to Port Malliot, and there we waited for almost an hour on a hard bench for the Citroen autobus. Then it was a two-hour ride through the clear morning sunlight, out past Versailles into open farm country. We glimpsed haystacks, clumps of trees, stone buildings with courtyards enclosing chickens and straw and geese and children. On the bus was a voluble Frenchman in a beret with hands that flew, first one then the other, with every word he spoke. The words poured forth like a series of minor explosions. When not talking, he read *L'Humanite*. Everyone who got on the bus at the little towns talked a long time with the driver over the fare, where to get off, etc. Obviously, it was the thing to do.

The driver was indignant because the voluble one and a young fellow, taking advantage of a prolonged argument the driver was having with a quavery old lady who was getting off, got out and refreshed themselves at a café. There was much discourse, and you'd think they were ready to fly at each other. But when the voluble one finally got off with his satchel bulging and spilling out bread, the driver wished him a happy vacation most merrily.

We wove in and out of little towns, honking our noisy way down narrow curving streets, and on to Chartres. Built in the 13th century, the cathedral is a fine, restrained, simple and magnificently impressive affair. Inside, the gothic arches recede along the entire length of the nave from the entrance to alter. The stained glass and sculptures are the only relief. The glass is beautiful with blue, red and yellow light glinting through patterns of intricacy, like snowflakes under a microscope. The use of contrasting curves and angles, the repetition and the cold purity of perfection are simply amazing.

We ate a meal in a small café on the town square. A quiet back room opened at the far end into an area of rabbit hutches. The food was grand: chicken, mashed potatoes, tomato, salad, good wine, and fruit for twelve francs apiece, all well worth it. Then we had an interesting afternoon in the back garden of the cathedral overlooking an airport. Women were knitting, while children played busily at making a house out of the little bit of loose surface sand over the hardpan. They scraped the top dust with their little shovels into ridges to make rooms. French children all look very old-fashioned.

September 1, 1936. In reading a copy of *L'Humanite* the other day, I came across a large ad for a Grand Fete Sunday at a place called Garche. We didn't know what to expect but decided to go anyway. We wandered around this morning looking for a bus or some means of getting there. Not surprisingly, Kenneth was unenthusiastic but was not grumbling out loud. While waiting for a bus the first thing we saw was a truckload of people with red flags flying. The next thing was a boatload of same with more red flags and lots of singing and shouting. So first thing we knew we found ourselves on a bus loaded with picnickers bound for Garche.

There was a steady stream of buses, taxis, trucks, and every sort of vehicle going in the same direction, and as we grew closer, great crowds walking, all with some bit of red: red berets, red shirts, red ribbons, badges, paper hats, etc. As it happened, I had my bright red shirt on, and Kenneth wore a dull, red tie. Garche turned out to be an enormous beautiful park with a woodsy smell. There must have been 25,000, maybe 50,000, people there, all in holiday mood. There were whole families, plus groups from factories, girls with their beaus, and children of all ages.

It was a brilliant, moving spectacle. We got there about eleven and already large numbers had found a spot to picnic and established themselves for the day. Ropes were tied from tree to tree to make enclosures, and then any superfluous clothes were hung over the ropes giving shade and privacy. There was much bread and wine in evidence. People were carrying long baguettes and were tapping trees with them and waving them in the air as they gesticulated while talking.

The heart of the affair was a huge enclosure to which two francs admission was charged. It was a space about as big as the U. of W. stadium ringed around with booths representing socialist causes. There was everything from booths extolling the Russian Soviet to games that involved throwing balls at Hitler and Mussolini and other less recognizable targets. In the center was a pavilion with loud speakers from which singing and orchestral music bellowed forth. There was some good singing, and the band playing, of course, the Stars and Stripes Forever or another one of those damn Sousa marches. A high four-sided platform was decorated in tri-color with the Soviet hammer and sickle and typical posters of fighting youth. Red flags flew from countless poles, and red balloons were sent into the sky.

We left about one o'clock, neither of us feeling up to the enormous crowds and noise. It was a mighty demonstration of where the political strength in France lies today, I should think. It certainly made the fascist demonstration a week ago in the Champes Elysees seem puny in comparison. This was a cross section of French people; some factory workers, some middle class, many housewives and mothers. It was a decidedly respectable and ordinary crowd, boisterous and happy, but not with the belligerence one senses in America at such gatherings. The fete was sponsored by the daily newspaper, L'Humanite.

This is our last night here in Paris. We leave tomorrow noon for Dover. It will be nice to be near the ocean again. I think the salt air will do us both good. The Paris streets are pretty dirty and dusty this time of year and the city air is sometimes not the freshest.

September 3, 1936. Our sailing was delayed, so we are waiting here in London for our ship home. We found a letter in our mail from Mark. I had written him from Paris.

Dear friends:

I had intended telegraphing, but your fine letters have come so I'll write just to wish you Bon Voyage and tell you how much I regret not being with you in London and to see you to the train. If I helped in any way to make your trip pleasant, well, I'm the one who is glad.

I want to answer your letter very carefully but can't now as I am packing to leave tomorrow for Manchester to see Bahais there. I am enclosing a pamphlet that I want you to please read carefully. It's the only one I have but I think it explains my thinking very well. And will you read *Moscow Mirage*? I know you are both idealists, but so were the earldom of Russia!! It is fine to rid humanity of the present crop, but when godlessness is taught to the young, they are godless and will remain so. There is much humanity must learn of religion and its cyclic emergence and of its inner unchanging condition and its outer one, which lives and dies as does all else.

It is interesting how the art you have seen reflects a state or a time that still moves us while the political features are much relegated to the background. The great art to me has come out of the inner and meditative side of man and rises there far above the current conditions. Margaret may hate this statement, but I feel it is true, never the less. I must and do realize I sound careless of conditions, but I doubt if problems are solved in the flame of their initiation.

Do kiss the Seattle hills for me, the drifting clouds, and the sun that seems to set into eternity. Remember me ever so lovingly to Ted [Abrams] and do give my best to Dr. Fuller and others who might be interested. It seems rotten not to see you after this fine adventure but do keep in touch with me. Perhaps I shall see Seattle again, but I hope under more direction. A fine trip home.

Love to you both.

Mark.

16

J UST THREE YEARS AFTER what now seems like a surreal dream, that September day at Garche, Poland has exploded in flames. My mistake, America. I said it couldn't come, and now it has. We all had hoped that it couldn't. There would be appeasement once more. Something would happen, some miracle. Hitler would be shot or overthrown. But war couldn't come again. Not war. Not in a world just beginning to stagger to its feet from the blow it got twenty-five years ago. So we all listened to the radio commentators and news broadcasters: Raymond Gram from Paris and William Shirer from Berlin, Elmer Davis and H.C. Kaltenborn. And they all said the same thing. There was the voice from London, clipped, British, expressionless. "This is London" ..... pause. "The British parliament met this morning to discuss the latest developments." Notes, notes, notes! You write me, I'll write you. Notes are flown across the channel while the world waits and waits with ears glued to the radio. "We interrupt this program to bring you an important bulletin from Columbia's London news rooms," the words pulsate through a million ears in beer halls, at hot-dog stands, in tightly wedged houses along city streets, in far-flung farm houses and in cabins by the sea.

But one week and one day ago they made up their minds, and on that Sunday morning the radio gave forth Mr. Chamberlain's soft-spoken declaration: war with Germany. It was Sunday morning out here on the Pacific Coast, and in all the homes we women moved about the kitchens making toast and coffee and listened with a cold chill down our spines. We wondered what it all meant, what it really meant and would mean in the days and months to come. And there was an ominous threat, a feeling that this day was the end of something, perhaps the end of an era and the end of a part of our lives. "They'll be writing books about 'the years between'," Kenneth said at breakfast.

The day war was declared in Europe was warm and sunny with that wonderful early September promise, and we took Tobey with us to Puyallup to see friends and their new baby. Some friends from long ago were there with their children, grown long-legged and whom I hadn't known existed. We sat around and admired each other's children and the new baby. But no one mentioned the war, except when I said I supposed they had been listening to the radio. No one responded, except the girls I used to know. One asked, "did you listen?" And the other answered, "<u>Did</u> we <u>listen</u>!" But that was all anyone said.

Coming home through the valley on the old Tacoma road, the farms were somnolent in the late afternoon light. The truck farms worked by the Japanese are a miracle of beautiful even rows, everything growing strong and green with no weeds nor anything higgledy-piggledy. And always somewhere down the rows were squat, brown-clad figures of men and women, their heads hidden by big shade hats and looking for all the world like little gnomes crouching over the earth. The Japanese live all through the rich fertile farm valleys south of Seattle, and some of the white people hate them, because they work so long and so hard and live so frugally. But their vegetable stalls in the public market are always the finest in design and color, and their lands are always cared for the most beautifully. There should never be hatred for a job so well done.

The next day was Labor Day, and Kenneth and Tobey and Mike and I walked along the waterfront almost the whole afternoon watching the slow holiday activity: the loiterers, the small fishing boats at rest, and the big sea-going boats at dock, and smelling the oddly pleasing variety of shore smells. On the way home we drove all through the skidroad district, clotted with groups of gray men with so many beautiful, anguished faces. The old red brick and gray stone buildings with the high arches and splendid architectural detail were a backdrop to the men, huddled and lost. I noticed that the old Lyric Theater was empty, and I said to Kenneth that it should be turned into a museum.

What moments of grandeur it had known when Seattle was a stripling and the gold-seekers stomped the streets.

So there was war, but the first shock wore off and life went on as before, and the war became remote and unreal. But I couldn't stop crying in the theater when the last minutes of peace from Europe were shown, and there was a shot of street crowds falsely alarmed by an air raid, scurrying for shelter. A woman hurled her two children to the sidewalk and attempted to cover them with her own body, a gesture so instinctive, primitive, and pitiful; so helpless and brave against such completely insane wickedness. How can there be such extremes in man? How can he breed his young and love them and shield them and the next moment go forth to do mass murder? How can this be, and what does it mean? Does it mean things will never be any different? And what does it leave us to hold on to, to believe in? Well, the nearest answer to me right now is to believe with all my capacity in what I have that I love, and I mean really love, not what I covet or own.

Knowing that war had started again cast a strange, confused light on everything. You felt like an actor going through your lines on a stage where the backdrop has suddenly begun to go up in smoke. The fateful voices of the correspondents: "This is London" ...... the newsreels of the first bombings, the confused street crowds.

Stay out of it, my heart whispered; stay out of it, keep a part of the world for the future. "What do you think?" I asked the freckled, gray-eyed iceman. "Are we going to get involved?" Apprehensively, I awaited his answer as he chipped the shiny splinters of ice to make the block fit the icebox. "Damn right we'll get into it. Ain't a chance in hell of staying out." Then reflectively, "and I think we should; it's as much our fight as anybody's."

Everyone asked it of everyone else. "Naw," some would say, "let them fight it out amongst themselves this time. Or, "it's not a real war at all, it's phony." Or, "if we'd just keep our noses clean, if that damned Roosevelt would mind his own business and quit shipping stuff to Britain."

But an evil premonition has come to live among us. Our next-door neighbor said in the course of a backyard conversation, "you know, I have the strangest feeling that we're right back in 1914." There were three of us talking as we dug in our flower borders; all of us with children, and after that we hadn't wanted to talk anymore. The smell of the wet earth had lost its magic.

Most of the artists we know think America should stay out of it. Some of them because they are sure it is a "phony war"; some because they are completely pacifistic; some because they can't see any sense in this particular conflict.

There are more artists painting in Seattle than at any other time in the past; there is a sense of awakening and discovery. Morris Graves has lost interest in the big, heavy, dark landscapes in oil and the figures and still life he has been doing for the past five years and is experimenting with exquisite small temperas of animals, birds, and bugs which he calls "Message No. 1" and other such cryptic titles. Mark Tobey, just returned from England, is developing small, complex forms into intricate, all-over patterns and calling them "Broadway", "Electric Night", "Drift of Summer", and "Forms Follow Man". And he is doing a series of market sketches, drawings in blue paint of the people and places characterizing Seattle's great Public Market.

Seattle's Japanese artists continue working in their grayed colors and close values, transposing city streets, mostly the section of town where they live, into personal canvases, poetic and devoted. We see Mr. Nomura on occasion, but the group has stopped calling socially. As the world's crisis grows more acute, they seem to become more guarded, more remote.

Guy Anderson has gone to Spokane and is teaching in a W.P.A art center, creating a ferment of activity in that eastern Washington city. That government-sponsored program has given painters a new assurance and has confirmed their belief in the importance of their work. But the handwriting is on the wall. Sensing the end of the program, the artists are falling prey to jealousies and fears. And behind it all is that greater apprehension: the instability of the entire world.

Most family people among our friends are more conventional than we are. They make money, own large houses and fine furnishings and the right things for the table. Sometimes when I return from their homes, I find myself surveying our junk-store possessions with a jaundiced eye. To his credit, Kenneth never feels this way, perhaps because he accepts himself so thoroughly.

I stared out the window on this October morning, a morning just brushing off the cobwebs of an early fog. A male and female Chinese pheasant flew over the fence into the yard and stood like part of a medieval tapestry beneath the drifting leaves of the wild cherry hedge. I called Tobey, lifted him in my arms, and from the window we watched the handsome birds as they cautiously moved among the fallen leaves, pecking for bugs or seeds, then alert and motionless with upraised heads. My eyes wandered to the contours of the Cascades through the yellowing leaves of the wild cherry trees, and my mind drifted to our Shangri-La less than two hours away.

17

NO MATTER WHAT SORT of dwelling I shall ever inhabit, never again will I experience the delight of that small, gray, shake-covered cabin at Robe Ranch. Like a hound on its haunch it sat on a steep south slope of a shoulder of Green Mountain, its long front legs in the form of cedar poles upholding its tiny, railed balcony. The view from the balcony was prodigious. To experience it, however, we first had to cut away the clinging, octopus-like tendrils of a hop vine and the unruly top shoots of a cherry tree, which had been planted directly below the cabin and which had flourished without benefit of pruning for some thirty years. Its twelve-by-sixteen foot interior of whitewashed boards and caulk scarred flooring held everything a human being could possibly want, we ardently believed. The cast iron cook stove kept us warm on the coldest winter nights; the roof shed the most determined mountain cloudbursts, the iron bedsteads and thin mattresses provided divine slumber and the happiest of dreams. Even the outhouse, which leaned a little and had no door, was attractive. It was new enough not to have developed too much of an aura and was facing up the hill through a sparse setting out of happy young fir trees planted by Wirt Robe to replace the giants he and his brothers had harvested.

We had paid Wirt five dollars of the $25 annual rent and we finally took possession on a mild winter weekend in late January. We made the fifty mile trip on a Saturday morning, taking with us groceries, blankets, dishes, pans, oil cloth for shelves, white wash, soap, bleach, disinfectant, scrub brushes and all the old cleaning rags we could lay our hands on. Not that I am a fastidious housekeeper, quite the opposite, but the Lewis family, including three boys between the ages of nine and fifteen, who had just moved out, had given the cabin hard use. What with the table, the stove, the beds and the clothes hanging on nails along the walls, there was literally a space of about three square feet where the family could move around. A Lewis family evening at home meant that at least two of the circle had to go to bed in order to make room for the rest.

They were former Texas ranchers, driven from their land by dust storms. They had taken to the road in a jalopy, and had kept going west and then north until by some strange guidance they had landed in a region about as remote and as different from their starting point as they could have found. From dry, hot, open country they had migrated to an enclosed mountain valley with an enormous annual rainfall that was cold and wet in winter and cool and moist in summer. Mrs. Lewis would say, "sometimes I think I can't stand it no longer, and I wish I could jest push them mountains right back out of sight and let a little air in to dry thengs out." As she stretched her great arms in a graphic gesture you looked for the mountains to topple.

Apparently the problem of how to dry things in that tiny cabin cancelled all thought of washing clothes nine months of the year. The solution was to wear jeans until they dropped off. The Lewises were as glad to get out of the cabin as we were to move in, as the vacating of the larger ranch house by the Barrett family gave them five rooms and cold running water for only $4 a month. There would come a day when we would move into the main house, but we had no idea then of ever achieving such magnificence. The cabin on the hillside was quite enough.

We plunged feverishly and happily into cleaning, whitewashing, floor painting and tin can raking. The ground within throwing distance was strewn with many years' crops of bottles, cans, worn out shoes, parts of stoves and a general welter of discarded paraphernalia which the elements were doing their best to digest. As we worked, the rusty kitchen range sizzled and popped its rations of split, dried hemlock, giving a fine, even heat. A high film of gray cloud hovered over the sharp, white peaks of Pilchuck, Green Mountain and the Monte Cristo range at the head of the valley, some thirty miles away. Gradually, during the afternoon, billowing masses of low clouds surged into the valley from the southwest, and by late afternoon rain pattered steadily on the cedar roof.

By the middle of March we had enjoyed several long weekends at Robe Ranch. The winter had remained mild, with moments of pure springtime in February. We had started a garden on the lower slopes of the hillside, the first of what were to be many hassles with that toughest of all weed enemies, quack grass.

One changeable day in March, moments of bright, warm sunshine took turns with showers, and at times snowflakes, that fell in playful swirls through the cherry blossoms. By evening a drumming rain was falling, and I read aloud by the kerosene lamplight while Kenneth painted. Before long, what with the soft noises of the fire and the raindrops, the words my eyes were seeing could have been Sanskrit for all the meaning they registered.

When I picked Tobey up to move him from our bed to his own cot before stumbling into bed, I noticed a small dark object on the sheet. I watched it for a moment uncomprehendingly, as it scurried toward the edge of the bed. Then my spine did a caterpillar crawl. With my thumbnail I clobbered 'The Thing.' I had encountered an aspect of nature's seamier side. Tobey's cheek was swollen and red. I called Kenneth. "Look!" I said. "Is it what I think it is?"

"Oh, hell," he said. "It's a bedbug." While I held Tobey he lifted the mattress, peered under the blankets, and searched the walls. There was no sign of any pals. "What will we do for the rest of the night?" I said drearily. "Shall we bundle him up and start for home?"

"Not in this rain," Kenneth said emphatically. "Maybe there was just one. Can't be many or we'd have seen some sign before this. We'll burn some more sulfur candles tomorrow." The night passed slowly and was a misery. In my imagination I felt things crawling and nipping continuously. Unable to stand it any longer, I would grab the flashlight and shine it frantically under the pillows and blankets. But I found no evidence of the intruders. Kenneth slept soundly. He had the enviable facility of sleeping through anything including the major earthquakes we had experienced years before in Mexico. Sometimes he had to read half a book before going to sleep, but once he was unconscious, a mule or the Queen of Sheba could crawl in beside him and he'd never know it. As for me, I was about ready to give up the whole backwoods venture. Nature, I was willing to allow, must have its harsher aspects;

it must at times be fearsome, threatening, and destructive. But not, please, this furtive, creeping loathsomeness.

Morning found me wide-awake, hollow-eyed and impatient to begin the day's efforts to liquidate our invaders. Dawn was anything but rosy-fingered, but rather was soggy and gray. I was relieved to hear the small voice from the cot announce, "Had a nice s'eep", which was Tobey's way of saying, "let's all get up now!" We fed him, then hurried into Granite Falls to buy sulfur candles. I was embarrassed asking for them, and went to some pains to explain to the totally uninterested clerk how we were taking over this cabin we weren't too sure of and thought just to be on the safe side we'd better fumigate before moving in. We went through the routine of chinking up the cracks around the windows and doors of the cabin, lighting the candles in their boxes of sand and locking ourselves out. We could not enter the cabin again until evening. We faced each other in the pouring rain and conjectured how best to put in the day. Neither of us mentioned returning to the city.

To Susie's, we decided, for a warm and consoling atmosphere, to say nothing of the hotcakes and coffee. Susie had moved to a larger place, about a half a mile down river from her former location. In the short time she had occupied the new quarters she had made them cheerful and thoroughly comfortable. Cleanliness and simplicity were the keynotes, the one touch of décor being crocheted curtains held in place by small pie tins painted red.

From the front windows one saw a striking view of Mount Pilchuck across a wide, flat orchard bordered by the river. Today, however, the mountain had retreated behind an opaque hood of mist. "Look who's here," Susie greeted us, "so early in the day. You folks must have got up before breakfast this morning. Or did the rain wash you right out of bed?" She was pulling golden loaves of bread out of the oven. Near the back window in a worn maple rocker her mother sat knitting.

Susie chatted steadily while she worked. Her mother occasionally laughed or snorted at what she said, but was not talkative. She was small, very quick and alert in movement; with shrewd amused eyes behind her glasses, and a fluff of unruly white hair. She was a great, great grandmother and, since her husband's death a few years back, had operated by herself, the cabin camp across the road by the river, changing the title from 'Dad's' to 'Ma Baker's Pioneer Auto Camp'.

The Bakers had arrived in the valley at the end of the century with their three little girls and had homesteaded 160 acres near Turlo Creek. They had crossed the plains in a covered wagon. To complete their journey, they converted their wagon to a sled and hauled their belongings into the valley on skids drawn by oxen, as the primitive road was so deep with mud no wagon wheel could turn.

As she cooked our breakfast, Susie imparted the following items of news. Her husband had shot a bobcat, measuring six feet from nose to tail, in the chicken yard, and he'd gone into Everett to collect the bounty. Kate Knowlton had stayed over the night before last on her way to Monte Cristo. The new ranger at Verlot said they were going to open up selective logging in the Monte Cristo district. Her family was going to have to postpone their five generation photograph until the granddaughter had her baby, as she was "too far along to look good in a picture". I had promoted the photo idea and we were financing the effort.

I wanted to ask Susie's advice about our dilemma, but I hesitated to mention such a sordid subject. I finally stammered, "Susie, what do you suppose we found in our cabin last night? A bedbug." Mrs. Baker snorted and her shoulders shook with inner laughter. Susie looked up, smiled and said calmly, "You did? That's rather uncommon around here. Back east there's a lot of those things, but out here they've never really got started much." I told her about our sulfur candle burning, of our certainty we had successfully fumigated, and of my despair at finding the beast. "We're burning six sulfur candles again today. Do you think that will do the job?" I asked. "Well, it may kill the grown ones. But I understand to really get rid of them you have to burn the candles three times in succession about ten days apart. That gets the new ones as they hatch out."

Susie brought us a platter with a stack of thick, fluffy light brown hotcakes and another plate of fried eggs and crisp bacon slices, a bowl of home-canned peaches, and tall crockery cups of pungent coffee. Mrs. Baker stopped rocking, let her knitting rest in her lap and said in a tone of amused derision, "Why, I remember one winter when my husband was mining we had to move into a run-down cabin and we got snowed in for about three months. When spring come a fellow who lived about five miles down the trail dropped by on his way out prospecting, said, 'well, for land's sake, are you still living in this shack! I'd a thought the cinches would have drove you out months ago.' I said to him, 'Cinches, my eye. Any old time I let the cinches drive me out!'" She ended as abruptly as she had begun and vigorously resumed her rocking and knitting. I gathered cinches were the preferred terminology. 'Bedbug' was a city folks' label.

Kenneth said, "It won't be too much of a chore burning the candles three times. Then we'll be sure, anyway." Susie looked at him a moment, started to say something, then apparently changed her mind. "We'll hope so," she muttered. I was reassured by Mrs. Baker's comments but only a little.

We spent the long wet day at Susie's, helping with dishes, peeling vegetables and chopping stove wood. While Tobey napped, we visited the nearby ranger station where we spent an hour studying the relief map of the region, speculating on possible trails yet unexplored. The names were magical to us: Twin Lakes, Glacier Basin, Sheep Gap, Pinnacle Lake, Meadow Mountain, Upper Whitechuck Meadows, Kennedy Hotsprings, Poodle Dog Pass, Crested Buttes, Foggy Peak, Goblin Peak. We realized with delight that we could follow trails for years without repeating our footsteps and that each new spot would have its own charm or grandeur. We left for the cabin in the evening with Susie cautioning us, "you want to be careful about carrying those things back to town with you. They can get into your clothes or blankets you know."

"It smells in here," Tobey complained sleepily when I finally tucked him into his bed. He and Kenneth slept soundly as usual, but the remaining traces of sulfur irritated my lungs. In spite of the fact I didn't see how anything could be alive after what we'd put that cabin through, I couldn't help surreptitiously turning on the flashlight under the blankets and spying under the pillow from time to time. I slept deeply toward morning, and when I awoke a determined sun was raising banners of steam from the soaked earth. The daffodils were lifting their soggy heads, and the new green leaves of the ubiquitous willows glistened. By noon the ground had dried enough to work in the garden.

We burned the candles at ten-day intervals and burned them an extra time for assurance. We blinked our smarting eyes and congratulated ourselves, as we aired the cabin after the fourth candle burning ceremony; at last the whole disagreeable episode was over.

"But," I marveled to Susie later, "why didn't the Lewises warn us or attempt to get rid of the pests themselves?" "I'm sure I don't know," Susie sighed. "I can't understand it myself, but I guess some people accept the bedbugs like we accept the rain."

Those first two years in the hillside cabin at Robe Ranch constituted a period of discovery, rich and exciting. Back country life was completely different from city life, and as there was no through highway, traffic was nearly non-existent. Visitors to the south fork of the Stilly were limited to a few old-timers who remembered the days of the railroad and the mining boom at Monte Cristo or those who had heard of the area from old-timers talking about the past. While a new blacktop road as far as the Verlot Ranger Station was under construction, the only one in use at the time was the original narrow gravel affair, which followed every twist and turn of the river. It ended at Barlow Pass, some thirty miles from Granite Falls. Occasionally, the road followed the old railroad bed; a few of the timbered structures still remained from former trestles that had criss-crossed the river.

Ancient forests stood on scattered tracts throughout the valley, but for the most part the growth was young, having sprung up after the first period of logging was concluded during the decade before the First World War. However, as Robe Ranch adjoined National Forest and timber company lands, the wilderness was close. Logging in the National Forest was limited to the 'cutting of individual ripe trees', consistent with the wording of an Act of Congress. As the lumber industry was in the doldrums with the dearth of building brought about by the Depression, there was almost no pressure to begin big time cutting in the National Forest. The logging of smaller trees on private land for pulpwood was usually a family affair: a father and son, or a husband, wife and sons affair. Such operations provided only a marginal living.

Wirt Robe's crew of pulp cutters dwindled soon after we moved in, and soon no one but Mr. Lewis and his oldest son, Mike, were still logging. Mrs. Lewis and the two younger boys carried out the home chores -- looking after the cow and the rabbits, the woodpile and the garden, tending the pump and avoiding housework. Stanford and Robert were Mrs. Lewis's own sons, Mike being the son of a previous union of Mr. Lewis.

The expression "to wrest one's living from the soil" had hitherto been a vague abstraction to me. I had seen country cottages on small plots of land between Puget Sound and the mountains, acreages too small for truck gardening or dairy farming, and I had always wondered what on earth these people did to keep alive. Now we learned, first hand, from the Lewises. For here was a family who had come to a strange country flat broke in an ancient car that was ready to bite the dust. They faced all the problems of a completely new start in life, having no assets but their muscles and their ingenuity. Their first break was in finding old Wirt, who was willing to accept them at face value, provide them with a roof, loan them tools, and advance them groceries out of his 'store'.

As soon as they could, they bought a fresh cow, a pair of rabbits and a few laying hens. They accept everything they are able to get their hands on. Mr. Lewis fishes and hunts. Deer are plentiful; bears are so numerous they are pests; and the rivers and creeks yield trout.

Whenever they heard us driving into Robe Ranch, Mrs. Lewis and the boys inevitably stationed themselves near the gate to their yard. Mrs. Lewis often pretended to be busy in the woodshed; the boys lined up waiting to greet us. There were questions and talk while we unloaded groceries and blankets from the car, and then, as we started up the hill to the cabin, Mrs. Lewis would think of something to detain us.

"Say, I mustn't forget to ask, did you want a rabbit today, 'cause if you did I could start right now preparing it?" Or perhaps, "say, jest a minute, Mrs. Callahan, I got a little bouquet for you. The spring flowers are comin' out real pretty now the sun's showin' a little warmth." As I lingered she drifted into a long, colorful narrative, her monumental figure clad in tight faded overalls, her hands gesticulating airily, the fingers prettily, almost daintily curved. She would smooth back a stray wisp of her dark, straight hair, which was wound into a knot at the nape of her neck, with the elegance of a grand dame. I always longed to see her regally dressed, pouring tea with all the accoutrements, for the ladies of the Daughters of the American Revolution.

Wirt Robe remained a rather shadowy figure during our first year of acquaintance. I was a little intimidated by his forbidding appearance. His sharp blue eyes peered through the lenses of his bifocals. He was a tall man with a lean, high cheek-boned face, distorted by the scar that marred one whole side. His aquiline nose and Abraham Lincoln chin completed an expression of granite-like sternness. The unkempt, straw-like hair that strayed from under his battered gray hat and the traces of grime embedded in the creases of his aging skin somehow did not detract from the dignity of his bearing.

One fragrant day in April, when the daffodils were flowering and current and cherry blossoms were fluttering in the fair weather breeze from the west, he came to the gate, or rather the gap in the split cedar fence where the gate had fallen away. He explained that he was going to restore the gate so the Lewis's cow would no longer have entry to our yard. I was puzzled about the old car door under his arm, complete with ruined upholstery and hardware, until I realized the door was to be the gate. He hung it somehow on the cedar post, and it stayed shut of its own weight. There it stayed as long as we did, and longer, until it dropped to the ground, where it probably still lies under many years' deposits of leaves and earth.

I went down to the path to inspect the new gate and to thank our landlord. He was leaning, as though tired, on one of the fence posts. His pipe was in his mouth, but it wasn't lit. I asked him if anything was wrong. He pushed back his hat, scratched his forehead and pulled his hat back into position. "Oh, I dunno," he said in a despairing tone. "It seems to me things are all wrong. I just come from my brother's funeral down in Everett, my brother, Roy. He was the youngest of us four and the best man of us all. He had lots to live for: family, friends. He was first-rate, Roy was. I got nothing that makes any difference, nobody that would even know if I was gone. Why couldn't it have been me instead of him?" This was the only time I ever saw Wirt express grief, even in all the months of his own dying. He rubbed his scarred nose, spat, scratched his head again, and shuffled off down the path to his own tiny cabin. I didn't understand until much later, when I learned how radically he understated his own emotions, how deeply moved he was at that moment.

18

GRADUALLY WE CAME TO know the people and the places of the Stillaguamish valley. This was a process that could not be hurried, and we were happy to let discovery unfold at its own pace. Kenneth found that the closeness to nature and the simplicity of life contributed powerfully to his painting. Tobey played delightedly with frogs, garter snakes, baby field mice, and snails, paddled in the river when it was warm enough, and tagged after the Lewis boys in their farm chores. As I am a born squaw, everything about the life seemed right. I like splitting wood, hauling water, hanging clothes and picking berries. I like being in a place with no distractions where I can savor the special quality of each day as the seasons roll along. This to me is a birthright, which so many unknowingly sell for a mess of chrome and plastic junk.

One morning, recently, while watching Tobey on his stomach on the dirt path below our porch, intent on the comings and goings of a trap-door spider, I wondered how much of this childhood would remain in his memory. As I poked around in my own childhood memories, I wondered what I had forgotten. I have not forgotten the back yard of the rusty house on 73rd near Greenwood Avenue. We called it the rusty house, because it wasn't painted.

We lived an entire three months in the rusty house on Phinney Ridge in Seattle while our house three blocks away at 138 North 76th was being finished. The year was 1910. One day as my brother and I sat in the back yard among grasses taller than our heads we discovered a big new plant with round pink blossoms. We pulled on it. The tough stem resisted. We pulled harder. Bob sat on one side of the plant and I on the other and we pulled at a separate stem until they gave way and we fell over backwards, still clutching the mutilated clover. This is my first remembrance of the miracle of laughter. The unexpected could bring laughter or tears, but this particular 'unexpected' involved no hurt. We lay back in the tall grasses with the smell of crushed grass all about us and the buzzing of insects in our ears, the sun warm upon our faces, and laughed helplessly in shrieks until our faces were wet with tears.

And a little later, a little taller, there are household objects I clearly remember. Among them are the round oak dining table, which could be split for additional leaves; the wood-burning heater stove, the treadle sewing machine, the 'funny man' chair with its carved oak seat and round laughing face for a back, the birdseye maple bedroom set in my parent's room and, later, the bed I slept in with the round iron framework. The latter had vertical bars that I attempted to curl my hair around, twisting it and lying very still, imagining the ringlets I might unwind in the morning.

Other recollections are tentative, but with flashes of experience sufficiently extraordinary to catch and cling to the structure: memory-like fragments of a kite in a treetop long after the laughter and tears of the child who flew it have died away; or the time when, as a toddler, after a fretful day of fever, my parents took me for a brief ride in my carriage, thinking the air might cause me to sleep better. Do I remember, or is it hearing the incident told? We came upon a small street festival with an organ grinder and children dancing. They were at first distressed by my insistence upon joining the fun, but they assented rather than cope with tears of rage. I clambered from the buggy and stomped about with my eyes shining and a gleeful smile on my face, waving my arms in time to the music. When we returned home, they took my temperature immediately, fearing the excitement had increased it. On the contrary, the thermometer revealed a normal condition. I slept perfectly that night, and there was no return of illness. Whether remembered or acquired, the incident was probably my earliest expression of a lifetime love affair with music and dancing.

I can remember every show I saw as a child: vaudeville, movie or live drama. First there was the anticipation, telling the big news to one's friends and enjoying their envy, then the utter transports of sitting through the actual event, followed by the long-lasting memories and the recounting of the details to anyone who would listen. I saw my very first show, a combined vaudeville and movie billing at the old Pantages Theater on Third Avenue and University Street when I was five years old. Our parents took my brother and me to an evening performance, probably because they couldn't get anyone to babysit as my mother was normally an adamant sender of children to bed early.

The glitter and strangeness of the interior of the theater were overwhelming. The unfolding of those heavy red plush curtains disclosed an inner curtain covered with advertisements for everything from corsets to cough medicine. I thought it would never, never rise on the opening act. But rise it did, and from that moment on I was a quivering mass of delight and impatience -- delight over each performer's entrance and impatience for the next one to commence.

The movie, however, which customarily preceded the vaudeville show, left the deepest impression. Wormwood was the title; what went on I have no idea, but the ghostly jerky figures on the dark, flickering screen, constantly lashed by diagonal streaks as though a heavy rain storm was happening, cast a spell. It is hard to understand just why. But the scene that has never left my mind showed a dead body floating face up down a dark river, no doubt a lovelorn suicide. The white blob of that Hollywood dummy's visage still rides that nameless river's currents in an occasional nightmare of mine.

The next time we were taken to a show was about a year later, and this was a matinee with my mother, my brother, and myself in attendance. Again, it was vaudeville at the Pantages, this time preceded by several short movies, none of which enthralled me, as I can remember suffering with impatience for the real people to begin their acts. This time it was a comedy team that left the indelible stamp. The actors were made up like Chinese and had long braids. Their nonsense involved a couple of balloons, which would escape their grasp and rise to the ceiling of the stage, whereupon the Chinese would say, "Meely-go-up." Bob and I were to get a lot of mileage from that particular scene in the coming year or so.

There were many things I loved as a child. I loved the members of my family, but I was not conscious of it. It was more an abstraction. But certain things about them I definitely loved. For example, my brother and I would get to laughing together during after dinner romps, while Mother and Father were washing the dishes in the kitchen and the lights in the living room were off with only the firelight peopling the walls with fine mysterious shadows. "Quiet down," our mother would call, "with so much laughing there will be crying in a few minutes." But we would go on scurrying about on hands and knees under tables and behind chairs, colliding, writhing, and laughing until we were limp. It was often wintertime with the sound of wind and rain outdoors. All too soon, we would be hustled through the folding doors out of the warm coziness into the unheated hall and up the stairs for a bath and bed.

I loved my mother when she sang while going about her housework. "Oh my darling, oh my darling, oh my darling, Clementine," she would warble. Seeing Nellie Home was another favorite. I found her gorgeous when she dressed to go to a party in rustling skirts, her eyes very bright, cheeks pink, hair piled high, and a faint fragrance in her wake. But at such times she was pre-occupied and distant. And I remember when she talked to the pets in a high, teasing way, and when she made cookies and strung popcorn and cranberries for the Christmas tree.

I loved my father coming home from work, walking briskly the half block from the streetcar, always glad to be assailed by the racing children. I loved smelling the male smell of tobacco, office, and occasionally the mysterious scent of liquor from a clandestine nip for which he was bound to be scolded if he kissed our mother.

I loved the smells from the kitchen of Sunday dinners being cooked: a juicy leg of lamb or roast beef or stewing chicken. I remember the smell of cut grass; the look of a box of paper dolls or a doll's trunk full of folded clothes; gutters running with water, slippery to slide down; frozen puddles and the patterns when you struck them with a rock; the big yellow maple leaves of October, their smell in the rain and the lovely shapes like hands spread out; and finding shaggy mane mushrooms under wet leaves in the fall.

I hated the nights when we were left with Ruth of next door as babysitter, because she was told she could leave as soon as we were asleep. Mother believed firmly there was no such thing as robbers, burglars, sluggers or any of the doubtful characters the kids I knew could tell you about. Even at the height of the slugger scare, along about 1914, when the neighbors all installed slide bolts with chains that would allow the door to open only three inches until you knew who it was. In addition they kept clubs of assorted sizes handy, however she refused to be bothered with locked doors or other precautions. If we objected to going to the store after dark, she would exclaim, "Nonsense! Ridiculous! Just behave yourself and you'll be all right. Just imagination, that's all these stories are. Or people wanting attention."

As it happened we never had a burglar or any other type of marauder, except one time when a neighborhood tramp she had fed finished his sandwich and coffee by saying with a leer, "Wonderful food, wonderful coffee, nice warm kitchen. And now how about a little kiss." Apparently the alacrity and energy with which she ordered him from the premises scared away her visitor permanently. She told the story for years as a great joke on herself.

But I had none of this staunch attitude. Once the door had closed on my departing parents, off to an evening of bridge, I steeled myself to stay awake by every device I could think up. The Chinese acrobats served me well. It was still pretty fresh material when one of those dreaded evenings arrived. We were fed and bedded down some time before they left. I watched my mother swirl about in silken skirt, in and out of closets, dabbing a final bit of perfume, catching up a scented hanky, trailing lovely smells and cooling breezes in her hurried goings and comings. The good night kiss was lovely for the delicate trace of powder, the extra fluffiness of the pompadour that her light brown hair made above her smooth, high brow, and the little caress of her fingers across my hair as she urged me to be a good girl and go right to sleep, and she'd remember all the funny things to tell us at breakfast.

The door was no sooner closed than I called to Bob. "Meely go up." And we were off. We worked over all the possibilities, which were increased by the demise of a couple of balloons we had been given at the show, one of which burst (his) and was forever dubbed "Fatty"; the other escaped by floating into the upper atmosphere. This one (mine) became "Meely go up." Finally, however, every new hilarious angle I could think of regarding "Meely go up" and "Fatty" failed and I had realized reluctantly that Bob, who had inherited my mother's basic trust in the absence of hobgoblins and monsters, was sound asleep.

Dreadful world of night silence, dreadful effort to stay awake. Strain and fight to keep eyes open, seeing shapes in the almost dark. Hearing the evening noises: wind whining above the hill top houses, inexpressibly mournful dogs barking their lonely vigils, an occasional crackle of the fireplace in the living room below. My wakeful state faded and there was a merging of reality and dream. The sudden telltale click of a door latch snapped me awake. "Ruuth!" Stiff with fright. Had she managed to sneak a getaway? Door closes softly. "Goodness! Aren't you asleep yet? You be quiet now and go to sleep."

Hmmm, not if I can help it. Play games. Fix your face into the way other faces are. Long upper lip and nostrils pulled in like Zulu Zonker, who sat in the back seat of your row in old lady Dee's room. Corner of the eyes pulled down like Gerald's, who made deep snuffling noises and then swallowed so hard his adam's apple bounced up and down. Smile up on one side of the face like it hurt too much to do it up on both sides -- this was the principal, Mr. Jassel, who kept a rubber hose in office for the bad big kids. Bug your eyes like Seventh grade teacher Sophie Lauks, called by all, Loafie Sox. Push your ears out straight, push your lips out thick, and bulge your stomach like Fatty Chew. Squint through hair over eyes like Benny Saw -- savoring each of these transformations, wondering if this was the way they felt, whether you were making yourself really feel like you were inside all these people. What would it feel like to be inside somebody else? Why am I inside me? Why did God make me different from others? Or does everybody think God made him or her different? What does 'I' mean? What is there special about I? Does everybody feel there's something special about his or her 'I,' even those tough Leary girls, who shouted "snot nose" and threw rocks harder than the boys?

I am running like Violet Porter with my head tipped to one side and I am being chased, but the terror dies away, for suddenly I can span a block with every running step, floating along at any speed I desire, so easy, so free. Jolt. Wide awake. Silence. "Ruuuuuth." No answer. Louder, as loud as I can call without waking Bob. No, she got away. Alone in the vastness of night. What time is it? Is it nearly time for them to come home? Or will it be hours and hours? The back door rattles. The stairs creak. I forgot to look under the bed and in the closet before the lights were turned off. Pull the covers over your head, only your nose out. You could smother, so your nose must be out. And don't move. Just lie very still and don't breathe very much. Hold your breath and listen. That far away rumbling, is it the streetcar? Oh, it is, closer, traveling very fast, closer, closer. It's at our street. But it isn't slowing. Oh, it's gone past, fainter, fainter, into the distance. Silence again.

Once, when the fear becomes too pressing, I call softly, "Bob." How absolutely and terrifically wonderful is the thought of hearing his voice. But he sleeps much too soundly and I don't dare shout him awake. He would tell. And he'd never stay awake anyway. "Maggie got scared and woke me up." No, no, it would never do. Another streetcar and this one whines to a stop. A brief stop, then clanging and an accelerating grind of wheels on tracks as it takes off, its comforting noise again becomes stillness. But the sound of footsteps on the board sidewalk comes closer. Filled with confidence, I leap from bed and look out the front window of my parents' bedroom. Two figures, indecipherable in the misty night, walk on past and disappear down the street. The night becomes only the rhythm of streetcars, alternating to and from down town. I get to know expertly which way they are going and listen for footsteps only from the outbound cars. But sleep finally conquers trepidation.

Our house was built on a hill, on top of a ridge. The sun came to us in the mornings from over the Cascade Mountains and sank in the evening below the Olympics. The mountains seemed as far away as the sun and as mysterious. They were merely something that furnished us a view, over which visitors exclaimed, telling my father, "it's a nice little home you have here. Splendid view!"

Green Lake was down the hill to the east, as was the public library branch; in the valley to the west were Ballard and the mills, whose smoke we could see. At night in the stillness there was the sound of the trains shunting about in the lumberyards. And the mills never rested in those days, for the big trees from all around the raped countryside seemed endless, and the city was sprawling in all directions. Every child grew up to the sound of hammers ringing and saws rasping and knew the delight of playing in half-constructed buildings, pungent with the smell of raw lumber. Little girls pinned long curling wood shavings to their hair for Mary Pickford curls, and little boys pocketed bent nails and odd bits of wood and hardware.

We were once waiting for the streetcar, my mother and I, on the corner of Second and Pine where there was a small green park and benches. A man lay as though dead, stretched out on the bench. Suddenly, as I stared at him, he fell onto the ground, rolled a short distance into the gutter and lay there with his eyes closed and his arms over his inert head. "He's drunk," my mother explained in tones of horror. I felt a faintness and sickness rising in me as I stared at this strange lifeless being who was living, yet dead. I felt a cold dread to the depths of my being, and I was unhappy for hours; the vision was never erased from my memory. "Don't look," said my mother. "Horrid!" But somewhere in my general dismay, I felt pity, rather than scorn. And this was the hardest emotion of all.

The same feelings racked me when I saw a small white kitten being pursued by a group of noisy boys, armed with sticks. The kitten scampered up the trunk of an apple tree and crouched in the fork; boys poked with sticks, attempting to dislodge it; kitten climbed higher and the boys' frustrated shouts and savage caperings intensified. That picture stayed with me, haunting my mind in the moments before sleep overtook me. I included all lost kittens in my prayers. In visions I rescued kittens, night after night I shielded kittens in my arms, gave them soft beds and large bowls of milk. I was not brave enough to intercede with a gang of boys, not so much fearing physical hurt as the brazen assertion of my own personality. But I derived consolation from my imaginary deeds.

Our house on Phinney Ridge was typical of hundreds of Seattle's middle class homes of the day. Those who had already made fortunes from this new, raw land were building mansions on the hills close to the center of town: First Hill, Capitol Hill, Queen Anne Hill, and some more modest ones in the districts of the newly located University of Washington, northeast of Lake Union.

My parents operated on no long-range plan; they did what seemed feasible at the moment. When a client offered to pay my father for a legal job with a plot of ground rather than cash, which he was short of at that time, my father agreed without quibbling. My parents then set about finding a contractor who would put up an adequate dwelling for themselves and their two children.

Our street had yet to go through the grading and the sidewalk building process with its attendant assessments. But my parents told themselves it was a coming district, bound to build up well, what with the splendid view, closeness to a good elementary school, and the fact that "you found a better grade of people in the outlying communities."

Our house was the second in the block to be built, but soon others sprang up, each a bit different in style. All were made of wood, all were painted brown or gray or white, and all were one or two stories high and contained from five to eight rooms. Each house had a covered porch and a basement. We had no attic. Basements were merely dug out of the dirt and not lined with cement. They were scary, dark places, draped with cobwebs and smelling indescribably damp and musty. I hated to be sent to the basement for canned fruit or eggs from the water glass barrel because of the imaginary terrors lurking in the darkness. To make it bearable I would sing to myself the Sunday school hymn, "God Will Take Care of Youuuu," while my heart pounded and the scutter of a mouse made my hair stand on end.

Basements, however, were fine places to hide in the various versions of hide and seek we used to play, and in the company of one or two whispering, snickering hiders the dark corners we crouched into were no longer fearsome. Even the boogey-men we invented, who lived in the knotholes of the teeter-totter board and whom we saw running in and out of the basement, weren't ominous, but rather only deliciously spine-tingling. The trouble with these inventions was that they returned to stalk you when the comfort of company was missing. Even without the menace of the comic books and the concocted fiends on the animated cartoons, we managed to people the world with lively demons. The ogres of the old fairy tales served as stimulating models. Just why human beings create these bugaboos for the disturbance of their security is a mystery. Young people love to scare themselves, and this goes for adults, also. The specters created in all seriousness by adult minds outdo any of the fantasies indulged in by children, original sin for example.

People tend to humanize everything, which is probably why some cultures animate things with gods or devils. Every item in our house, from the relaxed, fatherly Morris chair to the tall, frowning hall tree, bristling with coat hooks and holding in its lidded seat a jumble of overshoes, had for me a personality In the beveled glass mirror of the hall tree I first discovered vanity, surveying my adolescent features for some faint resemblance to the be-curled, painted masks of the movie stars we worshipped in that day.

As far as we were concerned, our parents' choice of neighborhood couldn't have been finer. Its future didn't materialize in quite the style my family had envisioned. Not even the row of frame houses, all alike in their tan paint and only about four feet apart, which sprang up across the street, offended our aesthetic senses in the least. In fact, the addition of a somewhat transient population in the neighborhood was refreshing for us children. There was always somebody moving in or out of the homely little replicas, and we kept track with avid interest.

The Greenwood district afforded plenty of hills for coasting and roller-skating. In close proximity were woods, vacant lots galore, plenty of trees for climbing (in the future Woodland Park), and a lake (Green Lake) within walking distance that was good for swimming in summer and skating in winter on the few occasions when the weather was cold enough.

The house, itself, possessed sufficient charm to endear it to a child's heart. The ever-inviting street bordered a yard, big enough for play and unfenced. In addition to the basement we had a fireplace, and a deep recessed window with a seat whose lid opened to contain our toys. A wide, square opening connected the living and dining rooms, and swinging door divided the dining room from the kitchen. The front porch was deep and ran the width of the house; it had a hammock and two rustic chairs, one with arms and the other a rocker without arms, which by diligent rocking we could make travel the length of the porch on rainy days. This invariably brought loud commands from our mother to cease, as it left marks in the paint on the porch floor. The back porch was a spot of great charm. It was small, latticed on two sides with an opening for the steps. It contained the icebox, woodbin, garbage pail, and other bins for vegetables. I don't know why I should have been so fond of it. Perhaps it was the way the light entered through the lattice.

My recollections are interrupted when Tobey tires of the trap-door spider and moves up the path toward the outhouse. Back to Seattle tomorrow -- oh woe.

19

TOBEY IS SLEEPING IN his crib in the south room upstairs. Mike is sleeping in the old Morris chair on the orange serape. I am writing at the round oak table. The Cascades are barely to be seen in the haze – long have they been without snow, this year being unusually warm and dry.

House payment, $20. Gas, $5.50. Lights, $4.00. Phone, $3.75. Coal bill, $25. Groceries, $15. Catch the department store bills on the 15th, let the dentist go until next month. Maybe next month we can afford the bulbs and the shrubs I wanted to put in this fall. Twice a month, between household tasks, I sort out bills, survey our liabilities, and think longingly of adding to the microscopic savings account but discard the idea as impractical for the present. I consider going after some sort of job but always decide that being a full-time mother is more important for the time being.

Kenneth is still working at the Seattle Art Museum, a job that appeared at a crucial time, as if by magic, when the Town Crier finally knuckled under in the mid-thirties after trying valiantly to meet the riptide of the depression. George Bernard Shaw has said the only solution for the dilemma of the artist in a world where his work is not valued is a part time job. He is left free to create without being hampered by having to peddle his product. Of course, no artist feels he is really contributing to society except by painting a picture, writing a poem, or composing a symphony. But there is something to be said, too, for the experience of working with other human beings whether it is checking groceries, driving a cab or teaching. It takes the artist outside his own ego, and this is quite a journey.

It is one of those mornings when nothing works out. I haven't paid down the garage bill or the water bill or the bookstore. I made out a tentative budget for the next paycheck and for the one after that. I calculated that we should be able to pay up back bills by that time. Experience tells me it won't work out that way, but it gives me a sense of order to put the figures down.

Mark and Kenneth and I went to see *The Light That Failed.* Friday evening. We had our usual dinner in the grill at the Olympic and the debate over what to see. This time I tried to hold out for *The Shop Around the Corner,* but Mark insisted on *TheLight That Failed* and the first thing we knew we were at the doors of the theater. Not bad either -- Ronald Coleman was really magnificent and the artist's life was handled rather well for the period and all. Mark was swept away by one beautiful shot of a man on a horse with light flooding a battlefield, saying it was like an El Greco painting. The movie was crowded with kids, as Friday is their night in all American movie theaters, and their rowdiness, and mindless laughter about everything was upsetting. "You wonder how they have enough sense to get them through their lives!" Mark said. "How I hate them, no feeling for anything, no sensitivity, just speed and smart-alecky talk," he concluded.

Mark is still not feeling well. He is not painting and feels baffled. He made a painting from one of the market sketches and said it came out fairly well, but he just doesn't know what approach to take with his art. Kenneth said that he thought this was a difficult problem, but that it was a period necessary for digesting and waiting for the right thing to surface and that he shouldn't limit himself to just making 'market pictures.' Mark said, "Lord no," he didn't want to just make market pictures.

After the movie we talked of the importance of light, and Mark wondered why no one since Cezanne has tried to use light. Why didn't Oriental artists have use for it?

Walking from the show to the car through the warm evening we looked at the red, white and blue dresses in Frederick's windows and were repulsed by the 'military influence' and amused at the extreme hats. I asked Mark if he were a woman would he wear one, and he said he didn't know. It wasn't a very good time for being frivolous, was it, he said, as the headlines were of a new Russian offensive by the Nazis and more ships sunk.

Back at home we had toast and chocolate by the fire. Mark liked Kenneth's new portrait of the man in the gray hat, one of the best, he said, and I agree. He made some pungent remarks about a few other paintings. "Take the house out of the one of the man pumping water," for example. "I find myself pre-occupied with the house when what I want to see is the man -- then I see the door, and first thing I know I'm wondering who lives there."

It was just last week that Bill Cumming and Kenneth took over kitchen duties while I tended Tobey and otherwise collapsed on the couch in the first stages of a bad cold. We listened to Bruckner's Fourth on the radio with Bruno Walter. I was in pretty much of a daze, but I liked what I could remember. Bill was playing himself in the role of romantic young artist, telling of "living in a state of intoxication all week", of working all day and at night, prowling about the streets alone, "running and skipping and letting out little rat squeals of joy, and singing and laughing aloud."

But just last night Bill was here again with the report from his doctor that he has TB. He is to find out the results of the x-ray today and another test tomorrow. He is feeling pretty romantic about it, being more than ever the poet and artist, starving in the attic. But he's pretty genuinely perturbed too, and is saying, well, if he had it, he would go get a pick and shovel job. "Important to get plenty of outdoor exercise. " So I lit into him again about not eating properly or keeping regular hours, etc. I really don't know what is to become of him. He brought over a book of Hart Crane's poetry, and I'm reading *The Bridge*, which is real poetry all right. I love Bill, but maybe he is doomed. His painting is getting more interesting all the time, but he's got something in him that keeps him from living up to his capacities. It's a terribly strong, negative thing that won't let go of his vitals. I thought maybe it was just loneliness, but now this, too…

Many are asking the question of whether democracy is worth preserving now, and my own answer is 'yes'. By democracy I mean essentially the Bill of Rights along with an economic democracy we've never before had. I would like to see an economy without private ownership of natural resources, and one that moves toward public ownership of essential industries and banking. I believe just as firmly that homes should be individually owned, more so than at present, and that all the communist hooey condemning as bourgeois the collection of possessions should be rejected. I believe it is a natural and wholesome inclination on the part of human beings to accumulate things from their journey through life, maybe just so the trip won't be so damned lonely. Fortunately, Kenneth's and my mania along these lines coincide in paintings, books, and archaeological specimens. Natural objects we find on our trips such as fungi, rocks, and driftwood also occupy our shelves and tabletops. I don't understand why most people spend so much on rugs, furniture and dishes when they could just as well do with more modest items and have money left for paintings or sculptures or collections of books and records. For me these are the only things worth having, once you have the essential comforts.

For me, this war we're fighting is all tied up with the freedom to do what we want to and say what we want to and think what we want to, and I don't see anything for it but to fight until the other side is defeated. Then we must keep on fighting the forces among ourselves who would cheat us of the fruits of our victory. I began to sense about two years ago that what Hitler and his party represent is more than a political menace. It more represents something approximating the 'forces of evil' in the old biblical sense. We all felt so damned enlightened in the 20s and 30s. We became convinced that there was no such thing as evil or good. At least we said we were convinced, but perhaps we weren't at all. I can remember fleeting thoughts and doubts on the subject.

I am sure that it is possible to have a fighting belief in the dignity and beauty and wonder of life – human, animal, and plant; that is, to have an appreciation for the universe in all its immensity, variety and minuteness. I am also sure that these feelings are part of any worthwhile morality or system of living, and that only under democracy is there the possibility of this sort of system developing. I believe anyone who considers himself apart from the world and its struggles, who feels justified in looking down on any element of life, be it an animal, an individual, or a race of people is lost, lost, lost. I don't think our lives are long enough to achieve true humility, but we must try to develop in ourselves the capacity for humility. It is what opens us to the earth's natural blessings.

The Battle of Britain is raging. Perhaps soon it will be the Battle of America. What will be salvaged? Through all things breathes the prayer that the war will end soon. Let something happen, some sudden turn of events that will end all the horror and bring about a decent world again. The Russians and the Germans are apparently carrying out the most appalling slaughter of all. Goddamn the smug souls who lick their chops and wisecrack about hoping that neither side runs out of ammunition. There was a certain grim I-told-you-so feeling among we scorned liberals when Germany opened the eastern front against Russia. The communist party in this country immediately put a stop to its sabotaging of the war effort and began blowing on the fires for all they were worth.

Winter Plea, 1940

It's true John Donne,
No Man is an island
And those across the seas
For whom the bell tolls -- or no bells toll
Are me: and all the 'mes' and 'thees'
Are one great flowing stream
Today made foul with hate
And all the loathsomeness the world might dream.

But then is this not also true?
If one black hate pollutes us all
Then one bright love
Can be a cleansing, too?

If so look not at the headlines

Screaming sterile fears,
Nor at the comic ugliness
Offered in the merchandise marts
Shoddy substitutes

Offered by those whose noses are constantly
Beneath the scrawny tails of the money gods
Shoddy substitutes designed to appease
The dire hungers of men's bodies
And their longing souls.

Look instead to the earth's gifts, at a stone's modeling,
The unfurling of a chestnut leaf,
At microscopic form
And the Milky Way,
Rim of our galaxy.
Look into the eyes of animals as they seek your own,
And at the beauty of old faces
And old hands;
Look into the eyes of men of all nations,
Without fear, without prejudice,
As the child looks;
Then the wonder, long dead, will come to life,

Man's spirit still is brave,
Still can toss his noble head,
As nostrils catch scents of spring
Of hyacinths and daphne,
Tree leaves, fungus, and ocean beaches;
Man's heart still skips a beat
To see his toddler faring forth
On tiny, stomping feet.

Tobey delights me these days with his distinctly elfish quality. He tries to sing constantly now and can almost hit a tune. His standbys are Brother John and Row, Row Your Boat. He speaks quite plainly, but it's still y for l and 'Kensus' for Kenneth and 'tuntul' for tunnel. He had quite a time one day and was all ready to throw a tantrum because he "can't know how to say it," trying to say tunnel like we do. He still says sink for think, sank you, etc. Tonight, when we left for the library, he brought a paper bag full of toys to the door to give us (a trick he does quite often). Kenneth said we'd bring it back soon, and he said, "no, don't bring it back, give it to the dull ones" -- (the old dull people we're always going to see). When he woke up this morning he wanted to know if I was "going to any old dull places today?" No. Well, was I "going to any fine places...?"

20

IT'S SEPTEMBER, 1941. THE war goes on, and nobody knows what to think except the communists, and they have been told. The Germans are still pounding at Moscow. The Russians are apparently fighting a great fight. If the British are deliberately holding off from the Western Front until they are sure Stalin is finished, then it will go down as the greatest double-cross in history. But the news is so censored that nothing is known for sure. I do think this country should be in it. I want to see the whole thing over as quickly as possible. Please God, may it be over before our children here are endangered. One must always keep the thought that if body and mind and family can be kept intact, if there are food and shelter and love, we must not ask for more. I wish I were more patient and radiated more good feelings than I do.

Joe Cohen and his Vera appeared out of the blue one evening recently. At first it appeared to be a friendly visit, "so sorry not to have seen you for so long" and all, but the real purpose came out before they had been here long: a detailed and lengthy resume of the communists' position at the moment. In a way, it annoys me to think that just because they feel they are going to need their 'fellow travelers' in the days to come they can take up lost friendships where they were tossed aside some months or years ago and make use of them again. I am convinced this was the motive for the visit and not friendliness at all. Vera was wonderful. Joe should leave her home out of self-protection. She kept saying all the wrong things, and such stupid ones;

I got embarrassed for her and for Joe and pretended to help her make a point. I had wished intensely to have a talk with Joe, because I felt he could reason somewhat on his own, but aside from presenting the party arguments far more logically and intelligently than the others, he was the same as all the rest, swallowing it all whole without question. Maybe they are right, but they are going to have a tough time making most people think so.

Anyway, maybe I don't know what my stand on the world situation is, but I am for the Puyallup Fair. We had a magical day there: Kenneth, Dick Bennett, and I. We arrived in the heat of the afternoon. Everything was as usual: the small souvenir stands lining the approach, the milling crowds within the high whitewashed fence, the trampled ground, and the paper littered floors of the display buildings. The feeling of contagious merriment, of carnival gaiety, was not forced but pure and spontaneous, and this year's Western Washington State Fair was as fine as I have ever experienced it.

We sat on the narrow and increasingly hard boards to watch the show, the first year we have indulged in grandstand seats. We watched a swell rodeo with fancy riding, bronc-busting, bull riding and steer wrestling, interspersed with a variety show that included trapeze artists in pink tights, a dog act, clowns, comedians, tumblers, and horse races. And over all the wonderful afternoon light flooded the great green circle, illuminating the movements of horses and riders. A wonderful synchronization it is, the rider and his horse. As the event ended, the low tree-covered hills against the horizon, the reflected light and shadow ever changing and slowly growing more dim and golden, all made a marvelous backdrop to the event.

When the show was over there was dinner in the big, whitewashed loft cafeteria, jam-crammed and noisy. Afterwards, we walked about among the animals, experiencing that unspoken sense of communion with their great beauty. How I love the dappled Percherons with proud, arched necks and the nervous, sullen racehorses, the Karakul sheep with their golden eyes, the gentle, patient cows, sometimes with calves, and the families of pigs. I love the Puyallup Fair.

Kenneth has gone to Fort Casey, as he is organizing art classes for the soldiers. A request for this came to the museum. The artists are to donate their time, and Dr. Fuller will pay the expenses. It may only be that they are hard-pressed for any amusement in the isolated localities, but it is encouraging that military men in wartime will even acknowledge that art exists. He and Guy went this time, the first. He won't be home until midnight. I rather like being alone evenings. I thought some of calling Mary or Morris or George but couldn't resist the thought of solitude and perhaps getting to some writing.

I have the brave and sturdy Barrett family strongly on my mind tonight: Ethel, Everett, Herbert, John, and Loretta. Life at Robe Ranch must have been a lonely one for her. He didn't often get leaves of absence from his lookout, and she made the trip up only once during the season, and then he was called out on a fire 10 minutes after she had made the steep, hot climb. They have left Robe Ranch now and gone to Los Angeles. It's too rainy a fall for outside work in the mountains, and he is one who must be on the move every so often. It is in his blood. They left in their 15-year-old car with goods packed in a homemade trailer, planning to camp while en route. Lauretta is not two years old yet and just toddling. A note from Oregon says all is well so far. Everett wrote in an earlier letter that they wouldn't be able to come to Seattle for a day before going because $2 or $3 worth of gas might determine whether they got to LA or not.

It's hard to put into words what I sense in them. They are truly gentlefolk, who love the country. Their boys have the best manners I've seen in children their age. They are natural in their hospitality and possess a keenness for living. They prefer physical hardship in the country to slow death in a city. He didn't finish grammar school, but his sense of values is right, so much more right than that of the average college graduate.

"Yes," Everett had once said in answer to my remark that it must be terrifying sometimes to look about and realize that no matter where lightning chooses to spark a fire, it was his job to get to it and put it out. "It does scare you some at first but after a while you get less scared and finally you feel privileged to have a job protecting these forests."

Last weekend we went to Betty Willis's cabin at Agate Point. Mark went with us, and three of Betty's girls were there. Mark surprised me in that he enjoyed everything and came back relaxed and "all ironed out". I had worried that he might not like it at all, due to the presence of so many children, including little Tobey. He told fortunes for us Saturday evening, seeing wonderful things for Kenneth and me. Betty was pretty intense when he read hers. She is far-gone on him, I know, and I came to see the interpretations of what he said flashing through her mind, hopefully. He did say some rather leading things. I'm wondering how much of it was deliberate. He was most charming all weekend: helping with cooking, joining the girls' shadow shows, amused at their masks and costumes, digging clams by lantern light after midnight, reading poetry the next morning and walking to the charming old Chief Seattle Store and Trading Post. I wonder if he is trying to position himself for some arrangement with her. It would have to be marriage, I suppose. It might work out very well.

We got the invitation for the tea at Mrs. Baillargin's home today. She will be exhibiting Kenneth's drawings of mountains and trees he did this summer. I wish I didn't have to go. She's invited seventy-five of the crème de la crème of Seattle society. I hate the thought of going, yet I'd like to see the drawings up. I am sure they are great and will be recognized as such some day. He is working on groups of people in relation to mountain landscapes lately, but hasn't had much time to paint.

Mark told me that he had commented to Morris that in every community of artists there had always been a 'mother' to them, and that I fulfilled that role here. She must be a woman of creative talents who allows them to be absorbed in their work. It is rather pleasing to me to be thought of thus, but it would be more satisfactory to give vent directly to my desire to write. I hope the one will serve the other in time. I do have a deep affection for Mark, Morris, Bill, and, even in a way, Leuben. Bill is doing some good paintings lately: flat geometric renditions in dark, rich colors of some of the architecture around his apartment. Morris said the other evening that he intends to cram all the fantasy he can into a given area. I wish this would purge his system of it, for I feel he is coming to a dead end. Mark certainly reached a peak this winter in his small market drawings. If I had the money, I would buy the whole series. If I had the money, oh god, what wouldn't I do? Not that either of us pines for it, but it would be swell to be able to buy a record without the gnawing memory that the fuel bill and taxes and what not remain unpaid.

Kenneth's first words Sunday morning (December 7) were, "It's a beautiful day." We got going early and caught the ferry to Betty Willis' place again. It was a fine lazy day, with a walk on the beach netting us some beauties of drift wood, and no news until about four o' clock when the girls came rushing in, breathlessly: "We're at war with Japan, they've bombed Pearl Harbor, sunk two battleship," etc... And now the tide of war has washed over the world's last peaceful shore. Since Sunday, we here on the coast have lived in a world of radio announcements of blackout details, latest bulletins, rumors, voices, voices, voices relating, urging, impressing, commanding. And tonight the President sealed our fate with these words: "it will be a long war and a hard war until the enemy is broken." With the threat of air raids here people spent the first night of the blackout with amazing calmness, except for the mob down town that had a fine time smashing plate glass windows of stores in which lights had been left burning. What a chance to shed inhibitions. And, apparently, many a fist was filled with the pretty things left exposed.

My own concern has chiefly been in keeping any note of alarm from reaching Tobey. I feel such heartache in seeing that pink little face with the wide eyes emerging from the covers, having said his "now I lay me..." and "see you in the morning." Tonight he told us to be good kids when we left him. And no fears of the dark -- that is so wonderful. May he never have fears...

Mrs. Bruce exemplified the reaction of many of our neighbors when she described what happened to her seaman husband after Pearl Harbor. "Well, he come home Tuesday night. They was held up four days in Ketchikan, Alaska after the government ordered them into port, and they couldn't have no lights, and they wouldn't let nobody go ashore or nobody come aboard ship after dark, and they didn't have no lights at sea all the way down. The passengers didn't like it, but Mr. Bruce said it didn't make no difference to him. They don't use no light anyway. The watch goes by their compass, so as far as they're concerned they'd rather the lights was off all the time. But he got a cut on his eye, going up on the bridge in the dark. It's just on that there eyelid. It ain't nothing serious... But say, you should have seen his face when he seen

I had everything packed and the covers over the furniture and all, and the clothes hamper full of towels, napkins and tablecloths. He said, 'What are you doing, May?' And I said, 'I want to go to Spokane. I can't stand it here no longer. I'm weak as a cat; I want to go over to my sister's.' And he said, 'But May, do you think I'm going to leave my home and let them damn Japs get it? The people in homes got nothing to be afraid of anyhow. They'll try to get Boeing and the Navy Yard and all them defense industries first, and anyway if they got as far as here they'd get to Spokane, and there's nothing for me in Spokane, and you won't catch me leaving my home to the Japs.' Oh, well, them fishermen -- they ain't afraid of nothing. And when he looked at the clothes hamper you should have heard him laugh. Well, anyway, the government has taken over all the Northland Company's ships, so all the boys are off, and he won't be going to Alaska anymore. But he's paid up his dues in the Boilermaker's Union and he's going to get a job in a defense industry, maybe Boeing or Todd. I guess it ain't any too safe there, though. Ain't it awful that one man like that old Hitler can tell everybody what to do and make them do it? Well, they're afraid they'll get shot if they don't, but then, he's the devil, and you can't get away from the devil. Well, anyway, Mr. Bruce will be home nights, and I won't have to go through what I went through before, calling the company every day and not getting' no information on the ship, cryin' my eyes out all night. He's an awful good man, Mr. Bruce is, and I've got a lot to be thankful for that the Lord give me such a good man."

It's January... Even with the war going on, spring stirs up the same old instincts. I'd like to go get pussy willows and dig up the ground and take a long rambling walk on the waterfront and on up skid road and all over First Hill and then have dinner somewhere. The memories of the days when I worked on the *Crier*, frightening as they were, with budding social and political consciousness, the Depression and all, are actually 'haloed' with a carefree, happy-go-lucky aura that could belong nowhere but in the past.

We start taking first aid classes tonight at the museum. Dorothy Malone's exceptionally intelligent sister Kay Chatterton will do the instructing. This is going to take up two evenings a week. And Kenneth has the job now of assembling the artists into some sort of organized and functioning body to aid in civilian defense. I hope to hell he can keep some time for painting. I guess I will never have time for anything but my own particular little treadmill. The squirrel on the wheel, that's me.

I simply couldn't write during the blackout days and all during the shock following Pearl Harbor. I find it very difficult to even mention it. What made it so frightening was the unreality, the unknown, and the nightmare quality of waiting. And waiting for what? And when?

Guy Anderson has signed up as a conscientious objector and is waiting for the results of his actions. He even objects to non-combatant work if it is done under the military. I hope this won't mean segregation in a camp. If he could do some sort of farm or hospital work under civilian direction this would seem best. I think it is all very well for people who can take this stand. I feel the principle is worth serving. But at this point I can't feel detached from the main human stream sufficiently to do so. Mark is firmly convinced that it's all working out according to Bahai predictions, and that a world society with a new religion will be the answer. George Mantor goes on buying record albums with almost fanatic zeal. He owns all the Mahlers now. Morris is having success in New York at the Museum of Modern Art; the show in which he is included opened yesterday. A *N.Y. Times* correspondent called last night to get information. We are wondering what Morris will do with the money he apparently is to get from the sales.

We've been stocking up some canned goods, a little sugar, etc., due to prospects of future scarcity. I wish they would ration things before they run short, as it is so unfair for those with lots of money to be able to stock enough supplies for the duration. But as long as everyone else is doing it, I feel better having a few things put away. We intend to put in a garden – Guy, Bill and Celia Leary and us. I hope we can really raise some vegetables this year, both in town and at the Robe cabin.

21

Mrs. LEWIS' VOICE HAS been flowing into this soft, opalescent evening with the steadiness, relentlessness and monotony of a riveting machine. This time her words were addressed to her husband, who has said nothing through it all until about five minutes ago, when he burst out with "Goddamn it woman, shut up!" This response slowed her up a little, and finally the flow trickled into a moment's quiet. Her sermon had to do with some change in their plans suggested by Mr. Lewis, I gather, for I heard something about the year and a half she spent alone and what an experience that was, and lots of "I'll do what I can, buts" and "furthermores". She has an emphatic way of talking at all times, to put it mildly, a rich throaty drawl that clings to the vowels, and a picturesque vocabulary that has us all straining our ears for prize sayings every time she goes on a tear.

"Stanford-an-Robert," she called one evening, "supposin' you just get busy and clear everything out of the pathway here that might trip up a body comin' in along about half dark…"

"Stanford-an-Robert, you better listen to what I say, or if you want to hang it up on a nail and fergit it, that's all right, but just you wait an see if I fergit it…"

She said last night after dinner that she hadn't "skinned the table yet…"

Overhearing Stanford cussing today she threatened to split his tongue and scrape the edges… also today, "don't ever you fergit yer

169

talkin' to yer mother. It'd be just as easy fer me to whack the dust outn yer britches…" She said one time, when giving Tobey potato plants to transplant, that if he "wanted to entertain them potatoes" she was all for encouraging the effort…

Mr. Lewis is a scrawny, leathery individual, a quarter-breed Cherokee Indian who, Robert informed us the other day, has had four wives. "The first one went insane from sinus trouble, the second one died on him after about two years, and the third one died on him, too. Fourteen years ago he and my mother got married." The fate of the second two wives may be the reason for his choice of the present Mrs. Lewis, whose look and build would seem to guarantee that she wouldn't "die on him" for a fair spell…

This evening is like being on the inside of a moss agate. The ridges of treetops make criss-cross patterns through the mist up the valley; a slow haze of wood smoke drifts peacefully from the ranch house. But what an unpeaceful family is to be heard down there just now. Robert is doing the dishes. "Git at them dishes, Robert, and don't you go fer to sass me neither or I'll take a good big club to ye. If you boys won't do what yer supposed to do so as I have to do it fer ye, then you can do what I'm supposed to do," and Robert goddamning and son-of-a-bitching with all the viciousness his 13-year-old nature can cook up.

Stanford for the second time just queried his father thus, "god damn it, ain't we goin' to get no supper aroun' here tonight. Ain't we goin' to git no supper aroun' here tonight. God damn"…

It's later and Kenneth has gone down to the ranch house to get Tobey, who's right there every time for the milking, and Mrs. Lewis has been talking to him ever since he got there. The Lewises will be moving out soon; the signs of restlessness are in the air. The patch of pulpwood they have been cutting for Wirt is just about cleared, and they have saved a little money. The ranch house will be vacant, and I know we will have first claim to succeed the present occupants. Wirt almost promised as much when we paid our last rent money. The prospect of again cleaning up after the Lewises isn't exactly enthralling, but the appeal of the house overrides any such unpleasantness.

We will miss the virile family from Texas. Stanford and Robert have grown into gawky adolescence, Jessie into a young man, away a good deal of the time, doing what we never know. The younger boys are our constant companions except for the times when their mother's orders can't be dodged. They have shown us secret ways to get to the river and to Green Mountain, short cuts in the dense woods we never would have discovered. They both swear with the uninhibited manner they have heard all their lives. Their vocabulary is small but vivid and functional. The tenor of their lives is pierced at all times, like a road sign punctured with rifle shots, by the stentorian tones of Mrs. Lewis, calling "Stanford-an-Rooobert!" Her voice carries up to the top of the hill, down into the swamp where they fish, into the woods on the far side of the pasture.

I have enjoyed long, animated gardening sessions with her over the last two years. She never works at gardening unless I am there, and then her pecks at the earth with the spade are only a pretense. She is a lonely woman. "Now I don't mean to be telling other folks how to do their own affairs, but there's really no call for you to be stooping over like that when you can use a long-handled hoe and git them weeds out jest as thorough." The garden patch is on a hillside facing southeast directly below the ranch house. Nothing ever materializes in the way of produce because, although she spends days plowing with Old Betsy the sway-back white horse, Mrs. Lewis never gets around to planting anything. And the thirty square feet she allows us to cultivate at the far end of the patch has such poor soil that nothing but quack grass and dandelions figure it is worth the struggle. The plowing sessions are noisy affairs. In spite of Mrs. Lewis's shouted threats, Old Betsy occasionally stumble's to her knees. When that happens she rushes around and backs under the mare's front legs and with brute strength raises her to her feet. I sometimes think the job would be facilitated if the harness had been draped around her ample body, and Betsy took the reins.

The climax of our association with the Lewises occurred one weekend in October. We drove into Robe Ranch on a Friday afternoon to a scene of smoke, hot ashes, charred embers and wildly excited Lewises. The boys and Mrs. Lewis, all talking at once, told us that Mr. Robe's homemade automatic oil stove had exploded. The contraption consisted of a can of oil with a hole in the bottom suspended over an old iron heater. The hole was just big enough to slowly drip fuel into the flame. His cabin and store had burned like paper, and the Lewises had been frantically trying to keep the blaze from spreading to the elevated gas tank nearby. They had prevented the catastrophe that they at first believed to be inevitable. The adjoining hay barn had not escaped the inferno however. Wirt, who had gone into Everett that morning, did not yet know of his loss, or in a way of his miraculous luck, as the blackened base of the full fuel tank attested.

"I've been atellin' him time and time agin' that the oil drip rig would cause a fire sooner or later," Mrs. Lewis said. "He goes away and leaves it goin' full blast. He's a careless man for fire, anyway, always having that old pipe stuck in his mouth upside down and spilling kerosene around every time he fills them lamps." She placed a fluttery hand over the broad expanse of her breast, and with the other smoothed some flying wisps of hair from the big knot of hair at the back of her head. "I still feel shaky," she said, "thinkin' what could have happened. The way I feel, kind of wobbly in my knees, reminds me of an accident happened back home when I was a girl. Except for today, I've never been so downright scared."

She stood by the charred, still smoking ruins, with the autumn twilight deepening and looked off toward Pilchuck as she lived again that early fright. Sensing the story would be a long one, Kenneth and Tobey and the two boys began unpacking blankets and cartons from the car and carrying them up the hill to our cabin.

"It was whin my Uncle Lambert cut hisself in the head. He fell across the big saw and he was bleedin' so bad they had to do somethin' then and there, because there jest waren't time to git him to no hospital. Well, I was a good piece off from the house and run across that field like I never run before. I was clean out of breath when I got to the house, and not feelin' so good anyhow -- it was that time of the month -- and my mother give me two big buckets and said fill them at the well and git back on the double, so I run again to the well, and clambered back with them buckets weighin' me down, and, I tell you, I couldn't hardly git any air -- half sobbin' I was with every breath.

"They stopped the blood as good as they could with wet rags, and then sent Cousin Jim on horseback for to get Doc Purdue and have him meet us at the crossroads store, because they'd be a place thar and stuff for to sew up the cuts. So we put Uncle Lambert into the wagon and drove to the store, about five miles it was and not too smooth a road neither.

"Well, they took him up to the room above the store and laid him on a table and the doctor got things sterile for the stitches. His whole face was wide open from his scalp down to his neck. And all of a sudden when I was astandin' there watchin', I got dizzy and everytheng turned black and the next thing I knew I hit the floor full length. It was funny because I guess I fainted, but I kin still remember how hard I hit that floor, and how the whole building shook. I knew every single thing in that old store, and I could hear every blessed one of them as they fell onto the floor down stairs. I jest shook that old building such a jolt that I heard every thing in that store fall from its shelf and I knew the noise each thing made, a bong for this and a ring for that, a tinkle for this and a thud for something else."

There was something regal about her as she stood in the gathering night, the little spirals of smoke curling about her in the movements of mountain air: her great frame; the wide, flat breasts, the vast girth of stomach and the square, muscular thighs filling the faded and patched bib overalls and work shirt with sculptural symmetry. As always, she gestured airily with her big hands and daintily curved fingers.

The war began for America that winter, and by spring the Lewis family had moved to a patch of land closer to Everett, where both Mr. and Mrs. Lewis took on jobs in the vast Weyerhaeuser mill. She came to visit us later and was rhapsodic over the sociability of working with other people and the magnificence of two paychecks. The boys, however, overwhelmed with their new freedom, were involved fairly constantly with the juvenile authorities until they were finally absorbed by the military.

The saga of the Lewis family came to us in bits during the subsequent years. We heard Mrs. Lewis was in ill health and that she and Mr. Lewis had broken up. I pictured her in a lonely but, I imagined, majestic decline. I underestimated her powers. On a summer day after the war, a proud and beaming Robert Lewis visited us at our cabin on our own land. He introduced us to a taciturn, buxom Mrs. Robert

Lewis and a chubby infant half smothered in blankets. His mother? Oh, she was fine, just fine. Married again with two babies -- both boys -- and living near Arlington.

And so, it became our turn to inhabit the main ranch house. We accomplished the move early in the spring of the year that Kenneth went to work for the Forest Service during the six-month season when they needed him. He continued his curator's job at the museum during the winter and helped with defense work that arose, including the coordination of artists throughout the state for posters, teaching at military posts, etc.

His first Forest Service priority was to man a gate near Barlow Pass at the head of the valley. The gate was designed to keep out saboteurs. Kenneth was required to check anyone wanting access and to keep an eye out for incendiary bombs floating into the area on weather balloons from Japanese submarines off the West Coast. He lived in a tent next to a rushing stream called Perry Creek. Other duties included manning the fire lookout at Barlow Point, keeping the telephone lines free of branches and fallen trees, and patrolling and clearing trails in the area.

Guy Anderson, after being granted conscientious objector status, joined us at Robe Ranch. He rented the cabin on the hillside just below our original one. Richard Bennett, the illustrator and author of children's books, had replaced Malcom Roberts and later Morris as a companion for Guy. Due to gas rationing as much as anything else, I hadn't been to Seattle that summer of 1942, but I finally had to go in to run some errands. It was the first time all summer I'd seen anyone much except Guy and Dick, and Mark a couple of times. I wanted Mark to come back with us, but I doubted very much that he would. He's afraid of life in the country. It's too primitive. He has rented the "ginger bread cabin" from Wirt and spent some nights up there always with a companion. But the last time he slept there alone and he emerged visibly shaken by the experience. Nature in the raw for Mark Tobey means dinner in the open at a city park such as Golden Gardens or Volunteer Park.

When I had my first careful look around the ranch house on a day of pouring rain in early March, I wondered whether we were getting quite the privilege as the promise of a fireplace, a separate kitchen and two bedrooms at first suggested. Mrs. Lewis's custom of pinning the legs of the rabbits she cleaned to each side of the projecting cupboards over the sink and letting the spatters fly where they would had made itself felt over their two years' occupancy. And when the weather had been cold enough to endanger the lives of these convenient, edible little reproducers, they had been brought into the house. Whether for warmth or for shelter, they had apparently favored a position under the beds. Heaven knows, a broom would never have molested them there! We scraped and swept out enough droppings, beautifully aged, to fertilize rows and rows of Victory garden vegetables. Everyone was encouraged to grow a Victory garden, so called because in theory they freed up food for the troops overseas. Such gardening during the war did produce an enormous quantity of homegrown vegetables, gardeners, and backaches. Its effects are still in evidence among some families, in which at least one member developed a chronic seasonal urge to dig, fertilize and plant in rows a great many products offered in season at every grocery store at negligible prices.

First of all, we visited our friends the exterminators in Seattle. Please, would they allow us a few cyanide bombs (illegal in King County and a much more effective treatment than sulfur candles, we learned) if we promised they would be used in another county? They allowed. We carefully guarded the undertaking from Wirt, as we were certain he would be hurt and possibly offended at the suggestion of any such insect infiltration.

I remember the day, one of our first weekends at the ranch, when I had gone down from the little cabin on the hillside to buy some grocery item we had forgotten to pack. I waited in the murky little room while the old man poked about in his assortment of gunnysacks and cartons assembling an order for a small boy, sent with a list by his parents. His father was apparently one of Wirt's pulp cutters. As Wirt completed the list the boy, staring into a sack of rice, asked with the bluntness of a child, "say, have you got bedbugs?" Wirt's reply was an insulted and emphatic negative. "Well," said the boy, "there's all these little black bugs in the rice and the beans."

"Oh those," Wirt scoffed, "why they aren't anything. They're just some kind of little bugs; get into everything. Harmless. Hell, no, those aren't bedbugs. Just get into the dried stuff. Always do. Everything. Get in everything..." He continued to mumble after the boy had gone happily on his way, followed by a slightly embarrassed silence as he handed me my few things.

We gassed the house on a day when Wirt was away. For extra protection we followed a neighbor's suggestion of placing each leg of the beds in a small dish of kerosene for several weeks until we were confident any bugs were history.

Our first Robe abode had its water faucet some fifty feet from the door of the cabin. It provided a trickle for our buckets. The return trip was up a steep little bank. Close by was the cement-walled storage tank. Its shake roof gave it the superficial character of a wishing well. Gravity provided a fair stream of cold water from the well to the ranch house. I remember being impressed when Mrs. Barrett told me the first time we ventured into Robe Ranch that she had running water in the house. "It's fine," she said, "except when the pump breaks down."

Hmmm. I had vague apprehensions. "Does the pump break down often?" A troubled look replaced her slight smile. "Fairly often," she said. "And they don't always get around to fixing it right away." Her warning notwithstanding, as long as we were in the little cabin and the Lewises were in the ranch house, the pump never let us down. I kept close watch on the supply in the storage tank, and when the water got low I'd notify the boys or Mrs. Lewis and within a day or two they would 'pump up.'

"Stanford-an-Robert, you boys git on down thar and git that pump to workin', or we'll jest see who's boss around here."

The water system originated with the snows on Green Mountain. Melt water splashed its way down a steep, rocky creek-bed through a forest of enormous old growth trees, mossy fern draped banks and across a small valley where it was lost in the jungle-like willow swamp of an old lake bed. It finally made its way through a narrow channel Wirt had dug to divert a part of the stream to the mouth of his pipe. Then there was the matter of getting this lovely clear water through the pipe and up the grade to the tank perched on a hill some 200 feet higher than the source. Between the house and the water channel was the pasture and some 300 feet of dense second growth hemlock forest.

In the midst of this dark little forest reposed a monster: the pump, a contraption Leonardo would have admired, I'm sure, for it was nothing if not ingenious. It was the result of a community of minds, namely Wirt Robe, his advisor in mechanical matters and neighbor, Leonard Ottaway, with bits of advice from the Lewises thrown in. Bolted and tied to a wooden frame, its basic ingredient was a Model A Ford engine. Added to this was a crank starter from a much older Model T Ford, a suspended five- gallon can for a radiator, and another five-gallon can for fuel. A transmission from a Chevrolet truck, I think, had been adapted to the main carcass. A great many loopings of hose, lots of loose nuts and bolts, oceans of black oil and grease and some sort of pumping mechanism from lord knows where completed this unique invention.

When it fired up, a series of startling explosions were usually followed by a sonorous chugging of the motor that echoed from mountain to mountain. A few minutes more and we would hear the reassuring sound of water gushing into the storage tank. Water was plentiful the first few weeks we lived in the ranch house. The storage tank was full, and I used rain water from the mossy barrel just outside the kitchen door for most washing purposes. Then, one day, we had visitors from the city who were inclined to be a little squeamish about some aspects of country life, such as outdoor toilets, no icebox, and flies on the window panels. I noticed a peculiar and disheartening smell from the water when I turned on the tap in the kitchen. I let it run a bit and something very like bits of fur and small bones were forced from the faucet. One of those precocious field mice had somehow entered the pipe and there had been gathered to its maker. I explained to the women that the water system wasn't working, filled the bucket from Guy's outdoor tap, and resolved to cope with the problem when our guests left for an overnight excursion.

But once during that afternoon I entered the kitchen just in time to see Wirt, who had been doing a little cement work between the kitchen door and the woodshed, down the last of a large glass of water obviously just drawn from the tap. Horrified, I tried to stop him, but it was too late. I told him in low tones what had happened, hoping the shock wouldn't be too much for him. He squinted through the empty glass, his expression unchanging. "Oh, yes," he said. "I thought it had a kind of different taste. Well, I guess it won't hurt me any. I poured myself a tumbler full of kerosene once from a jug I thought was a water jug. Drank the whole thing before I knew. Tasted pretty fiery. But when my throat cooled off I never noticed it did me any harm. Maybe all them Wahoo Bitters we made during prohibition have given me a galvanized stomach."

The guests departed as the warm glow of the late spring afternoon lay like apple jelly on the green pool of the pasture, the tips of the trees and the snowy peaks of the mountains. Wirt and I set about clearing the pipes of their obnoxious contents. We ran water until the tank was nearly dry, but still the offensive odor lingered. I was to leave the next day with Tobey to spend a week or so with Kenneth at the Perry Creek gate. Almost ready to admit defeat, I decided to try the water one last time. I turned the tap on and out popped a long gray tail. Giving it a slight tug what was left of the mouse plopped into the sink.

What a relief! While we were gone, our guests Emily McIntyre and Louise Gilbert, both painters whose husbands were away with the Armed Forces, were going to stay at the ranch, look after the garden, do some sketching and rehabilitate their city-tired bodies. I felt it was important to leave things in working order. Emily and Louise became regular visitors at the ranch during the war years. They rented our original cabin for a time. Emily eventually purchased her own land nearby, which was a good thing, as her heavy drinking had become a serious problem by that time.

22

An Offering

Panting,
After the steep climb
Up the side hill to the house
Along the raspberry bushes
Under the August sun.
Wirt comes to the back door,
Where the broken screen
Allows only the most ingenious of flies to enter,
Reaching out both hands
Forming a cup
Filled with purple plums
From the slender tree in the meadow.

Our ASSOCIATIONS WITH WIRT Robe covered a period of about eight years, not a long time in terms of the number of years we had lived. He emerged, however, as one of the most powerful characters and influences among all our contacts. Why? Perhaps because this man was a part of America in her golden days, her days of freedom, of expansion, of belief in unlimited wilderness frontiers and inexhaustible resources. But so were many others. Perhaps it was that, lacking nothing in intelligence, ability and humor, he was able to discard so much of the conventional claptrap of society and to live his life independently. He made his decisions in the light of one thing only; what did he want to do?

However, Wirt was a very lonely man, about as lonely as it is possible for a man to be, but he didn't suspect he was lonely. He had two surviving brothers. He and his oldest brother had been estranged for many years and never saw one another nor communicated -- political differences, Wirt said, was the reason. Another brother visited at the ranch on occasion, but the two had little in common, for Campbell was as domestic, well ordered and conventional in his life as Wirt was the opposite. It pained Campbell, I suppose, to witness Wirt's renegade ways, but he was loyal and made a visit at least twice a year. He was a neat man with a clean collar, well-brushed hair and polished shoes. He had been superintendent of a Sunday school in Granite Falls for thirty years, a fact that he mentioned to us the first time we met him.

When I commented on this bit of family information to Wirt he mumbled under his breath a bit, then said, "Oh, I dunno. I always figured Campbell was religious enough for the whole family. I never went to church myself. Got prejudiced early in life by a pious aunt. She was my father's sister, Aunt Mary, and she come to visit us at home in Ohio pretty often. She'd never do a lick of work, just complain about the food or the room wasn't warm enough or something else all the time, and here was my mother with her big family to take care of and her health breaking down as well. But Aunt Mary never missed a sermon. Always tried to boss us boys. She'd come into a room sniffing. 'Somebody's been a smokin' in here,' she'd say. Oh she was a terror, that one, never met a person more selfish in all my life, nor more 'churchified.'

"Then she took to bringing all her washing over for my mother to do. She'd never give her nothing for it, except maybe an old dress or something she'd got tired of. My mother'd say 'Sure bring it on over, I'll be glad to do it,' her with her big family to wash for. She was a great one for believin' in Hell, Aunt Mary was. Maintained that if a tiny baby died without being baptized it would burn in Hell forever.

Well, I decided if God would do a thing like that I wanted nothing to do with him anyway." Wirt spoke rapidly, his words tumbling out in a deep, rumbling voice. His big hands gestured occasionally, the fingers thickened and stiffened from hard, outdoor work.

"When we moved out west I thought, 'hurrah, that's the last we'll see of Aunt Mary.' But one winter she come to visit us in Granite Falls. Picked out my mother's and father's room, said that's the one she'd like for herself, please. Said she'd decided to spend the rest of her days with us. One day she come into a room where I'd just been smoking a cigar. She sniffed and she sniffed. Then she asked my mother, 'Is Wirt in the habit of using tobacco?' 'Why yes,' my mother said. 'He's practically never without it.' Well, that did it. She decided she simply couldn't live under the same roof with a tobacco fiend, so she packed up and moved back east. Mother told me later it was the only time she was ever glad one of her sons had taken up smoking."

Wirt's contacts with the local people were few and confined pretty much to expedience: selling raspberries and strawberries, borrowing and lending tools, etc. There wasn't much social life of any kind in the valley. The few scattered individuals and families teetered on the edge of complete isolation. Until Wirt's nose cancer got so unsightly that even his old pinochle cronies in the Corner Tavern stopped showing up for the Saturday afternoon games, he made a regular social trip into Granite Falls once a week. For this purpose he washed, shaved, wound a dejected black tie around his grizzled neck and slapped an old brown fedora over his straggly hair. He was so regular a customer that a chair had his name carved on the back. With his corncob in his mouth, he would depart in his Model T pick-up. In spite of the tendency of most of the male population of the town to get drunk of a Saturday night, to my knowledge Wirt never did. He would rattle back to the ranch early and was always up at the usual hour, somewhere around dawn the next morning.

One exception to Wirt's aloofness regarding valley people was Leonard Ottoway. Leonard, a man with a hulking big frame, had been the victim of a logging accident. He had a frail, anemic-looking wife, Dorothy, who, nonetheless, had a great deal of pluck and several little children. Her apparent lethargy hid an iron spirit. This was the Leonard of the great pump-monster in the woods below the ranch house. That contraption was a work in progress as long as Wirt lived.

"I never was much of a mechanic myself," Wirt would say. "I never could understand how them motors work; but Leonard, he can make anything run."

Leonard could and did do anything for others, and he never had a dime. Wirt joined most other valley folks in criticising Leonard's domestic situation. "He don't have to keep the wife and all them kids in that messy little place, so damp all winter. They're always sick," Wirt would say. "Why don't he build a good sound house with room enough for the family? I notice it was easy enough for him to get all them kids. Now why don't he take care of them like he ought to?"

Leonard and Wirt had a complicated, never-ending swap deal going on; sometimes it seemed like Leonard got the best of it, sometimes the other way around. Things probably evened out over time. For instance, Leonard bought some of the hay from Wirt's pasture each year, mowed it and packed it off to his and Wirt's barns, but money never changed hands. He maintained the water pump at intervals, repairing the unique, hodge-podge of machinery when necessary, gave Wirt a hand with the Model T in a pinch and showed up for wood sawing at least once a year. In exchange, he borrowed Wirt's tools frequently, sometimes forgetting to return them. Just as frequently, Wirt had a substantial meal with the Ottoway family together with a little precious sociability with no one looking critically at Wirt's unwashed condition.

My appreciation of Wirt came in bits and pieces. Before I began to understand his complexities, some of his notions worried me a little, his hatred of dogs, for example. You'd have thought he'd have wanted a dog for company, being alone so much of the time. But he couldn't bear to be near them. "I don't know why I feel that way about dogs," he said one time. "It might be because I saw a mad dog once when I was a kid back in Ohio. It was frothing at the mouth, and I saw it bite a man, and the man died. I can't remember whether I liked dogs before that or not. I can't remember ever liking them."

He had apparently made up his mind at the start to tolerate our wire-haired terrier, Mike, although he would quite frankly have been happier with us had we been dogless. His first encounter with Mike had not been a good one. He and Kenneth were talking just outside the door of his hut, and Mike approached on the alert, sniffing here and there. He was about to lift his leg against an open crock of rather dirty looking water standing at the corner of the shack, when Wirt let out a roar and sent a kick in Mike's direction. "Goddamn dogs," he grumbled, "always pissin' in my drinking water."

His hostility towards dogs did not extend to other four-legged mammals. I remember watching from the ranch house one day when he confronted two deer in the garden area behind his shack. The doe stood between Wirt and a yearling, eyeing him now and then. He took a few steps towards her and both creatures looked quickly toward him, ears alert, eyes round and curious. They watch him a moment, chewing steadily, then bent their heads again to the cabbages. "I ought to get my gun and shoot you both," Wirt rumbled at them. "Don't you think I'll need those cabbages this winter? And how about my strawberry patch? All the work I done, weeding and putting up that fence, and you go stomp it down so's you can eat up every last leaf and berry. How long do you think I'm going to stand for that?" As he talked the deer looked up occasionally, sniffed the breeze, threw their ears about, and went back to their nibbling.

Those cabbages aren't going to last the three of us very long," Wirt said. "There's some hay in the barn, though, and if you'll promise not to raid my strawberry patch next spring I'll make a path right to the barn door. I need the exercise anyway," he added, as he pawed about in the side shed where he kept his tools when he remembered to put them there. Most of the space was taken up by an old metal bedstead and mattress, which the field mice had torn almost to ribbons. It was a mouse bonanza; their favorite nesting stuff. And generations of the tiny beady-eyed beasties had snuggled gratefully into dark corners made warm, soft and cozy with layers of the fluffy, old cotton filling. The mice accepted Wirt much as he accepted them. He once told me that as long as they refrained from chewing on his hair at night, they were welcome to a reasonable share of his food and shelter.

He found the shovel he was looking for, leaning in a corner with a short-handled hoe and an almost toothless rake. Laboriously, he climbed the steep hillside between his cabin and the barn, a haphazard, but sound structure he had put up following the fire. Although the fire had burned all his belongings -- what clothes he wasn't wearing at the time, his bedding, all his cash except what silver coins were pocketed by the Lewis boys -- he had accepted it philosophically, having been burned out several times before. He continued disposing of burning matches with an unconcerned toss, and he could often be seen striding through the dry August woods with his lighted pipe clutched between his teeth, upside down as often as not.

The dim light inside the barn revealed a sizable mound of sweet dry hay. Old Betsy, the mare, had died midwinter the year before, her teeth so ground down she could not digest her food. He stood a moment in the twilight, leaning on the spade. "I miss you," he said, "you Old Betsy. I used to wonder who would last the longest -- you, the Model T, or me. Well, it's between me and the Model T now." He thought of trying to get another horse, mainly for the companionship, but remembering how every horse he had owned died off and left him with the problem of disposing of the carcass, he had resisted so far.

He had spent lonely weeks in the swamp, keeping the fire burning about the remains of poor old Betsy. Remembering the battered white coat, the pale eyes and long white eyelashes, he couldn't let scavengers do the natural thing. The stubborn old critter would wander off and get stuck in the swamp. Stubbornness was a quality Wirt could understand and feel akin to.

As he left the barn, he propped the door wide open and, going down the hill, he shoveled a clear path through the slushy snow. "It's one place the cougars won't track them down," he said aloud. He made a practice of talking aloud to himself, as he had a theory that the sound of the human voice, even if only your own, was a healthy thing to hear, and that vocal cords if left too long unused might go rusty and refuse to function at all.

"There," he called to the deer, when he reached his cabin at the base of the hill again and leaned the spade against the wall, 'now I've made it for you, I suppose you won't ever use it." The doe had found and nosed out an apple from under the snow and was rolling it about with her tongue, her eyes rolling, too. "Looks like your teeth aren't any better than this old plate of mine," Wirt said as he turned toward his shack. After losing his place near the ranch house in the fire, Wirt had moved into an abandoned pulpwood cutter's shack at the base of the hill. It was no bigger and no fancier than his previous home and he abandoned the idea of maintaining a store.

"Folks say to me," he said meditatively one day when he had come into the kitchen for a drink of water, 'Wirt, if I'd 'a been up here in the early days like you were I'd be rich by now. All that land, all those trees, there for the taking.' Well, I could have been rich, I guess -- knew plenty that got rich, knew 'em when they didn't have a thing. I knew Cobb -- built that Cobb building down in Seattle -- I knew him when he was just a logger, like myself. Knew others like him, started out working in the woods but they knew what to buy and what to hang on to. Oh, I've made lots of money, but I always spent it or lost it. But I dunno -- I could never see much reason for money. It brings troubles and worries."

Another time, after Wirt and I had spent the morning weeding the garden patch the Lewises had vacated, I invited him to lunch. He weeded by sitting down between rows, his knees arched over the row between his feet and his seat. Thus, he would inch along the sidehill, wielding a short-handled hoe (the short-handled hoe as in, "Has anybody seen the short-handled hoe, I had it yesterday and I left it right here by the rain-barrel when I come up from the garden," etc.). With one hand he steadied his pipe and with the other he wielded the hoe, letting the loosened earth rain over him as the breezes tossed it. Expecting the usual excuses for turning me down I invited Wirt to share sandwiches and soup, and to my surprise, he accepted. After lunch, I cleared the porch table while he filled his pipe, first knocking it against the weathered porch railing. He lit it, puffing tenderly with his scarred lips.

"We used to have jamborees," Wirt said as if to himself. Crows cawed stridently over the young trees across the pasture. Flies buzzed on the inside of the torn screen door trying to get out, and on the outside trying to get in. Tobey slowly ate the last of his chocolate pudding, loitering in order to put off naptime. "What's a jamboree?" he asked through a barricade of pudding.

Wirt looked absent-minded and didn't answer. I waited because I knew he was remembering something. "Ran into a little boy once, nearly knocked me down with his tricycle," he said. "I pretended I was mad. Whose little brat are you?" I said. I used to like to say that to kids just to hear them get sore and answer back, "Aw, shut up" or "Who wants to know?" and such. This kid looks at me through his glasses for a minute, kind of blank, and pipes up, "I'm Mama's little brat." His shoulders shook with laughter under his worn and dirty cotton shirt. "That was in one of those towns I hit with old Professor Casanova."

"What's a jamboree, Mr. Robe?" Tobey asked.

"Oh, when I was young we used to all get together, have a great time. Dancing, singing. I used to play the banjo, Frank'd bang the piano and Tom Bird would fiddle. We played for all the dances around this part of the country. Folks had good times in those days, always danced all night, sometimes two days, three days. I swear I played the banjo once for forty-eight hours without stopping, guess I just sort of played in my sleep. None of us had any idea what we were playing, but folks kept dancing. Wouldn't let us stop. Jamboree." Tobey's wide eyes were beginning to close. I took him out to the washstand for a slight going over, then tucked him into sheets still fragrant from drying in the morning sun.

I thought this would be a good time to hear more about Professor Casanova. Having had no company for a spell, Wirt might be eager to talk. When I returned to the porch, however, he was already down in the garden, slapping away with the short-handled hoe. He had finished the soybeans and was starting the sugar beets, a product he was experimenting with due to the shortage of sweets caused by the war. I decided that perhaps the evening would be a more appropriate time to share some memories, and I called down an invitation to Wirt to join us for coffee after dinner.

His reply was inarticulate, but that evening after dinner, Wirt did join us and we got a rare glimpse of his past. Morris, Guy, Emily, Kenneth and I were sitting about the table on the porch. He told us his story with no regret or apology. Gingerly fingering his battered, cancerous nose, he began. "When Doc Snyder down in Snohomish sewed up the cut I got from running into the corner of the door, he said it would leave a scar that I would never get rid of. I said, 'Well, Doc, I guess one more blossom on this old pumpkin vine ain't going to make much difference.' Despite constant dosing with iodine, it never did heal right," he said.

The bats had emerged from whatever recesses they spent their upside down days hanging in and fluttered noiselessly about the porch after moths and other night insects. A large owl lit on the tilted top of a young hemlock nearby and motionless, silhouetted against the darkening sky, awaited the rich abundance of field mice soon to begin their nocturnal scamperings. Kenneth lit a kerosene lamp, and Wirt continued.

His first real venture into show business many years before was with "Casanova" -- Professor Casanova, ventriloquist and magician and ex-Grand Army man. Wirt manned the door while Casanova did his act, and at the cue he had to rush back and get into costume for his blackface act. "I put on black face and got out there onto the stage. Oh, I dunno, I tumbled over the acrobats' ropes and took a lot of falls. The harder I'd fall, the more they'd holler, Lord, I took some terrible falls, enough to kill a man, and the audience, they just kept a laughin' and a'hollerin'. I could talk pretty good nigger talk, because I'd been raised with them, and I kept a patter going all the time." After a few puffs on his pipe he continued. "It was a nigger gave me my first banjo and taught me to chord and pick. My father hated it and said I would never amount to anything playing that nigger music. I guess he was right."

Casanova hadn't changed his line in 32 years. Wirt asked him once if he didn't get sick and tired of the same old thing, saying he couldn't sing the same song twice without wanting to do a new one. And Casanova got so sore and said it was his show and if it wasn't good enough for Wirt he could get out. Casanova was an awful old crab, and a terrible drinker, used to drink up his own share of the money and most of Wirt's too. If Wirt held back, Casanova would kid him about sending his money home to Mama, and Wirt would say all right take it, take it. But he always held out thirty dollars or so that Casanova didn't know he had.

They traveled mostly through Utah, Colorado, Arizona and New Mexico. Casanova would always go to the schools in the towns he visited and hand out free tickets and handbills to the teachers. It worked. The teachers would go and take their kids. The students would bring their families. Once Wirt had to make the visit to the school for him, and he had to walk up and down the street five times getting up nerve enough to enter the building. "You know, that awful show – the nerve of that man handing out these flyers in schools. During the evening, Casanova did various tricks. One involved passing around through the house, saying, 'take a card.' He was very clever at forcing the card he wanted taken. Then he would make the right card come up out of a water tumbler. He would get some poor sucker from the audience to pick the queen of hearts. The queen would come up with her back to the audience the first time, providing for cracks about going back down and coming up right, etc. It was Wirt's job to pull on the delicate little strings that manipulated the cards.

Wirt finally left Casanova because he got too mean. He bawled out an audience because when he called for a couple of kids to come up to the stage to help out on a trick, none responded. The townspeople were going to beat him up that night, but Wirt talked them out of it on the basis that he was just an old man, and a Grand Army man at that.

After leaving Casanova, Wirt made his way to Washington State where he hooked up with a medicine show run by a Doc Ennis, who claimed to be the son of a famous surgeon. He was missing one arm, which he said he lost when assisting his eminent father in an operation. A patient when going under anesthetic moved convulsively, knocking the hand of the doctor, who slashed his son's arm so badly it had to be amputated. Wirt said the way he actually lost it was by getting drunk and falling off a train down by Auburn. The train cut off his arm. Wirt's job was to play the banjo in blackface from the back of their wagon until a crowd gathered, and then Doc Ennis took over flogging his Wahoo Bitters (a concoction of mostly alcohol and opium). On one occasion the sheriff of a southeastern Washington county arrested Wirt for embezzling money from a bank in Missouri. They kept him in jail forty-eight hours until he insisted on getting a hearing, and they found they had the wrong man. The sheriff had been told to arrest a tall man with front teeth missing, a fellow who had been appearing in the Palouse country. Wirt missed a county fair due to the incident, but accepted their apology and $2 for a bottle. He told them they were getting off cheap.

He built the theater in Granite Falls and all the good shows came there, because Granite was known as a good show town. He also had a saloon in the early days in Granite. It had a piano player, barber, and a bar with beer, wine and whiskey. It was called Collar, Robe and Burns. He gave it up because his mother and father disapproved of saloons.

"Well, I figure if I'd any ambition there was a few things I'd have been a success at. One was a big league baseball player, another a minstrel man." A short guy once begged him to team up with him, said he'd been looking for a tall man to work up an act with for years, but Wirt was making a good living in Granite and had no desire to strike out again. Another time he was begged by a boxing promoter to go into professional boxing. "Oh, I'd put on the gloves a few times, and we'd give each other bloody noses, but I could never see the fun in it." Promoter Smith (whose son became a Seattle mayor) would say, "Goddamn it, you got good foot work and a wonderful reach, and you'd be a great boxer."

When he was about 65, he intended to get himself a gila monster, some snakes and tarantulas and such and travel through the small towns. He figured it would be a good living for an old man. But "a woman got to talking about muskrats, what a heap of money there was in it. She said all you needed was a swampy place." Well, Wirt thought about his brother's Robe Ranch swamp and took her up to see it. She said that it was the perfect place to raise them. Brother Campbell said if Wirt wanted to buy out half of the homestead for $1500 he'd sell. After a short negotiation, he put up the money and has been there ever since. The muskrats all went through the holes in the fences the first year, but he still talks about damming up the creek and getting them back.

The coffee was cold and the stars bright as Wirt got slowly to his feet, said good night, and headed off to his shack. When we learned that his 80th birthday was looming in July of '44, we decided there should be a party. I thought it would probably mean something to him, as I have never seen him so beaming as on one of those accidental social occasions earlier that summer when some drop-in visitors had come with guests from New York. One of the visitors was able to bring true music out of the old pump organ, and a feeling of festivity had developed. Wirt, hearing the music and laughter, had found a pretext to stick his head in at the door, and not only came in but stayed and more or less took over the party.

We sent him down for his banjo, which he was only too glad to resurrect, and he rendered "Why'd You Go and Make Them Goo-Goo Eyes?" in his best medicine show fashion, hoarsely and off-tune, but with boundless zest. He told jokes, whether anyone listened or not, that dated from the days of the traveling shows, jokes he got for the most part from a publication of that period called Madison's Budget, a sort of almanac, I imagine. And, to everyone's thinly veiled horror, he brought a jug of his blackberry wine, dusty and cobwebby as anything from a choice ancient cellar, but not for the same reason. It was sour and murky, but under his pressing generosity we sipped at it bravely.

It was worth every puzzled and uncomfortable expression on our visitors' faces to see the light in his blue eyes as he said good night.

He added, as he started down into the blackness of the little path to his cabin, "I'm going to write to Tom Bird and Frank Jordan and tell them all about it. We had a jamboree, yes sir, a real jamboree. Tom and Frank said we'd never have another one -- Well, I'm going to write them." A day or so later, when I brought up the idea of an 80th birthday party, Wirt declined saying the only people he might want to see were far away. Wasn't there anybody in Granite he might want to invite? His reply was inarticulate as he wandered off to the barn. So died the idea for Wirt's 80th birthday jamboree.

23

RASPBERRY BUSHES, SOME TWENTY rows of them, grew on the hill beside the house at Robe Ranch. The dense bushes topped six feet in height, their branches intermingling between rows. The droning of bees was heavy in the summer afternoon. Clusters of red berries hung like jewels from the vines. They fell into a jar at a touch from my fingers, fragrant little thimbles holding a miracle of tangy sweetness. When six jars were filled I placed them in a kettle of water over a burner on the kerosene stove. We kept it on the back porch so we wouldn't have to light the wood range on hot days. Sugar I used sparingly or not at all, as stringent sugar rationing was in effect. When it was possible we shared our sugar rations with Wirt who ate very little and needed the energy. We used a dreadful substitute for sugar in baking and canning. Wirt's gray, home-boiled syrup from his sugar beets was the worst of all.

I had the raspberries packed away by the time Tobey awoke from his nap, and there was still enough afternoon sun left to make a swim possible. The Forest Service swimming hole at Verlot was about three miles up the river. I tried to arrange gas rations to include afternoon swims there. We parked the car in the clearing in front of the Forest Service headquarters, a cluster of handsome gray-green cedar board buildings and walked the leafy trail to the river. Toads as big as my hand and small frogs hopped about our feet. Thrushes sang in the high, green recesses of the hemlocks, firs and maples.

As we neared the river, the branches of the trees parted on a light-filled clearing. A few women sat in a group on a patch of sand among the boulders. Some of them were knitting, while an energetic bevy of children splashed in the moving green waters of the river. It was a tranquil scene, a living French Impressionist painting, filled with the softness of summer, the serenity of relaxed young mothers in starched cotton dresses and the high spirits of healthy children. Why wasn't this enough? Why war?

These were mountain people. I knew that to them I was still a foreigner, a flatlander, and their greetings, while friendly, weren't exactly enveloping. I always took a book, and when my swim was over I lay flat on my stomach in the sand, the sun warm on my back and my book open in the shade of my head. This way I could listen to the small talk of the adults and the shouts and prattling of the children without having to make the forced conversation which would have followed the inclusion of a stranger. I could be of it and not of it, which pleased my lazy sense of sociability. In time we would become friends, but this couldn't be rushed. I marveled at the clean, starched clothes they all wore, for there was no electricity in the valley. A few of the households had kerosene washing machines, but most of them relied on washtubs, their muscles and stove heated irons. The washtub and muscles was my system, but starch and ironing were beyond my capacity and inclination.

On the way home I stopped at the Ottaway's place to drop off some raspberries. I decided to drive down to the house rather than park on the road. This decision always involved certain risks. The deeply rutted and rocky driveway, all but grown in with car- scratching salmonberry bushes and fir boughs, had barely enough room at the end to turn around. Not enough if anyone else was visiting or if Leonard had acquired a recent addition to his vast collection of dead cars and other machinery that occupied the swamp land around his home. Today we were lucky. Leonard greeted us with his usual warm enthusiasm.

After accepting the raspberries he launched into his usual apologetic monologue about the state of his house. He took me over to look at the foundation of the small building where he had pulled away some siding. He pointed out that the cedar blocks supporting the floor beams were "still in pretty good condition," but avoided mentioning the crumbling floor boards, their remains apparently held up by the linoleum layer above. "It's discouraging. You can't really build onto this shack, with the creek so close. And it would cost more'n it's worth to move it. Nope, better wait 'til we can put up a whole new outfit, concrete blocks maybe. Then you've really got something that'll stand the wet." A large creek ran within six feet of the house and an outhouse was perched over it. Just above the outhouse a large wooden waterwheel powered an old car generator that produced enough electricity to operate a few lights and a radio in addition to a supply of piped water to the house.

Dottie had been watching us from the porch. "I want Leonard to build us a log house. I always did want a log house. This shack we're living in now was only intended to be a honeymoon cottage. But along came the first baby and we went right on living here, and then the second and still we stayed on, and now here we are with four, and they're just getting too big for this little place. Seems like a log house would be cheap and they sure are nice and solid."

We turned down an offer to come in for coffee and as Tobey climbed into our car Leonard leaned in the window and offered a final thought. "Dottie ain't got much meat on her, but she's stronger than she looks." I contemplated Leonard's last observation as we bumped our way up the driveway to the main road.

The trip to the mailbox three days a week was usually made on foot. But on days of particularly chancy weather, Wirt sometimes used the Model T. One morning after a late spring snow, Dick Bennett came down the hill from the cabin he shared with Guy. Noticing Wirt fussing about his truck, Dick asked if he could have a ride to the mailbox?

Wirt said, sure he could if the truck would start. He slapped the seat to scare the mice out of the cushions before installing Dick on the passenger side. He then kicked the blocks away from in front of the thin worn tires, jumped into the driver's seat and the Model T started creaking and rattling on its first trip since the snow began. Halfway down the slushy slope, between the picket fence on one side and the abrupt rise of the hillside, the motor started with a terrific snort and roar. And it kept going, though coughing dreadfully. At the foot of the grade there was a moment of uncertainty. With pipe clutched tightly between his teeth, Wirt administered the gas in heavy doses. Over the rutty little side road and out onto the Green Mountain Road the truck bounced, bound for the county highway. The old man relaxed, sailing along in triumph. A cold draft floated up Dick's pant legs from the space where the floorboards had fallen through. He found it disconcerting to look down and see the ground speeding along below with only some rusty metal in between.

Wirt was graced with selective hearing. He didn't seem to notice the truck's deafening racket. Dick whistled nervously to himself and was amazed to have Wirt turn suddenly and shout over the uproar, "You've got to stop that whistling. I can't stand it any longer. Drives me crazy." Dick stopped whistling, but it was all he could do a few minutes later to make Wirt hear him as he shouted that the truck's rear end was on fire. Wirt finally stopped the truck, got out, and tossed some mud on the burning truck box where an exhaust pipe had apparently started a fire. He grinned at Dick, climbed aboard and off they went again.

They rounded the last bend in the road and left the dense forest. Wirt made out the figure of Frank Bower, bachelor logger, waiting by the mailboxes, presumably for a ride to work with whomever might come by. Frank lived alone in a small cabin down by the river. Wirt parked the truck in the gravel pit just off the highway, left the engine running, stuck some rocks against the tires and sauntered over to Frank. Dick went to check for mail. Frank was a union man. The very word 'union' was anathema to Wirt, a Republican by inheritance and an individualist by nature, by choice and by God. The two men met without smiling. Frank was nearly a foot shorter than Wirt, black-eyed, high-cheek-boned and thin-lipped. He was dressed for logging in tin pants. His canvas waterproof jacket, open in front, displayed a faded plain wool shirt and yellow-green suspenders. His lunch bucket and corked boots were parked on the shoulder of the road.

"Glad to see you out, Wirt," Frank said. "How are you getting along?" he asked in his deep voice tinged with what may have been a Czech accent. "Ooh, I'm like the old darky who said that if he lived through the first day of the New Year, he generally lived through the rest of the year." Frank didn't bother to laugh; he'd heard it from Wirt so many times. "You fellows back to work again? Wirt asked.

"Thought there might still be too much snow in the hills." "This is the first day back," Frank said. "We've been off three weeks now. That's a long shutdown. Your money begins to run out, you know."

"Oh, hell, with the money you fellows make these days you ought to be able to retire. Twelve-fifteen dollars a day -- why good God, there was never a man earned that much money, I don't care how good he is. It's all those damned unions -- bunch of racketeers. Prices going up so the rest of us can't afford to eat hardly." "Well, Wirt, maybe you'd feel different about it if you was working in the woods yourself. Them fellows with wives and kids to support -- buying food and shoes and paying doctors -- it's different with them than with old bachelors like you and me." Frank had a way, while talking, of raising his glance to the eye-level of his companion, then letting it fall slowly to belly button level.

"My father supported a family of five kids without ever getting any wages like you union men are getting," Wirt responded. "Everything's just easy-come, easy-go these days; tax the people and spend the money. Raise wages and raise prices. If I was able to work for wages now I'd refuse to take that much money. I wouldn't be worth it, no man is." As Wirt got hotter under the collar his words came in a faster jumble.

A car appeared far below, where the road curved out of sight. "Here comes Leonard now, no chains neither. He won't be able to stop on the hill here, so I better start walking to the top. So long, Wirt. Take care of yourself." "Hi, Wirt. Need anything?" Leonard shouted, leaning out of the rusty Chevrolet, which was skidding by so rapidly Wirt could only shake his head and wave his pipe. Wirt stood by the mailboxes, watching until Leonard made it to the top of Robe Hill. A moment later, the mailman's car showed up over the top of the hill and descended, chains rattling.

As the truck bumped back to the ranch through the little black forest, Wirt felt a warm surge of affection for his venerable Model T. "I'll never drive one of those gear shift cars again," he shouted to Dick. "I used to drive a Chevrolet, and it's still parked in the shed by the rabbit house. I drove it into Everett nine years ago and I started to park it there on Chestnut Street. I was close to the curb. I thought it was in neutral and I meant to put on the brakes, but I guess I stepped on the gas, and it must have been in gear, because she jumped just like a horse right over the sidewalk and into a plate glass window. Just lucky nobody was in the way because they'd have got killed for sure. I paid for that window and drove that car back here, parked it in the shed and it's been there ever since. I swore right then I'd never drive one of those gearshift cars again, and I never have. They're too dangerous."

As he drove up the final steep little curve to the parking spot, a very brief, very intense snowstorm turned the air into a dense, swirling mass of enormous snowflakes. The feathery fluff obscured the old man's vision completely, plastering the windshield with a wet white blanket. "Got back just in time," he said, as he chugged to a stop on the level. "I'll just turn her around now and get set for next time." With a sudden loud roar, the truck leaped forward, climbed three feet straight up the gravel bank, turned a somersault and settled down on its battered top. Its spindly wheels turned slowly in the frosty air. A few big puffy flakes blew into the hole where the floorboards would have been and settled on Wirt's pant legs before the blizzard stopped, as suddenly as it had begun. A shaft of sunlight found its way through the scudding clouds, lighting the old man's bare head as he fumbled for his hat. A pale Dick Bennett crawled out on his hands and knees swearing silently to never accept another ride with Wirt.

24

By THE SUMMER OF 1942 we had hiked and explored Mt. Pilchuck and its lakes, Glacier Basin (above Monte Cristo), Canyon Lake, Coal Lake, and the meadows of Mt. Dickerman. One of our first explorations was of the glacial valley above Silverton. I first heard the name Silverton from Kenneth in far away Mexico in 1932. It has become one of our favorite hiking destinations. Silverton was a mining boomtown in the late 1800's. But now it has only a handful of residents. Some ten miles below Monte Cristo the tiny community spans the Stillaguamish River's south fork not far from its headwaters. There are about thirty houses still standing, plus the vacant Double Eagle Inn and the still active Eric Shedin's Tavern. The buildings, all survivors of the boom era, are beautifully weathered and nestled at the base of nearly vertical cliffs. The valley there is just wide enough for the river, the gravel road and some 300 hundred yards of bottomland across the river.

Erick Shedin's Tavern is a slightly leaning frame structure about twelve by fourteen feet, containing a small bar, a glass case with candy bars, a shelf of cigarettes, an iron stove, and a hand-made Swedish style rocking chair that attests to Erick's craftsmanship. On the wall are signed photos of Democratic congressmen and President Roosevelt. Erick, now past 70, and his brother, Albert, 10 years younger, have been living at Silverton for about 25 years. When they first moved there a bearded Dutchman named Carpenter, but never called anything but

Carp, was about to go broke on his tiny grocery store. Erick bought the store and took Carp in as a companion, friend and helper about the place.

Carp was sometimes more a liability than a help. One time when he was alone, tending the store, a small boy asked hesitantly for an ice cream cone from the gruff old man. As Carp stuck the scoop of ice cream onto the cone he didn't notice that his long beard had somehow been incorporated . When Carp thrust the whiskered ice cream cone at the boy, he looked at it, then at Carp, burst into tears and ran from the store. I gathered from what Erick said that Carp was the butt of many practical jokes over the years. Once Albert built a tarpaper bear in an old orchard across the river. A nearsighted Carp grabbed his rifle and fired off several shots before he realized he had been fooled. In spite of such tricks old Carp was well looked after by his tormentors.

"Well, old Carp, he's a Dutchman," Erick sighed, "but I would do anything for anybody if they needed help. In this world we have to take care of the children and the old people, isn't that right?" Erick talks vehemently, with a strong Swedish accent; his eyes are crystal blue and his face deeply sunburned. He loves to tell stories, which are usually built around difficult situations he's dealt with. "You gotta be tough," is Erick's usual conclusion to these tales. "You gotta be tough," has become one of our family maxims.

Stories are told over and over around wood-burning stoves and kerosene lamps during the long, stormy winters. Most of these mountain folks have Alaska and prospecting in their early lives. All have hunting and fishing, not as sport but as means of providing food, or in the case of cougars, the $50 bounty. Killing animals as sport is repugnant to them. When they kill a deer they use every scrap of the meat and their rage churns at hunters who cut out the choice parts and leave the rest in the woods.

We stopped recently to greet Erick and Albert on our way to Silver Gulch. The two brothers were perspiring in the morning sunshine getting their woodpile restocked and seemed glad enough to take a breather inside. "Erick, you're thinner. You've been working too hard," I said.

"Yah, yah, I know. Once I weigh 240 pounds, now I'm down to 160. Never weighted such little before. Well, my back, you know, where the log hit me that time. It bother me quite a bit. And my diabetes come back. I got it cured you know drinking huckleberry tea. Then I eat some candy bars and sugar and drink some beer. Well, it got kind of bad again, and now I got to go back to the huckleberry leaves.

Erick's grandmother in the old country taught him his knowledge of medicinal plant lore. Huckleberry leaves, she taught him, contain insulin. His own experience has born out the truth of her teaching, for without ever having a shot of insulin, he did cure an advanced case of diabetes. All he had to do was refrain from sweets and alcohol. "Now is the time I should be gathering the leaves," he said, troubled, "now before the berries form. But the red-berried bushes "they're the best, more insulin than the blue" are scarce around here. " They grow lower down, and it's hard for me to get to where they are." Later when the berries form, they take some of the strength from the leaves. We promised Erick some red huckleberry leaves on our next trip. As the tiny leaves shrivel when dried, it takes quantities of them to last a season. These, incidentally, are not the tough shiny-leafed huckleberry that florists use with flowers; this bush grows in the deep forests, where it joins the vine maple and devil's club to form a lovely, green, horizontal leafiness. The berries, both the red and blue varieties, make excellent pies and jellies. Red huckleberry and wild blackberry jam is a superb combination.

Erick was warming to the conversational possibilities and told us of an experience he remembers with particular horror, one which occurred about twenty years ago at a time of a mid-winter flood. There were several feet of snow at Silverton, but a warm spell had brought about a sufficient thaw to send the river on a rampage. The Stillaguamish took the bridge out at Silverton, which isolated the one dweller on the west side from his few neighbors on the east bank.

"When we finally got to old Sullivan, he had been dead three or four days," Erick said. "We called for the coroner to come to Verlot, then it was up to Albert and me to get him down those twenty-five miles on a sled". Their greatest difficulty was at the river crossing called Red Bridge, called so because there was once a red bridge there. There's a gray bridge now, but the name remains the same. "When we got to Red Bridge, the crossing was about a foot under water. Well, we were up against it, so Albert, he pulled and I pushed from behind. About half way across the sled slid off into the current and dragged me with it. I fell forward, right across the corpse, and there I was in the water, hanging onto the corpse, and Albert pulled us both."

Erick stopped to spit before he continued,"Well, we got out all right, but I was pretty wet, and we still had five miles to go before we reached Verlot. The coroner was there waiting for us, and by that time Albert and I were so tired and cold, we decided to go into Granite Falls with him and get dry clothes and stay over night. The driver couldn't take more than one of us in front with him, because, according to him, it was against the law, so Albert, he had to get in and lie down in the back alongside the corpse".

"The undertaker met us at Granite Falls. He opened up the back of the van, and Albert he sat up and started to get out That undertaker got white as a sheet, and his eyes bug out, and he said, "Hey, it's coming to life!" We had to laugh then, because I never saw a man look so scared. I tell you, Albert was mighty glad to have that ride come to an end."

We finished our stubbies of cold beer and bid the Shedin brothers goodbye. Kenneth, Tobey, Guy, Emily McIntyre and I crossed the dusty road to begin our hike. Silverton's trails all start across the river from Erick's Tavern. A narrow suspension bridge over the Stillaguamish bobs around beneath your feet. I always look closely at the rusty cables and wonder if the whole affair is adequately inspected. I have a deep-seated suspicion of all hanging bridges, a suspicion that has become imprinted on my brain since the steel and concrete Tacoma Narrows Bridge turned handsprings and catapulted into Puget Sound a few years ago. I don't like people bouncing on suspension bridges either, so I wait until everyone is off the bridge before I pick my way gingerly across, carrying my dog Pixie who shares my feelings about anything moveable underfoot.

Our plan was to climb to a mine about a mile and a half up the trail toward Silver Gulch. Over the suspension bridge we went, then along the path past half dozen or so vacant cabins, their shake or board exteriors as weathered as driftwood. We continued through thick alder that occupied what a few years before had been a gravel road, up a steep grade and around a sharp bend. There it was, as impressive a scene of wreckage as you could imagine. Great hand hewn timbers, parts of machinery, cables and splintered shakes were strewn about, partially buried by the tremendous winter slides, which had crushed the structure. The wooden skeleton of an ore concentrator was still partially intact.

It's an inviting place to climb around and explore. The steep climb up the sunny slope rewarded us with beautiful views. As Tobey and I sat on a silvery old 12x12 outside a deserted mine we were serenaded with the song of a waterfall from the small creek that poured from the gaping mineshaft and splashed on the shattered rock below. Dripping with icy droplets, the mine exuded a damp cold breath that blotted out the warmth of summer.

We had walked up the road and found several kinds of lichen -- silvery gray, yellow/green and rosy gray . We arranged them on a piece of silvered board and called the others to admire our creation. Patches of blue sky gave way to an occasional sprinkle. The mountain across the river was a giant wearing a hat of mist pulled down about its ears. It was all very wonderful.

Kenneth and Emily painted inside a little abandoned miner's cabin. Emily hummed tunelessly. Every so often the door through which they looked blew shut. Kenneth was annoyed but Emily kicked it open and didn't mind.

Emily can be exceptionally good-natured at times. I thought of the previous night when Guy, Emily and I had gone to Granite to a tavern and the dance hall. The Corner Tavern is a smoky little place with darkened wood paneling, and natural cedar shakes. It's like Ted Abrams' Seattle house inside. It was amazingly alive compared with bars I've visited in the city. The patrons included grandmothers and grandfathers and all down the scale to as young as they let them in. Emily's good nature again shone, and we all had a swell time.

She has an uncanny ability for rounding up rationed items and furnishes us with a   touch of luxury up here in the nature of extra gas coupons, butter and great thick steaks from her supply officer husband. He has access to such luxuries, some of which we enjoyed for our Silverton hike lunch. She has also bought whipping cream from a farmer who lives on the beautiful little farm across Swamp Lake, the name we gave a small pond, about a mile west of Robe Ranch and just back from the road. We've always loved it but never knew who lived there. It turns out to be an old French couple called the Sauniers. Emily's new property borders Sauniers. Discovering who they are has solved our milk, cream and butter problems while at the ranch.

As the sun slid behind Silver Tip Mountain, we gathered our things together and made our way down to Eric's tavern. I fervently hoped the rest of our summer would be as much fun as that day at Silver Gulch, even though Kenneth would be off by himself on his Forest Service job most of the time.

25

THE SUMMER OF 1942 slips away. I was thinking today how wonderful it is to be able to be in the sun unclad from the waist up. It should be part of everyone's life. Until people grow more in accord with nature again the world will be full of troubles. I took Kenneth back to Perry Creek Sunday evening after the weekend here. He has a perfect place to stay -- if the bears don't eat him alive. He says they are thick around there. But according to the man from the new government plane spotter's lookout on the hill above the ranch, they're thick around here, too.

Kenneth lives in a tent with an earth floor over which he has spread some cedar shakes. A cone- shaped stove and a cot are his only furnishings. Perry Creek goes dashing by a few feet from his tent and the forest rises all about. There's a lovely carpet of needles, and the air is beautifully clear. He's done a few paintings and started several others. They all look like he, again, has a grip on things. There must be a periodic freshener, almost a rebirth. And when it comes it must be welcomed and appreciated, or stagnation takes place.

One more day until the new gas-rationing card is good. You figure time by ration books these days. Susie and Bob and Leonard Ottaway are very sensible about the rationing business. None of them are hoarders, but they make sensible allowances. Susie says more and more people are collecting silver dollars. They come into her place and ask if she has any, to which she replies that there isn't much silver in circulation because certain fools are collecting it and putting it away. "Well," said one man, "I was about to say that I'd trade you paper money for them. I'm saving them myself." "I was about to say," replied Susie, "that if there is such demand for silver dollars then I'll sell them for $1.25." "Oh," said the man, "that would be a dirty Jewish trick." Stupid, it seems to me and Susie, to put one's faith in a silver dollar. If things get that bad, we're all in it together and silver won't mean any more than paper or anything else.

As I was typing the above I suddenly became conscious it was getting dark and no black and white spaniel here at my feet. Emily moved up to our old cabin for sleeping and painting purposes and has taken Pixie for protection. That left me only Molly, who is normally my shadow. Calling her brought no results except a suspicious rustle in the raspberry bushes, so I went up to Emily's to see if she was there. But no -- Emily said she had taken off after something, "undoubtedly a bear," a short time before. Meanwhile there was enormous crashing in the bracken and salmonberry bushes that have grown over the path to what was our hillside terrace last year. The crashing stopped, but no Molly. I had visions of Molly lying cut and bleeding, slashed by a bear, or tangled in stickers and unable to move. There was much calling and listening, after which a panting and tail-wriggling Molly appeared from the direction of the outhouse, undoubtedly having been on the trail of some night bird. In the meantime darkness had descended. Molly now lies peacefully under the table as I write.

It seems ages since I've seen Kenneth, but it was only yesterday. We waited at the tent for a half-hour or so for Emily and Morris to return from an antique hunting expedition to Monte Cristo. I worried about Tobey having such a late supper and getting to bed late after a strenuous and long day. In the evening chill, I lay on Kenneth's narrow cot in the tent with the fine little cone-like stove burning. Tobey stuffed it into inactivity with bark, causing a wonderful wood smoke smell in the tent. Kenneth read to me the diary notes he has been keeping. He writes them to refer to later and for us to read aloud the small hard to remember things. They finally returned about 7:30 and we made haste to Susie's for a belated dinner, then home to put baby chickens and Tobey to bed. Later we reviewed their loot from the abandoned houses of Monte Cristo: a chair, not bad but with a loose back; a small table, which Morris kept because it had achieved the proper amount of weathering cherished by him; kerosene lamps; and other assorted pioneer knick-knacks.

Morris left for Seattle this morning after going on an orchid-hunting expedition with Mr. Robe (they found a few blooming). Emily and I rehashed the episode of Morris' latest visit, over numerous cups of coffee following lunch and while picking raspberries this afternoon. We feel there are subversive motives in many of Morris' remarks to Guy, and we're afraid these might have an adverse effect on Guy's newfound paths in painting. Morris' comment on the mining painting, that "the symbolism was lost in the too sensuous color," and regarding the parachute one that "the drapery was nicely painted" were both calculated to hit Guy in certain sore spots, which Morris knows better than anyone how to get at. He is a little puzzled, I think, by the general lack of attention paid to him by Emily and me. We both have been very casual toward him, and he is used to the worshipful goings on of Denise Farwell. We all talked around the fireplace last night until midnight about world affairs: the significance of Mussolini's demise, what about after the war, what about the Catholics, etc. Morris is strongly anti-Catholic and has been since we've known him. I suspect it comes from family conditioning rather than discovery.

We also discussed Virginia Boren and her divorce and remarriage. We wondered about its influence on her career and on Seattle activities, good and not so good. We discussed Nancy Ross, about whom Morris seems a little disillusioned, presumably because she had abandoned for now her book on pioneer women to do one about the W.A.A.C.'s (Women's Auxiliary Army Corps.). Emily and I agreed in general about her book, *Farthest Reach*. We think she is writing only for a small group of New York sophisticates and talking down this region as just a quaint and picturesque place full of scenery and 'characters'.

I dreamed about my old friend Edie Porter last night. In the dream she was a W.A.V.E. (the Navy equivalent of the W.A.A.C.'s) wearing a gorgeous uniform, sort of white with a chartreuse business on the chest. In my dream I was thinking what a perfect thing for

Edie to do. It's <u>just</u> the thing she would do, and the beautiful uniform so suited her.

The relationship of Emily and Guy is a story I had hoped to write this summer. It would be a coming together, a blending, a clashing of wills, then a divergence. The blending could be permanent like that of D. H. Lawrence and Frieda, but I think Emily's drinking is too destructive. Anyway, it's August already and I haven't started to write the story.

To live completely in the present is so important. But it is particularly difficult when every day is so unpredictable. I resent the hysterical quality of life around here lately; the drinking and restlessness Emily brings. She is close to being an alcoholic, but, like others we know, she won't believe it. An occasional drink for relaxation is fine, but it should never be the big thing of the day, nor hold so much importance.

It's only about a week since I wrote the above and sure enough, the story of Guy and Emily seems to have worked itself to a violent climax. I'm not surprised. I was at Kenneth's camp Saturday when it happened, and I am very glad I was there. For one thing, it might not have happened had I been here at the ranch. I knew it was inevitable, but I would not have wanted to witness it.

I have reconstructed the events from conversations with all the participants. Emily arrived from town in the middle of the afternoon with four quarts of liquor, which were soon guzzled. Things were a little difficult and kept getting more so as more liquor was drunk. Emily went down to ride Wirt's new horse, slipped off onto her back and broke her ribs again. Guy and Emily's friend, Louise Gilbert, found a door to carry Emily on, and Guy and Wirt started out for the house bearing her between them. However, Wirt slipped and fell. At that point Emily got up and walked up the hill with Guy's help. A shaky Guy and Louise got her into my bed and finally settled into a late supper. Then Emily got out of bed, went out to the front porch and was going to jump off the railing backwards onto some boards with nails in them.

I don't know the motive. She had been railing and tantruming and talking suicide, which she does when drinking. Things became more and more violent; more liquor was drunk. Emily alone consumed almost two quarts in the hours between 3 P.M. and 4 A.M. Everyone became sick. Louise was hysterical. Emily became violent and berated Guy for being weak and getting sick, etc., etc. Guy escaped to the woods and came so close to a bear he heard it snorting. Emily searched everywhere for him. At one point she climbed up over the wall onto the porch, broken ribs and all.

In the morning Emily woke bright as a berry, but Guy and Louise were wrecks. They called Emily everything they could think of including a little Hitler. How they ever made it up to Perry Creek by 1 P.M. I don't know, but they did. I knew the minute they got out of the car something had happened. Guy just told me the complete story tonight. Emily is feeling a little smug about it, I think. This is the sort of thing she thrives on. But it breaks other people. I hope she gets diverted into some other channel before any more of it happens here. It violates the whole spirit of the ranch.

The funny thing is, I almost came home last evening to escape drinking and possible fights at the road camp, as the foreman and the new bulldozer operator stayed in camp with a case of beer, and Kenneth feared the worst (a crew is building a road into Monte Cristo). As it was, I stayed and they were quiet as could be. We all had a fine sleep, and the rain of the last several days, which turned into a downpour last night, cleared into a beautiful dawn, sharp and feeling like autumn. Later in the day we had bright sunshine, fine for tanning. Emily is much subdued today and in some pain with her ribs, especially as she has a tickling cough. Each cough brings a grimace.

As I type on the porch, I can hear Guy up at his cabin sawing on the new cello that Emily bought him. What a gesture! He plans to trade her a picture for it. Oh, if there could just be a little more fortitude and calmness and a deeper, more enduring love among people!

26

I ASKED WIRT THE time yesterday. He pulled out his watch from grimy pants, squinted at it and said "I'm like the folks who wanted to find out how much a hog weighed. So they tied it to a stick, found a rock that balanced and then guessed how much the rock weighed. I look at this old watch of mine and then guess what time it is." Wirt wants me to go blackberrying tomorrow. What he really wants is company and, no doubt, help. He goes somewhere up on Green Mountain to chase more water down our creek every year about this time. I am going berry picking soon but I promised Kenneth I'd go see him at Perry Creek. And from the looks of Tobey I've got to get him to the river soon. He is black and the water tank is about empty.

We had a good couple of days at Perry Creek. After a river bath, Tobey had a wonderful time 'fishing' in a pool on the Sauk River with a pole and string. Butterflies were tied to the end of the string, which the fish would bite off. The line had no hook to catch them, but it kept him occupied for hours. A high point of the day was when Tobey walked with Kenneth to inspect the phone line. A porcupine appeared beside the road, and Kenneth and Tobey were able to walk right up to it without it being startled. They watched it eat fireweed for awhile before it waddled off into the woods. Tobey has been doing an impersonation of the porcupine eating ever since. He demonstrates just how close they got to it -- "look, here was us, and right there was the porcupine." Back at the ranch, I finally had a rare afternoon of blackberrying, but with Ethel Barrett and the boys rather than Wirt. They are living nearby again, as Everett is back with the Forest Service. She still has something of the quiet shyness of a woods animal. She has a soft voice and soft curling hair, just beginning to turn gray. Her eyes with laugh crinkles at the corners always appear a little frightened. I'm amazed at what these people have been through, and how they have remained as yet undefeated. I'm glad they're back in the area.

We took the Green Mountain trail and found wonderful berry patches. It was a perfect day for picking, shady and cool, with the sun filtering through soft grey clouds. At one point I heard Tobey several brush patches away talking to someone. Thinking it was me moving about on the other side of a berry vine covered fallen tree, he chatted away. When I reached him I saw a black bear scooting away from the other side of the vine-covered stump. Tobey was unfazed but sorry he hadn't seen the bear! The positions you get into when picking are definitely uncomfortable, and I'm still sore. I saw the beady little blackberries in my mind's eye until I went to sleep last night. I picked half a water bucket full. The flavor is as magical as ever.

Today Wirt was beaming under his old scars and dirt, because he and Gypsy, his new horse, are all set up for winter. She has a barn full of hay; he, a shed full of good, dry wood. Frank Bower and Leonard helped saw it up today. I furnished sandwiches and cake.

Later that same day, Guy and Tobey and I had a lavish dinner on the porch, including freshly picked beans from the prolific little low bushes down in the garden. Tobey had spinach, the first the garden had produced and almost the last. He said it tasted fine to have spinach again for a change. Then he had his fig bars and was induced to wash his own hands and face, and was finally ensconced in bed. He has quite readily accepted the fact of the chickens in their coop at night instead of in boxes in his bedroom. It is easier on me not to have to carry them into the kitchen, then out again in the morning. And not have to clean up the spilled straw and chicken manure if they managed to get out during the night.

After we finished dinner we sat on at the table for about two hours, watching the moon come up, one of the most dramatic performances the old boy has done yet. It rose from the middle of the range of mountains at the end of the valley, first just a pink glow, then a sharp sliver of radiance and turning rapidly into a great orange sphere. At first, it silhouetted the valley between two peaks, then an entire mountain peak. It looked enormous and very orange because of the fall smoke low in the valley. Everything was marvelously peaceful.

Emily and Louise left this afternoon, and so did Jim and Theresa Stevens. Guy says he is definitely through with Emily and all that she represents. I think she feels now that Guy is afraid of her, and she gets a sadistic pleasure from playing with the idea. She has said, once openly and other times inferring rather jokingly, that she is basically sadistic. The strange thing is that she can be so lovely and so warm and simpatico that you find yourself liking her immensely, and yet there is always this uncomfortable threat of what she can become.

I am sleepy and I'm fairly sure the mice or pack rats or whatever lives in our attic aren't going to let me sleep very soon. They don't even wait until things get quiet to start their activity. They are pattering around now, but they're nothing to what they will be later when they really get to moving the furniture around. Guy heard them last night and was sure a bear was pawing out back, trying to get into the cooler, gnawing and clawing at the door. It is incredible the noise the mice make. I went up awhile ago and put a little tin of poison seeds on the floor. I hope they take the hint.

Theresa asked today if I have no nerves at all. How do I always manage to be so calm and undisturbed about everything? Jim said, "Yes, we always picture Margaret riding out the storm." Well, I liked what Jim said, but I felt Theresa was taking a jab at my housekeeping or something. She said she couldn't possibly spend a summer here like I'm doing. I said, "How are you going to spend time in a logging camp with Jim, then?" (She has been saying how they simply had to arrange this soon, so he could get back to serious writing). Well, she thought she would write, too, in that case. She just can't accept life and relax in the real meaning of the word. Emily and Louse also say I don't seem to have nerves. I don't think I am any more insensitive than most. Perhaps I am more sensitive in that I can't bear to have things upset by making a scene. I have bad times during the winter, as Kenneth knows all too well, and the stability I usually feel has much to do with Kenneth's calmness.

I do think it important for Jim to get back to writing something significant. Something in league with *Brawny Man* or the *Paul Bunyan* book rather than the timber industry propaganda he's been writing lately. I know he has it in him.

This evening was so beautiful after today's rain that it hurt. Before going to bed I walked down to the garden, which is lush. The moon hung in a cloudless twilight dome. Pilchuck glowed faintly pink and was almost bare of snow. Moonflowers were opening, exuding their beautiful fragrance on the evening air. I have been showing Tobey the moonflowers since they started blooming. How he loves it when they jerk as they unfold.

Moonflower

Under all the clamor
there is the music of the universe,
not always to be heard,
rarely to be seen,
more often sensed,
when the spirit opens,
as does the moon flower,
when its lemon pale petals,
cradling the day's heat,
feel the presence
of evening's cool moisture and
open mysteriously and receptively.

27

SEATTLE, FEBRUARY 12, 1943. It's the first spring-like day since Christmas. It's been clear and warm in spite of a slight north wind. I dug in the garden in my shirtsleeves and dripped from the brow. What a blessed feeling. I used to wonder why older people were so anxious for spring; it's a sure sign of approaching middle age, Mrs. C.

Everett Barrett, former Barlow Point lookout man who introduced us to Robe Ranch, came to see us last Saturday. Out of a clear blue sky came a ring on the doorbell and there stood Everett. It's been a year and a half since the family set out in their old car to beat their way to California. He'd been working at Douglas Aircraft down there and was transferred for a time to Denver before wandering back here. He's a born wanderer and although without formal education has thought out a lot of intelligent sensible ideas all by himself.

He came Sunday and Mark was here, too. In spite of the enormous disparity in their backgrounds and lifestyles, they hit it off amazingly well. Mark liked him and he liked Mark. They had an interesting exchange of views, talking of social opinions, religion, world remedies, nature, the arts, and the character of various parts of the country. Everett is now a mechanic at Boeing, putting engines into Flying Fortresses. He may try to get on with the Forest Service at Verlot again next summer.

Betty Willis and I visited Bill Cumming at Firlands T.B. Sanatorium yesterday. He and I argued in the old way about an article in *The New Republic* favoring a return to moral and ethical values and discounting the political solution. Bill's been reading Lenin and Marx for the first time and is a dialectic materialist with a vengeance. He believes whole hog. Bill's wife Ginny is in the picture again. She wants reconciliation and another chance. Bill agreed to it. I guess I have forgotten a lot about that age, but I will never understand the lure of a future life with Ginny after such an unhappy past relationship.

Tomorrow evening the group meets at Mark's to work on symbolic visual statements about the war. Expected at the meeting are the Camffermans, Guy, Dick, Kenneth and I.

Kenneth has been so busy working out the composition of a group of pictures that Mark has been using for discussion in his Saturday art classes, that he hasn't had time to do any war sketches.

This winter is marked by war, worry, edginess about the draft, and occasional colds. On the positive side are our contacts with Mark, Betty Willis, Guy Anderson and my friendship with Emma Stimson. And, topping the list is Tobey, who turned five in January. He's a constant delight with some new quirk every day. Lately he has taken to asking me at odd times if this is all a dream we're having or if we are actors in a show with people watching.

He's outdoors now with the children in his old green jacket and red logger's hat. He plays with the baker's little girls, the truck driver's children (mainly Donny Skinner), the hod carrier's boy, and assorted others. Talk about a proletarian start in life. Donny is the favorite. He's seven years old, in the first grade for the second year, not awfully bright, but a good kid, easy to play with, good-natured and with a sense of humor. He eats dinner with us every night now. He just started coming and has continued. His sister Joan came a few times and started bringing her baby sister Darlene, but I drew the line. Joan tried to queer the deal by reporting to me that her brother has accidents in his trousers every day at school. I took Donny aside and told him always to ask to be excused and make a beeline for the bathroom, and he has been getting along better. I think he was afraid to ask the teacher about leaving the room.

Tobey's interaction with the neighborhood kids inspires me to record more recollections of my own childhood in north Seattle. Children in those days (circa 1910) had to rely more on their ingenuity than they do today. There weren't any radio shows with "Sky King" or "Hi Ho, Silver" emanating from the speaker. There were so few cars that they didn't count in a child's scheme of things. And movies made very rare visits to Greenwood's neighborhood theater. So, for all practical purposes, our fun was up to us, and like all children we played traditional games and drew upon vast reservoirs of creativity.

What used to delight me most of all were the occasions when a whole gang of kids would be available for a game of Run, Sheep Run or Sheep in My Pen or Fox and Geese. The first two of these old-fashioned games had everything including strategy and teamwork. I've forgotten some details of Fox and Geese, but it involved chalking white arrows on sidewalks or walls for the fox to follow. I have vague memories of the game petering out disappointingly before the climax was reached. The search too often ended in failure for the fox because the geese, having grown tired of hiding, had gone home for rest or sustenance. But the excitement in Sheep in My Pen involved grouping around the base, which was always the big maple tree down in the field. We watched for a signal from a hider-out; then, having received one, tried a desperate dash for cover before 'the farmer' saw you and called out "Sheep in My Pen!" Oh, that was excitement supreme. Conspiracy is thrilling to every child.

It has been years since I have heard a child's voice ring out "Run, Sheep Run" or "Sheep in My Pen" or have seen the white chalk arrows beckoning the fox to the hunt. Something must have taken the place of all this magic, but what it is I haven't discovered. Hide and seek was of course a standby, because just a handful of kids was enough. It didn't require preliminaries or organization. Baseball was chronic during spring and summer. Mostly scrub was favored, although if there were enough of us we chose sides. It seemed we were always being called to dinner just as we had worked up to bat. A "wait 'til I get my ups" was the plaintive plea, while baked potatoes withered in their skins.

Both boys and girls played these games. There were more of the former in our immediate neighborhood. In fact, the two sisters, Evelyn and Frances Hagen, and I were usually the only girls with about a dozen boys. Sometimes the Swedish girl, Edith Bekmann, joined in, and for a short period there was Brunhilda Iverson, but she moved away. The girls were usually accepted as equals by the boys. On those occasions when a group was all girls, only certain games were played. Hopscotch was one of these. I liked marking out of the play area with a stick on hard packed earth and landing a piece of broken glass in the right square. Other girl's only games were jump rope in season, statue, and London Bridge. Strange the way certain games were assigned by unspoken consent to certain places and certain times. School ground games, such as "Drop the Handkerchief", "Farmer in the Dell", "Go In and Out the Window", and "Blind Man's Bluff" were fun on the school grounds, but we never played them away from school. A game I used to adore to play on the beach on summer evenings was "Three Days", but we never played it in the city.

Aside from games, a spontaneous enterprise would periodically engross the entire neighborhood. While it was underway it was totally absorbing, and when it was through it was completely through, as dead and forgotten as an old feather hat in the attic. I remember one such time. It was a warm, peaceful day in mid-June, and great activity was taking place out in the backfield. Old planks and hunks of wood, cans of nails, and tools of various kinds were being hauled from woodsheds and basements. The air was full of sawing and hammering, and the shouts of Ralph Keilholz could be heard as he bossed the job. He was the smallest kid in size but with over-sized brown eyes and vocal cords.

"Hey, not that way —over here, over here, I say. Oh for cripes sake —gosh all heck Ole, hey Leo -- put down them nails -- can't you see they're fallin' out the bottom of the bag? Here's a can -- put em in here -- aw criminy -- there they go -- all over the ground —pick em up, you guys -- come on now -- gosh darn! Hey, Curley -- come back with that saw!" The grown-ups all expected Ralph would grow up to be the boss of a road gang, but he evolved into a quiet little man in an engineer's office.

Then, one morning there was a procession through our yard and into the field of many small boys with delight written large on their faces and hunks of soap in all their pockets and hands. "Get some soap Maggie and come on" they said. There wasn't a laundry tub in the neighborhood that wasn't raided, and to what a noble purpose! The contraption was a sort of simplified Coney Island roller coaster, a high slide, perhaps twenty feet high at the start and sloping dizzyingly for forty feet to the ground. The slide board had raised tracks that accommodated little wooden sleds. The idea was to slick the track up plenty with soap, and then flop onto a sled and away you flew. While a touch rickety, the structure lasted about a week. By that time something else had come along to fascinate us.

Another time we made our own merry-go-round in Leo Bladic's back yard, a rig like a teeter-totter. It revolved about a center post when pushed and would get going very fast when well weighted at both ends, with, say, three small bodies to an end. The pusher's job was hazardous as the go-round soon was revolving too fast for the pusher to keep up. One had to make a dash to safety. One day my dash was not fast enough, and first thing I knew I was being helped to my feet by very solicitous playmates, who eyed the lump on my head with awe and said nothing. Dazed, I went on home, resolving not to mention the incident, as I knew that its revelation would mean no more merry-go-rounds. My bump was not noticed during dinner, and I was congratulating myself. While drying dishes and putting them away in the pantry, Leo, Carlyle, and Ralph came silently to the back door with eyes round and serious. "How's Maggie?" they asked my mother in hushed tones.

28

AFTER A COUPLE OF false starts, Tobey is launched on an all-day school schedule in the first grade at Stevens School. Miss Adelsberger is his teacher. On his first day there, some two weeks ago, he came home at noon, completely disgruntled -- didn't like it, didn't like the teacher, wished he was back in Mrs. Nygreen's room in kindergarten where you could do what you wanted. Quite a jump, from kindergarten with its lack of restraint and Mrs. Nygreen's liberalism, to Mrs. Adelsberger's discipline and stern methods of imparting knowledge.

I was going to let him stay home that afternoon but the teacher called and said, no, he must return. She adopted a tone implying that I was also a wayward child, but I controlled my irritation for Tobey's sake. I had already objected, but without success, to the mid-morning glass of orangeade because it is a synthetic product, not real orange juice. It was her custom, she said, and that was that. Well, Tobey returned with me as escort, feeling more like jailer. He begged me tearfully not to send him, and it was hard resisting his pleas, particularly as I shared his dislike of the teacher after our telephone conversation. We talked on the way back of life not always being what you wanted it to be. It took all kinds of people to make a world, etc. "Just be good to the teacher, do what she says, try to like her, and all will be well." I was feeling like a stinking hypocrite the whole time.

On the way home I thought about my own first days at school in north Seattle so many years before. I was five and a half when I started Greenwood School, and I attended the entire eight grades in the same building, a fortunate experience for any child, I am sure. There was no kindergarten then. The school building was seven or eight blocks away, a ten-minute leisurely walk or a three-minute sprint. I can remember no emotions on starting school. The leave-taking from home is a blank, although my mother said later she watched me start out with the customary tears and regrets thinking, "there goes my baby." Evelyn Hagan, who had already been to school one year, took me with her. I can remember neither trepidation nor anticipation on the walk to the two-story schoolhouse, a very imposing-looking building to me then.

But a dreadful experience came later that day. The various classes were released at different times, whenever the first day's business of roll call and introductions were over. Our little band of first graders must have been the first out for we straggled through the doors to a vast and supremely empty school ground. Strange territory stretched away in all directions, and I hadn't the vaguest idea how to find my way home, as my classmates headed off purposefully in all directions. Feeling infinitely small and bewildered, I started climbing the hill leading to Greenwood Avenue. We had come to school through a forested shortcut, and I apparently ruled that out as impossible wilderness to traverse alone.

I must have reasoned that by going straight to Greenwood Avenue and then heading toward home I would sooner or later get into familiar territory. The plan worked. What is strange to me about this memory is how completely alone and helpless I felt in what seemed a terribly vast and hostile world. Why shouldn't I have felt comfortable surrounded by friendly if unfamiliar souls, any one of whom I could have turned to for directions and aid? It seemed true to most children that they instinctively feel nothing but unfriendliness when left alone with strangers. I am sure that many of the nightmares later in my life are traceable to those few moments of feeling lost. In childhood, experiences can take on an exaggerated dream-like quality that disappears as the ability to reason takes over. But the emotions they triggered recur in the realm of dreams.

Miss Dahl was my first grade teacher. She was slim and had goldy-red hair. I thought her exquisitely pretty and loved her dearly for her gentle, quiet manner and the sweetness of her smile. She won my heart completely the day my head hurt and she held me on her lap and said the little brownies would chase away the hurt. Very lightly she beat a little tattoo on my forehead with her fingertips while I sat in a heavenly stupor. Finally, she said "There! The hurt is all gone." She sent me back to my seat in a delightful daze, and I was as one apart the rest of the day.

All through childhood, and indeed in later years as well, I was cursed with a shyness and sensitivity, undoubtedly an inferiority complex, but why? Not that I went about with an inner gnawing unhappiness. On the contrary I seem to have been quite happy most of the time. But there were occasional difficult situations, which tortured me and left memories. Whenever they crept to the surface they brought hot blushes and a sinking feeling in my solar plexus.

One such situation occurred at the Methodist Sunday School. My father's family is the only branch of my parentage where religion is connected to churches. And the hold the Episcopalians had on him was not very tight at that. We were sent to the Methodist Sunday School for the simple reason that it was the only institution of God within walking distance. In retrospect, I think one reason my mother favored the district they chose was the absence of Episcopal houses of worship.

Anyway, I had just come through the only serious illness of my life thus far, pneumonia, and it was my first trip to Sunday school in two months. As it was Mother's Day, there was a special program scheduled, and it was thought I would be entertained.

In spite of the fine weather I was bundled into a dark brown winter coat, rubbers and a knit cap, and as I walked my knees wobbled slightly. As one entered the long narrow building with Greenwood-Phinney M-E Church painted in black over the double front doors, there was a necessary pause while one's eyesight adjusted to the pale gloom, within; not a gloom dramatically filtered through stained glass saints, just ordinary gloom. The only light came through small opaque windows high on the sidewalls. The only other light was from dim electric bulbs hanging from the ceiling and shaded by conical green glass hats.

The pews and benches were varnished dark brown; the worn boards of the flooring were without carpets. The altar, raised a foot, had a varnished wooden railing with gates at the two aisles. Faded green carpeting floored the altar. In one back corner there was the old organ, the foot-pumping variety, and in the center was the pulpit. On special days there were flowers. The Sunday school superintendent was Mrs. Williamson, wife of the grocer, who carried the religious burden of the whole family on her shoulders. I remember hearing it said that the poor creature had a great cross to bear in the willful heathenness of her husband, who rested after six long days wrapping up coffee and oatmeal and pounding the cash register by sleeping all Sunday morning.

For so ardent a Methodist, however, Mrs. Williamson was not the hard-bitten variety, and I remember her as being always patient, kindly, and sweet to children. She sang hymns in a voice so ringing it fairly drowned out the best efforts of the combined Sunday school. The hymns were lots of fun. We were allowed pretty much to select our own hymns. Our favorites were 'Showers of Blessings', 'God Will Take Care of You' (this is the one I used to sing to myself when sent upstairs or into the basement or to the store in the dark), "His Yoke is Easy, His Burden is Light', and 'Stand Up, Stand Up for Jesus'. They were rousing, happy tunes, all. I thought them beautiful music and would sing them gustily about the house later in the day, which my mother would stand as long as she could and then put a stop to. I could never understand why she didn't think the songs were pretty.

On that fateful Mother's Day, Mrs. Williamson announced the special program: a comic poem to be recited by her little boy, Ralph, who stuttered. It was a sentimental verse sing-songed in unison or thereabouts with the youngest of the pretty, curly-haired Phillips girls. And then there was to be a song by Mrs. Burns' class. Lost in the excitement of it all; I was brought to by a great thump of my heart. This meant me. I was in Mrs. Burns' class. But I didn't know the song. All about me, girls were getting to their feet, smoothing down skirts, starting up the aisle. Horrors! Why hadn't anyone told me? And here is what I will never understand. Why didn't I stay in the comfortable obscurity of my corner? But no, the instant reaction was to bluff it out. Tottering, I got to my feet, winter hat, coat and rubbers still shrouding my skinny figure, and followed the others to the platform. I saw Mrs. Burns' eye me as if something was on her mind, but it wasn't until I was arrayed up there in full view of God and his congregation that I realized this was a specialty number by three members of Mrs. Burns' class. It was not an ensemble, as the announcement had indicated. My suffering sidelong glances also took in the fact that the other three girls were dressed alike in pink and white frocks, and that each carried in her hand a bouquet of flowers.

Even so, I didn't give up gracefully, acknowledge my error, and retire to my place in the audience. Stupidly and in acute agony, I stood there through the whole frightfully long affair, and when they joined in chorus, I remember making my lips move as though I knew it too. And if anybody thought there was anything funny about my being up there, they were mistaken! My embarrassment must have been as painful to the rest of the class as it was to me, as the subject was never mentioned. I sat down when it was over and maintained stony silence, hearing nothing the rest of the session. I never told my family about it, and it wasn't until years later that I was able to talk about it at all.

February 10, 1944. We are waiting to hear whether the draft board will accept Kenneth's request for a deferral. I hope, I hope, I hope. He passed the physical and written tests that qualify him for the Army, Navy or Coast Guard. But the ranger at Verlot encouraged Kenneth to apply for a deferral based on his age, one year from being too old, and his government job with the Forest Service. He will write to the draft board on Kenneth's behalf.

Mark is planning for his one-man show at Marion Willard's New York City gallery in April. I am almost sure it will result in some good returns for him. Betty is leaving for New York tonight, taking some of his paintings with her in case dealers, buyers, etc. are interested. This may be the beginning of some recognition for Mr. Tobey. If it is he will take himself right back there, I am sure, and probably get his life all messed up again.

It's April already, a long time these days between jottings. I think it's that underneath everything there's the rottenness of the war and all the stench it brews. The work it takes to maintain a routine in this atmosphere leaves little impetus for writing. However, I will try to summarize the last couple of months.

Mark is having his show in New York. The Art Digest was critical, calling the work "moonstruck" but as likely to win favor as the recent Graves show. The New York Times was more favorable. But we have had no word from Mark or Betty since the opening. We're all wondering about sales. I doubt they'll be able to understand Mark or his paintings back there. They won't appreciate all of it, I know. And I don't know if that matters. The things have been created, and they will live.

Since his draft deferral, Kenneth has been at Verlot. He writes from the woods that he is painting evenings, he thinks not badly. I hope that means damn good. It's been so long, what with the Weyerhaeuser mural and the rush at the museum, since he's been able to do anything. He often includes illustrated notes for Tobey when he writes.

Eleanor King is in the hospital. The doctors think perhaps she has undulant fever. Guy spends all time possible with her. I can't quite see the end of this relationship. I don't think she has the warmth Guy needs.

Today a Mr. Lumle from Lincoln High School gave a talk on birds at Stevens School. Mrs. Adelsberger urged me to hear it, in order to be able to talk birds with Tobey, who is becoming an expert. Their mutual interest in birds has smoothed the waters. Strange, the things one finds oneself falling into. There was the evening of folk dancing at the Y.W.C.A. induced by Eleanor; the evening recently at the First Christian Church in support of the Committee for Racial Equality, and now a talk by a fanatic on the subject of bird life. I will say Mr. Lumle has mastered the art of whistling their calls. He can do the robin's mating song I have always loved during the green moist evenings and dawns of early spring. And he did tell me it is the varied thrush we hear in the deep woods during the summer. The long, minor, haunting note on a slightly declining scale is the essence of the summer in the thickness of the forest.

Lumle had the children in the palm of his hand. They laughed uproariously at his jokes and ooh'd and aah'd over each new color slide. Oh well. I expect I will be attending odder groups before Tobey is much older.

29

EVER SINCE TOBEY'S FIRST adventure with the fruits of the soil -- a premature pulling of potatoes when he discovered, by accident, they had such nice little balls on the roots -- he has shared with me the delight of gathering things that grow from the ground. As well as cultivated crops, we collect salmon berries, blackberries and huckleberries, and fruit from abandoned orchards.

But the subject of mushrooms was always fraught with uncertainty and suspicion, partly because most of the pioneers in the area are scared of "toad stools" and unwilling to consider any for food except perhaps shaggy manes, meadow mushrooms and occasionally morels.

A book from the library covering the whole field of mushrooms has turned me from an abstainer into an eager neophyte. The author clearly defined the poisonous family of Amanitas: the snowy white angel of death, the tawny panther amanita and the exotic fly amanita with its flame red top and leprous scales. The latter is a growth so flamboyant it might as well flash POISON from its brazen face.

I decided to try a few others if I could find them and be certain they fit the book's description. The three I found most alluring were chanterelles, sulfur polypores and savory pleurotis. Chanterelles, said my authority, were apricot-colored, smelled slightly like apricots, and were distinguishable by a particular fluted shape. Sulfur polypores were described as orange on top, sulfur-yellow beneath, growing in shelves on dead trees and apt to be found in great quantities if found at all. The flavor, said to be rather like fried chicken, sounded most tempting.

The savory pleurotis, it seemed, was small and porcelain-colored, ribbed underneath and also to be found growing on semi-rotten logs. It is one of a larger group known as oyster mushrooms, and is sometimes called angel wings. All three were reported to be agreeable to our habitat. While some authorities cautioned never to eat mushrooms found in the woods, as this was the favored home of the deadly Amanita family, I resolved not to be cowed by any such blanket warning.

August was a wet month that year. We often walked the path to our swimming hole (and bathtub) in a warm drizzle. We searched in vain for our target mushrooms but, finding nothing, our attention shifted to other matters. One morning, Tobey and David Perine burst into the kitchen holding something before them in their cupped, wet hands. Big-eyed, they spread their spoils on the table by the window -- mushrooms! A lovely pale violet one and a red one, both white underneath, and a porous monster, sulfurish on the bottom, red on top and inky green where it had been bruised. Then I caught the scent of apricot. "Is it a chanterelle?" Tobey asked eagerly. We examined the plump, inverted cap, the rounding fluting running into the stem. I sniffed it. "It does smell a little like apricots," I exclaimed. The children sniffed and agreed. "Where'd you find it?" I asked. "Down there in the woods. Along the path to Green Mountain," Tobey said. We promptly went out to look for more and the yield was spectacular.

The path was actually an old skid road that had been used for logging forty years before. The road let in just enough light through the dense tall second growth to please the chanterelles. We found them singly and in fat clumps, varying from buds to full-grown, some of them four inches in diameter. Their tawny gold color fairly shone against the carpet of wet green moss or dark brown duff. The boys darted about searching among the trees. By the time we reached the spot where salmon berry brush and young alders had overgrown the old road, making the going too hard, we had a fine lot.

On the way back we passed Wirt stacking wood alongside his cabin. Always curious, he squinted at the bulging sack. "Whatcha got there?" he asked, taking the opportunity to straighten and work the kinks out of his back. "Chanterelles," I said. "They're a particular kind of mushroom supposed to taste very good. Have you ever eaten them?"

His interest waned rapidly. "Oh, I eat them," he said. "They grow all around after a rain." He pointed to a spot near his steps where some wood had been stacked. The ground was covered with a brownish fungus, decidedly a different species. "They're all about the same," he said in his growly voice. "I dunno why I eat them. They only taste like rotten wood."

Wirt's attitude toward food was casual, to say the least. Through some miracle he claimed never to have eaten a poison mushroom, never to have contracted botulism from his home-canned vegetables or been sickened from his week-old clam chowder. He never, until the illness that kept him confined the last two years of his life, had had anything wrong with him except the occasional session of violent stomach cramps. The affliction, he said, was hereditary, having plagued his mother for many years. I had to wonder whether she ate mushrooms indiscriminately, too. The remedy he had found to be a drink of whiskey, which he kept on hand for such emergencies. Wirt didn't look like an aesthete, but except for his pipe of Grainger Rough Cut, he was one. His physical tastes were the most simple I have ever encountered. And his willingness to eat "toad stools" was rare among his contemporaries.

We found savory pleurotis to be worthy of its name. Again Tobey made the first discovery, bringing home a hat-full of the delicate, shell-like things. In his eagerness he even trimmed and washed them, which, with pleurotis is an extremely dull chore, as they have a way of growing around moss and sticks. "I got them all from one log," he said triumphantly.

The chanterelles we cooked in butter and ate with meat. The oyster mushrooms we sautéed in butter or stewed gently in milk and ate with crackers. The consistency is not unlike that of oysters, but there is no similarity in taste. In fact, the taste of the oyster mushroom is not like anything you can imagine. It is truly rare and more like a fragrance than a taste. And they *are* the most poetic looking creations, with their purity in color and form, the upper side smooth, the underside daintily fluted. For their habitat they like downed logs not yet too advanced in disintegration . They grow layer upon layer from the sides of the log, horizontal to the ground.

One afternoon, shortly after our black forest road had been widened by the government for logging on Green Mountain, I was walking into Robe Ranch from the mailbox. I noticed through the trees, about thirty feet from the edge of the road, a glow of color more concentrated than the occasional patches of August sunlight. I investigated. Surely our somber Northwest woods could never have produced the orgy of exotic growth before my eyes. Growing on the six-foot stump of an old growth Douglas fir were layers and layers of huge fan-shaped fungus, brilliant fiery orange on top and pure sulfur yellow underneath. Attached at the base, they rippled out, slanting slightly downward. The largest were nearly a foot wide and perhaps eight inches deep. From two inches thick at the point of attachment they tapered to a narrow rim. Sulfur polypores! They could be nothing else.

Following the suggestion of the book, we fried outside strips two inches wide in butter, first dipping them into egg batter and cracker crumbs, as you would treat veal cutlets. The cooked mushroom was more like meat than any other mushroom, more like chicken or veal. There must have been nearly ten pounds of them, and they were just at the right stage to be tender and delicious. We ate them for several meals and shared them with a few brave friends in the valley.

At the time I didn't realize how lucky we were to have found the polypores before they became too old. The next time we came across a supply of them, we found, after all the rather complicated cooking process that they were disappointingly dry and woody, not far removed from Wirt's "old rotten wood." Sulfur polypores are temperamental; they seldom appear twice in the same place, and there seems to be no consistent way of locating them. We have over the years, found dried remnants of great colonies of them, like white bones at the base of the stumps. We have also found quantities when they were maddeningly just a few days too old to be good eating. Not more than three or four times have we had the luck to gather them in their succulent prime. These have been memorable gastronomic occasions.

Mushrooms once brought us a friend. Barney Crane was employed by the Forest Service at Verlot when we first discovered the valley. He was one of three or four year-round workers at the Verlot station, obviously a man with a calling, the calling being nature. Barney was as average a man as you could find in appearance. He was of medium height and built with light hair, thick glasses, and blue eyes, which, if you bothered to notice, had a provocative mocking glint. But he was an unusual man in other ways. Fanatically devoted to the mountains and forests, he knew his way around places where no trails had ever been blazed. In addition to his intrepid mountaineering, which from time to time contributed importantly in saving the lives of the lost and injured, he was like us, given to playing classical music on his windup record player, and was also an amateur painter.

He was, however, quite elusive and unsociable, and while always courteous and friendly, couldn't be reached. He was regarded by his fellow workers as grumpy and moody. To us it seemed we had a good deal in common with Barney but we couldn't find the key to his door. It wasn't until two or three years after we first met him that we learned Barney had lost an eye when he was still in high school and wore a glass eye, about which he was extremely sensitive. We had never detected this infirmity. The loss had for some reason caused him to give up his piano studies. Barney's mountaineering, in our estimation, became even more admirable considering his handicap.

One day in August, on our return from a hiking trip, we stopped at Susie's for dinner and presented her with a quantity of sulfur polypores we had gathered on the way back. Barney and a group of Forest Service employees were just finishing their evening meal. "You don't mean to say you eat those things!" he exclaimed when he saw the brilliant mushrooms. Only too happy for an opening, I told him what they were, where we had found them, how to prepare them, and anything else about mushrooms I could think of. He said little, only looked slightly incredulous, but two weeks later I was surprised to see a Forest Service truck drive into our road, from which emerged Barney and another station employee. We've got something we want to ask you about," he called. The something was a great find of sulfur polypores. They had come to be reassured that they were the real thing; partly too, I think, out of pride of discovery.

We had a long talk about the mountains Barney knew so well; how to get from this lake and to that one without the benefit of a trail. He knew the way from the west side of Mount Pilchuck, through a draw, to the little known south side with its many small lakes and meadows. He was obviously disturbed about plans then just getting underway to carry on extensive logging operations within the Mount Baker National Forest and, more specifically, in our home territory, the Monte Cristo district.

Knowing the tendency of the old-timers in the mountains to guard jealously their secret places, we were deeply grateful to Barney for telling us as much as he did. We felt we had made the grade in his estimation from idle and despoiling city folk to 'belongers' in the valley.

We felt something else, an underlying sadness in Barney's attitude, which we were inclined to trace to the inevitable changes he could foresee: the encroachments of the world on his wilderness privacy. He was extremely modest about his rescue work, as indeed are all the Forest Service men. He talked about it, if questioned, as rather a bore, a nuisance, but a chore that had to be done. Actually, there was no provision at all for this type of work; it was strictly extra-curricular with no pay of any kind, not even the comparatively low Forest Service salary. Rescue work had to be undertaken on time off, or time spent during work hours had to be made up. It was not considered part of the regular duties of the men in the department.

I asked Barney why he always volunteered. He said, half jokingly, "Oh. I figure it's a kind of insurance. Maybe if I get lost or hurt some day, someone will do the same for me." But Barney never collected on his insurance. The following winter, an unusually cold and snowy one, we were horrified to read a small item in the *Seattle Times* telling of the death of B. Crain (misspelled), a "logger" near Granite Falls. Strychnine was the agent. He left no note. I never see sulfur polypores without thinking of Barney and wondering.

It is so quiet tonight; the sound of my typewriter is startling. The ranch house is dripping with the nostalgia of a departing summer. The evening is a rare one, with a little more than half a moon over the peak of Pilchuck. The air is warm and still, full of elusive fragrances and the slight rustling noises of small night things getting their activities started.

The summer of 1944 has been a continuation of the last one with some new personalities entering stage left while others exited stage right. But changes have been hovering in the wings. Wirt has been in and out of the hospital and his promise to sell the ranch to us at some point has been eroded by the presence of, until now, uninterested and unconcerned relatives. I've been investigating another piece of property nearer the river.

In the 'good news' department, Kenneth has new digs. The Forest Service has built a guard station at Barlow Pass. Twin bunks, a wood cook stove, cold water and an icehouse provide relative luxury. The trail to the lookout begins at the back of the station. Very rough roads from Barlow Pass to Monte Cristo and down the Sauk River to Darrington have been completed recently. In the culinary department there is the discovery of the wild mushrooms. And Kenneth and Guy have done some good painting this summer. I wonder if Mark has also. We have not heard a word from him since we came up here.

The summer has had its share of comedy, a good many annoyances, and portions of tragedy, pathos and poetry. There has been a good deal of confusion in the kitchen over meal getting and dish washing, and frequent wrangling over who had what blankets, with Dick and Tom regular pack rats about the subject. Guy was having to sleep in all his sweaters and coats and I in my bathrobe. I guess poor, thin Eleanor was cold some of the time, but she never complained. She wept when saying her farewells last evening and embraced me fervently while tears rolled down her cheeks. It put me into a state of furious embarrassment, which set me to stammering a lot of idiocies about being a good sport and everything working out for the best, etc. She replied with only that wan and knowing smile, so full of brooding tragedy.

Things closed most pleasantly with a fine evening Friday. George Mantor read aloud from Walt Barnett's collection. Sunday was a fine summer day, flooded with really warm sun. We had a long afternoon at the marvelous new swimming place on the river we recently discovered. It is really perfection: deep pools and shallow ones, a sandy beach among the boulders and a long bar across the river with white sand next to a beautiful rocky hillside with enchanting miniature gardens. It has everything.

Guy, Elanor King and George left for town last night. They took Dick, Tom, Marjory Nestor and kids to the bus. That leaves only Tobey, Wirt and myself on the old homestead. Tobey's asleep and I am for the first time since early June, relaxed in the luxury of being quite, quite alone; however, the luxury is tinged with certain sadness. It came on so suddenly. I need Kenneth around I guess, and tomorrow we will go to Barlow where he is working.

A chilling scream interrupted the above writing last night as I took advantage of the last light of the day to type outside at the porch table.

It seemed to come from the swamp where the boys fish. The violet green swallows were tucked in for the night under the eaves above my head and abruptly stopped their little cooing noises when the high-pitched cry pierced the evening quiet. As I listened it came again, exactly like a woman's scream. Tobey was in bed and Wirt had gone to the Ottaways for an evening visit. "What was that?" Tobey asked when I tiptoed in to see if he was awake. I told him I was going to go down to the swamp to see if someone needed help. I told him to stay in bed and I'd be right back to report.

With fear and trepidation I took the axe from the woodshed and made my way down through the garden, over the fence and across the field. It was getting quite dark along the little forest trail that ends at the large beaver dam where Wirt had once planned to raise muskrats.

I called out "Helloos" in a quavering voice hoping I wouldn't again hear that blood-chilling cry. No response. "Hellooo, is anybody there?" No response. I listened intently but there was no sound, no frogs, no night birds, just an unnatural, ominous stillness. Often glancing over my shoulder, I hurried back to the ranch house. From the edge of the field I could see a small head peering over the edge of the porch.

I bundled Tobe into the car and we drove up to the Ottaways. Just as we reached their driveway, Leonard and Wirt drove out onto the road. I described what I had heard, and they both exclaimed in unison that I had heard a cougar scream.

This morning we walked down to the swamp, and Tobe made his way out onto the beaver dam while I waited at the trail. He soon came hurrying back with something furry dangling from his hand. It was the back half of a rabbit cut as neatly in two as if by a cleaver. He said there were fresh cougar tracks in the mud on the dam. I had apparently interrupted the big cat's meal. I've never heard a wolf's howl, but I'm sure it could be no more chilling a sound than the scream of a cougar.

30

It's 1945: A CHILLY early January at the ranch with no snow. The boys are in bed, Tobey and a friend from Seattle, David Sjostrom. Molly is in the Morris chair and Mitzi is on the couch. Me, I'm in the basket chair before the fire. The mantle lamp is giving a good whitish light.

Big changes are stirring. Wirt's promise to sell or give us the ranch in his will seems less likely as time passes. For one thing, I doubt that he has a will of any kind. His niece's family, which has shown no interest in Wirt in the past, is more in evidence recently, and I suspect the worst of them. The thought of losing access to our beautiful valley is too much. So I have snooped about the area for cheap property that we might be able to somehow afford. Kenneth does not feel we can afford anything, and to put it mildly was not supportive of my explorations. But not being one to be put off by practical considerations, I persisted, and the results have been exciting.

After crossing the highway at the mailboxes, the trail to our river swimming hole passes through an old apple orchard with a burbling artesian spring in the dark forest behind the small clearing. Frank Bower says the orchard on the original wagon road into the valley was the site of an early homestead. The last occupants were members of a large Negro family who were burned out (no explanation) around 1920. No one has lived there since.

My curiosity led me to the courthouse in Everett where I discovered that one Frank Rush owns the property. I telephoned Mr. Rush in Arlington and made two delightful discoveries that day. The first was that the 160-acre homestead included not only the orchard but also all the land between it and Robe Ranch. The dark little forest we drove our Model A Ford through to deliver the blueberries many years before was all part of the 160 acre homestead. But the really exciting discovery was that Mr. Rush was willing to part with the place if he could get enough money to pay the back taxes and provide him with a little extra. He allowed he would have to charge a thousand dollars for "the whole outfit".

On the one hand a thousand dollars was an impossible sum to ponder. On the other it did not seem to me to be an unreasonable price for such a beautiful place to build a cabin. The associated wooded acreage has no monetary importance but ensures the privacy important to both of us. The orchard is virtually at the foot of Mount Pilchuck with only the river between it and the property. The river is only a 10-minute walk away instead of the half hour or so from Robe Ranch. Perhaps best of all is the wonderful crystal clear icy spring that explodes from the hillside in the woods behind the meadow. Its riffles and pools define the boundary between the orchard and the forest. Small trout are apparent in the pools much to the delight of Tobey. The only fault about the place, if it is one, is the lack of any unobstructed view of the mountain. But I am sure that with the removal of a few carefully selected trees we can have a vista nearly as good as the one from the front porch of the Ranch.

After many a contentious discussion with Kenneth, a plan began to emerge. Guy Anderson was also alarmed at the prospect of being forced from Robe Ranch. The idea of buying the Rush place together evolved. Despite Kenneth's protests I approached my father who was able and willing to loan us 500 dollars to be paid back in installments. Guy obtained an equal amount from his mother and we drew up papers and closed the deal. Kenneth is sure we will "never live long enough to repay the loan".

We have signed an agreement with Guy that if either of us ever decides to sell, the seller must allow the other first refusal at the original price plus a fair amount for any buildings. Guy has begun to build already. He is not incorporating a proper foundation, using instead cedar slabs on large stones. But we've decided to build on a shale and concrete foundation. I remembered how Leonard's foundation had rotted without proper footings in this wet climate. So the slow process of hauling suitably flat rocks down from Green Mountain began. We've also scavenged some windows and lumber from abandoned buildings. Our cabin will be built at the back of the orchard near the creek. A view of Pilchuck over the old veteran apple trees will be stunning when a few big Douglas Firs come down.

Wirt has burned his hand and arm putting out another fire that got away from him. The injury didn't heal properly, and I finally talked him into going to the doctor. We delivered him to the hospital in Everett where the staff insisted he bathe before they would treat him. Wirt was incensed, especially because a large Scandinavian female nurse insisted on helping him. He later told us that he had never had anyone help him take a bath since he was a baby and he wasn't about to start then! But apparently to Wirt's chagrin, the nurse won out. Unfortunately the wound became infected and Wirt had to return for more treatment later.

Back in Seattle, we received the following two letters from Guy at Robe Ranch where he's staying while working on his cabin. One describes helping Wirt after his return from the hospital in Everett. The second is about the construction of his cabin at the other end of our orchard.

Robe Ranch, January 1945

Dear Margaret and Kenneth,

I would have given a pretty penny to see the manipulations that preceded Wirt at the bath. Never have I seen such a transformation as that which appeared at seven last night. His relatives managed to unload him quickly enough back at the ranch, probably with a sigh of relief. Frankly I don't think much of that bunch. It seems they might have at least kept him for a couple of days and then brought him home and helped him arrange himself a little more conveniently.

The first day with hot applications I would say offhand to have been a complete failure. By six o'clock tonight he had managed to get only three on and read all the rest of the time. So after I went to town and got his provisions and bandages etc. and got the wood and water and his dinner, he got to raking over the coals of his life. So I made him the proposition that he could carry out the doctor's instructions or I would quit the ranch cold and leave him to his own resources. Of course I wouldn't nor did I make it quite that bluntly, but he is acting better this evening and working at his towels. He says the doctors these days aren't very caring, not like the old time doctors, those good old days before anesthesia.

Things went very well this past week at the ranch and I had a simply divine time painting all day, and finally, I believe, I have pulled together and brought to a conclusion one of those dreadful monsters I have been working on. Nothing extraordinary, but something, and it does look quite complete. Did you see Mark's "Tattered Man" in the recent *Art Digest* with a very fine write-up? Unfortunately, the rest of the magazine is so cluttered with that typical crap that they run in full color, that in spite of the small reproductions of a few things I think there should be a concerted complaint about all the dregs of the earth they scrape up to run.

There is a light fall of snow this evening, and I think to see it in this fantastic setting is mystically beautiful. The deer have come back to the meadow. They come out of the rusty ferns at the border ever so cautiously and walk over ever so delicately to nibble the apple trees. It hurts me at the ankles to think of Eleanor boiling their feet (salvaged from a hunter's kill). But with her rattles, if she can dance the dance of the thousand little sharp hooves, then maybe the hunter is vindicated. But I think maybe he isn't.

What I'm really writing about is Margaret's illness. Do take good care and none of this overdoing stuff and being too nice to people. From Wirt's description of your nurse, I took it to be Marg Nestor. I hope so, as she is a good one all around. So probably see you in a couple of weeks.

So for now and best,

Guy.

Robe Ranch, January 1945

Dear Margaret and Kenneth,

At last we have winter and the snow is getting quite deep, but it is ever so beautiful, and the wood supply is lasting with constant adding to. Are you still on the mend and is the little hospital trip over yet?

I've been as busy as a beaver, night and day, these past couple of weeks. The plywood is finally all in place, the floor is down (wet boards), and very rough shelves and places to store junk are in place. A slapstick movie company should have been on tap to film the plywood ceiling go on. Never have I been so completely exasperated and at nerve ends. It was something awful. Just as a 4 x 8 section was about to go in place and I would be holding my breath ready to drive the first nail, down would come the whole thing on me, hammer and nails flying all over. I broke three windows and almost knocked my whatchits off, falling straddle of a saw horse. Well, finally my friend Lewis came to the rescue, and things went along quite merrily from then on. And I made a plank door that doesn't hang just right but it's heavy and opens and shuts almost all right. And now for that monster of a fireplace, which has to be finished or there just won't be enough heat. If anyone ever tells you that it's easy to build a house by yourself, just tell him or her to go jump in a volcano.

By the way, the snow is falling now. I don't know when this will get to the mail box, not that it matters, but I would like to hear how things go by all of you and when to expect you so I can have the Robe house warm.

So, hope things are going well.

Guy.

February already, a month of low vitality, too long with no sun. The flu that Guy spoke about laid me out in mid-January, and, after two weeks of choking chest congestion, fever, and night sweats, I am crawling about again, but very tired. If it hadn't been for Emily MacIntyre (not Marg Nestor) coming over every day last week and carrying on for me, so that I could stay in bed, lord knows what we'd have done. Granted, she has neither job nor family; still, there aren't many who'd have done what she did so willingly. What an anomaly she is.

I am waiting to hear from Vanguard Press on the "Cascades" job. I had to send them some old stuff from the *Town Crier* days as samples, and it may not do. If not, what the hell. Morris's second show is on at the Willard Galleries, presumably knocking 'em dead again. Mark is to have his in April. Guy sold $1,065 worth of paintings at his museum show, and Kenneth keeps hearing encouraging things about the ones he sent to the galleries. Such a flurry! I wrote a fan letter to E.B. White today, something I've long wanted to do.

Mark and George Mantor were here last night. Mark was looking well, but worrying over a slight lump below his right eye. He had a letter from Betty Willis in New York, which he read from, she being in better spirits since his pictures arrived back there. Mark hopes he won't ever have to paint under pressure for a show again. I predict more success for his coming show than the last one had. We discussed the vagaries of the art critic. Coates devotes his whole *New Yorker* review this week to Morris, "The Bird Man". Mark and we are wondering how none of them seem to be bothered by thinness and lack of structure, composition and background in Morris's work. Mark respects critic MacBride as a seasoned old man, but resents his comment that Mark's things should be reprinted on silk.

Later, Mark was wondering how anybody could know how he or she wants to paint, as I have heard him wonder so often. "I love Inness and his moods," he said, "and then I look at an abstraction, and I like that, and there're Turner and El Greco, and I can look at them and see how great they are. And the more I think about it, the more I don't know what I want to do." He has said repeatedly that he must do some more important painting from now on. Looking at our one of the men around the stove in the store, he said he would like to see it about four by six feet. "Now, wouldn't that be something for me to try to figure out -- that many people in a composition that size." The thought was overpowering. He says that he does not want to be known as a painter of that type of Americana, although he knows he can do it as no one else can. "Perhaps I've seen too many awful paintings of that sort of thing; Benton and all that crowd."

Later, we got to clowning around with the little white Angora goat rug that Dorothy Malone brought to our Tobey. Mark put it on his head bandleader style and struck a pose. He loves to do things like putting on funny hats. Then George tried it on; then it had to be put on Kenneth.

Summer, 1945.   It goes on and on; unrelenting rain here at the ranch with a real storm yesterday afternoon and this evening. The boys have been very good about making up things to do, and all dispositions have been good for the most part with only occasional outbursts of exasperation. It's really like being marooned on a tiny island. All we need is Sadie Thompson and the missionary.

I wouldn't mind a card game in this kind of weather. I think games are a wholesome diversion, and one can avoid so damned much talk as we usually seem to get into. The mood of the valley is very strong during this kind of weather. The trees are hanging their light green tassels in a sort of waiting, heavy immobility. The low mists are moving up and down and around like aimless, imprisoned spirits, seeking some way out of the encircling mountains. The steady, riveting staccato of rain is forever heard on the roof.

We went to the Darrington Timber Bowl the other day, and a good day it was. We stopped in Arlington at the second hand store and picked up a mirror, a table to be cut down for a coffee table, and an ironstone bowl. The Timber Bowl had a nice spirit: gay, colorful, simple and folksy. There were quite a number of Indians, and the queen and her princesses were dressed in blue jeans, plaid shirts, and red hats. Contests included a kids' shoe race, ladies' nail pounding, chopping and cross cut bucking for men and women. The natives were prominent in all races and contests. Tobey and David were busy in the merry-go-round and games department. David won a red balloon; Tobey, to his disgust, won only a soap dish. One of the women who lost the nail-pounding contest complained loudly to the judge afterwards saying of the winner, "them nails ain't drove flush."

Guy's been staying at his old cabin at the ranch during this wetness. It's pretty soggy down in the orchard. This morning after breakfast, Guy and I and the dogs piled into his Model A and went down to see if anyone had arrived at Emily's, as she and Mark and Per Halston were supposed to be up this week-end. There was much cleaning up and fixing up, particularly on Guy's part, and then they didn't show up. This is the second time Mark has done this. There was no one around at Emily's, but we salvaged a dented one-pound coffee can, never opened, that they had dropped and run over on their last trip. Then we went down to our salmonberry lane, but the berries were too soggy and lacking in sweetness. There was an occasional really good one, but mostly they were mediocre. There has been practically no sun since the middle of June. Anyway, I had a bath in the river this afternoon, the air being warm enough. The water was cold, however, and the river was higher than ever.

Kenneth about 1930

Margaret's handwritten note to parents

Tobey with Morris Graves' puppy, Edith, 1938

Patriotic Tobey in 1942 on the 'terrace' behind the first cabin at Robe Ranch

DEAR. TOBEY —
I have been on a [train]
to see about [painter] a [picture]

and will be [house] soon

you be a [face with halo] and I will

buy you a [package]

love [face]

A letter to Tobey at 2407 Ward Street. ca 1940.

Mark Tobey's 1940 painting, *Around the Stove*

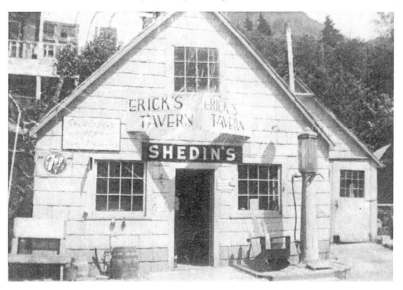

Erick's Tavern at Silverton

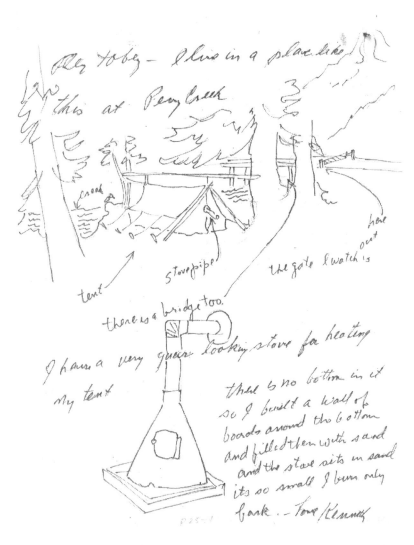

Forest guard Kenneth's base at Perry Creek, 1943.

David Perine with shakes split from cedar slabs dredged from the creek behind the house. Behind David the van body/tool house provided an irresistible mural surface for Kenneth.

Earl Storch, Dick Storch, and Vic Hill

Dorothy and Leonard Ottaway

Kenneth and friend in the orchard next to the van body converted to a gazebo after its murals were vandalized.

The cedar fence in the Robe orchard before it was moved to 1138 17th Avenue in Seattle.

Margaret with Earl and Maudie Storch on the trail to Twin Lakes

31

IT'S BEEN ALMOST A year since I've written in my journal.
I have always had trouble writing when outside events are frightening
or depressing. The world situation is certainly both of those. When
Kenneth and I got back to the ranch house the other day, Wirt was
waiting on the front porch with the boys to tell us that an atomic
bomb was about to be dropped on the island of Bikini. There had been
several delays of this event, but on March 4th it was finally happening.
We went down a little later to listen to his battery set and heard the
announcement of the dropping. It was a tense and unlovely affair, and I
hated everything about it. Inside Wirt's cabin the dirt has gathered to an
astonishing thickness. He has little bowls of dirty water that he's saving
for future washings and the inevitable dish of margarine, crisscrossed
by fine lines where he has scraped bread over it. With the steaminess
outside and the dirt and smell inside, it was just about too much. On
the radio there was that awful ticking of the countdown drumming
right on through the static and the excited voices. Then the word that
the bomb is away, she's dropping, and "there she goes," then again:
"there she goes." There were two explosions, apparently. I think of the
terrible implications of the whole thing. And there is Wirt with his old
ears plastered to the radio, saying, "I wouldn't like to be the fellow that
dropped that bomb." He too was a little worried over the possibilities
of things not going right and some dire catastrophe happening.
There is a certain relief that we're still here, although the radioactivity

business isn't too comforting. I read an article this morning in the *Seattle Sunday Times* that disgusted me into severe depression. The Red Cross is attempting to work out cleaner and purer international rules for warfare. God, there is nothing about trying to work out a plan to eliminate war; just rules to bring the laws of war up to date. I suspect them of being tools of the cartels and munitions industries.

Another reason for my lack of writing is that we spent almost every spare minute last summer and weekends since, gathering building materials for our cabin down in the orchard. Endless hours were spent hauling shale down from Green Mountain. After rationing was lifted we made many more trips up the mountain than when we began. And now, all week, we've been working on the foundation of our cabin, "we" being Guy, Kenneth and I with Dick Bennett looking on. It's at the other end of the orchard under the apple trees. Guy sets the rocks in place; Kenneth mixes and hauls cement in the old wheelbarrow, and I haul buckets of water from the creek to the site. Tobey and David amuse themselves as always by building brush houses, fishing, and scurrying about through the forest. It is quite a magical spot for boys to spend the summer. Tobey will never forget these days, I am sure. If this life gives him a real regard and love for nature, it will be the best source he could have for happiness.

Summer has really come, along with health and sun and a certain amount of time to be quiet and think. Maybe I can write, if I can decide what it shall be. I don't think I can analyze and dissect living people. I would like to take on the lives of the painters I know, but the risks are too great. Perhaps though, I could do it just for myself. Then there is the possibility of a novel based on an autobiography or a novel based on the sufficiently disguised artists. We'll see.

There was a gorgeous, rocking, swaying earthquake this morning about 9:15. I was standing by the sink wiping things down with the dishcloth, and I thought how dizzy I was feeling, but that it would no doubt pass; a most peculiar, ineffable feeling. Kenneth called from the front room, "feel the earthquake!" and then it got really very rocky, and I went outdoors and watched the trees tossing their branches, as though some giant had them by the trunk and was trying to shake down fruit. I called the others to come on out, as I was afraid a beam in the house might work loose, and they finally came, Tobey looking a little worried, and he and David wanting to know what caused quakes. The swaying must have lasted all of two or three minutes. It was like standing on the waves of a solid sea, which of course is just what it is. It was the strangest, undulating feeling, kind of wonderful and awe-inspiring. I wonder how much it was felt in town. It seems as though we're having these quakes quite often of late. God knows how we'll be affected when they get through playing with the atom bombs on the Bikini atoll. The idiots! The best news in the world right now would be if they would call that little party off as a completely worthless and definitely catastrophic bit of high folly on the part of low minds.

Twenty-two days without rain, another record and so different from last year. Out here on the porch there is greenness and veiled sunlight. Pilchuck is clear to the top but clouds are slowly gathering. Rain has been threatening for days but holding off. A Forest Service truck is here, and the greenery is scorched all around the lower fence because Wirt got the idea of burning off the shrubs and bracken. He says the fire was accidental and has an elaborate story all worked out. The deer were sneaking under the fence, and he must have just thrown his match into the dry grass. He went to chase the deer, and when he came back it was blazing. So Kenneth and two U.S.F.S. employees, Wes Harlander and Ken Wallin, have been working with axes and shovels and a water pump all afternoon. Wirt is hacking away at the weeds in the garden, happy as can be to have all this company and activity going on around him. It's a good thing we came up from the work in the orchard and could alert the Forest Service. He insisted there was no danger, but when we arrived there were stumps smoldering all around and a very brisk breeze blowing right in the direction of his little house and the surrounding forest. The idea of burning up in his sleep doesn't bother him in the least. We are a little puzzled as to why Guy hasn't shown up recently. Morris is at his Woodway Park acreage, which is probably why Guy is staying there. We took a look at his place and at Emily's last night and all seems to be intact and unmolested.

September 12, 1946. It's been a week and a half since the fall return to Seattle. I'm catching up on washing, cleaning, ironing, and the weedy, neglected yard. I miss the Robe Valley and yearn for the haunting loveliness of the old orchard, with its intermittent thud of early apples falling to the lush turf, the musical burble of the creek in the dark forest behind the house, the enchanted spot by the river where the demolished cabin stands, bereft of its beautiful shakes (now fronting our cabin), the great, aged maples turning slowly golden, the leaves slipping through the still, late summer air. There were magical swims with the river low enough and warm enough for comfort; the river tamed after its turbulent spring. Tobey learned a lot about swimming. He gets his head under without fear, and even dives a little.

The river had changed its course radically during the previous winter, giving us a bigger gravel bar, a new little sand beach on the near side, and piling the sand up several feet higher on the far side, where it had also added a giant spruce snag to the scenery. Its roots perch on the rocks; its trunk stretches across the sand bar. The large pool to the left as you leave the woods path to come onto the beach is completely wiped out. The little isolated pools here and there in the rocks at the beginning of summer were marvelous for shallow bathing.

I had a swim on Labor Day, and many, many days before that. Packing shakes from the abandoned building was hot and strenuous, but the spot was so charming a place to be that memories of the work are all pleasant. We would take our lunch, work all morning, ripping them off, knocking out nails, and packing them along the trail; then we'd have our sandwiches and a swim first, perhaps, if it were very hot. Then it was more work, after a good deal of talk, then a mid-afternoon swim until time to go up and get dinner. What a life! Idyllic! And so simple. What more do people want? It is a temptation to sell this house and take whatever we could clear, after paying up what we owe, and take our chances, living by painting and writing. We could live cheaply up there. Someday, I'm sure that's what we'll do.

The Leaf

Is this significant?
A yellowed alder leaf
Floats down the Stillaguamish
In August,
Suspended
Below the surface of the light-pierced stream,
Water,
Mellifluously green,
Melodiously flowing
Over trout-patterned rocks and sand,
On to deeper pools
Leaving on the granite bosom of the shore
Foamy bubbles, twirling a waltz,
Coasting in from the singing riffles
Upstream.

One sits upon the sun-hot rocks
Remembering
The floods of spring;
Then thundering tons of bilious melted snow
Came roaring down,
Tossing that hundred feet of snaggy spruce,
A monstrous carcass,
On the rocks where it's now high and dry.
A cougar walked it recently and
Paused mid-bridge
To leave his royal dung.

Rain and thunder,
Wind and thrashing bough
All played their parts in full orchestral glory,
Crescendo of the Gods.

Now the andante,
For strings and gentle reeds and timpani.

On this same river
Which, three moons back,
Careened a giant Spruce,
There now floats slowly by through dappled shade,
A yellowed alder leaf,
Prismatically entombed.

32

"THE CALLAHANS!" AND ORRE Nobles pounced upon us with the avid joy of an old tabby after a mouse. It had been years since we'd seen him. His hair had turned pure white and receded a little, and his face and brow were very pink. He'd finally finished his house, which perches daintily with its scalloped trim on "Profanity Hill" above the tough part of Seattle, the hill just above the police court. The house always reminds me of that joke we heard during the war about the training camp: the barracks being just a bunk and window, bunk and window, then bunk and lace curtains, bunk and window, etc.

He was all agog over Betty MacDonald's success with her *Egg and I* book, remembering that sister Mary had come to his place on the canal for her honeymoon with that nice, quiet Dr. Jensen. What a funny girl she was, always saying stink in the oddest places. His old friend Mrs. Pixley had sold her house on 15th in the University District to the Bards and they'd never paid her any money because they were so poor, and Mrs. Pixley used to look at him with a glare and snap, "*your* friend, Mary Bard!"

The occasion was the preview of the Ambrose and Viola Patterson retrospective with dinner first at the Isaacs. Margaret and Peter Camfferman, Mrs. Griffiths, the Conways, the Pats and we were there, and of course Orre. It was very pleasant to see Pat's older paintings. I'd love to own the snow picture of Trinity Church, two of the Paris ones, and the brilliant, freely painted one of La Push.

Orre came up as I was talking with Pat, exclaiming in that idiotic, gleeful manner, "this is a wonderful show! There's something to please everybody." And remembering the snow photo in the newspapers, he commented about what a fine Christmas card it would make. Pat looked over everybody's head and, blinking rapidly, said, "yes, yes, well, thank you. Yes. There is a little of everything isn't there." And Orre said, "well, why *not?*"

Mark was here Saturday evening, the first time in months. He brought a book called *Black Elk Speaks* inscribed to Tobey, and he also brought his best manners. We talked of the idea of working out a book together of his lectures on interpreting pictures; what art is all about, etc. I think it could be done, together with a folio of prints from color plates. He may go to England in the spring or summer. He's angling to go back to Dartington with the Elmhirsts. I wish he could forget all the gallery business and just get back to painting. But he worries that sales have dropped off. He says he hasn't sold a picture in New York for a year. Still, he maintains three separate places. His rents and heating expenses alone must be well over $200 a month.

Morris, according to Mark, has been seeing little gnomes, who come on birds' feet and peer into his door, whispering, "ask for a booooon". He gilded his beard for Christmas and made appearances everywhere, including the Garden of Allah nightclub. Theresa wants to do a book on Mark, Morris and Kenneth. But Morris assures her he is not interested in an art career or publicity. He has a great mission to accomplish. He is getting more and more messianic as he prepares for his Japan trip.

Kenneth is working much too hard of late, I'm afraid. Perhaps during spring vacation we can take a few days off and relax in the country. It would be marvelous if the weather were good. He and I were in the market for lunch today – upstairs at Mannings, all done over with new walls, new tables and chairs and, best of all, new windows you can really look out of. The marketers eat there, with much exchange of camaraderie.

Well, I am 43 today, and tomorrow Tobey is nine. The only thing that troubles me about the years is the way work doesn't get done. And of course occasionally the "abysses" William James mentions in his heroic chapter called *Death and the Importance of Living*. It should be required reading for everyone.

Morris is off to unknown parts again, probably New Orleans. Strangely, as happened before when he and Mark had been seeing much of each other, there was no communication between us and Mark, but now that Morris has left, Mark is much more friendly. Maybe it's just that Morris supplies the companionship he needs, and when he goes, Mark looks elsewhere, and there's no more to it than that. But we fancied he was feeling hostile toward us.

He and Guy were here at lunchtime yesterday. We were looking at Henry Moore's things in *Life* magazine and the Penguin book. Mark feels there's something strange and wrong with Moore's feeling toward women. "When I look at all these twisted forms, with the navel all pulled out and the tortured things he does with them, I say to myself, what *is* it between himself and women? What is wrong? He must hate them to do these dreadful things." I said I thought he tried to ally all forms in nature, seeing the female form in relationship to stone and driftwood, etc. No. Mark thought it something deeply psychological and unresolved in his own nature. I think homosexuals too often resent any preoccupation with fertility.

Kenneth seems diverging lately from his many-peopled, chaotic universes and is doing small things with small groups, getting interesting texture and more solidity and sculptural feeling. I approve. He talked to the Study Guild Tuesday. He made the point about all real art being both universal and anchored in the artist's region. The Guild finally bought a painting. Also, a Dr. Foxworthy bought one of the little logging accident works. I think we still have the one I like best.

Art School

"What would you paint, my bold young man?
What in the world would you paint?
The delights of the eye?

258

The clouds in the sky?
The boats on the sea?"
"Ah, fiddle-de-dee!
Something more rare,
Like the little white square
On the white piece of paper for me."

"What would you paint, my tired young man?
What in the world would you paint?
The turn of the thigh, the pulse of a heart?
A child, a Madonna, or maybe a whore?"
"Oh, God, what a bore.
The things you suggest,
It is quite manifest,
Have been painted too often before."

"What would you paint, my sad young man?
What in the world would you paint?
Still life with a bottle?
How light and shade mottle?
Sin tempting a saint?"
"Oh, use some restraint!
When all's done and said,
I refuse to be led.
What's the matter with just painting paint!"

The Valentine fever is on, said Tobey this morning, in giving orders for how many, preferably one cent ones, he would require. "The trouble is there are too many girls that like me, and I don't like them." "How do you know they like you?" "Oh, they write me letters, you know, notes in school…" "What do the letters say?" "Oh you know, 'I like you' and stuff like that." "Don't you like any of the girls? Which ones do you like best?" "Oh, I kind of like McCaleb, but not very much. No, I don't like them very well." "What other boys do the girls like?" "They like me and Jack Bernard – there are two, you might say, gangs of girls at school and one gang likes Jack and the other gang doesn't, and the gang that doesn't yells names at him and the gang that does chases them and they're always having battles." He says the girls are always chasing the boys, grabbing their caps and throwing them. Then the boys can't get even or tell because that would be tattling on a girl. It all sounds pretty familiar. The pattern doesn't change much.

Probably because I long to be at the cabin, but for whatever reason, there is a strange dead atmosphere about Sundays in town. I don't like them. I have always felt the same restlessness. Kenneth is painting upstairs, as always, and the awful drone of the radio goes on and on. I don't know how he can stand it but he's never without it.

Kenneth must have read long-distance what I've been writing, as he turned off the radio. Now I can hear the piano from next door. The Reverend Dunstan, incidentally the only other non-Catholic among our neighbours, is a fairly accomplished pianist from the sound of it.

Our latest house at 1138 17th North suits us. We are only a few blocks from Kenneth's job at the art museum, and Tobey can get to school without crossing that dangerous 23rd avenue at the top of Montlake Hill. We are putting in a larger window in the east bedroom upstairs. Kenneth will then have a lighter, brighter studio with a clear view over Lake Washington to the Cascades. We also have our own garage in the alley overlaid by a rampant Concord grape vine.

It has been a busy winter. Great Books is every two weeks, the Americans for Democratic Action (A.D.A.) meet monthly and currently there are Tuesday concerts of Mahler with George Mantor officiating. He buys enormous albums of 12 inch 78 records and, once we are ensconced before the fireplace with drinks and cigarettes, George demands absolute quiet while he tends the phonograph. The effect is pretty close to an actual concert with more creature comforts.

Morris came by to tell us he's very depressed over the article in *Time* magazine. He would like letters to be written and I wouldn't mind registering my own resentment over the statement about artists avoiding steady work, as though painting wasn't work. It is true that he has avoided getting a regular job to support himself while painting, but the idea that painting is loafing isn't fair. The business of Morris cutting himself off from all social responsibilities is, however, difficult for me to accept. His refusal to co-operate in any way with the draft board during the war is only one example.

The last Great Books session was on Montaigne. We concentrated on different approaches to education. Are the schools doing a good job? No, said most of us. The fear of exploring ideas so evident in adults now has a devastating effect on the young. Their emptiness is pitiful to behold. The discussion moved from education to fear. What it is, and who fears what today. Miss Brown as usual offered a positive philosophical opinion. She is an interesting individual, small of stature, about 60 I think, and so alive and full of spirit. An old time socialist, I suspect. The leader is a retired Navy commander but he has escaped stultification. He thinks and has integrity and a nice sense of humor. We love this group and have most happy experiences there.

Kenneth's Belgium show is on presently. There was a lengthy comedy of prologue: cables, wires and letters about shipping and timing etc. We keep hoping to hear of sales from the show, but so far only one, for 16,000 francs, whatever that might be in dollars. His paintings say so much that human beings need to know in these times. That their content can go over with the public is my prayer. He's now working on the Washington state capital dome mural sketches. He has developed a good thing around the seven days of Genesis.

I have come to love the market again, and the brief meetings with Don Mars are a part of it. He sometimes works at the horsemeat market and on other occasions I see him at the fish market. We have the most pleasant exchanges. He is struggling to get through law school. I suppose he will be at Gonzaga University next winter, and I'll miss him. I'm hoping he and his girl will come up to the mountains for a day this summer, as I would like to get to know him better. I really want to know more about the market from the inside, and he has worked there since he was a boy. He's also done commercial fishing, another world to know.

There are so many wonderful people in the market. Mary Jensen and I had a long talk recently with Mrs. Morgan, an 89-year-old flower seller. She has a German accent, prominent pleading eyes, thin lips and a sharp jaw. She sells thin bunches of dried grasses in containers. Her stall would make a great portrait: old black-brimmed felt hat, green coat, green bench with grasses and bouquets, and the backdrop of the market.

We also talked with the Norwegian antique shop woman, she all pinned together at the neck with an old silver buckle. An amazing hat, set high and square on her head, was decorated with a tinselly band all ruffled and double ruffled. Out of the blue she said, "We've all got to die. No reason to be afraid. It's just the mystery behind it."

Mark was here last night for another art criticism session. "I like this," covering part of a Kenneth painting, "but then something happens in here. I don't know what." And on another one: "You have to break up your green house, can't be all green. You've got all your interesting forms below. Down in the lower half it's a pretty rich dish, and then above, it just becomes an ordinary bill of fare..." and so on. He read an interesting letter from Betty Willis in which she concludes, "Modern art is dead, long live art." Mark's comment was "I'd like to ask her who she thinks the offenders are."

After we went to bed, I read to Kenneth the article in the June *Harpers* on Einstein's theories of the universe. This is the concluding one of three. I'm sure his descriptions come closer than any of the other scientists to the real nature of things. His unified field theory is, I think, what I've been sensing for some years. That is that everything is part of the same thing, just variations in the concentration of mass. I am also reading astronomy and finding it fascinating. What vistas. And so few are alive to it. I think of Sophocles' ultimate message: Look, wonder, think.

33

SUMMER. 1947. WIRT IS in a rest home in Everett. Leonard found him under his stove with his feet sticking out. "What are you doing under there Wirt?" asked Leonard. "Checking the stove. What the hell do you think I'm doing," answered Wirt. Actually he had a stroke of some sort and had collapsed in the garden patch at least two days before. When he woke up he crawled from the garden into his shack and figured he might survive until the Callahans or someone showed up, if he could push himself under the stove to keep warm. When he tried to get out later he was stuck. He had no idea how long he had been there under the very cold stove where Leonard found him. We were in Everett the other day and called on him at the rest home. We again heard the story of Ella Turner adopting the homeliest girl in the orphanage because no one else would. Says Wirt, "She turned out to be a real beauty, a *real* beauty." He is about the same, other than his nose cancer is progressively worse. He said that if we ever want an old Winchester 22 rifle to ask Frank Bower for the one he *loaned* him years ago.

We hiked the Coal Creek trail to Coal Lake today, about three miles from the highway, through a stately forest. The trail is perfect. It's covered with a matted black duff embedded with tiny hemlock cones and twigs. It springs you along from step to step for one stretch. Another section along a steep slide requires caution. The lake is in a basin, walled by steep cliffs. It's wooded on one side and on the other an old avalanche of boulders disappears into the water. At the far end there is a beautiful growth of young Alaska Cedar at the base of the cliffs. Trilliums are blooming profusely in the rock gardens at the approach to the lake. Behind us where we perched on a log to take in the beauty was a stand of venerable Mountain Hemlock. Over two feet in diameter, they were there when Columbus landed. The lake was clear and green and ice cold. It should be good swimming in another month. Tobey and Dave Perine caught a few big trout.

We had a sad little meal at the Ottaways this evening, and the boys caught a lot of fish up the creek behind their clearing. Talking with little Mrs. Pomeroy was also great fun. She's a small dark woman of spirit. Her husband is in bed following a third heart attack. They have the little cedar mill in back of the Ottaways. Her daughter, a tiny thing, drives a ten-wheel army truck full of cedar. The daughter, city-bred, and son-in-law have settled in the valley and love it. They wouldn't go back to the city for anything.

The fourth of July brings back memories of my childhood. I think often of our family's summers at Ellisport: the charm of the woods, the beach, the big dining room, the wonderful meals, the little girls I liked to play with. At the after-the-afternoon-nap gathering we were all combed, washed and dressed in starched clean gingham dresses. Margaret Corbet's curls always looking perfect with the comb marks showing in their damp, dark crispness. We spent endless hours with small dolls, making clothes, dressing and undressing them and playing house. I remember the magic of an old snag with a ladder up it and a platform at the top, among the leafy boughs of a huge tree. Yesterday was the first real Fourth of July Tobey has had, and then it didn't compare with the glories of my childhood at Ellisport with the roman candles, sky rockets, pin wheels, etc. But anyway, they had firecrackers and sparklers, the first available after the long war years. Last night, after a session of fishing in the swamp, they made a ceremony of the sparklers, running with them through the pasture, whooping and leaping. They looked like enormous animated fireflies throwing off sparks, fluttering over the meadow in the twilight. The sky was clear, and Jupiter was luminous, moving ever toward the west, where the first stars Arcturus and Antares were glowing faintly.

Kenneth has made the boys a raft, which will navigate the creek among the marsh grasses and tangled willow growth. The beaver dam has increased the amount of water down there. Last evening we spent the hour just before dusk with them. There were a few clouds, pink with the sun's late rays. The tops of the evergreens surround this basin-like hollow, which once was a lake at the end of the glacier. It's so easy to become lost in the speculation of earlier times, to imagine the great glaciers into existence, grinding down the gravel, piling up their moraines, icy streams flowing from their dripping maws.

The area is still changing rapidly in geologic time. I was talking with Grandma Otto recently in her little frame house near Susie's. The cranberry bogs of her youth sounded fascinating. They used to take their children and lunch and go behind their place for a day and pick cranberries. The berries rested on the mossy peat and could be picked up by the handful. "It was like a different world back there," she said. "Beautiful view of the mountain, no trees, a small lake with fish. It's all changed now…" Today the whole area is a willow swamp with beaver dams and clumps of large spruce and cedar.

The other day we went into Everett to see Wirt again. We took him socks and magazines. He said, "Oh, I'll never be able to read all those. I'm slipping fast lately – can't last much longer." His voice has become weaker, but his mind is just the same, except that time doesn't mean anything now. He asked again if we were living in the new house yet. We mentioned Australia and he said, "Oh yes, that was where the wart hog came from." He had seen one in the San Diego Zoo once – so homely you couldn't believe it – all over warts as long as your finger. He said, "I looked at it with my mouth open, and the wart hog looked kind of ashamed." Then he drifted into the following scenario: "…like the man who came across another man and said 'I always swore if I saw a man uglier than myself I'd shoot him', and the other man said, 'Well, if I'm uglier than you I don't want to live, so go ahead and shoot'."

April 1948: Our house is "finished". That is, the shakes are on the roof and sides and the second floor is laid. The partition containing the closet, kitchen cabinets, and ladder to the loft have been built. The sink is in, and the upstairs walls are finished with shiplap. We can see the running water of the little creek from the back windows and from the front it's the old apple trees. We'll see Mt. Pilchuck when the trees across the road are cut down.

Wirt is still in the rest home and is insisting he wants to go back to Robe this spring. One side of his nose is nearly gone and that spot on his upper forehead is still burning. He works crossword puzzles, reads through a magnifying glass and plays solitaire. He is happier because the Swede who snores is gone. "Never could stand a Swede anyway," he growled. The only reason the Swede snored, of course, was to plague Wirt. The rest home nurse thinks his time left is short. I don't want to think about it.

A logger named Earl Storch has been trying to arrange a tree-cutting plan with Mr. Hansen, the owner of the property between the river and us. He came around this afternoon to say he would start taking the trees off this week. At last we will be able to sit on our porch and look at Pilchuck. How wonderful that will be.

It's August already and, while the rain falls, the loggers fall the trees that block our light and view. It is amazing how many small problems they are having setting up their equipment and falling the trees. "They" are Earl, his brother Dick, and a towhead in a pink plaid shirt and red cap named Vic Hill. It turns out that this is the first logging job for their small "gypo" outfit. They have a tiny donkey engine, Ford V-8 powered with two rusty old cable spools, mounted on twin skids. I've nicknamed it Dinky the Donkey. Their logging truck is an old bakery van. Earl gave us the van portion to use as a tool house. The remaining truck bed looks too small to hold the logs they plan to pile on it but we'll see. As the trees come down the difference in the outlook is so wonderful I keep going to the window and gazing. July was three times wetter than normal, and August promises to be the same.

A major disaster was narrowly averted. We watched Earl top the spar tree, a large Douglas fir on one side of the clearing created by the fallen trees. As we watched through field glasses he moved his steel spurs with careful deliberation, sure of each step. With easy grace he dodged around to the opposite side when the top cracked off. He has a strong, handsome face with a wide mouth, olive skin, dark hair and metallic blue eyes. Even with the strain of chopping while belted to the top of the tree his face remained serene.

After Earl had topped the tree he climbed back up and strapped and spiked a small block that held a new steel cable to the tree near the top. It was then Vic Hill's job to be pulled up the tree by the cable in a homemade "boson's chair". Attached to a harness around his waist was much heavy gear including a larger "bull" block, tools and cable ends to be attached to the tree top as guy lines. Just as he reached the small block at the top, the new steel cable snapped. Vic grabbed at a stub of a branch with one hand and somehow let his harness and all of its attached hardware loose with his free hand. Within a second or two he lost his grip and fell slowly backwards, completing one complete somersault in the air before disappearing into the limbs and jagged stumps at the base of the tree 70 ft. below.

Earl had been operating the winch to pull Vic and the load up the tree. Kenneth, David and Tobey had been standing in our yard watching. Before Kenneth or Earl could reach the base of the tree, a very pale Vic was making his way toward us under his own steam. His only obvious injury was a nose scratch. When he reached the road, clearly shaken, he said, "I guess I better go to the Doc and get checked out." He had indeed survived the fall without injury. Earl later completed the rigging with a different cable, but I couldn't watch.

Today the loggers' wives (Mrs. Storch and Mrs. Hill), the Storch baby and the Storch father – all came to call, ostensibly at first to see the men, and the spar tree Vic fell from, but it was lunch time so they all came in and we had coffee and sandwiches. The talk became very easy and pleasant. Mr. Storch is a beautiful old man with a kind sweet face. He must have been handsome when young. They are all most kindly, humorous about their work, venturesome, serious, yet ready to laugh, interested in making money but not absorbed by the thought. Mostly they're concerned with the business of living. It's all very refreshing. The wives and husbands love each other. They adore the baby, but not fatuously. They are devoted and loyal friends and they have a good time. The whole experience of the logging and getting to know these people has been most happy and restoring of faith. I hope I can do a good article on "the boys" and that Chet at the *Seattle Times* will accept it.

It is apparent we are to have no summer. I'm resigned and I must get as much writing done as possible. The boys are finding chanterelles. We barbecued salmon last night, Indian style, with alder wood, and spirea sticks for skewers. Entirely succulent.

Just when we were becoming increasingly depressed by the rainy summer, the rains have increased. It has become so wet it is all of a sudden intensely dramatic and interesting. I spent the entire afternoon standing about watching "the logging". They attempted to haul in some logs that were recalcitrant due to siwashes (strain caused by cables sliding around stumps or tree trunks). Dick and Vic were down in the brush chopping away branches and setting chokers. Earl was running the donkey. Speaking of the little donkey lacking in power, yelled Dick, "that thing wouldn't pull a hat off a hat-rack." Earl's response was, "try getting the choker off those stumps and put it around some logs for a change." Vic told me again about the "Molly Hogans," the "school marms," "siwashes," etc. and said most of the logging terms couldn't be spoken in female company.

August 30: The end of the logging and the end of our summer. We had a party at our cabin Saturday night, one of those happy affairs, everyone quite high. Played lots of records, Benny Goodman, with dancing and laughter. Earl is a lovely dancer with ballroom manners and a way of clapping a little at the end. I could hardly bear it. I really never expected to be danced again! Dick Bennett did a real Irish jig and everyone clapped. As the night grew late we tried a Spanish flamenco and the Borodin classic on them, and they all decided promptly to go home. Said Vic, "It sounds like concert music to me." I had wanted very much to get our water system and septic tank in this summer, but painting sales were slow. So maybe this fall, or if not, next summer for certain.

34

THIS STORY WAS WRITTEN in March, 1949. Winter was tottering but still in the saddle. It details a typical weekend at the cabin........

Once more we were bound for the mountains, for our 160 acres in the valley, which we hadn't seen since a Christmas tree-cutting expedition early in December. Nature was still groggy from a knockout freeze. Our normal mild, moist climate had given way to zero temperatures, blizzards, and harsh, dry air. Accustomed to fog, rain, and occasional nippy frosts, we found both our lips and our dispositions becoming chafed and rough.

The trunk of our '39 Ford was loaded with sleeping bags, blankets, cartons of food; the back seat with boys and dogs, two of each. We were wrapped from the cold like a bunch of mummies, but still we had to keep knocking our toes together. "You boys would be warmer if you'd sit close together in the middle of the seat," I suggested, but this of course was impossible, for each had to be by a window. Tobey and David had been neighbours and schoolmates since the first grade and were like brothers. Although Tobey was an only child, the threadbare condition of our hall and stair carpet could attest to how seldom he had been inflicted with that status. Two Davids were his best friends, and David Sjostrom provided the companionship this time.

Heading out of Seattle by way of the university district and Bothell, we scanned the roadside for changes produced by the weeks we'd been city bound. A huge slide near Woodinville had wiped out the railroad tracks. At Machias, the Pekoe's (for years our source of fresh brown eggs) fine brick fireplace was all finished. The poor old, black bull was still chained by his nose ring to the post on the banks of Bear Creek. A few doors and windows were installed in the place we called the "Jukes house," a real slum, overflowing with children and rough adults. We were told that Pa had sold everything removable to raise money for liquor. A section of guardrails was knocked out on the "crooked mile" just before Granite Falls, where a log truck had once again spilled its load. Some huge shaggy rounds of fir salvaged for firewood were still strewn among the flattened roadside bushes.

At Granite Falls, the last town on our route, we stopped for last minute purchases. While David and Tobey lit out to buy comics, salmon eggs for bait, and ice cream cones, Kenneth picked up a few cans of beer at the Pioneer tavern, and I dove into the warmth of Pruitt's Grocery. I was paralyzed from the long, cold drive, but my spirits were soaring, as they always were when we reached this final crossroads outpost. Foothill towns like Granite Falls have an atmosphere very much their own, quite different from valley and shore settlements.

Two men in the beat-up clothes and shapeless hats of loggers were comparing notes on donkey engines, while their wives prowled about among the shelves, squinting at canned and packaged goods with the intense concentration of any careful shopper.

I asked about the Jim Creek project, if work had opened up there. The Navy was building an enormous radar and broadcasting station said to be the biggest in the world in a canyon about thirteen miles southeast of Granite. Some three hundred acres were to be cleared of trees and stumps and sprayed with chemicals so that no vegetation of any kind could exist.

"Oh, they're going ahead with the job, all right," Tom said, shaking his head, "but it isn't doing Granite Falls any good. The government went into Everett and hired construction workers to do their land clearing. The I.W.A. is picketing the place, but so far they've refused to hire any loggers."

The two men were listening, their faces heavy and solemn. "Why, Chrissake, it ain't construction work any way you look at it," one of them said. "It's straight logging, that's what it is. It's falling, bucking, choker setting, loading – and if that ain't logging, I'm a lady barber."

"They got plenty construction work without hiring them fellows to do their logging, too," the other said. "The goddamn cable is two miles long; they're stringing it from one mountain to another, two thousand feet high. You know, I heard they'll be able to broadcast anywhere in the world right from them towers."

Kenneth came into the store wearing his glowering, 'you're-taking-too-long-to-shop' expression. There were times when he was convinced that everything, myself included, was engaged in a monstrous conspiracy to keep him from painting. Mr. Pruitt was checking the items, mumbling to himself. "Let's see now – bacon, hamburger, milk buttermilk, matches, peanut butter, canned milk, brown sugar, bananas, kerosene – sure that's all?"

Wrestling the load into the trunk, Kenneth grumbled, "You'd think we were staying for three weeks rather than three days." Even after eighteen years of marriage he had never quite lost his resentment at life's necessary encumbrances. He had a wistful sense that you should be able to just walk out of the house, into the car, and arrive at your destination with everything magically arranged ahead of time. The boys, bored with waiting, were locked in a wrestling hold, the dogs watching them apprehensively. "No scuffling in the car,' I said automatically, hoping I wouldn't have to repeat it more than three times. " We aren't scuffling," Tobey said, his muffled voice coming from somewhere under David's left leg. "Gimme back my comic!" David yelled.

I had carried on a losing war against the reading of comics in our household. Kenneth insisted it would do more harm to forbid them, which would give them an exaggerated importance. He said that, if he has books, companions, contact with nature, games, crayons and paints, the comics and radio programs can't leave too big an impression. It's only when the rest of their lives are impoverished that these things become a menace. I came to agree after seeing the fascination with which children who were forbidden comics at home sat on the edge of Tobey's bed and devoured his old ones by the hour.

"I guess we'll have to stop at Jack Webb's" Kenneth said, with barely restrained exasperation. "The gas tank's almost empty." Minor obstacles such as this brought out the beast in Kenneth, but in the face of major calamities, he was the unruffled philosopher. The usual quota of jalopies, mud-splattered logging trucks, trailers, and miscellaneous small trucks were huddled about Webb's Texaco Station like mute patients in a medical clinic.

"While you're getting gas, I'll run over to the Storches for a minute. I want to leave these books for Danny." "Tell them to come up tomorrow, if they feel like it," Kenneth called. The Storches' small, neat house, square and white, was just around the corner. Earl Storch was hammering at something on the motor of his truck, parts of which were strewn about the ground like autumn leaves after a gale. He grinned, waved his free hand and shouted, "Hi! Goin' up the line? Maudie's in the house. I'll be in after a minute."

Maudie, sitting on the chintz-covered couch, below the tasseled mirror, was half buried in knitting stuff. She was a small, pale, intensely feminine person. It seems that men and women in rural communities often hover at the extremes of masculinity and femininity. The curves of their lives meet only in domestic functions, and then swerve in opposite directions. The men find companionship with other men, working, hunting, or playing poker. The women gather with other housewives talking offspring, attending showers, or playing a friendly afternoon game of poker. "See the sweater I'm making for Earl!" Maudie said proudly, smoothing it out to display the intricate pattern. It was dark blue with two deer worked into the front. "Come and see how I dyed the bedroom curtains," she said, carefully laying the knitting on the couch. "Danny is asleep, but if we're quiet, he won't wake up. He's had the sniffles."

Danny, not quite two, slumbered soundly in the pink and blue world of his crib. The walls of the bedroom were hung with family photographs, several of Earl in his Air Corps captain's uniform. A rather regal wedding pose of the two, with Maudie splendid in travel suit, orchids and a new hair wave, sat on a dresser. The groom had comb marks showing in the slicked-down hair and a smile lit with pride and confidence.

Earl, a mill town boy with a high school diploma and a passion for flying, had gone into the war a buck private and had returned a captain in the air corps with six months' experience as a combat pilot in the Pacific. Carefully put away in a bureau drawer were the official photographs of his missions. He had shown them to us after considerable pressure had been applied, saying little and wearing an intense and vaguely troubled frown. I admired the freshly dyed curtains and tiptoed back to the living room.

Earl was lighting a cigarette and warming himself by the shiny brown wood heater, the chimney of which ran into a closed-up fireplace of varnished cobblestones. "Well, we sold the mill," he announced, grinning briefly, then frowning. I said I hoped they got a fair price. The mill had been the culmination of a post-war dream. The handsome officer returned to the hometown he had left as an awkward, mill hand kid. There would be no more working for wages as his father had done; no kicking around from job to job during the depression. He'd be his own boss, build his own mill, have his own logging operations, pile up some money quick, own things, travel, send the kids to college.

He'd built the mill all right, and with the help of their wartime savings, had financed his logging equipment: truck, donkey, rigging. And luck had provided an initial opportunity: a fine patch of old growth trees. But looking about for more timber, he found saw logs were hard to get. Too many other young men had hatched the same plan, and the big mills were buying everything they could lay their ever-ready contracts on.

"Yeah," he said soberly, "some Everett fellows bought the mill. They think they can get enough logs to keep it running. Well, I hope they're right." He paused. "Syd Holmes will be running his outfit again in a week or two. Wants me back as sawyer. I don't feel like I can pass up 450 bucks a month just now, so I guess I'll wait until fall to go to school." School was an accounting course under the G.I. Bill: an opportunity I had encouraged, but was abstract and vague to Earl, and time was running out. Wages were still good, when you could work. Logging wasn't a bad occupation if it was steady; I'd heard Earl and his friends say. But the wives would always respond, "I want Earl (or Vic or Dick) to get out of the woods before he gets his. It's too dangerous."

I saw the car through the window and as a long honk split the air, I said good-bye, calling back, "Kenneth's in a hurry. He said to tell you hello and to come on up tomorrow if you feel like it." "It's Mama's birthday tomorrow, so my family will be coming here for dinner," Maudie said. "Stop in on your way back to town."

In these isolated regions where large families are clustered, birth, illness, and death are woven into a tapestry, sparse in pattern, but rich in overtones: the ceremonial days, the winter's firewood, getting meat for the locker, seasonal canning, whiskey on Saturday night, the long boredom of enforced idleness, moments of release through getting drunk, making love, and over it all the powerful association with nature. These meanings are lost in cities where special occasions are often relegated to casual gestures.

The foothill towns these days with the old growth trees almost gone leave the people scrambling for the meager yield of the second growth forest. These pioneer settlements are clinging to their existence with their fingernails, jumping from season to season like Eliza on the ice floes. The character of the people is written in the weather-toughened faces of the men and the sorrow-marked faces of the women; faces reflecting lives lived without the protective screen of modern city facades.

The town of Granite Falls is laid out on a flat between the Pilchuck and Stillaguamish Rivers. Here, over a forest trail, the Stillaguamish Indians packed their canoes from one river to the other. The first white settlers named the site Portage, but the majesty of the nearby spot where the Stillaguamish hurls itself over a series of water-sculptured granite terraces prevailed with the villagers, and they changed the name to Granite Falls.

Our car, feeling its load, plodded patiently up the long grade of the Sand Hill. The dogs suddenly snapped out of their snooze and quivered with excitement. They stuck their snoots to the breeze, vibrating their black nostrils and alert tails in a frenzy of recognition, for we were nearly there.

"My ears popped," Tobey announced. "So'd mine," David chimed in. We all felt the same inner excitement the dogs were showing. "Look at Swamp Lake," David shouted, "it's still got ice." Broken patterns of slush covered the small lake. Across the water the Saunier's homestead farm nestled among the evergreens. Shrewd old Joe Saunier had the biggest trees in the valley, and he said flatly that nobody was going to cut them. He had a peculiar conviction that trees were important to the health of the land!

At the crest of Sand Hill the air had a new, exhilarating quality. From here we saw once again the whole sweep of our valley, tree-textured and mountain-rimmed; a view so familiar yet always new and, except for the ribbon of road, as wild as if no one had traversed it. Until seventy years ago, no white man had.

Among the trees the snow lay in thin, irregular patches, but on each side of the road was a two-foot bank of dirty slush, pushed there by the snowplough. Both our driveway and the original road to Robe Ranch opposite were blocked with snow. "You can go ahead and get the fires built," Kenneth said. "I'll dig out a place to park and the boys can haul the stuff in on the sled."

The narrow driveway ran with streamlets of thawing snow water. Overhanging boughs of hemlock and cedar dripped icy droplets down my neck. The air, damp and aromatic, reached deep into my lungs. Cakes of wet snow still sat like brooding hens on the flattened salmonberry bushes at the side of the road. Catching hold, I gave it a jerk and it sprang into the air, generously baptizing me with a cold shower.

The road forks, one branch leads to Frank Bower's solitary cabin, an old mill pond and the train tunnels through the river's gorge. The other fork leads across a small plank bridge over our gushing creek to the clearing just beyond. Nature was still asleep. Only the movement of water was alive, an incessant harmony, trickling, murmuring, dripping, and gurgling. The orchard clearing lay at the extreme southeast corner of our acreage. Covering about two acres, it was level, grass-covered, and flanked by seventy-five foot conifers on three sides with the other side facing Mt. Pilchuck.

As my cold hands fumbled with the key in the padlock of our shake-covered cabin, the splashing murmur of our creek behind the cabin competed with the rushing of the Stillaguamish behind me. This corner of our land was on a shelf, which, some hundred yards from our door dropped away to the riverbed. Between the river and us lay a small strip of forest, a backwash that Tobey called Long Pool, and a thin arm of tree-covered land. This, we hoped, was sufficient protection from the threat of the river's might, which each year washed away great chunks of earth from the overhanging bank.

Before building the fire in the kitchen range, I examined a cozy nest the mice had built in the firebox, one of their favorite building sites. Most artful, it was put together of soft bits of cotton cloth, Kleenex and kapok. If there were babies, I'd have to save the nest, but there weren't babies this time. I recognized stuffing from my mattresses and pillows, fragments of thread from my dishtowels, bits of sheepskin from the lining of Kenneth's shoe packs and generous touches of my wool mending yarn. No bird ever built a more enticingly soft haven than these very cute, black-eyed, white-stomached, pink-eared pesky little creatures.

Plenty of dry cedar kindling and a squirt of kerosene soon had the fire crackling, both in the range and the airtight heater at the opposite end of the room, where a fireplace would be when we got the time and money to build it.

The cabin had a good smell when it had been shut up for awhile: of split firewood, the rust and ashes of the stove, and kerosene. No musty smell at all, maybe because of the large windows and the south exposure. The air, however, was colder inside than out. When the fires were going well and drafts adjusted, I went out to look around, deciding to leave the door open for a while.

As a matter of ritual, I visited the source of our creek. It gushed from the foot of a high bank about fifty yards in back of the house. To get to it you crossed a narrow, crudely built footbridge over the creek, skirted the mirror-clear pool with its clumps of water cress, wild parsley and skunk cabbage, and followed the tumbling stream through a dense grove of cedars, happy as clams with their feet in moisture and nearby the tall stumps of their parents, some fifteen feet through, were still standing or tipped on to their elbows.

From several places the clear water gushed forth in springs of various sizes. Miniature waterfalls and tiny trickles hurried over mossy boulders to join forces in the main creek bed. The stream boiled out year around and was always ice cold. I often wondered if the glacier had left ice under Sand Hill that chilled the water as it retreated from the base of Green Mountain. I dipped a cup into one of the freshets, and as I drank I remembered the time in Mexico seventeen years ago, the hot, dusty street in Oxhaca. How I had longed for such a drink!

I walked over to Guy's cabin at the other end of the orchard to check on possible winter damage, and there seemed to be none. No broken windows, no trees down, no evidence of roof leakage. No broken limbs on the apple trees; their unpruned, spreading branches sometimes cracked with a heavy snowfall. They weren't very good apple trees, except for the big Gravenstein by the house, but they were old and mossy and bloomed in such pink magnificence that we couldn't bear to supplant them with more choice varieties. Most of the trees were an early species, which all ripened at once in August, and then, too eager to get their seeds to the Earth, proceeded to drop and rot all over the place; a sweet feast for the yellowjackets, ants, chipmunks and deer.

Our woodshed, a haphazard structure of cedar poles and shakes, was well stocked with dry cedar for kindling and mill ends for the drum heater. I carried some of each into the house, which was already becoming warm and comfortable. I put some canned soup on to heat and returned to the creek to fill water buckets.

The boys arrived, out of breath, with the sled piled high. "Things kept spilling off and the snow was either too soft or not enough of it," Tobey complained. "We're hungry. When's lunch?" "Can we go down to the mill pond and fish?" David asked between pantings, his voice high with insistence. "We'll see after lunch. The pond's probably still half frozen. Help me unpack and we'll eat right away." Kenneth arrived with a large load of sleeping bags. "Lunch ready?" I'm hungry."

Tobey, warming his hands over the heater stove, said "We saw a grouse. She came right out in the road in front of us and walked around like a tame chicken. *Can* we go down and fish at the mill pond?" "Help put things away. Take your sleeping bags up to your room. We'll see after lunch, how the weather is."

The upstairs room was a long narrow space under the half-pitch roof. Although we wanted more the less-intrusive look of a flattish roof, we'd had sense enough to take the advice of valley people who insisted a steep pitch was necessary, because you never know when there'd be a winter of deep snow. The very next winter the snow had piled up to nearly six feet and we'd thanked our lucky stars and the valley people for their wisdom. The first time a sudden whoosh of snow slid off the shake roof was in the quiet of an evening when my mind was far away reading a book about galaxies in outer space. The noise and the vibration gave me such a start that I was left limp as a rummage sale hat. But we decided that further avalanches, though startling, were preferable to getting up there on the steep slope and shoveling.

Lunch over, it was beautifully quiet, the boys having gone to the mill pond near Frank Bower's to fish. The pale sun was breaking through the clouds with mists rising against the mountains upriver, a sign that tomorrow would be clear. Kenneth was set up for an afternoon of uninterrupted work. Luxuriating in the silence, I relaxed with coffee, a cigarette, and the large stack of mail our R.F.D. box had yielded. First were several copies of the *Granite Falls Press*, a four-page weekly with a boiler-plate insert, which brought me up to date on local matters, such as the meetings of the " Home Demonstration Club", the delicious ham dinner enjoyed by the Lions' Club as guests of the " Lady Lions", the picketing of the Jim Creek project, the P.T.A. cake sale at Pruitt's store, vital statistics of the countryside, and the enlightened opinions on world matters of a surprisingly well-informed columnist.

Other publications arrived unsolicited, such as a farm magazine largely devoted to news of the highly efficient poisons being developed to combat insects, weeds and blights. It left me with an uneasy feeling about its effect on nature's intricate system of checks and balances. There was a vitriolic little paper called the *Yellow Jacket* published in North Carolina by a vicious, if minor, Hitlerian of the American South, who lashed about in ten-point type with all the fervor of a gas chamber deputy. Completing the stack were the usual advertising flyers. The latter kept the flames in the range a-leaping. No wonder there's a market for pulp logs, I thought. We live in the age of pulp, in the resounding era of waste paper. The hollow wizardry of the direct mail specialist has become one of the major manifestations of twentieth-century American culture. If we couldn't burn it we would soon be up to our ears in it.

Late in the afternoon, Kenneth came in hauling the start of a large painting, oil on canvas, and asked if I would like a little bourbon and swamp water. He had used the general structure of one of our river rocks as a world where groups of naked figures were merging in attitudes of toil, conflict, and compassion. He set it down and stood looking at it, and I knew I was supposed to say something, but at this stage there wasn't any use in saying anything critical. If I did, it would be the wrong thing and too intrusive, so I said it looked to me like an interesting start. He said, yes, he thought he could make a good thing out of it. I knew how he felt, needing a response, really an echo of his own absorption, but nothing to distract him from the concept which held him.

To a jigger of whiskey he added fresh, cold water from the spring. On the old stem-winder phonograph, a Victrola cabinet model of the late '20s with mahogany veneer, Kenneth put the opening record of Mozart's C-Minor piano concerto. We had played it at Robe Ranch during one of our first years in the valley, and it had become a favorite of all of us. It belonged to the mountains in a very special way.

We listened to Mozart and watched the wind in the tree branches. The isolated, tall fir across the road waved like a symphony conductor in eloquent gyrations, tossing its ragged branches in rhythmic invocation. "I hear the boys," Kenneth said. "I was just wondering if I should go after them. It's starting to rain." They burst in, stamping feet, breathing hard, and both talking at once. "Naw, we didn't get any fish, but we got some bites. And David fell in up to his knees. And the jar of salmon eggs fell through a crack in the raft, so we had to use some bugs we found in a wet log. And we saw an animal. I don't know what it was – too big for a muskrat – but it swam right up to the raft; then it saw us and looked so surprised and dove quick out of sight like this…" Tobey gave a graphic imitation of the surprised animal, opening his mouth wide in a silent scream. "I think it was an otter because it was slick, like a seal," Tobey concluded.

"You oughta see all the trees the beavers have cut down. Big ones, big as this," David said with hands describing a circle two feet through. "We found all kinds of that jelly stuff full of frog eggs, lots of it, all kinds of it." "Your jeans are wet," I said. "Take them off. There are dry ones upstairs. And change your socks if they're wet. And hang the wet things behind the stove. Don't leave them in a heap."

Scratch, scratch at the door. The dogs burst in, wet as fish, frantic to run about on something dry, telling us with rolling eyes and lolling tongues of their afternoon's adventures. "Don't let them on the bed or chairs," I cautioned. After a good deal of preliminary scrambling, they settled down by the drum heater and for several minutes there was the regular sloop, sloop sound of tongues licking wet fur. Sometimes they licked each other, sometimes themselves. It didn't seem to matter. There were those among our friends who couldn't quite see why we wanted so many animals, and there were times when I thought they were right. Especially, as our animals knew their place so well, and their place was our place. We seemed to acquire animals as ship bottoms acquire barnacles. But being without them would be like being without fingernails or eyelashes.

Molly was a Springer Spaniel with fur as silky as thistledown. She was black and white with a white streak between her eyes, which spread into the black of her forehead, like the eye in a peacock feather. She was deceptively high-minded in appearance, canny, disobedient though loyal, stubborn and a hypochondriac. Mitzi, the offspring of a Bedlington Terrier I had found in San Francisco and a short-haired pool-room character who jumped the fence, I suspect at Pixie's invitation. She was delicate and small-boned with sparse, mousy-gray fur that tried to curl like a Bedlington's but could never quite make it. She would pout when jealous, squinting her eyes and sticking out her lower lip. She was silent and stoical in pain, an eager greeter, and a little mixed up as to whether she was dog or human.

The wind continued to rise as we ate dinner by the subdued, white light of the kerosene mantel lamps. We could hear the blasts approaching from a distance, a powerful chant, and then suddenly they were on us, whistling and roaring, with creaking and snapping of limbs and, occasionally, the shattering crash of a tall tree, snapping in two or uprooted and falling. The excitement of the storm made us quite silly. Kenneth felt so expansive he offered to help with the dishes, but mainly, I think, because he wanted to talk about painting.

"I think I can really paint some good pictures this summer," he said, flipping the dishtowel about inefficiently. "The trouble is it takes so long to learn. But I am finding things out a little all the time. If I can just live long enough, Babe, I'm sure I can paint something really good." "I'm sure, too," I said. "Just put the dishes on the shelf. I'll put them away." Our cupboard space was cramped because by the time Kenneth had hung the two end doors on hinges, he was tired of the process and just nailed the middle door in place. He said he was going to put it on hinges someday, but it was one of those things, like cleaning the basement in town, that if mentioned would cause him to look beyond me into space, twitch his eyebrows, wrinkle his forehead and mutter about how he never had any time to paint.

"I want to do a lot of painting from nature this summer," he said, savoring fully the delight of the prospect. "Straight sketching, things I can develop into paintings later or use as sources. It's the only way you can keep your forms from becoming stale and arbitrary. You'd think I'd studied and drawn enough rocks and trees and mountains, but if I'm out of contact with nature for awhile, my work begins to lose something."

When the boys were done up in their sleeping bags, Kenneth and I put on our tin (stiff canvas) coats and went out into the misty darkness for our customary evening walk. For light, we used a "bug", which is a candle stuck through a hole in the side of a tin can. The bottom of the can acts as a reflector, and a wire handle completes the package. It was economical and amazingly effective. We walked up the "old highway", now our driveway, which becomes a grassy trail beyond our orchard between the "new highway" and the river. We stopped at the Kosmowsky place; a deserted house and clearing high on a bluff directly above the Stillaguamish where the river makes a big bend. The waters had eaten their way through about twenty acres of the old homestead in recent years and were still gnawing ravenously at the clay and gravel of the bank. The two-story pioneer house, built in the 1890s when the Monte Cristo Railroad was under construction, would go soon, too, for the edge of the bank had crept to within ten feet of its gaping doorway. The railroad bed below had washed out long since, as had the foot trail, over which pack trains had carried piecemeal the makings of the boom mining towns of Silverton and Monte Cristo.

In the wet, dark night the house loomed a darker shadow and the fruit trees postured indistinctly, and with their gnarled branches looked like witches playing statue. I could practically feel the ghosts breathing down my neck. We followed the bug's circle of dim light across the soggy grass to the edge of the cliff. Kenneth turned the bug away and after a minute our eyes could make out the form of the river's majestic curve, the lighter form of the rock and gravel bar across, then the darkness of the trees abruptly at the margin of the river bar. Pilchuck was obscured in the gloom.

"Somewhere up there behind that muck there's a three-quarter moon," I said. "It should be directly over Pilchuck." "I guess that's why it's such a light night, for such a dark night, if you know what I mean." Kenneth smiled. Our thoughts drifted to the valley people who had gone recently: Wirt Robe, Susie's husband Bob Buchanan, Barney Crane. It was hard to think of the valley without them. These were the early trail builders, the men who had cut the old growth trees with their muscles and hand tools and had aged as the second growth had come into maturity.

"By God, Ken," Bob Buchanan had said last summer, full of beer and feeling jovial. "They're talking about a state park up there on Pilchuck. Ski lodge and all that stuff. By God, maybe we're not such damn fools as they said we were for hanging on here in this valley." But that sort of thing really hadn't anything to do with why he'd stayed in the valley, or why any of the handful of scattered individuals had stayed. This applied particularly to Barney Crane, whom the war had taken far away. He'd returned to the rain he cursed and the trails he'd loved, clearing them of their windfalls each spring when the Forest Service put him on the paid staff again – the just barely paid staff. Barney was gone, too. Suicide by poison and not even a note was left.

"It's very strange about Barney Crane," I said aloud. " I still can't figure it out. He was a man who loved the mountains and the forests. He wasn't the type to do a thing like that. Life couldn't have been that bad, as long as he could count on summer coming again and the snow melting off the high trails and all the trail-less places only he knew how to get to."

The sky began to break apart; shreds of swiftly moving mist skimmed past an El Greco moon. We could see more clearly. A doe stepped cautiously from the black woods and stood at the edge of the clearing, sniffing the breeze. She saw us but was not particularly concerned. "I'm glad the dogs aren't with us," Kenneth said, as we watched her walk, slowly and stepping high, across the faintly moonlit grass, cross the road and disappear into the trees on the other side. "She's hanging around waiting for the first of my strawberry leaves," I said. "But that's all right, I guess."

The wind wrestled us as we walked against its blasts on the way back to the cabin. The road puddles in the light of the bug were ruffled erratically. "It's the end of an era for the valley," Kenneth said. "We were lucky to get in on it when we did. There'll never again be the kind of forests and trees that there were," I mused.

"Nor people either," Kenneth replied as we entered the snug warmth of the lamp-lit cabin, shutting the door a little reluctantly on the night of tossing clouds, moon, wind and rain. And the ghosts came right in with us, a genial company.

35

WE TOOK THE LAST of our belongings out of Robe Ranch. Such a poor deserted spot it is these days. The boys went to the swamp while I dug up the lilac bush Mrs. Lewis and I planted beneath the apple trees. I transplanted it to the place down below and the alpine juniper from Mt. Dickerman is now in the rockery in front of our own cabin.

Our move to the other side of the highway has brought us in closer proximity to neighbours we knew only in a casual way before. Old John Albright is one such. He lived in a shake covered shack on an old homestead just east of the Kosmoski place. John stopped to chat awhile the other day. He spoke vitriolicly, as always, about the state of the world, the skullduggery in high places, and the knavery of big business. His remarks were peppered with profanity, restrained a bit because of my inhibiting female presence. As he spoke he jabbed at the soft earth of the bank at the edge of our orchard with his stick, a slightly curving peeled branch of cedar. He dislodged grass, a creeping twinflower plant, a small nest of delicate brown mushrooms and, finally, to his and our surprise, a large brown toad, still inert from hibernation and seeming more dead than alive.

John is an old-timer in the sense that he has lived in the valley since the early settlement days around the turn of the century. His father had worked as a logger when Robe was a mill town that sprawled over the ravished land, denuded of virgin forest. Now a bachelor in his early sixties, John divides his time between his town house, conveniently situated near the main dump in south Seattle, where he carries on a desultory career in salvage, and his forty acres bordering the Stillaguamish.

"Oh, goddamn it," he said, poking viciously at the earth, then bending over to drop a globule of spit squarely into the hole he had made. "I don't know what to do about my place up here. I think I might try to sell it. This goddamn country ain't fit for a man to live in. It's so cold and miserable and rainy most of the time you can't work outside. Then summer comes along and the weather turns so Christ awful hot you can't stand it, and the flies and mosquitoes and gnats chew you to pieces. Why, migod, you go down to Canyon Creek and the goddamn bears they're so thick they come and eat the berries right out of your pail."

All the time he was talking he kept jabbing at the dirt with his stick, leaning to spit in the hole, knocking dirt over where he spit, then digging a new hole for a fresh spit.

"Seems like when you come out of Granite Falls and cross over that bridge over the Stillaguamish, well right there, that's where the iron curtain comes down, and from there on it's every man for himself. Why, goddamn it, there's no law up here. You leave a place alone for a week or so and like as not when you get back, your place is emptied out and tore to pieces by thieves and vandals."

John is a tall, thin man, round-shouldered and round-headed. He has a paucity of scraggly, brown hair, thin lips, narrow gray eyes and long eyelashes. His eyelashes curl straight up, touching the wrinkled lids, giving him a sort of elfin look for all his grizzled qualities. He's a bitter man on many subjects – government, business, and foreign nations out to bleed the United States, loggers (they'll cheat you out of your last nickel), but perhaps most of all on the issue of sportsmen.

"Seen many deer around this year?" he asked, raking around among some small stones with the tip of his stick. "I guess somebody shot that tame little doe used to come around my cabin the last couple of years." He jabbed, spit, and jabbed with an extra spurt of venom. "Sportsmen!" His small gray eyes grew flinty and his thin lips became an inverted arc. "Where's the sport in it I'd like to know. They sit around behind stumps and wait for the deer to come out of the woods and drink out of the river, then they blast away. Why, goddamn it, you know what I seen a fellow do once? He was rowing a boat on a lake, and some dogs chased a young deer down to the water. The deer started swimming out to get away from the dogs, and the shitty louse of a man waited till it was a few feet from the boat, then he pulled out his gun and shot it. Why, goddamn it, I wouldn't do a thing like that if I was dying." You could almost see the steam come out of his ears he got so hot thinking about it.

The sign lettered in red paint with large smeary letters and tacked to a tree at the entrance to his acreage read, "cut no trees if you don't want to get shot." And, nailed to this sign, was a square of paper that warned, "don't molest this sign, you dirty brat. I know who you are and I'll turn you over to the Sheerf. John."

We first became acquainted with John Albright during a summer at Robe Ranch. There were a good many children and animals around, which apparently spelled sociability to a young female Boston bull terrier that suddenly began to appear around the place, all wriggles and ingratiating manners. Wirt Robe, who couldn't stand dogs, but who put up with ours simply because he couldn't see an alternative, took after the Boston with fury and the biggest rocks he could find, which didn't faze the dog in the least, for as soon as the track was clear, there she was again, squirming into figure 8's and wrinkling her upper lip in an embarrassed smile.

A black '32 Hudson sedan drove in one morning, battered and full of squeaks. "Seen a stray bulldog in here?" asked the driver, leaning out the window and making a rather weak effort to sound pleasant.

Then he spied her as she pranced around the corner of the house. "There she is, the little sonofabitch," he shouted, inaccurately. "Come on, Pat, get in here. She's the damnedest little tramp," he explained. "Fellow gave her to me. I keep her tied up most of the time, but sure as hell she gets loose she runs away. I think she gets lonesome. I'm out cuttin' pulpwood most all day. By god, I thought she'd be good at guarding the place while I'm gone." He held the door open to Pat, who jumped into the back seat where she sat squarely in the center, regally erect, and gazed out the window at us with an expression of almost complete resignation. It was definitely "Au revoir, but not good-bye."

This was the first of several identical episodes, except that profanity flowed a little more freely as the visits grew more numerous. Late in the summer Pat stopped appearing, as did her owner. I met John one day in the grocery store at Granite Falls and asked him how he had finally solved the problem of keeping Pat home.

"I didn't," he said. "I had to give her away, the crazy little tramp. She didn't like to be alone. Long as I was there to keep her company she'd hang around. Thing is, I hated to go away and leave her tied up. Well, I give her to the Kennedys. There's always somebody around that place, and they got a kid and that's what she likes."

"She's a good dog," I said. "We got to like her nearly as much as we do ours."

"Oh, yeah, she's a good dog, all right. Smart, too. Goddamn if I don't think she knew everything I was talking about. Gets lonesome around the shack without her."

The next time we saw John was a weekend in October. Saturday afternoon we went walking, deciding to make the loop up the river to John's place and back along the road. He was putting new shakes on the roof of his two-room house. We didn't have to look very high to talk to him because the roof was low enough to reach from the ground to the eaves. The shakes were hand split, thick, and a bit wavy. He was nailing them over the old roof, which was made of shingles.

John kept on with his work as we talked about the usual subjects, the weather, his health (back bothering him a good deal), and the goddamn high prices. "It don't make a bit of difference how many raises the unions get, all the money goes right back into the pockets of the rich anyway."

"How's Pat getting along with the Kennedys?" I asked. John stopped pounding, looking down at us. Slowly drawing a galvanized nail from the corner of his mouth, he said, "Didn't you hear what happened to Pat?"

"No. Haven't been up that way for a time."

"Well, she's dead. Shot." John climbed down the ladder. On the ground he stood facing us. His thin hair, not yet graying, was disheveled; his small gray eyes beneath the pixyish lashes stared through us and seemed to hate everything they saw. With difficulty he pulled one shoulder back, then the other, until he was standing nearly straight. "Yep, bygod, Jim Kennedy shot her. Of all the lousy, dirty goddamn tricks! Seems he couldn't keep her from killing his chickens. Well, he should've said something to me. I'd have taken her back. Hell, he said he wanted her, said she'd be a good companion for the little girl. I guess she killed two chickens, but that didn't give him the right to shoot her. Not the way I see it."

Not having a stick to jab the ground with, he kicked a clump of grass free from the earth, bent and spit into the hole. He kicked dirt over the spit with more than ordinary feeling and he continued to kick at the ground and to stare at something unseen as we expressed our condolences.

Guy has decided to sell his half of the property. His interest has shifted to the LaConner area where Morris has been living most recently. Guy wants $1,000 for his cabin on top of his $500 share of the property. Kenneth is livid, as he thinks Guy is gouging us. Fortunately, he hasn't had time to dwell on how we'll get the money to buy Guy out, as he went to the opening of his show in New York. He's back now and it looks like a success. Maybe we'll be able to buy Guy out after all. The trip east and the opening was a big experience for Kenneth. He likes Maynard Walker tremendously and also the director of the Metropolitan, Francis Taylor. They are the main ones. He's a poor reporter but more details will come out in dribs and drabs as time goes on.

36

JUNE 14, 1949 AT the cabin.   We're almost into another summer. It's Sunday evening and Tobey, David Perine, the dogs and I are in residence.   Kenneth went to work in town with Sherman Lee. Dr. Fuller hired Sherman as Assistant Museum Director. The Lees talked old Albright into selling them the river front portion of his property, and they are planning to build there this summer. They drove up when we were still at breakfast. I dove into the house and smoothed up the beds. Kenneth shot over to Guy's cabin and shaved. It was the fastest shave anybody ever had.

We had a pleasant but vacuous day with them. I sense a lack of vitality. There is no spark. No spontaneous laughter. They probably think the same of us. He said he used to like Turner "before I became more conservative." I have a feeling his politics shift with his career. There is a heaviness about both of them.

Tobey and David are taking turns posing for each other. Tobey has drawn David rowing, hunting etc., and now wants him to pose swimming, but David said it was too cold to take his shirt off. In coaxing David to pose he said, "if you'll pose for me for half an hour, I'll carry your pee can down in the morning." At one point he had David standing with his hands behind his head. When he had drawn David down to his waist he said, "you'd better button up, I draw anything and everything."

I do miss Kenneth when he's gone. The first evening is always particularly lonely. We went up to Robe Ranch last night after dinner. No one was around. We picked a few berries. What a desolate feeling! The cabins and barns are flattened; now just heaps of shakes. The ranch house has a large hole in the roof, and the grass and brush have taken over. It shouts its lack of Wirt.

Pilchuck wears a pinky mantle this evening. I had a drowsy day, even though I slept nearly twelve hours last night. I shopped in Granite this morning at the girls' store. It's unusual for a grocery business to be run by two bachelor women. I must do a story on them for the *Seattle Times.* I also called on Jean Hill. Her house is in turmoil as usual, but some of the long talked about work has been done. The kitchen floor has linoleum tile and the bedroom is painted pink. Her doctor says she must have an operation this year or her intestinal damage from previous pregnancies and her war years as "Rosie the Riveter" could turn into cancer. Vic is logging in Sultan and leaves at 4:30 in the morning. She said she and Maudie Storch will come out to spend a day soon. It occurs to me that small town or rural people are often much nicer than their homes, while city people's homes are nicer than they are.

The Ottaway boys stopped to play with Tobe for a while on the way to Frank Bowers, where they leave their milk cow to graze during the day. Bobby always says, "I haven't forgotten that trip to Heather Lake." We must remember to include him in other hiking trips. Like so many local kids he never gets into the backcountry around here, maybe because there's so much wilderness in his back yard. Looking around the house he observes, "you guys got three doors, we got two." A little later he said, "we had some kittens, but something got them." I said I didn't know they had cats. "Sure, we got Tiger and we got Floozie; it was Floozie had the kittens." We learned that the third oldest, Vernie, has stitches in his head from getting snagged on the water wheel and being carried around for about five minutes, something banging his head on each revolution. "He's lucky to be alive," said brother Bobby.

Before they left the oldest boy, Stanley, said his mother had told him to ask us to lunch Wednesday. I protested that Dorothy had too much to do to be fixing us lunch etc. Stanley said, "Well that's what she said, and I guess she's got her heart set on it."

I walked down to the millpond with the boys this afternoon. The pond is a charmed spot almost a block long and not much over six feet in the deepest parts. Yellow pond lilies and darling frogs, swimming like little boys, scatter the surface. Lots of birds sing from the alders, willows, cattails and elderberry bushes along the shore. Brown and orange salamanders surface for a gulp of air, turn and wiggle back to their large submerged logs left from the days when the pond was a storage place for the original Robe mill 50 years ago.

We poled the heavy old raft around a while, then I went home along the road with the salmon berries ripening on either side, the lavender daisies blooming and the evening light shining through the big trees. There's a feeling of summer at last. I had almost forgotten what it can be.

We made our call on the Ottaways. I had written her a note that we'd be there, but not for lunch. She was frosting a white layer cake with flaming pink icing and candy trimmings when we arrived. In the small room off the kitchen, an oak table was covered with unwashed dishes. Every item of furniture was covered with dishes, clothes, packages of food, soaps and so on. Their only girl child, Ruthie, was sleeping in a new bedroom. Skinny little Dorothy has a suspicious lump on her stomach again, which I tried not to stare at in a fascination of horror.

While kids swarmed, I dried the dishes. After the boys fished a while, we ate cake and talked. She finally made a guilty reference to the lump. "I told Leonard he had to keep his hands off me until he got some protection, but he said, 'oh hell, you're still nursing so you couldn't get that way now.' I told him it would be born before Ruthie was a year old, but he insisted. Now he keeps saying, 'Well, there won't be any more.' That's what he said the last time. I keep hoping it's a tumor but I guess I'm just not lucky enough to have tumors. I have these cysts on each side but they aren't this big." She hemorrhaged badly after the last baby. Lord knows what will happen this time. Sometimes I wonder if Leonard is subconsciously trying to kill her off. She certainly is the type who can roll them out. I doubt if she's ever miscarried, and yet she looks so weak. The varicose veins in her legs bother her more and more. Leonard's latest purchase is a battery powered radio-phonograph and one Bing Crosby record. "It only cost $32.50," says Leonard.

Now Ruthie and Vernie both have stitched-up heads in bandages. It seems Stanley was swinging the bush knife and clipped Ruthie on the temple and ear. Leonard is terribly tired when he gets home, and the fumes from the power saw bother him. He and another faller are working on a cedar 16 feet through. I hate to see those giant Pilchuck cedars go.

The *Everett Herald* has not run my letter so they are not publishing positions opposing the Mt. Pilchuck ski area. Guess I'll send the State Park people a copy.

To Whom it May Concern:

Mt. Pilchuck as the scene of a state park is an appropriate and worthy project, but I would like to throw in my vision of such an idea, which differs from the ski lodge concept so widely discussed. Snohomish County has in Mr. Pilchuck a unique possession, a virtually unspoiled wilderness area, a complete mountain with all the attributes of a major peak (except glaciers) yet on a friendly, approachable scale, and within easy access of major cities.

I propose keeping this mountain as a natural wonderland in its primitive state, with minimal development other than bridle paths, hiking trails and shelters, maintaining the remaining virgin forests intact, its lakes in their pristine beauty, its rocky cliffs free from the blast of dynamite for roads.

Western Washington has many scenic roads for car travel and many ski areas and potential ski areas, far surpassing anything Pilchuck could offer with its inconsistent winter snows. But imagine a 75-lake mountain with old-growth forests, wildlife, glacial cirques, streams and waterfalls in its original state of creation, virtually in the back yard of major population centers! This is a treasure few countries can boast. Hundreds of mountain enthusiasts who have enjoyed the Heather Lake trail in years past have been grimly disappointed this year to find the site devastated by a 320-acre clear cut where the trail once meandered. This is a small sample of what a large area of Pilchuck will look like if contemplated logging plans are carried out to pay the expense of an automobile road to Cedar Flats.

Recently, a book was published describing the wildlife to be found on Mt. Pilchuck. Certain species are unique to this mountain. To change the natural habitat is to take a chance on wiping out these shy forms of life. In this mountain, Snohomish County possesses an attribute priceless and irreplaceable. Keep it as a wilderness; build trails to the lakes, build a spiral trail to the summit. Build a system of shelters. We will all be far richer in the long run.

Leonard and the four older boys dropped by. Leonard had been down helping Frank cut hay. He got to talking about his invention, a glass coffin with a lead seal. "Sort of loaf shaped." Should retail for not more than $50. He again pondered on what life is, how cheap, how easily destroyed, how wasteful. "More than a million sperm in one discharge. What are we here for? According to nature, only to reproduce. Nothing else, just to reproduce." He told me about the Granite Falls high school girl raped by two boys, the boys being held by police. Leonard hopes they get off because "the girl probably flirted around, teased them too far." One of them held her while the other one "fixed her". "Well, they say a girl is about as hot as she'll ever be at 17." The girl had a sister that was always "flirting, tossing herself around," etc. I gathered Leonard had a barely suppressed desire to "fix" the sister.

Tobey and David Perine came home from fishing at the mill pond the other day with a story about Frank Bower. He has always been friendly when he sees the kids passing by his riverside shack on their way to the pond. But on this day David needed an outhouse and thinking, when no one answered his knock on the door, that no one was home, went around to the back of the house to find the little one holer. Emerging from the tall salmon berry bushes, a ferocious Frank confronted them. He told the boys <u>never</u> to go into the brush behind his house. I learned from a chuckling Leonard today that Frank has been making whiskey in a still near the outhouse for years and has bear traps scattered around the area to catch any snooping "revenoors."

A startled Tobey tried to change the subject by asking about the .22 rifle that Wirt had mentioned in the rest home. Perhaps feeling a little guilty about his outburst, Frank disappeared into his shack and returned with an old single shot, octagon barrel Winchester, which he passed over to a very excited Tobe.

It's quiet now. No sound of rain: Kenneth is just going to bed over in his corner. The boys are blotto upstairs, that first deep slumber. The dogs are now coming over to get on my bed. Mitzi has complete assurance of welcome. Molly decides on the basket chair with her usual grunts and lapping while in the process of getting settled. Clothes are drying on a rope that Kenneth has stretched across the room. We found out today that our land taxes are overdue for three years and we are being penalized. Guy and we each owe six dollars, a bargain.

37

SEATTLE. KATE KNOWLTON CALLED. After about thirty minutes of her rat-a-tat-tat talk she said she had seen Morris and Guy's show in Bellevue. She said, "that one of Guy's was pretty interesting. It was called *Search for the Morning*, and it was a man, he looked to be a Negro or something, all wound up in a cloth, like a sheet I guess, like he was sleeping. Well it was pretty comical. I said to the man there, 'It looks to me like that feller had three operations; one at the neck, another in his middle parts, and another on his ankles.' Well, he was all tangled up in this sheet and there was a lot of other things. I don't know what they were, but it was pretty comical." She's worried about Susie, because she drinks coffee all day, and her ankles are puffy and her circulation is bad. I think she's right about that, too.

We've become good friends with Mitch and Ludy Jamieson. As a military artist he went ashore with the first American forces, recording the violence and madness with sketchbook and pencil. Later he turned them into real paintings that are terrifying and fascinating. Mark took us all to the Meany Hotel for dinner and we came to our house afterwards. A pleasant time it seemed to me and Mark was in good spirits. He likes the idea of a school with himself talking on values in general and Mitch teaching techniques. It could really work all right.

We talked during the evening of teaching, of what's wrong with the attitude of the young. Said Mark, "They want to know everything right off, without the long process of learning. They want to know the trick, the secret formula. Why, I used to love an apple so much I would set it up on a plate and paint it and paint it, and I didn't know anything about colour or abstraction until I'd painted for years. I just used to paint in reds and greens and blues or any old thing. I learned by doing and by loving things enough to want to paint them. But the young don't want anything but formula. It's a mass age and a godless age." He also talked about Morris and Mrs. Fredericks. "I know she has a feeling about him, I could tell it by the sound of her voice when he came in, just the way she breathed, "Morris!"

A few days later we had dinner with the Jamiesons and Guy, this time at Mark's. Mark has made his house into something more livable. He's painted walls and ceilings light gray, and placed his objects about. We ate in the kitchen by candlelight. It was pleasant, but Mark did several things that annoyed me, perhaps not fairly. One, his having no sympathy or interest in Eugene Linen's situation with the Seattle symphony, while to me his replacement is again the distressing story of the native son unappreciated for his unmistakable talents and achievements. It's another example of a less aggressive personality being shouldered out of his just desserts. Also, he turned on me when I was recalling the time he was cleaning out his studio before going to England. He told us we could salvage what we liked out of a great heap of drawings that were to be thrown away. He said nastily, "Remember too, dear, that I left things with you on several occasions," inferring, I suppose, that we are keeping things he intended to take back. Both Kenneth and I are positive he never "left" anything with us, except once a role of canvas, which Kenneth later shipped to him in England. But I suppose these moments are bound to occur, with the uncertainties of approaching old age, and the dying out of production. But Mark has limited his horizons in a most arbitrary and unnecessary fashion, it seems to me.

I hope our friendship with the Jamiesons will mature into a lasting association. They can be thoughtful and they can laugh.

It's the middle of March. A winter as discouraging as this one is hard to write about, but I feel I should for the record's sake. It started with Marj Nestor's death in the early fall, then my father's illness, which frightened me so. Next it was my mother's fall and the terrifying Friday the 13th blizzard trip to the hospital. Ed was having angina pain, which the daily trips driving over the ice to the hospital didn't help. Then came the long convalescence, the daily reports of pain and no improvement or very little. Mabel is still crippled, apparently now with arthritis. The final nightmares were Kenneth's teeth extraction and his back trouble. He has his front teeth out next week and gets his plates.

Finances are the same sad story. First there was $400 for the oil furnace (replacing coal), then $400 for the car, now $300 for his teeth. And prices are going up steadily. The museum is still paying pre-inflation salaries. Fuller announced an employee contribution type of retirement plan. If Kenneth works there until he's 65 he will get $120 a month. It's peanuts. He will get more from the state old age pension, I think. On the other side, the Metropolitan Museum has bought a painting and a drawing, $950 altogether of which he should get about $625. Actually, the money from sales he has made this year just about pays the extra expenses. I think perhaps he really should teach. It would give him more time to paint and better pay and security.

I must write to Mildred Oaks. We were out there a week ago Sunday; a pleasant day outdoors in the garden, dinner of rabbit and a special barley dish. Too much liquor was drunk, however. Glen Trimble was there. I think I like her; her look of extreme erudition has always intrigued me.

I've been reading Liebnitz on metaphysics. In his mind there is no conflict between science and religion. He believes the answer to the question of good and evil is that evil must happen at times in order for greater good to come, and that our finite minds cannot understand the overall plan. I'm sure most of us have conjectured about an overall plan and either accepted or rejected it. Could there be a heaven if there was no hell? And must we not all have our share of both in this life?

There can be no saints without sinners. Of course many of us would rather there were neither, but if you really think it through, without good or evil we would have none of the values we have. Life would be an entirely different thing, and while it would perhaps be possible to have such a life, to construct it in imagination is difficult because contrasts are eliminated, and how then to form values?

The world continues to move toward more and more insanity it seems to me, after each reading of the news. There are announcements of billions more for military aid to non-communist countries. It's always military aid. Nothing short of a popular revolt can halt this cancerous growth.

Great Books opened with *Moby Dick* . It was strange to hear the different interpretations. The great white whale represented evil in the author's mind. To me it represented the natural order and Ahab the man out of step with nature. Ahab the disordered element possessed by devils.

I had a recent conversation with a friend named Becky Heidlebaugh, whom I like very much but disagree with very much. She thinks great books should be read as archaic works, not to be applicable now. I disagree entirely. The universal qualities in these works are what are important. The same things are mysteries today as they were in Aristotle's time; the same values important; and mankind has yet to embrace basic truths or he wouldn't be in the increasingly worse mess he's in. For me life is still fundamentally as great a mystery as it ever was. I think we should welcome the mystery and accept what we are given to know. We should search for knowledge, but not exploit our findings without extreme caution.

Tobey is in his last year at Stevens, very tall, up to my shoulder, weighs 115 lbs., size eight and a half shoe. He still has the little boy look to his face and possesses a good deal of stability and common sense. He is selected to do the errands such as going downtown to the central office with the weekly school savings deposits. I asked him about Georgia Morrison yesterday and he said, "Oh, we snowballed her… *nobody* likes her anymore. She's so darn stuck up; goes around kicking everybody, thinks she's so smart." Next fall it's Edmund Meany Junior High. I suppose adolescence will have a good many difficulties.

I can easily recall my own struggles during those years after our family changed neighborhoods.

It's so hard to know what one thinks about life and its meanings. I am not a steadfast soul by any means, and my doubts sometimes overwhelm my faith. Yet I think my faith is generally stronger than my doubts. As Tobey grows into adolescence and I see his problems and yearnings, I remember acutely my own unhappiness, which tends to become obscured by time, and it's hard to know which was uppermost, the happiness or the achings of the heart. I think with tremors of the many, many sorrows he has to face, and I pray from the depths of my being that he will have the faith and the strength to surmount them and to go on believing.

38

J UST BEFORE MY JUNIOR year in high school, when I was fourteen years old, we moved from Greenwood on the northern outskirts of Seattle to the Ravenna Park district in order to be nearer the University of Washington, where it was intended both my brother and I should obtain our so-called higher education.

Intensely loyal to the neighbors I had known since I could remember, I fought the whole idea of moving with every ounce of venom I could summon. I would return at every opportunity, I vowed, to the homes of my old friends, a group of families, the women of which devoted their spare time to the Woodland Park Methodist Episcopal Church, in which cold draughts and the erratic heat produced by the pot-bellied stove chased each other through and among the vibrations struck by young and old throats lustily intoning favorite old hymns. The men were too tired from their labors to do anything but spank their kids and read the newspapers.

I had no wish to know anyone in the new neighborhood and was overcome with adolescent pouts of bitterness at any suggestion from either parent that I try to make friends. They pointed out with relentless regularity the girls near my age living in the vicinity, but I wouldn't have made an overture for all the Marguerite Clarke movies laid end to end and handed to me on a silver screen.

Then one summer evening, as I was about to start across the wooded ravine, now called Ravenna Park, to get our daily supply of milk from a man who had a cow (a chore I secretly loved, but protested on principle), two girls burst suddenly into our yard from the grove of fir trees adjoining the house. That is, one of them burst into sight, exuding confidence. The other, larger, hung back until at the exasperated urgings of her companion to "come *on* – you said you would," she *came* on, but with hanging head in a manner that might accompany a thumb in mouth, heel twisting Hollywood movie routine. I greeted them with apprehension and curiosity on our front porch, and, awkwardly, with much arm-flailing and giggling on the part of Claribel, the larger of the two girls, we made ourselves introduced after a fashion.

My mother appeared and, delighted to see some signs of ice breaking, nudged me to ask the girls into the house. The smaller girl, whose name was June Pfeiffer and who lived only a half a block away, had all the assurance Claribel lacked. She was still in short skirts and had a twist of curly hair held by a ribbon at the back of her neck. Claribel's skirts were halfway long, and her brown hair was gathered in a figure eight on the back of her head.

"Where do *you* live?" I asked Claribel, after June had made known which house was hers. "You know that house on 65th Street that looks like a caramel? I live in that," Claribel said, and from then on I began to like her enormously. They asked me to go swimming at a place they called Amosford the next day. "I don't think I can," I said. "Why not?" my mother asked quickly, overhearing from the next room. "Well, I think my bathing suit has a hole in it." "Sew it up then," my mother said. "At Amosford nobody cares if you have a hole in your bathing suit," Claribel said, laughing an infectious, clear laugh. "Nobody's there but little boys and theirs always have holes.

Twilight was about to become darkness when we remembered the milk trip. My brother wasn't home, so it was up to me to go through the woods, which would be thoroughly dark by the time I made the return trip. June and Claribel said they would go with me, and we started down the path through the summer's leafiness, the air still so warm we had no need of jackets.

With the constraint of first meeting and my mother's presence removed, the two girls lapsed into their natural manners, which involved much giggling, lunging about, and mysterious references to boys. We picked certain things to smell, certain others to chew and would suddenly break into flight.

I had been used to girls three or four years older than I whose conventional behavior was ironbound, girls whose dizziest moments were enjoyed within the confines of a church meeting or a Sunday school picnic. I had made every effort to convince the bigger girls that I was as old as they were, and nothing gave me greater satisfaction than to be mistaken for 17 or 18 when I was 13.

This sort of uninhibited romping, while causing me to feel stiff and not with it, still promised something good, an unshackling of bonds I had found boring without knowing it. I began to feel a return to the unself-conscious merriment of true childhood. But it was combined with that new, mystifying and alluring quality identified with adolescence.

I did go swimming with June and Claribel the next day. They came to get me about nine o'clock, shortly after breakfast. The day promised to be breathlessly warm, like an overstuffed bosom. We stopped at Herman's Corner Grocery on 65th, where we purchased dill pickles and sliced ham for sandwiches.

"T'ick or t'in?" questioned Mr. Herman, peering from spectacles, his greasy black hair combed sideways over his round scalp, as he poised at the slicer with a slab of ham in hand. He had a furtive, querulous manner. He never failed, I discovered, to precede his slicing with the same question, and so we nicknamed him "Tickortin." Claribel went into ecstasies over the dill pickle keg. From the green, briny depths Mrs. Herman, a rosy-cheeked, near-sighted woman, extracted three large, juicy specimens. She plopped them into a pint carton, meanwhile asking as many sly and probing question as she could think of about neighborhood affairs. She lived on gossip.

Who's your best beau now?" she asked Claribel, looking from one to the other of us with her squinty blue eyes that held more of a bite than a twinkle. "Is it that Willard Lasley or is it Harry Buckley. I seen you with both of them lately." She winked at June. "My boy Harry says he don't stand a chance with her. Says she don't even speak to him when he's out delivering groceries." "He just doesn't hear me for fear I'll ask him for a dill pickle," said Claribel.

We made sandwiches at Claribel's house, the small-scale English Country architecture of which had a cluttered charm, but which was badly heated. Here I first met Mama. She was canning in a small kitchen on a coal range some wild berries that Fred, who was Papa, had brought home. There was chipped ivory paint on the cupboards, and the linoleum's pattern had long ago been worn away. A great number of potted plants rested on the windowsill and indeed any level spot not otherwise occupied. The sink couldn't have contained another unwashed dish. Open jars of this and that, some of them with spoons idling in them, stood among breadcrumbs, tealeaves and cheese rinds.

Mama said, "How do you *do*!" looking down at me from her great height out of deeply set gray-blue eyes. Her hair and features suggested the Gibson girl on a grand scale. "So this is our new neighbor we're all so happy about!" "But Claribel, dear heart! Whatever possessed you to bring anyone in with the house looking so disreputable?" "Mama!" Claribel said. "You know the house always looks the same." "Why, dear heart!" Mama exclaimed reproachfully. "I've only been putting off cleaning until I could do a thorough job from top to bottom!" Mama and Claribel spoke always in exclamations. They argued constantly, with Claribel impishly rude and Mama grieved and reproachful. "Mama!" Claribel would cry, "Can't you make your blouse stay down inside your belt?" or "Mama!" The hairpins are all falling out of your hair!"

As we were leaving the house, each with our paper sack of lunch and our bathing suit, Mama called, "If I'm not here when you get back, put some potatoes on to cook so your father won't be complaining. I'm going to a Garden Club meeting. We're to have a tour of Mrs. Porter Beson Tudor's Lake Washington Boulevard garden with tea on the terrace." Mama never referred to her Daughters of the American Revolution and garden acquaintances excepting by their full three names.

The three of us walked up the 65th St. hill, crossed south to the Sacred Heart cemetery, trekked down the east side of the hill, followed along the rail tracks, an old skid road, and finally a cow path which skirted the Nicholas's peaceful farm, emerging on the sandy shores of a placid Lake Washington.

We were hot and somewhat tired. We all wore gingham dresses, under which we were equipped with considerable underwear including boned corsets, the garters of which held up brown cotton stockings. June still wore a Ferris Waist. All this paraphernalia we removed in natural little dressing rooms formed by thickets of Balm of Gilead, alder trees, and Spirea bushes. The walk, about three miles, had whetted our appetites, which were never what could be called dormant, and the sandwiches were burning holes in their bags. We swam briefly, first tucking our long hair into colored rubber bathing caps. It was the stage in bathing suit evolution when there were still residual sleeves and the pant legs hung three inches longer than the skirts, terminating loosely just above the knees.

All the mugginess of the day vanished with the coolness of the lake water. Summer haze veiled the horizon; the high sun's rays probed the green liquescence of the lake. Song sparrows caroled in the thickets. We stretched our wet bodies on the hot sand, and when the chill of the lake had left we devoured our lunches. This was a world, timeless and enduring. The prospect of two more years in high school stretched endlessly into our futures. A day then was a long affair, with time for whatever the fancy willed.

Some boys arrived in a canoe, among them Willard Lasley who was Claribel's love, or one of them. Willard unloaded the other boys and took the three of us for a ride, Claribel, laughing and lively in the bow, June and I, shy and cramped on the floor of the overloaded craft.

"Let's turn it over," Claribel said. The suggestion frightened me, but I wouldn't have said so. June said, "Take me in first." "Why, sissy, you scared?" Claribel said. Sensing our alarm, she and Willard rocked the canoe, almost capsizing it. June and I clung to the edges with a tight grip. I tried to laugh. "Please take me in. It's way over my head." June's pleading was almost tearful. "Look over the edge, baby," Willard sneered. "You can wade from here." True, we had drifted only a short distance and were in shallow water. "There's a drop-off here," June whimpered. Kids told terrible tales of drop-offs and quick sand. ("You gotta be careful if you don't swim good on account of drop-offs!")

Feeling ignominious but relieved, I waded ashore with June. Sitting on the sand with the warm sun on our backs we watched while Claribel and Willard dove and stunted like porpoises, their shouts and laughter skimming the lake.

That day for the first time I began to feel at home in our new neighborhood. That day also began a friendship with the Colby family and Claribel in particular that lasted until fate brought changes beyond our control.

A gas station has been built there now, where the old house stood looking, as Claribel always said, like a caramel, because it was dark brown on the bottom and yellow with dark brown stripes on the top story. It was fake Tudor with gables, and beams painted dark brown on the upper half. The fireplace was of clinker bricks. Scotch broom grew rankly on the terrace facing the street.

But now even the house is gone completely, and the bank it stood on has been leveled so that cars can drive into the gas pumps. The hill we used to walk over to get to the lake, the hill in back of the house, which was then all covered with fir, cedar, dogwood, alder, willow, and maple trees, is now shorn of any suggestion of woodland. It is comprised of streets and rows of fairly new boxy houses. You would never know now that three decades ago kids could climb up there and get Christmas trees, greens for holiday decorations, wild blackberries, autumn leaves, and spring wildflowers.

The destination of our walks was always the shores of Lake Washington, and that of course is all changed now, too. What used to be sandy beaches lined with groves of cottonwood and alder trees is now either the Sand Point Naval Station or private exclusive residential areas with building restrictions, racial taboos and beach clubs.

I wonder if it still smells that way of a summer evening now, the way it did when we would go swimming after dinner, at once heady and languorous with wood smoke, lake water, and young, waxy cottonwood leaves.

How very quickly those school years pass and fade in one's memory. I remember being appalled when I turned 17. Claribel and I were on the Cowan Park bridge, walking to school at Lincoln High, saying *17*, then pretty soon *18*, then in no time out of our teens and pretty soon old ladies of *30*! The thought gave me a feeling like the bottom of the world was falling out.

Now I am just middle-aged, and I still love to take long walks and swim in the cold water of Puget Sound or mountain rivers, and there isn't one single member of the Colby family left. It is strange, because they were a remarkably vivid and vital group. I never knew people to have so much fun and to react so strenuously to every little thing they came across in their lives. They were Mama and Papa and the two daughters, Geraldine and Claribel. Geraldine was about seventeen on that June day in 1918 when we met. Claribel was just going to be fifteen, and so was I. Our birthdays were but three days apart.

Nature produced the Colbys on a grand scale. Because of their unusual physical size, they always were a little apart from the average or the usual. And, as if she had regretted her own folly in producing these enormous specimens, nature concluded the whole affair by wiping it from the slate. Both Mama and Papa Colby were native San Franciscans. Mama was extremely proud of her and her husband's pioneer California ancestry, although he from all appearances couldn't have cared less. Mama valued her membership in the D.A.R. and attended their doings with painful regularity. She also belonged to Colonial Dames and a garden club. She would have been an Episcopalian had she not been converted to Christian Science when Claribel was a baby. Claribel, up to the age of three, showed all signs of following the family trend toward excessive size, but a siege of spinal meningitis, of which she almost died, rescued her from a fate she always looked upon as worse than death. She achieved a height of only five feet, seven inches and a weight of 160 pounds. The others were all above six feet and 200 pounds.

The medical profession, it seems, had given Claribel up, after conferences yielded no beneficial results and all panaceas had been tried. Someone suggested Christian Science, one of the physicians, I believe, and Mama, in her desperation, sought out a practitioner. The fact that the child recovered was proof enough to her of the religion's potency, and while she never was successful in eliciting the faintest devotion in the rest of the family, her own faith remained steadfast from that time on.

In later life, the goiter, which to others had been evident for many years, became so obstreperous that Mama sought out medical advice for the first time since the illness of her second daughter. A hasty operation was ordered, but Mama succumbed on the operating table on the way to surgery.

Two suicides (plus a third – Claribel's second husband) and death due to natural causes obliterated this family in what is popularly regarded as the prime of life. Considering that I had never known a house where could be found so many high spirits, so much laughter and freedom from conventional affectations, I was confounded by the whole thing

Margaret as Bohemian writer about 1925

Margaret and Kenneth bound for Europe, 1936

View of the Stillaguamish Valley from the Callahans' first Robe
Ranch cabin

Five generations of Bakers (Susie second from left)

Wirt Robe in front of his home/store

Bob and Margaret on the porch of the Greenwood house

Man With Grey Hat

Portrait of Wirt

Richard Bennett working on the porch of Guy Anderson's cabin at Robe Ranch

Portrait of Erick and Carp

Inside a Silverton miner's shack

Guy, Margaret, Richard, and friend in the Robe canyon of the
Stillaguamish River

The Bundy Family c. 1915

The Callahans with Richard Bennett and a friend at the river

Margaret and Molly at the swimming hole

Kenneth's studio at the 17th Avenue house in Seattle

Back door of the 'new' cabin

Mother and Child wire sculpture in the orchard of the cabin

Kosmoski house and encroaching Stillaguamish River

Margaret and friend at Greenwood shortly before the move to
Ravenna in 1918

June, Margaret and Claribel at Amosford, 1921

Margaret, Mary Bard and friends at Lake Washington, ca. 1922

From left to right: "Jack" Kenneth, David Perine, Jean Bedal,
Margaret and Edith Bedal in front of Yakbid camp at White Pass.

Callahans waiting for the Bedal sisters at Sloan Creek
campground

Margaret and Jean Bedal at Indian Pass near Glacier Peak

Forest Service employees Tobey and David Perine, 1956

Neil Meitzler's portrait of Susie with Mt. Pilchuck in the
background

Landscape of peaks near Monte Cristo

Margaret with Benny Goodman and daughters at
Goodman's Connecticut home, 1960

39

THE OCEAN AND SALT-WATER beaches have always exerted a pull on me. Kenneth also feels a strong attraction for the sea, partly due to his trips as a young seaman in the 1920's. Our contacts have been limited by our preoccupation with the mountains but we sometimes visited Dave Perine's parents, who owned a cabin on the beach near the north end of Whidbey Island. We often stopped in the little town of La Conner on our way to or from Whidbey. When Morris moved to La Conner followed later by Guy Anderson and Dick Gilkey, another painter who used to stay at Robe Ranch, we stopped there more often.

It was in the early 1950's that we went to La Conner for a different reason. Erna Gunther, an anthropologist friend, had been telling us for years of a special potlatch affair on the Swinomish Reservation across the slough from La Conner Village. She had told us intriguing tales of the annual dances and chants of the Swinomish. This time there were political implications for the future of the tribes. The dispute was over whether or not the members of the tribe should continue collective ownership of their lands or take up the government's offer to divide them up so individuals could sell or do as they wished with their own shares of the tribal lands. Timber and real estate values were increasing dramatically in the area, and this may have inspired the interest in the Indians' welfare by certain business interests and their politician friends.

We had intended to go to the celebration many times but something always interfered. Now Tobey was old enough to go with us, the roads were not icy and no one was down with the flu. Tobey had Philip Wamba, a Seattle friend, with him and they very gleefully anticipated being awake all night. The plan was to attend the ceremony and then drive back to the mountains when the dances were over. As we drove cross-country from our cabin to La Conner I thought back to a long ago visit with Morris in La Conner shortly after he had moved to the area.

It was late June or early July, and, although gray in the early morning, the sun broke through when we got to La Conner. The day slowly brightened and warmed a little as we sat on the board deck of Morris's kitchen. Peering through the twisted branches of trees stripped bare by caterpillars we could see the flat marshlands below stretching off to the rocky islands that mark the end of the tide flats and the beginning of Puget Sound. Those rocks stand solidly, dramatically, in space with light always changing about them, stunted trees fringing their rugged surface.

Morris was out when we arrived and we spent some moments admiring the new arrangement of his living room, enlarged by knocking out a partition. He calsomized the walls gray, the ceiling white, and painted yellow ochre on the doors and window moldings creating a wonderful background for his particular sense of decoration. A pink mobile hung over one door, a nicely balanced arrangement of planes suspended by strings and as usual there were flowers arranged for colour in the small pottery bowls from Japan and the tall purple vase picked up on one of the inevitable visits to junk shops.

I was raiding the big Royal Ann cherry tree when Morris's tall, bony figure pushed through the gate and down the path, all waving arms and striding legs. He looked fine in a sun-faded and worn dark blue sports shirt, a good colour against his smooth brown neck.

There's always a delightful sense of adventure when we plan things with Morris. After a short session on the now warm and sunny deck the unanimous decision was to borrow a boat from the old man next door and row down the slough to the rock islands, which had been tantalizing us. We took a short trip to the village center, which backs on the slough, to get food for a lunch and some canned dog food for Morris's dog Edith and his two baby crows. We slapped ham sandwiches together on the counter board in the long narrow kitchen, stuffed them into brown paper bags, shared what there was to carry and started off down the steep path leading from the deck to the garden below. Accompanying us were our dog Mike, Edith and one of her pups. The Siamese kitten and two crows we left behind.

As we made our way to the neighbor's place, Morris said, "Its been lonesome. I got to wondering last week how much longer I could stand it if someone didn't come. I got so desperate I paid a village boy's way to the movies the other night." Passing a row of small houses before we got to the cow pasture land, Morris added, "On the 4th of July an old man sat on the steps of that shack with a package of fire crackers, lighting each one and tossing it slowly and deliberately into the grass. When one didn't go off he'd wait a few minutes and then crawl up to it on hands and knees and re-light it. What a sight!"

Our way led between great fields of flowering cabbage and beets grown for seed, the purple veined leaves of the beets like apoplectic faces. We slid the boat, a frail flat-bottomed affair, down to the edge of the float after dumping the accumulated rainwater onto the beach. I sat in the back, Morris rowed and Kenneth knelt in the bow. The oars dipped with that wonderful rhythmic quality I have always loved. The tide was coming in and the swift current flowed against us. Morris braced himself and rowed hard. The reeds on the banks were taller than our heads, all combed in the same direction as the outgoing tide had left them.

We joked over the great strength it took to row. Morris threatened to make Kenneth get out and push. Leaking water was lapping about our ankles, so I started bailing with a small coffee can, without accomplishing much. Morris complained loudly about slaving while we rode in style and at the first opportunity he pulled the boat up on a bank of the slough. He and I got out onto the marshland reeds. Kenneth agreed to take the boat the rest of the way.

The mud under the grasses sucked at our feet. We climbed over the giant stumps and walked logs that had been washed in on the tide and left stranded in the muck. The contorted silvered roots of the dead giants stood starkly against the dark blue sky. I imagined that Morris's tall frame striding on ahead was Paul Bunyan, the thick growth of reeds a tangled forest. Morris is happiest making his way over trail-less country, regardless of the nature of the land. Trails others have made hold little interest for him, and this holds true throughout his character. We joined Kenneth at the base of the rock, moored the boat and began to climb up the slope, first passing a huddled group of simple shacks, faded and weathered, clinging to the soil like fungus. The route led around the side of the island, climbing steadily. Wild flowers sprouted everywhere and included a tough yellow daisy, a beautiful deep blue one, and a small white orchid.

We stopped before long on the green slopes above the water where the panorama of sea and islands spread out before us. We fished out the sandwiches while Mike chased butterflies and seagulls wheeled and called overhead.

"They started last night. It's going on now. Listen... don't you hear the drums?" The bosomy blond proprietress of the small hotel and restaurant at La Conner paused in the doorway of her empty café. She had just told us there was no food left. There had been too many visitors in town, fifty from the Makah reservation on the Olympic Peninsula alone.

The evening was cloudy, the waterfront street deserted. We picked up hamburgers and drinks at the drugstore counter across from the hotel. We ate hurriedly, excited, but a bit uneasy wondering whether white people were truly welcome at this treaty day commemoration.

We drove over the slough bridge to the community hall, a frame structure near the strange totem pole made and erected by artists under the W.P.A. during the Depression thirties. A hideously distorted face of Franklin Roosevelt adorned the top, grinning fiendishly over the countryside from his place above a number of carved animals and birds, each separate on the pole, rather than the traditional integration into a uniform design. The rows of small wooden houses, all alike, with the spire of the Catholic Church in the center, faced the tidal waters of the slough darkly and silently. Over the slough waters the Indian and the white villages stared at each other mutely. Only at the community hall were there light and noise. This was the first year the dancing had not been held in the old tribal longhouse with its central firepit , the smokehouse it was called for obvious reasons. Already a large number of cars were parked about the hall; we picked our way through the puddles and mud to the lighted entrance and through clusters of Indians about the doorway.

The atmosphere within was rather like that of a rural church supper. Dinner was in progress at six or seven long tables in the center of the large room. We stood for a while trying to look inconspicuous. The lack of interest in us was reassuring, and I edged farther into the room. People were leaving the tables, the few remaining lingering over coffee. The children were peeling oranges and drinking pop.

I discovered a bench with room for us at the other side of the room and beckoned to Kenneth and the boys. *Boom* boom boom boom *boom* boom went the drums. On the stage a group of teenagers was gathered about the piano, where someone was plunking Chopsticks. Dancers in the process of donning costumes wandered on and off the stage into the wings. We claimed our seats just in time, for the tables were now cleared away, the folding chairs arranged in rows, and the audience began to form for the program. The long benches against the walls were already filled. Plump brown babies, clean and well cared for, with slanting almond eyes, opaque and obsidian, romped over their young parents.

The speakers were many, starting with "our old friend Joseph Joe." "This day celebrates the day nearly a hundred years ago when our people signed over their great lands to the Christian invaders. At this time the government promised that $150,000 would be paid our people. A long time have our people waited for these unfulfilled promises to be kept. The Christian invaders have not kept their promises. We Indians have kept our word and we have lost the great lands we once owned in peace and happiness. The United States is feeding people all over the world but many Indians are dying of starvation. Two world wars have claimed our sons, and still the promises are not fulfilled. Now the federal government is going to take away our Indian supervisors and we will lose what little we have. This is a bad thing and we should try and keep it from happening..."

Next came the MC for the Neah Bay Indians. "My people have worked hard on these dances for you, but they have had time for only three practices. So we ask you to bear with us. This here first dance is a whale dance. The Indian he didn't just go and do a thing, he worked himself up first, to get himself ready, and so these people you might say are working themselves up to go whaling." The design on the curtain pulled open was beautiful and tasteful, the colors earthy, not gaudy, blues and reds and yellows, the design simple, traditional, thunderbird and whale.

The performance of the spirit sticks was particularly moving; a unique thing, half dance, half game, and with a strong air of magic over the whole business. The old man who controlled the sticks was introduced as the only remaining person who has the power. He chanted and pantomimed while the drums beat and two pair of young men, each pair with their hands on "the sticks" were apparently led around the circle by the sticks, at a running trot in unison with the drums. Arms outstretched, grasping the sticks, they seemingly were wrenched up and down by the power of the sticks. The sticks were shaped of wood into a square with rounded corners and a bar down the middle, the whole thing painted red. Each couple had one of these wooden forms; one man of each couple grasped the stick with both hands, the other with one hand, his other arm around his partner's waist. From time to time one of the partners would drop into the circle of watchers, and another would replace him. At the end, the drums ceased. The old man who controlled the sticks took them and was apparently thrown to the floor by their queer inner life, but managed after a struggle to get them back into their box, a decorated, ceremonial container. It was all very strange and very convincing.

It was at last the Swinomish tribe's turn to do its war dances. The old woman up the bench from us hastily daubed her face with black in the manner of many of the Swinomish dancers. Two very drunk young men worked their way through the crowd to our corner and stumbled to a couple of empty chairs. The air was by this time hot and the drums were booming thunderously, the primitive chanting of the Swinomish filling the hall with the fervor of despair.

Joseph Joe, said the MC, would lead the war dances. The heavy figure, unrecognizable in shredded cedar bark headdress and fringed costume, his face blackened and partly hidden by the streaming headdress, moved onto the floor alone, and slowly, rhythmically, stomped about in a circle, all the time shouting hoarsely in great, rending gasps from the very pit of his being; the sound could not be called singing or even chanting; it was animalistic, primitive, completely beyond my experience.

The blackened old woman on the bench beat her hand and shouted with him. The drummers and dancers were all concentrated in one corner of the hall, to where finally Mr. Joe, through with his performance, returned. The drums and shouting ceased, and only the spasmodic groans and grunts and wails of the performer in his state of trance and exhaustion filled the air

The drunks got uncertainly to their feet and, blunderingly but politely stumbled out through the standing people to the doorway. The eyes of the tall one were glazed as he ran the palm of his hand over his slack mouth. I was ready to duck as he went by, but he made it.

After each dance the performer was given a short spell to exhibit the results of his trance, and each seemed to attempt to outdo the others in the terrifying sounds they produced. A woman followed the second man, and the fourth dancer was also a woman. They were middle aged, heavy, and they hopped on both feet, rapidly, clear about the circle. The arms of the first moved from side to side before her in vague rhythm. The second thrust her arms in punching gestures. The hysterical noises produced by the women dancers were even more terrifying than the guttural sounds the men made.

I watched the faces of the two young couples seated near us, each with a chubby, pretty baby girl, the women with sweet faces and modish clothes, the men patient and somehow cowed. They seemed tired and perhaps a little bored. Past the second couple (they were seated on the bench against the wall) was an old woman with gray hair combed smoothly back from her brown and sublime face. She wore an expression of almost saintly nobility. With her was a girl of about ten, probably her granddaughter, and she too had a very lovely face. She had spent the entire evening on her grandmother's knee watching with grave fascination the baby belonging to the couple next to them on the bench. This baby girl had a red hair bow and a checked red dress. Her little mouth reposed in a constant smile; the smooth round cheeks were faintly pink through the brown skin. The grave child watched the adorable baby with a longing, unchanging expression.

Again, from the corner where the performers were gathered, came this heightened intensity, a savage, tearing, soul-searing wave of emotion that flooded the hall with a mood of primordial power. The beating of the drums and the stomping of the feet, together with the vibrations of the voices, revealed a fierce, rocking tumult of naked grief and vengeance.

I knew suddenly that I could stand no more of it. I had almost forgotten we were free to go, that we could by the simple movement of getting up from the narrow bench and propelling our legs to the door and into the night, shake off this world, which was not ours, but which had a connection with ours as disturbing as it was mysterious.

On the porch of the hall were stragglers who watched the excitement from a safe distance. Two pretty teen-age girls were talking with a couple of high school white boys. An Indian boy greeted one of the girls, asked her to go inside with him. "I'm sorry, I can't," she giggled. "We're with these guys tonight." A few feet away against the side of the building an Indian man was doubled over, limply; he had been vomiting and was still retching convulsively. No one paid any attention. Behind the row of cars two men hoisted bottles and gulped, their heads far back.

The wind from the southwest was warm, rippling the puddles, which caught the light illuminating the parking grounds. I tried to picture how it was before the invaders came. The cedar and skin huts perched between the dark wall of the forest and the restless tides, the bountifulness of nature, salmon in the bay and rivers as thick as beans in a pot, the foot trails in the forest and the canoes in the waters, the sunrises and the sunsets, the heat of noon and the moonlight coming to you straight from the heavens without a filter of industry's hot and smelly breath.

What is it about the white man, I wondered? Is it good or is it bad? Or is it neither? And is it with nature or against nature? The impelling energy, the drive, cannot be condemned in itself. But the Indians lived with nature, at times were cowed by nature, recognized their own dependence and made supplication to the gods of nature. The white man talks of conquering nature through science. Science is the white man's god. The Indian's society lasted 10,000 years here. Can the white man's possibly come close? All right, then, it's over and done. The white man took the Indian's lands and his very life, and it was robbery, let's recognize that. It's over and done with, but let's not add robbery to robbery. The Indian soul still survives. Today's old ones, remembering the old ones now dead, pass on the soul of the culture. And we must not from the tottering height of our manufactured world tell ourselves it is all stupid superstition, with no value. If we could learn to be quiet for a time and to strain our unaccustomed ears to nature's rhythms; to experience the wave's pulse, the wind's cry, the thunder's roll, the sound of seeds in a dry pod, the rustling of grasses around a forest pond – if we could be quiet and still for a time, we could perhaps recapture a thing lost to us, but perhaps not lost to the Indians.

It was two a.m. when we left the dancing. Our motor roared as the tires skidded in the deep mud; the sound of the drums was gone.

40

SEATTLE. TOBEY IS AT Edmond Meany Junior High this year. He's five feet six inches tall and wears a nine and a half shoe. His voice has changed and he seems so adult it is startling, yet it all happened imperceptibly. At the moment he is at Bobby Winks' house listening to, or I guess you say watching, Milton Berle on television. The Winks are the first in the neighborhood to own a T.V.

It is raining. I hear the water running off the roof from where the downspouts are supposed to be and never are. I am disgruntled. I want to write and I can't. Why? I feel so helpless about communicating. Do I feel too much or too little? I don't know. When I feel something intensely it is too hard to write about it. When I am depressed, I can't resurrect my feelings enough to record them. Yet I never quit wanting to write, and not just to publish. But to say what I think and feel is the hardest. I wonder what a broken heart feels like and if that is what I have. But I think not. There is so much I can't say.

I've just had a taste of that hour of solitude Lewis Mumford recommends in *Conduct of Life*. Then I picked up this record and turned to my writings of almost two years ago and I am shocked by my distress – yet I understand. I do hope I have grown calmer about the sense of writing-time being lost. The more conscious we are of lost time, the more we lose. The only time lost is the time spent thinking about it.

It is Sunday late afternoon. Kenneth has gone to dinner with Emma Simson at the Malones. I'm getting over the flu. I could have rallied and gone but think staying home is wiser. Tobe is out with new companions, the two Carols and Jim Grant. Last night he went to his first real party with girl-boy pairing. There was dancing, the first time he had danced with anyone but me. He seemed pleased with it all, and said the girls all asked him to dance. He didn't know why, "they must like to get stepped on." I think he has sprung into a new phase of life. I remember in the eighth grade when I first consciously had the feeling of belonging to a group. The little girls came for him last night in a parent's car. Both Carols small and pretty, one blonde, one dark. The blonde was in yellow organdy, the brunette in dark blue cottons trimmed with white, looking very sweet with flowers in their hair. It all seems quite strange, but this whole year has been a strange one. I think adolescence is harder on parents than kids.

Is this what it's like to be old and alone? I have tried to think about the old, ill and forgotten, and I've wondered what could be done for them. There should be pleasant quarters and good attendants and amusements such as convenient libraries and accessible art. What a world there could be! Without war, we could strive for a world without fear. We could nurture love and there would be enough for all. And if all were truly loved there would be no bad, sad or mean ones. Love and faith are the two keys.

Tobey, who was to be home at eight called, "Can I stay just a little longer at Leckbergs? There's a good canasta game going on." "Until 8:30 then. Home by 8:30!" "Please, I'll leave at 8:30." "No. Home by 8:30." So it's now 8:37 and no Tobey, which means he stayed anyway until 8:30. What can I do? Oh, I remember, I remember... the phone calls. *Is Bob there? No, he just left.*

Robe Valley. Spring slowly drifts in upon us, while the human species continues to mess itself up. Russia is bullying and we are bullying, each of us putting up a false front to lure other nations to our own pole; we aren't human beings dealing with other human beings, honestly and with integrity. We are a propaganda machine, ruthless and powerful, as lying as any roadside billboard, a nation of partial people, of fragmentary natures, as blinded in our way as the Russians are in theirs. What it will lead to eventually I can't see unless it is either a miracle of redemption and renewal, or utter destruction.

I sit on the doorstep in hot sunshine after a morning of spading. A thrush sang while I got half the garden turned over. Kenneth is doing things to the creek. He rebuilt the bridge yesterday. He has cleared out a lot of rotten wood below the bridge and enlarged the pool, which looks much more beautiful.

Tobey's girlfriend Jo McKenzie came with us to the mountains this time. She and Tobe are up the creek fishing. It's hard to know how to cope with such an affiliation when they are so young. She said yesterday she had always hated spiders and that a large ugly one was on Tobe's cheek while he was fishing, so she slapped at it, knocking his pole out of his hand and startling him. Said she, "he told me spiders were like everything else in nature and had just as much reason for being here as any form of life. He said everything in nature had a purpose and I was silly for being afraid of a little spider. He said the poor thing was probably much more scared of me than I was of it. He made me feel so bad I wanted to cry. I felt so sorry for the spider." Sometimes I really admire Tobe and think he has good sense.

Tobey and Jo are together constantly, I can't figure out just what their feeling is toward each other. I never had a similar experience. They seem to feel relaxed together, almost like Claribel and I at that age. Of course, having never had a "steady" boyfriend until I married Kenneth, I am at a loss. I don't know whether or not they are too serious for their age. I don't know if I should let nature take her goddamn course, or whether to interfere or what. It's actually true that I never went with one boy to the exclusion of others. In fact in college, we made fun of the whole idea. In the sorority we rolled our eyes at the rushee from the small town who talked about the "kid I go with". In fact, just the term "boyfriend" we thought funny and corny. Undoubtedly these two are more relaxed and happy than we were. But I have a feeling he is missing something. When we're in Seattle Bobby Wink and his friend come every day to borrow his basketball and have a fit if they get near a girl. They are so much more natural from my standpoint. We used to laugh at our romantic dreamings and ourselves. We were awkward and ungainly and reaching for the stars, either ecstatically or miserably. It seems to me his life is mundane in comparison, with his damn comics, radio, T.V. and weekly movies, and long telephone conversations with Jo.

Of course, he has had the mountains. And actually, until I was fourteen, starting my junior year in high school, I was quite, quite lost, pretending to be the age of the other girls in the neighborhood, who were 17 and 18. During the war years we took walks to Woodland Park with soldiers and sailors, whom my parents entertained for Sunday dinner. We were always yearning for and dreaming of romance in the form of "the knight on the white steed" or some other ridiculous idea we had from the books we read then. I didn't become interested in literature until I was fifteen. This constant effort to reconcile my viewpoint with Tobe's is a strain, but otherwise I have no way of understanding.

Seattle. I bought Debussy's "La Mer" and an album of early songs sung by John Jacob Niles. Some of the songs are beautiful, particularly "I Wonder as I Wander." It's simple but from the heart and full of mystery, ending on an unresolved minor that echoes the shrouded beauty of night skies and mountain solitude.

We've had good luck selling paintings the last few weeks and have a little reserve in the bank, about $1,000 for the first time in ages. Of course taxes are looming soon, but Kenneth has a show in April, which should net us some gain. . Just now he is doing a series of very small temperas on gesso or Japanese paper glued on board. They relate strongly to the ones owned by the Bloedels in Tacoma.

Contact with nature has brought about invention and magic in his painting. Its importance isn't understood yet except, perhaps by Maynard Walker. True advances in art are seldom appreciated until after the artist is aged or departed. This is inevitable and is not to be resented. The main thing is having the strength and faith to go on working. Maintaining faith is the most difficult of all. Kenneth's does not waver as much as does mine.

It has been a disturbing fall in many ways. Kenneth was asked by the editor to write an article for *Art News* that avoided promoting the usual big names. The responses to the article from Mark, Morris and Guy in the form of letters to *Art News* and verbally by phone, attacked Kenneth personally. It has left me with feelings of uncertainty about friendships and human relationships in general. I wondered if we had been at fault, and I searched into past events and attitudes. But I am certain that Mark, Morris and Guy are the unfair ones. I think they are somehow driven by their homosexuality and need to feel superior. But their anger and bouts of jealousy cause loneliness in me. As our friend Don Bear said in his letter, "Ah me! Caught between the fairies and the Pharisees."

But most disturbing of all, we recently learned from the mother of Tobey's friend Jimmy Foss that the boys stole two cars on evenings when they were supposed to be at the school gym playing basketball. Jimmy's younger brother spilled the beans. We are hoping we can believe Tobe when he says he will get into no further trouble. The whole thing could have been a major disaster, should there have been an accident, or should the police have picked them up. They have apologized to one of the owners here in our neighborhood. There have been nights of no sleep, desultory eating of food long cold, and emotional strain leaving us both older and with permanent scars. Tobe insists the acts were due merely to stupidity and to excitement-seeking and not part of a deeper rebellion or psychological problems. Perhaps we have all learned something; Kenneth and I to be more interested in his schoolwork and amusements; Tobe to be on guard against the sort of actions that can only lead to harm. Perhaps we all need to know how to pray. Reading aloud the 23rd Psalm helped us all that heart-breaking evening and the Lord's Prayer was a plank over the torrent.

Finally adjusting to his new teeth has been a long and difficult process for Kenneth, but should be easier from now on. At least my mother is walking around again and feeling a little better. Could it be that some of my anxieties might begin to dissolve?

41

YESTERDAY WAS WARM AND sunny. The Sherman Lee girls, Tobey and I went to Gold Basin to look at the slide. A virtual glacier of clay and gravel and sand, it's snout about a hundred feet wide and extending an equal distance into the river, forced the watercourse into the campground. Twice the Forest Service has had to blast a path for the river, and they think the entire upper campground is lost. It seems long ago that we met Everett Barrett here and were first told about Robe Ranch. It's another reminder, if we needed one, of how transitory everything and everyone is.

On the way home we stopped at the Ottaways. Leonard said right away, "How much did I get this time?" - a joking reference to the break in we had at the cabin. Our cabin was robbed just about five years from a previous robbery at Robe Ranch. This time they took everything: groceries, dishes, eatin' irons (as Susie calls them), rugs, blankets, tools, etc., plus a tent and camera belonging to Sherman Lee. I think Leonard knows damn well who did it, but it wasn't he, I am sure. Dorothy's hair has turned quite grey. She is skin and bones and her skin is grey, too. But Leonard said, pleased as could be, "she says if she could be sure she'd have another girl, she'd be willing... Imagine that? That's what she said." And Dotty spoke up then, "Well, I figure I don't need no more boys, but it's going to be a problem, just having one girl. There'll be nobody for her to play with." It never occurred to me that a family with six kids could have that complaint.

Last Sunday we went to the Darrington Timber Bowl with Ludy and Mitch. We met up with the Storches in Granite and drove to Darrington through Arlington. We sat in the dirt alongside the grandstand to get into the shade. We watched the tree topping, rolling pin throwing, women's log bucking and the log truck trailer backing. There were too many young mothers looking not more than fifteen or sixteen with two or three infants, real hillbilly types. I rode the caterpillar in the carnival with Earl, a fantastic experience. The spinning motion really takes me apart.

On Monday I went cherry picking. Maudie Storch made the arrangement. The cherry tree belongs to the Matlocks, who have a farm out in the Jordan Valley. It's a beautiful location. The ranch house is on a rise overlooking pastureland, Three Fingers Mountain and the backside of Pilchuck. It was a blue-sky day of sun and heat. There were chickens roosting and strutting and pecking and dropping everywhere. Mr. Matlock is fat, lazy and smooth of skin with a beard and hairy chest. "Be careful where you step, the chickens have been around the yard." An understatement! There was literally no place to step anywhere, including the porch and inside the house -- really distressing dirt. In the basement there was a heap of clothes to be washed that would fill a silo. The consummate dirt everywhere reminded me of the Lewises: a goo-spattered stove, an unspeakable bathroom that stank of small children, chicken droppings and unwashed adults, and over all the odors of sour milk and old grease.

Mrs. Matlock, fat and active, was heaving her great stomach, hanging breasts, mountainous butt and barrel legs around like a stevedore tossing sacks of flour. She has a good out-going spirit. I can tell she's out-matched, yet not giving up.

"I just don't get time to take care of the house or the canning I should be doing. I just can't bear to see good food go to waste with prices like they are now. I just get started on the washing or something and then the men call and I have to go run the tractor or help with the haying. Now tomorrow there'll be fifteen layers to butcher and all these cherries that should be picked before they split in the sun." I commented on the healthy looks of their four children. "Yes, the doctor at the Granite Falls clinic told me if all children were as healthy as ours he would have to give up doctoring and go to blacksmithing. I'm glad.

It makes it all seem worthwhile. We wanted three children, well the last one was a surprise, but the first three were planned."

They came from Oklahoma three years ago and (according to Maudie) paid $14,000 for the farm. Mr. Matlock is her second husband, younger than she, and is intensely jealous of her. If she stays too long after church gabbing with the girls, he trots into town after her. At one point he burst into "I Ain't Got Nobody". He has a lazy, low-down way of singing, a good mellow voice. He could make money in Hollywood. I'd like to be turned loose with a good cameraman in that backcountry.

While I picked cherries the chickens pecked them out of the box. "Look out, you won't have any left," Mrs. Matlock laughed. There was literally no place to put them where the chickens wouldn't get them. To pick the cherries her husband sawed off the branches while I sat on the ground on a cushion of chicken-doo and picked them at my leisure. "Won't it hurt the trees sawing them when they are bearing?" I asked. "I dunno, we'll find out."

October already. The perfect fall weekend in the country. I love the red and gold of the vine maples, the green and gold of the big maples, and the rich, deep gold of the cottonwoods, the dampness of their leaves underfoot. The southern sun sets in a blue and gold sky, the nights are sharp and cold, and during the day the sun is warm. The woods' smells are heightened and penetrating in the fall.

I walked a ways up the Green Mountain road. There were yellow violets blooming in certain warm spots. I never tire of the look of the mossy stumps, the matted deer ferns and the baby huckleberry bushes, so delicately green and so toughly alive. A passing hunter's car left a momentary taint so noticeable after the air's pureness. It made me wonder about the effect in town, where there is so much vehicle exhaust in the air all the time that we don't smell it. But up here I didn't want to breathe after the car passed until the air cleared.

Another sign of the times. At Bergan's Hardware Store we traded the gas lantern Kenneth's sister Dorothy gave us for Christmas for their last Aladdin kerosene mantel lamp, the type that gives such a nice even light for reading. Bergan's is closing out their Aladdin lamps because the electricity installed into our valley has eliminated the last buyers they had for them. Everyone has bought converters and now uses them as electric lamps, he says. Grandma Otto used to say she would never live to see a paved road, and then she would never live to see electricity. Now she has both.

Tobey shot his first live thing yesterday, a grouse near the Kosmowski place. I felt badly, but I don't believe he did. He de-feathered it before bringing it home. A plump creature, it must weigh about two pounds. I'll roast it today.

42

I T'S A MAGICAL EVENING at the cabin with frogs caroling, olive backs pouring out song after song, and robins clucking at the dogs and the cat. The rushing river is audible, as it is very high. Lots of snow melted today and yesterday. Tree tips are motionless against a pale sky.

The woods' smells are as heavenly as I've ever known them to be. There's been lots of sun and enough rain this spring; all is sublimely lovely. Nature has given so bounteously; we must feel very grateful to be part of it. Death is a part of it too, and must therefore be beautiful in its relationship to the whole. I am filled with joy on such an evening. A thrush just flitted past, so close it almost touched me.

The big fat toads are on the move. The snakes come out each morning now to bask outside the door and slither back under the steps at night. Numerous deer are around this year; two yearling does crossed the yard earlier tonight. I saw a porcupine up close on Green Mountain last Friday evening. It scrambled into the brush as we drove up. They can't hurry worth a damn.

It's nearly dark now and cooler. The thrush is still warbling. The robins are still annoyed with the cat. Reluctantly I must go into the house and light a lamp. I can smell the lilacs I picked at Robe Ranch. They are in the yellow vase, with that plant I think is called bridal wreath. Wirt used to say that the bush always made him feel sad, as he would never be a bride. How I love that place! Even though it's all mashed and battered, sad and overgrown, the old magic feeling is still there. The lilac bush is so tall I could hardly reach the blooms. The serviceberry bushes have become trees, a mass of white blossoms. The yellow transparent is covered with blossoms. I again dug a root of honeysuckle – I hope it decides to take this time.

Tobey and I scrambled down the steep bank to the river. The rocks on the gravel bed were hot with the sun, but the water felt icy. We climbed over the great jam of logs and wreckage of houses left by the flood, almost directly below our orchard. It must be a hundred feet long and fifty feet wide, a snarl of great trees, roots, lumber, timbers, branches, roof shakes, bits of household articles such as stoves and refrigerators. It's a great mess, which may be lodged there for decades or may be washed out completely in another season.

Vic and Jean dropped by. Vic's nose was all done up in gauze and adhesive following the straightening operation. It was broken last winter by a flying choker. He was really lucky it didn't take his head off. He has had too many close calls. Jean still hasn't had all the stitches out from her operation. She made $5 in a few hours peeling cascara bark last week. It is 20 cents a pound now. Vic hates breaking up the dried bark and packing it in gunnysacks. I said, "Can't you just jump on it like Tobe and Dave do?" "Christ, I jumped and jumped and stomped my guts out and we only got three more pounds in the sack."

We took dinner up the river above Red Bridge last night and picnicked on a gravelly bend in the river. The boys fished and we walked around through the forest. There were a number of unusually huge trees – fir, spruce and hemlock, some of them at least six feet in diameter. We found lots of dry wood for a supper fire strewn about on the wide gravel bar. The evening sun was beautiful on the tall old trees, illuminating the moss and lichen on the top branches.

Kenneth has gone back to Seattle with Louise Gilbert to do museum business. The boys have gone camping at Canyon Lake, the first time without an adult. I'll pick them up tomorrow. I was uneasy about it, but I have a lot of faith in Tobey's judgement. I am alone with the two cats and two dogs. It's a perfect evening, the mountain now gray after flaming moments at sunset. Everything is blooming; the air, fragrant. The thrushes are nesting now, so they only make little warning whistles. I can hardly bear to go indoors.

While driving to Canyon Lake trail today I had a strange thought. It occurred to me that my own existence really doesn't matter. I got an excited and elated feeling thinking of what will be going on when I'm not.

I feel rather dazed and inert today. Maybe I'm just plain tired as a reaction to the company yesterday – the Malones, Lees, Rourkes, and Fullers all here, making ten adults and four kids to cook for and serve, and talk to, etc.

Late this afternoon I went for a swim, hoping I might be revived, but I still feel leaden. Perhaps it has something to do with the particular company we had? The river is not really low enough yet. There is still a good deal of winter silt over the rocks, but much of the spring wreckage has washed downstream. It seems to me more rocks in our swimming hole than last year. I banged my toe on one, as usual.

We've started both the fireplace and water system. We found, upon Earl's advice, a Mr. Chapman, a cement and septic tank man, who is taking over, and seems a godsend. He is like a Dickens' character, perhaps George Weller, short, with a great middle bulk, very blue eyes, red beefy face, double chin, scant light hair. He talks all the time he's working, and where he gets the wind for the heavy labor and constant talk, with all that pot belly, I don't know. "There's a right way and a wrong way," he is fond of saying, and gives examples. To Tobey, bringing him rocks up the ladder, "you call that a *flat* rock? Now go down and get me a *flat* rock, boy." He tells about the man who made a well without covering it and the things that were found in it when they cleaned it. "Two dead snakes and about five gallons of earwigs and bugs, etc. It just shows what a person can drink and not know it. We drank water off of a dead rabbit for three weeks one time and never knew it." He startled me by looking square at me and saying, "Yes sir, I could pass for a bum, but I'm a college graduate. I could pass for a bum," he repeated, and I didn't know whether I should contradict him or not. I felt he didn't want me to, so I said, "Well, I guess I could too, in these clothes." A pretty lame comeback, but I was stumped.

He has installed three tiles, each 36 inches in diameter and about two feet in length, one on top of the other as a storage tank, making a high cylindrical container that is set into the bank above the spring. The whole thing, with plumbing, septic tank etc. will probably cost a little more than $200. The fireplace will cost $260. We're also doing a garage, which isn't costing a cent, as it is entirely constructed of cedar poles, salvaged boards and shakes.

This is the first summer Tobe has spent a stretch without another boy up here, but it seems to be working out well. He fishes with Sherman some, and works with Kenneth, and he and I do some things together. I guess he is beyond that stage when to be without another kid is to be lost. Dave Perine will be up about the 18th, apparently.

Tobe and I stopped into the lovely Currier farm this morning to pick another eight boxes of strawberries. They are better than ever, firm and sweet and still enormous. We must have picked together about 80 boxes by now, and we've eaten nearly all of them, too. We are both strawberry fiends. I plan to take some in to my family when we go to town Thursday. We must go in because of the Western Association of Museum Directors' meeting, which Betty Willis said we should attend – said it was important that we go this year, meaning probably just Kenneth. I am in a quandary about whether to go myself or not. Having nothing to wear, all the usual difficulties. I'd really kind of like to though, as this sort of festivity doesn't happen often in my life.

Entries to this year's Northwest Annual have been coming into the museum in droves and Kenneth has been working feverishly on the exhibit ever since coming home. Mark and Dame Pat Nicholson have rocks with figures in them this year!! I think Mark's idea is to confuse people with the idea that Kenneth got this idea from him. If so, he is getting awfully muddled in the head. Kenneth said he and Morris happened to meet at the museum, and the greeting was cool and brief. The basis of the antipathy artists develop toward each other is insecurity and lack of faith and belief in what they do. The insecurity stems not from economic factors so much as from lack of inner substance.

The difficulty the artist faces is that he must function emotionally when he is creating. He must necessarily think he is producing important work and that his vision is vital. But the transformation into his non-creative role, his 'living with others' role, is what gives us all so much trouble. He wants to be an artist but he doesn't want to take the consequences, which inevitably include a full range of reactions to his work, including indifference, active dislike, even anger, approval and very rarely, complete understanding. Insincere approval is as hard to take as disapproval. At least it should be.

I didn't go with Kenneth to the Museum Directors' meeting but the Artists' Equity dinner for Walter Isaacs' retrospective was one of those spontaneously happy affairs you wouldn't believe could happen among so many people who dislike each other for one reason or another. First, we had drinks at the Pattersons, the first time in many years, since Pat declared his feud. Two small whiskeys and I was high. Ray Hill and Dorothy Smith were being fey and gay. Thelma Lehman was bedecked in splendor with white flowers, and Joe Harrison was accessible enough that I finally told him he had taught me to think long ago in a contemporary literature class at the U of W.

Dinner at a restaurant above Lake Union was not served until nearly ten, so everyone got very high indeed, what with the sherry flowing all that time. Walter sang his 'Hatfields and McCoys, they was rugged mountain boys' song and Tsutakawa sang Japanese songs with closed eyes and gargly tremolo, and Pat sang his limping song, twollopy twollopy twa, and the happy little chappy.

Everyone expressed feelings of good fellowship, but toward the end Pat made it clear he was "sore again" because he's not in the drawing show Sherman Lee got together. I expected that of Sherman. If anyone has a right to be sore it is ourselves over what he did about the state capital mural project. He voted to reject all the finalists, Kenneth being the most likely to have won.

Kenneth and I have just come from a drive north of the city. The sun has shone all day from a cloudless sky, the air clear and edgy with a north breeze. On our drive we visited Northgate, the vast new shopping development of which I have read much hoop-la since it opened some months ago. Not being the let's-look-at-the-gardens or the latest-suburban-real-estate-development type I haven't before had the curiosity to investigate.

Northgate covers many acres, including several reserved for parking alone. Stores, ranging from the large Bon Marche department store to small florist and shoe shops, abound. The plan, completely modern, allows for a maximum of space, sun and convenience. Store windows face onto traffic-less avenues, in the center of which are raised bricked-in flower gardens. Lots of glass, brick and wood, and most importantly an over-all plan eliminating all haphazard confusion, distinguishes the area from similar shopping developments of the past. Here, I thought, is really a temple. This is no mere project for housing and selling merchandise. Northgate is a place for the worship of materialism.

At Northgate there is no sculpture, no painting, no mural. There is no concession to man's non-materialistic nature; no statement of ideals nor aspirations. It is an important omission and is not confined to Northgate. Art must be part of our culture if our culture is to survive and play a role in the awakening world.

John Stuart Mill's *Utilitarianism* provoked the usual lively, if indeterminate, discussion at the Great Books meeting last evening. The weather, incidentally, was so lovely and early summerish and warm and starlit, that I would say it was a great tribute to Mr. Mill that a roomful of individuals would forego the delights of the outdoors to gather and discuss his theories for two hours. Utilitarianism seems to be so foolproof, so complete, so thoroughly the intelligent solution to issues, and yet, when you bring it down to some specific problem you have the same old dilemmas. I foundered on the question of the

Korean intervention, regarded in the light of utilitarian justice. Having just about convinced myself that wars solve nothing, that the principle of evil for evil results in only an escalation of evil, when faced with the proposition of what then for aggressors, I hedged. I am certain of only one thing, which is, world government is the only solution to world discord and must be the prelude to a lasting peace. There is no other mechanism to insure peace. It is true, as Alice Harris interjected, that the aim of peace must also be in the hearts of people. But good will alone is not enough. Laws will not transform the nature of man, but they will serve to regulate his actions.

We hear that the Kosmowski place, or what portion of it remains after the river's depredations, will be foreclosed upon next year because no taxes have been paid since 1943. What the river hasn't taken away would be ideal to add to our acres and the Lees are interested in taking the other half. I must look up Alex Kosmowski.

The Lees are in full swing with their building having bulldozed the old Albright place. They sowed clover over the entire flat and built an outdoor fireplace and table-workbench combination. They planted a vegetable garden and some fruit trees and sorted their first load of lumber from the scrap heap of the small Granite Falls mill formerly owned by the Storches. As I feel somewhat instrumental in getting them started by steering them to the acreage I hope they don't come to feel disillusioned or regretful about it.

Their achievements so far leave me feeling inadequate as a gardener, but this afternoon I did turn over some of the sod around the raspberry patch. I clipped off the old dead spears. Gathering them up for kindling reminded me of Wirt and what wonderful heaps of those nice dry things we used to have for starting fires. It's funny how we miss Wirt. I can't think of anyone I'd be so glad to see.

Kenneth is in a good painting spell; bigger, more colorful, more geometric forms in oil on canvas. He wants to lose himself in something bigger than previous work; seeing man as having less importance in the whole scheme of things.

I was about to sit down at the typewriter this afternoon but I didn't. I thought, I'll just get started and they'll all be here; Kenneth in from his studio because he has come to a stopping place on a painting; the boys from the far creek where they have fished all day for the delicious small cutthroat trout. And we'll have a drink, Kenneth and I, while we wait for dinner to cook. This has been a cloudy-gray think-about-writing August afternoon.

Today I picked some carrots. And, as I picked the carrots, I picked through the years going back as far as my first memory, which was of laughter. This is what I shall write about first in my recounting of my life's journey: not of our tree farm, not of the Robe Valley and Granite Falls, not of the old-timers, whom I so love, but first of my young life. I must start soon...

This hot dry summer began with our week on Vancouver Island and ended with a hike into Twin Lakes. We had the idea of camping our way up Vancouver Island during late June and early July but a forest fire raged over 20 square miles in the interior, so we weren't permitted to camp and had to stick pretty much to the main traveled road. We went to the end of it, including the last 50 miles of gravel. We stayed at Kelsey Bay, the end of the road, for two nights at a place called the Salmon River Hotel. It is ordinarily a lodging for loggers, but as the fire hazard had shut down logging activities, they had all left and we had the place to ourselves. The rear of the squared off concrete structure overlooks the wide delta of the Salmon River. It enters the bay there through acres of salt marshlands that are nibbled through by inlets empty at low tide and running when the tide is in. Roots and trunks of trees are strewn over the marshes, which are packed with a carpet of dense reedy growth. On the stumps grow adorable gardens of dwarf, gnarled trees.

Our camping trip to Twin Lakes with Dave Perine, Tobey and the Storches ended the summer the last week in August. We all carried packs, except Maudie. It was the first time I'd traveled with a pack since before Tobey was born. There were times on the way up when I wasn't sure I could go on putting one foot ahead of the other. But always after a rest the machinery would begin working again. At that I wasn't as fatigued as the day we climbed Pilchuck without packs.

We started Saturday morning. I rode to Monte Cristo with the Storches, Kenneth and the boys in our car following. The road was dry and dusty, the widened stretch between Silverton and Big Four rough with big, loose gravel. The trail starts right in Monte Cristo and climbs without much relief until after you get to the halfway mark at Poodle Dog Pass, where a side trail goes into Silver Lake. There's a wonderful stretch of old forest this side of the pass, mostly silver fir and hemlock, great gray straight pillars of trunks, which I hope are not marked for an early doom. The logging continues at a terrific pace in the Monte district.

To get into the basin that holds Twin Lakes you must climb along a series of ridges a thousand feet above. Eventually, there is a moment when you realize that you are on the last ridge. Looking down you see the flat blue planes of the lakes like a pair of off-set Modigliani eyes staring up. How I longed for wings, that I might float downward, rather than tackle the step by step descent, for I was damn weary and thirsty, surprised by the lack of creeks or springs along the entire trail. At least during this dry season there were none. But step-by-step you go down an almost ladder-like steepness in places. Finally, with parched throats and fingers stained purple from blue barriers, Kenneth and I caught up with the others in an idyllic little meadow where water ran over stones feeding the roots of red and yellow lady slippers, gentians, mosses and lichens and the tough grasses of this upper world.

Granite chunks varying in size from small houses to tombstones were strewn over the shore and protruded into the lake. Between and among them had grown the greenest of meadow grasses fed by meandering streams from the permanent snow banks at the base of the cliffs. We crossed to the far side of the lake, where we found as perfect a spot as we could have wished for. From somewhere in the heights a small stream a few inches in width, traveled over the precipitous rocks until, reaching a ledge about twelve feet high, it formed a miniature waterfall ending in a pool about five feet across, then flowed on to form a series of pools stepping down before again falling to meet the waters of the lower lake. In this sheltered spot we made a rock fireplace just a few feet from the abundance of pure running water which formed separate basins for such purposes as washing faces, rinsing dishes, cleaning fish, etc. The fine perfume of heather, balsam and cedar was all about us, and everywhere we looked were the most idyllic of postcard scenes. The stunted trees along the edge of the lake had the strange, almost artificial character of stage sets. These mountain trees seem to be bracing themselves, anticipating the storms they know are coming when the brief interval of summer ends.

We're just back in Seattle from the cabin after a lovely November weekend. A full moon last night rose from the back of Green Mountain to ride down the mid-sky. We drove after dinner to the second logging block on Green Mountain, Kenneth, Tobey and I, and then walked through the forest to the next clear-cut. As we neared the end of the forest stretch, the moonlit clearing ahead was dazzling. We walked straight into the face of the moon, and it was like walking into glory. I've never had quite such a sensation. A barred owl was again hooting. We nearly always hear that sound on Green Mountain at night. I wonder why they do their strange, lonely call? It fits so beautifully into the mood of the mountain.

There was new snow on Pilchuck, and the moon was so bright it made flashes against the snow, so that the high part of Pilchuck was like a giant flashing crystal across the valley. Never saw this before. I thought at first it must be an optical illusion, but Kenneth saw it, too.

The bear hasn't been back in the orchard this past week, but the apple trees at Robe Ranch had a lot of dung under them, from both adults and cubs, and some branches were broken off. They'd been eating blackberries also, the dung being quite black.

During the weekend we went into Robe Ranch again. A car was ahead of us, and it turned out to be Ethel Barrett, her children and friends. I'm very fond of her. She and her family live in Edmonds now. Everett found work in some business on the waterfront there. They may come to see us in town, she said. Both Eugene and Herbert are in the service. I was thinking of the time we met Everett up on Barlow Point where he was lookout before the war, and how he was dreading World War II. He spoke of his two sons, whom he hoped would never have to fight. That was the day he told us about the cabins at Robe Ranch, and suggested we stop by and see his family. Which led to our long years there, and the finding of our present acreage.

I hope sometime I can figure out a way to communicate these experiences so they makes sense, a way that is honest and has form and recreates what has been so wonderful about this life and still is. Our experiences in the Robe Valley have provided episodes as rich as life could give, I think, and yet so frugal in every way, except in nature's own grants.

43

THE MOST WILD AND wonderful storm rages on this January morning, a long-winded one and I do mean long-*winded*. It's been going on intermittently for several days. Last night and this morning the gusts got up to 70 miles per hour. Clouds ride by like gray chariots, birds swoop with the currents and flutter madly against them. Robins can survive anything. Rain is blown in long horizontal streaks, the pine tree's branches are churning, the maples toss their black branches hysterically, and the two poplars on the edge of the hill lean heavily to the north. It's bleak and wonderful and I like to think of places like Neah Bay, where they say the gusts were up to 90, and the mountain heights, like North Lake and Twin Lakes. But I don't like to think of what the trees near our mountain place may be doing. I only hope they're still standing up and not draped over the roof of the house or studio. A small plane goes by, flying low – seems foolhardy that it's up there at all. There have been two bad crashes the last two days and many in recent weeks. The toll is nearly 300 deaths in the last two months from plane wrecks in this area.

I just read that the C.A.A. is going to launch a nation-wide campaign to revive interest in young men and women becoming pilots, as they seem to have lost interest in recent years. This pleases me, as I have long been convinced of the inefficiency and wastefulness of airplanes. They have done so much more harm than good. The hoped-for improvement in international relations has not come about;

rather, far more mischief. They use up resources at an appalling rate, and their few good points just don't balance the bad ones. It would be better to make more good ships and trains with low fares for those who appreciate travel and would spread goodwill, rather than catering to big-shot trouble makers who fly from place to place in a restless search for power and diversion.

I've been asked to talk to a women's literary and art group on Europe's contribution to us in turn for what we are doing for Europe under the Marshall Plan. It is rather tempting to work out something. I could preface the talk by saying that it shouldn't be a matter of giving each other something, but rather a matter of people and nations fulfilling their destinies along the highest planes already achieved in the past. Europe's great contributors to civilization did just that, fulfilling their capacities as human beings, not consciously making a gift to mankind. We, in sending aid to Europe, should not deceive ourselves that we are making magnanimous gestures of charity, only that we are attempting to preserve the values dear to us. If it is to make sense, we should know something of what those values are... philosophical, aesthetic, religious, and political.

I could quote passages from Montaigne, Voltaire, Locke, and Pascal. I could show reproductions of Renaissance painters and emphasize the concept of dignity of individuals through Christian philosophy, as we know it. The splendid architecture of the Gothic cathedrals epitomizes the heights of worship of one of the world's most civilized and complex religions. These soaring structures symbolize, among others things, man's love of fellow man, and good triumphing over evil. And, finally, in the area of politics – I could show how modern democratic ideals were developed as an extension of Greek thinking.

I think I'll do it...

This is the first time I've felt strong enough to punch a typewriter since the flu laid me low a week ago. I have been reading Scott Fitzgerald's *Crack-Up* (I read the novel all during the fever part of my illness) and also Malcolm Cowley's *Exile's Return*, and I have become saturated in that period. The disillusion of the '20s fits my own mood beautifully. There has never been such a calm, clear-eyed, devastating statement of ultimate disenchantment as Fitzgerald's. The Harry Crosby episode in Cowley's book I found thoroughly repugnant. He was merely a drippy little bastard son of the rich without courage; he couldn't imagine anything positive. There were some like him here in Seattle, only without so much money and without the dramatic flair. Jack Fisher with his Chrysler roadster, his limited editions and parties when Mama was away, was somewhat that type. During that period, we were living on the edge of that life, but I think we had more fun and real adventure.

The same was true in the '30s. They were all so hypnotized by each other's brilliance back east in the center of things. Out west we were close enough to nature that the worst of the idiocies were dispelled in the sane scent of ocean and forest.

Kenneth went to Portland yesterday morning, also down to Salem and Eugene. Tobey went to a movie last night and has been gone all day. He ate with Jo at her place and is still there. So I am finding out about being alone. There is quite a lot about it to learn. Not all bad, but not all good, either. To fortify myself I have a fire in the fireplace and the phonograph playing, just now a Prokofiev, before that Mozart.

I am glad I have lost that suicidal gloom of the last few days while being sick. Today for some reason everything is acceptable again, and I can look out the window and for no good reason feel happy. This, I think, is what the philosophers mean by "grace".

The business of being sufficient unto one's self is a puzzle to me, though it is recommended highly by the Hindu and other religions. Surely one shouldn't be all to oneself. Even the monks have their groups and their schedules.

The most stalwart souls are the lone ones living out in the foothills like old Mrs. Baker and Susie and Wirt before he died. No guilty consciences among them, I am sure. Alone in the mountain night, so far from the road, Wirt lived with the supreme blackness of the forest brooding over his shoulder, the stars on clear nights jangling in space - - jangling and dangling with their terrible brilliance and even the moonlight frightening with its artificial twilight and shrouding shadows.

He had only a small fire in the old stove and his pipe and, well yes, the battery radio. That must have been a great help. He must have looked forward with all his heart to our visits on the weekends, because he loved to talk. He never failed to communicate; he never lost his connections. He was a man alone and sufficient unto himself.

The daily activities of this summer of 1953 were dwarfed by two major events, one shocking, the other wonderfully reinforcing.

Soon after we moved to the mountains in June, Kenneth found a letter from Dr. Fuller in our mailbox. It told Kenneth he had been fired from his curator's job of 20 years at the Seattle Art Museum. I wrote the following letter soon after but Kenneth convinced me not to post it. I think he was hurt as much by what he felt was Fuller's cowardly way of informing him as he was by the substance of the letter.

My response:

Dear Dr. Fuller,

I could never, of course, convey the bewilderment and shock I felt when Kenneth told me the news of his dismissal from the Museum staff. As Kenneth's partner for the two decades he has worked at the institution, I have felt very close to the Museum, and I feel I cannot let the matter close until I have expressed to you some of the thoughts that have occurred to me in the last few unhappy days.

The feeling of being set adrift in middle age, with the necessity of starting anew, was, of course, frightening at first, but this is the least, perhaps, of the emotions that have swept over me. There was first the question, "Where have we failed?" I say "we" because our lives have been so closely intertwined.

I have throughout this decade of inflation used all my wits and physical strength to keep our heads above water, without asking for a raise in salary. With no household help at all and no modern equipment I have managed to wash, iron, cook and clean, and still have time to write an occasional article to keep up with the bills. Thank goodness I have managed to complete our house payments in town and to invest in the tree farm (our place in the country) for at least we are solvent as we face an indeterminate future.

These tasks I have done with a feeling, not of resentment, but of pride, for I was convinced the cause we were serving was so fine and lofty a one that it transformed menial and monotonous work into important service.

When asked to contribute to causes we believed to be worthy I have done so with work, as we have not had extra money.

On occasions when Kenneth has been offered positions elsewhere he has discussed the matter with me, and I have always agreed that our devotion and loyalty to the Fullers and the Seattle Art Museum and our love for our home region superseded the possibility of material gain.

As for Kenneth's work as a painter, neither of us ever felt, nor did we think you felt, that it interfered with Museum duties, but rather that as he was able to increase his stature as an artist away from home, that it brought credit to the city and the institution we so loved. We were convinced too that anything either of us could do in the way of writing, which furthered the interests of Seattle artists reflected in a significant way upon the success of the Museum. I believe as time goes on, historians won't find another who has done as much as Kenneth in this field except for your own most generous support.

I can easily believe that at times Kenneth might have become irritable, for I have seen him this way too, and know it is a result of nerves and tension and the strain of living two lives, of coming home at five from the Museum and beginning a five- or six-hour stretch of painting. He takes responsibility very seriously and I know that he has felt the burden of his department at the Museum rested ultimately on his own shoulders. When Walter Froelich, for example, was dallying about, wasting time, it presented a problem, for Kenneth's authority was not as clearly defined as his responsibilities. The last thing he ever wanted to do was to go to you with problems of this kind or to risk anyone else's job by complaining.

I have at times wondered if we were remiss in not attending previews more regularly, and whether I should have engaged in Study Guild activities. The reason I did not hinged upon our conviction that Kenneth's chief value was in the hard, substantial work he did and I chose to remain in the background. Many times after installing a show he would feel physically too tired to go to a preview, and there was the matter of appropriate clothes, which we didn't seem able to afford in late years. I would have been glad to participate in women's Museum activities, but we both thought it might just make too much Callahan, and better that I should widen good will toward the Museum by participating in other civic affairs.

We have known for some time that there was a movement in some circles to get Kenneth out of his job, strangely enough centered among the very artists whose work he in the past has done the most to forward. This began after his own national reputation improved and I think is obviously caused by jealousy. As William Blake said, "Like the poison in the honey bee is the artist's jealousy." Kenneth as an artist is of course not free from this emotion either, I am sure, but I am equally sure that in his actions he has never given vent to it.

As for your charge that he has not been sufficiently interested in the beautiful objects you so admire, I can only say that perhaps he is not so skilled in verbal expression, but that his weekly articles are a lasting statement to his feelings on this subject. He gave his life at a low remuneration to the cause of art, believing and still believing that all art is the same thing, living or past, and that a life dedicated to this cause is a good life to live.

I hope the changes in personnel will accomplish what you wish for the Museum in the future. I hope they do as much for the institution as those who have worked so faithfully during the first two decades of its existence. Regardless of your recent action, I shall always believe Kenneth's role to have been a useful one in the development of this fine project, and if it has not been so, I can only say, it was not due to lack of enthusiasm nor loyalty on either his part or mine. Sincerely........

The other event in late summer 1953 helped to soften the shock we had in June. For many years I had been told of an extraordinary woman named Edith Bedal, who had worked as a packer and guide in the North Cascades. She and her sister Jean were renowned as beautiful, competent, exceptional young women in the early days.

The daughter of an Indian mother and French father, Miss Bedal was reputed to be so beautiful, so intelligent and so skilled a woods girl that she became a kind of myth that I was afraid would be shattered if I was to pursue the reality. But I wanted to do an article for the *Times* and this seemed like a story that needed to be written. And we could use the money.

My decision to look up Edith was confirmed by a conversation I had with a camper I met at Monte Cristo Lake last summer. "Say, there was an Indian girl packer in the days when I was prospecting, and she was the prettiest, nicest girl you could imagine. She was the best packer anywhere around and she knew every trail – man or animal – in the whole darn country. No matter how much of a head start you'd have, Edith Bedal and the horses were always at camp ahead of the party. And she'd never pass you along the trail. One time a young forestry employee walked out and left a string of pack mules stranded in a mountain snowstorm. Edith went in and brought that pack train out. Another time, when a hunter was injured, his partner got scared and left him in camp. Edith went in and brought him out single-handed." The camper went on to say Edith was too modest to tell such stories herself, but he had reliable information from old timers in the area.

The camper's stories convinced me that I had to meet Edith, so I went to see her in Darrington last winter, and my only regret is that I hadn't done so long before. Far from detracting from my imaginative creation, she enriched it and brought it to life. The following is from my article published in the *Seattle Times* magazine section.

When the war began, she and her mother were living alone in the same shake-covered cabin in which she was born in the wilderness, about 18 miles from Darrington. No one lives at Bedal now, named for Edith's family. The cabins and barn have long since been flattened by winter snows. Her mother, Susie Wa-Wetkin, a Sauk tribe princess, died in the cabin after the war.

Nels Bruseth, a Darrington historian, says the Sauk tribe was dispossessed of its homeland in the early days by an armed white man who took over their land and lodges while the tribe was away picking berries. He burned their dwellings and upon their return refused them their historic domain.

James Bedal and his bride moved to their wilderness home in 1890. He had selected the site for the wealth of cedar timber, the beauty of the mountain surroundings, the Sauk River close by, and its safe distance from town.

Susie Wa-Wetkin Bedal bore and reared her four children without benefit of doctor. She taught them what she knew of Indian lore, the art of packing, trapping and basket making and another art too ,at which Indians excelled, that of living in harmony with nature. On snowy days when outside tasks were difficult, the mother told the children the legends handed down in her tribe for generations.

During the Bedals' years in the mountains, they saw two nearby mining settlements, Monte Cristo and Goat Lake, spring into existence and turn into ghost towns. While some of their packing was done for prospectors, most was for the U.S. Forest Service, Sauk River Lumber Co. and mountaineers, tourists and fishermen.

Although she doesn't do any more packing, Edith has never lost her love for the mountains; her favorite region is the White Pass country near Glacier Peak.

For Miss Bedal education is a life time process. She attended school in a shack the size of a breakfast nook. "How many pupils did the school average?" I asked. Edith smiled and replied, "Well, toward the end the average was about two, my sister and myself." Three leisure-time pursuits, aside from her hiking trips, are uppermost in Miss Bedal's interests. She collects albums of classical music, writes nature articles and assembles slides of flowering plants and scenes photographed on her expeditions.

While gathering information for the article I told Edith how much we loved the high country and our conversation worked its way around to the idea of our going together into White Pass. She said she would talk to her sister in Seattle and see if she was interested in one last trip.

She also knew someone with a burro that she thought we could use to pack the gear, and plans were laid for a trip later in the summer.

I kept an unfinished record of our trip in a notebook that was very worn, wet and grubby by the end of the adventure. From my notes I created the following account.

As we rounded a turn on the trail, along the steep flank of White Mountain, I paused, breathless for two reasons – the long climb we had made with packs on our backs and the spectacular beauty of the vista we now faced. I leaned on the branch I had been using as a walking stick, letting my eyes scan the spectacular landscape.

Then I saw it, a small brown patch on a bit of green meadow far ahead, and, rushing to get the words out before he should say it first; I said to Kenneth, "There it is – the shelter!"

We still had about a mile to go, but no more climbing, for the shelter lay a little below us. On either side of the narrow, rocky trail, the sides of White Mountain were almost perpendicular; a treeless, flower-carpeted, vertical meadowland. I couldn't look up or down without stopping and leaning inward, for fear of becoming dizzy and taking a header into space.

Like ants on a watermelon, we inched our way along the final stretch of our trip, with the lean-to always in sight, looking somehow so permanent and important for all its unassuming size and shape, the only mark of man in this vast, lonely world of wilderness. Where the trail crossed a moss and flower-bedecked stream we drank from its tumbling waters. Looking up we could see a thousand feet to the top of White Mountain; looking down we could see two thousand feet to the headwaters of the north fork of the Sauk River. To the east, south and west were ridge after ridge and peak after peak of the Cascade Range. From where we were, nothing in the world existed but mountains and valleys.

We soon came upon the White Pass marker, elevation 6,000 feet. We were on a section of the Cascade Crest Trail, the amazing footpath from the Mexican border to Canada. Below us to the east were the headwaters of the White River, which flowed into Lake Wenatchee in the dry eastern Washington pine country; to the west was the canyon bearing the Sauk River on its way through rain-soaked western Washington to the waters of Puget Sound.

We were in the North Cascades Wilderness Area, a vast section of rugged mountain land reaching about fifty miles south from the Canadian border. To penetrate this country you must walk or ride horseback. There are no roads; no planes are allowed to land. The Forest Service maintains a system of trails, but a great deal of the terrain is inaccessible and sections of it have never been explored. U.S. Forest Service trail crews maintain the trails depending on packhorses for supplies. The crews spend ten days in the mountains and have four days off.

Just over the shoulder of White Mountain Glacier Peak, the 10,500 foot high volcano, dominated the surrounding country; from White Pass it was obscured by the nearer, though lower, mountain.

We reached White Pass at 9 o'clock on a mid-August morning, having hiked since about 5:30 from our stop-over at Mackinaw Camp on the north fork of the Sauk. The sun was just emerging from the top of White Mountain. We had been wise to do the steep four-mile stretch in the cool of early morning, for that section switch-backs over a rockslide devoid of shade when the sun is high.

From the summit of the pass, the trail to the shelter diverged from the Cascade Crest Trail to drop perhaps one hundred feet to the shelf, which held the Forest Service shelter. This three-sided hut, about eight by ten feet in size, with its shed roof and sides covered with cedar shakes, was to be our home for the next ten days.

The shelter sat with its back to the west, for westerly was a great open sweep to the sea and from this direction would come the severe weather. In one corner was a raised bunk. A makeshift table of split cedar was the only furniture. Our shelter was named Camp Yakbid after a chief of the Sauk tribe.

Apparently the last camper had been caught in bad weather, for he had moved the rock fireplace from in front of the shelter to a spot under the roof and had quartered his horse inside. This necessitated a little work with an improvised broom of dead branches before Kenneth and I could lay out our beds comfortably. When the floor was brushed clean down to the hard, packed earth, and the fireplace reassembled outside in the sun, we made a lunch, for we were famished, although it was not yet ten in the morning. From our small, precious store of provisions we allowed ourselves a package of dried soup, a salami sandwich and coffee. Rills from melting snow banks supplied water.

Swarms of hopeful mosquitoes and deer flies prospected about us but our "bug juice" kept them from landing.

As we lunched and lolled in the morning sun, our physical weariness seemed to float away as did, indeed, all sense of care and worry, leaving only the sheerest delight. The air was scented with the blooms of millions of flowers; you couldn't walk a step without treading upon them. Along each rill were blooming the delicate lavender shooting stars, marsh marigolds and the earliest of the Lewis monkey flowers.

This trip into White Pass was a sort of culmination. For years during our wanderings in the Cascade Mountains we had heard of its beauty and special nature. But the trip, we were told, was a rugged one unless you could take pack animals, and this we had not been able to afford.

Then, when I met Edith Bedal, the seeds of the summer's trip were sown. I learned that Edith's mother was an Indian princess, Susie Wa-Wetkin, daughter of Chief Wa-Wetkin of the Sauk tribe. Her father, an early French settler, was rescued from drowning in the turbulent Sauk River by the Indian girl who was later to become his wife.

In 1870, Chief Wa-Wetkin with Chief Yakbid and a small group of Sauk Indians guided the first white men ever to penetrate White Pass and neighboring Indian Pass, a railway survey party in search of the shortest route over the mountains to connect eastern and western Washington. Fortunately the White Pass route was dropped in favor of a more direct route over Stevens Pass.

The account of the expedition kept by a Mr. Lindsay, engineer in charge, is unusually graphic for this type of recounting and relates dramatically the exciting ride in an Indian canoe down the Sauk rapids. Lindsay expresses gratitude for the bounty the Indians provided of smoked salmon and baskets of wild strawberries at a time when the expedition's larder was down to nothing at all.

Edith Bedal and her sister, Jean, who lives and works in Seattle now, are all that is left of the family of six who homesteaded on the banks of the Sauk River. While Jean adapted to city life, Edith belongs to the wilderness still. Around the fires in the evenings and on the trail during the days, I gradually learned the story of Edith's and Jean's lives.

When they were girls they worked as packers and guides. They had a string of six mules and their own lead ponies, and no trip was too long or too strenuous for them to undertake. Edith, when questioned about tales of her exploits in the early days, looked vague and denied any memory of such incidents. Whether due to modesty or lack of memory is unclear, but I suspect the former. Her memories are keen, however, of her childhood days at White Pass, of hunting and berry picking expeditions with her mother, who in turn related to her children her memories of such trips with the people of her tribe, whose hunting and berry picking on this land had been a part of their lives for many generations.

Framed pictures of White Pass adorn the walls of the simple room in the Darrington Hospital, where Edith lives. (She works as cook and general assistant to Dr. Riddle, physician in residence.) As we talked on the winter day that I had sought her out, Edith's eyes strayed constantly to the meadows and peaks in the photographs, and finally she said, "there is no place in the mountains as wonderful as White Pass. I spent my vacation there last year, and I hope to spend a longer time there next summer. The problem is to pack in enough food for a two-week stay because no one around here has pack animals any more. But last year we borrowed a little burro from a friend here in Darrington..."

From there a plan evolved. As things stood the day we were to start, Edith and Jean had a burro, Jack, for their provisions, and the four of us, Kenneth, our son Tobey, his friend Dave Perine and myself were to have another burro. But no trip would be complete without last minute complications: our burro developed sore feet, and we reluctantly left the pretty, gray creature to its peaceful pasture on the Sauk prairie.

The only solution was to get the supplies in on two trips, with the boys tending the burro. This meant thirty miles of hiking for them just to get to White Pass with the provisions: in with a load, back to Sloan Creek for another, and in again.

As the truck with the burro was late getting to Sloan Creek, Kenneth and I had gone on ahead with just enough supplies for a couple of days. We stopped off at Mackinaw Camp for two nights waiting for the others to catch up, then as the boys reached Mackinaw with their first load, we struck out again, this time for White Pass. The boys turned back to retrace the six miles between Mackinaw and Sloan Creek; at Sloan Creek the Bedal sisters were waiting with the rest of the provisions.

We assumed the rest of our party would divide the final lap, the trip from Sloan Creek to White Pass, and would stay overnight at Mackinaw as we had in order to get an early morning start to the pass, avoiding the sun's heat on the rock slide switchbacks. So I was surprised and excited at the end of a hot afternoon, as we were washing our supper dishes, to hear Kenneth exclaim, "here they come! I can just barely see Edith and Jean in the lead and the boys following with the burro!"

I felt deeply for them, for their heat and exhaustion; they had come ten miles, climbed five thousand feet, each with a heavy pack, and the day had been hot, with full August sunlight. Watching them inch their way toward camp, slowly but without pause, was exciting. Edith and Jean are middle-aged, like Kenneth and I, and neither had done much hiking in recent years. The boys, at 15 and 16, had of course terrific energy, but teenagers tire as fast or faster than we older coots who don't have to use a share of our energy to grow.

As they neared the pass, Kenneth went to meet them and share their loads. Their arrival in camp was a wonderful moment. Edith and Jean were still ahead, Jean walking along in spite of her utter exhaustion with casual dignity, as if taking a stroll in the park. Edith's eyes seemed to devour the place as they scanned every familiar contour.

As for Jack, he was really the big wheel; with me it was love at first sight. His big dark eyes were ringed with white in his black face, which gave him a clownish aspect; his long ears were as silky as a kitten's; his sturdy barrel torso and short but serviceable legs had a strong, dependable look. He was a sweet sight and quite a baby too, for petting. If he'd been encouraged, he would have gladly shared our sleeping bags.

That evening, right up to the time we blacked out in our mummy bags, stretched out on the balsam bough beds we had made on the floor of the shelter, was a kaleidoscope of vivid, dramatic impressions. Jean and I thought we would never get the dishes washed and put away, for the many times we were called to "come and look." The setting sun transformed everything with a molten amber light, as if the scene we viewed – the twisted old trees atop the ridge, the flower-studded slope, a motionless deer – were not sufficiently outstanding in the prosaic light of day.

We were the audience in a natural amphitheater, the sun from the west the giant spot, the shifting clouds the gauze filters, the doe our ballerina. When she had satisfied her curiosity, she turned and sauntered farther along the narrow animal trail until she reached the opposite end of the ridge where she stood in silhouette.

Jean and I had just got back to the cold dishwater when the sun began its display as it neared the western rim of White Mountain. Sunsets in the mountains, like sunsets at sea, are apt to be dramatic, but this one exceeded in grandeur anything I've ever witnessed. Contributing to the total effect were tremendous convoluted cumulus clouds on the horizon, and rising veils of mists in the near valleys, through which shafts and columns of light wove a shifting pattern. The colour of the light changed from pink to gold and far to the south a quarter moon gleamed a goldish white.

We went to bed at dusk and before we were asleep the fog we had seen rolling up the valley had swallowed everything about us in a thick blanket, which remained until morning. Several times in the night, strong gusts of wind howled about the shelter, blowing fine, cold droplets of fog over our faces. The occasional bursts of wind and the heavy stomping of Jack, who was unfortunately staked near enough to the shelter to chew on the shakes, which he did with seeming relish, made the night an intermittently wakeful one for me, but not distressingly so.

Fog still enveloped camp the next morning, but by the time we had eaten breakfast the sun had dispersed it. Immediately after breakfast the boys set off with Jack on the return to Camp Mackinaw for the rest of the provisions, planning to stay overnight at Mackinaw, fish the North fork that evening, start back early next morning and get the rock slide climb over with before the heat of mid-day. We were eating breakfast next morning when we again had the thrill of sighting the little procession far away on the trail around White Mountain: Tobey in the lead, Jack following, and Dave bringing up the rear.

Nowhere is life free from routine chores, nor should it be. Ours were gathering wood, building fires, cooking meals, washing dishes, hauling water, and washing out what clothes we weren't wearing. We also kept the dirt floor of the shelter brushed clean by sweeping with dried fir branches. To find wood we had to hunt about among the tough old trees along the ridge for windfalls. Their branches were so brittle we could snap them off without chopping or sawing.

We obtained drinking water from a rill fed by a snow bank, and we did our washing in a group of shallow depressions amply filled with not too stagnant water. These grassless dips occurred here and there in the meadows, sometimes filled with water, sometimes dry. Edith said the Indian theory was that bears rolling in them created them. From then on our bathtubs were called bear wallows.

Meals were adequate, if not stupendous. We had lots of dehydrated soups, fruits, vegetables, milk, sausage, eggs, corned beef, ham, rice, margarine, hotcake flour, bread, cheese and chocolate. We didn't oversupply, being chary of too much weight on Jack's and our own backs. But at no time did we have any worry that our food would give out. We were fortunate in having a sizeable snow bank near camp, which gave us good service as a refrigerator, for the sun shone bright and hot nearly every day.

Our first ramblings were short, exploratory trips about the ridges and meadows near camp. At White Pass, although the peaks surrounding are as rugged as mountain terrain can be, there are expanses of rolling, open country. The Cascade Crest Trail traverses the area north and south. Animal trails of deer, mountain goats and domestic sheep criss-cross every slope.

Kenneth and I were particularly fond of the old sheep camp on the meadows above the shelter. Tent stakes and poles marked the spot where the Basque shepherd had lived. You could follow his line of reasoning in selection of the place: the clump of trees as protection from the wind, the broad view, proximity of wood and water. Sitting there you could even imagine his thoughts. And here a constant breeze blew away the swarms of flies and mosquitoes.

The cinder cone was the destination of our first all-day side trip. "We'll make a loop," Edith said, "over the Whitechuck trail through Red Pass to the cinder cone and back along the headwaters of the Whitechuck River, skirting Whitechuck glacier and back over Skyline Ridge." She pointed out the twin humps on Skyline Ridge where the only possible crossing was. She showed us where we would work our way back along the northslope of the ridge, which was traversed by numerous steep snow fingers. We would take a rope, she explained, and a hatchet, for aid in crossing these snow patches.

The Whitechuck trail had not been recently worked and was in places alarmingly narrow, precipitous above and below for thousands of feet. At Red Pass we encountered our first snow; summer came later to this north slope. Anemones and glacier lilies were appearing as the snows receded.

We ate our lunch on a heathery knoll at the base of the Cinder Cone, an impressive geological phenomenon. It is so much newer than its surroundings and illustrates the very recent times when violent eruptions have taken place in the Cascades, themselves a comparatively new range, reckoned in geological time. The Cascades are indeed the last major mountain upheaval the earth has known.

The Cinder Cone is actually not a cone in shape, but a mound, about three hundred feet high, 800 feet long and 500 feet in width. It is entirely composed of lava pebbles varying in size from peas to grapefruits. It is dark purple brown in color, in contrast to the grays and whites of the more weathered surrounding landscape. Nothing much grows on it yet except scattered clumps of alpine flox, beautiful in its lavender blue against the rich brown of the cinders. One other tough little plant with a strong, spreading root system, probably mountain avens, has taken hold, so we witnessed the beginnings of vegetation on new rock.

As we wandered through the park-like country between the cone and the headwaters of the Whitechuck with its streams, waterfalls, clumps of trees and flowering meadows Jean and Edith exchanged reminiscences of their childhood, for this was country where they had made family expeditions.

"Mother and I came here many times," Edith said. "She loved it here. The berries were easy to find, and there was lots of grazing for the ponies." Throughout the trip Edith spoke frequently of her mother's ways of doing things. Together, until the chieftain's daughter had grown too old for such rambles, they had packed, trapped, hunted and picked berries; they had loved it all, as the haunting nostalgia in Edith's eyes revealed. Jean felt the pull less, and you knew her heart had become accustomed to the city. She, who had done no hiking for many years, became weary on these all-day trips, but never lost the easy swing of her walk, which was like a stroll even under exertion, and she was always ready for a laugh. Her contagious laugh came from deep within and shone in her eyes.

In the spreading basin of the Whitechuck, threaded by many narrow branches of the stream, which would unite farther down the valley to form a powerful glacial river, we scanned the towering cliffs of Glacier Peak for mountain goats and were rewarded by spotting two solitary animals and one group of five or six at the foot of a rock wall.

Ahead of us now was our climb up and over Skyline Ridge, without benefit of trail. The prospect looked forbidding to me, and I showed extremely poor judgment by following the direct route the boys had taken instead of going the roundabout way with Edith and Jean. There were bad moments when I wished for a few more fingernails for digging in. The perpendicular terrain was covered with heather, which is slippery and defies a foothold, but is fortunately tough enough to cling to.

The heather gave way to a rockslide, and this too had its precarious aspects, as the rock was loose and tended to slide. We got to the top of the ridge at last only to look down on what seemed even harder going. If the snow fingers had looked steep as we looked across at them from the opposite ridge, they looked impossible from above. As the sun had been shining on them, they were slick and melty on the surface. The boys manned the rope, one at each end of a snow patch, and by holding to the rope and digging into the slushy snow with each step I made slow but steady headway until we reached the last of the snow and could follow the sheep trails back to the ridge above our lean-to.

Jack greeted us on our return with long sad hee-haws, which were preceded by sniffs and nostril-quiverings exactly like the preliminaries of a child's sobs of self-pity. I wanted to take him in my arms and comfort him, but he wasn't quite *that* little.

Early the next morning, Kenneth and the boys set out on a twelve-mile hike to Blue Lake, anticipating excellent fishing. The boys were strong for taking Jack and making the return to Mackinaw by way of Sloan Creek instead of returning to White Pass. Edith and Jean and I were in no mood for another strenuous walk that day, and Edith was concerned there would be snow on the rockslide into Blue Lake, which would make it impossible to get Jack into camp there. It was agreed finally that they would return to White Pass in three or four days.

We had a visit from six horses and riders. Edith was starting up the trail from camp and called back that some riders were coming, so we got a good view of them. The visitors turned out to be the Melangs from Granite Falls and another man. One of the Melangs had had a mill with old T.K. Robe. His daughter has the very fancy ranch just out of Granite toward Vic and Jean's place – she was, I think, the oldest woman in the group. Their horses were handsome and they were too. They plan a trip from Stevens Pass around through this way in another week.

I only hope Kenneth doesn't have trouble on the snow slopes at Blue Lake with his bad hand, broken on an earlier hike, and I hope the weather stays clear or they could lose their way. The boys' big lumbering ways, their endless hunger, and the added work they cause will test Kenneth. I'll be glad to get them back, and I *really* hated to see them go.

Edith says a trail crew should be getting here soon. We are wondering if it will be tomorrow. If so, Dutch the packer and his mules will arrive today.

Last Sunday evening Tobey, Kenneth and I had walked up to the sheep camp. We saw a group of deer grazing and a spruce grouse doing his mating ritual – tail spread and swollen red nub above each eye. He would make four woomp, woomp sounds, very Indian chant-like sounds. She would answer with five. It is definitely made with the throat. He kept right on with his courting as we stood a few feet away. I haven't seen how the ruffed grouse does his thing – thump, thump, thump – but perhaps it is also with his throat and not by the beating of wings on a hollow log as some books say.

I like both Edith and Jean. They are agreeable companions, quiet and pleasant. They share the work. Jean has smooth, dignified ways. She is unruffled and calm always. She's not so demonstrative as Edith. Edith has a wonderful high giggle and both have a good sense of humor.

The day on the trail today was a good one. We covered about 12 miles. First we circled up White Mountain to Reflection Pond, situated in a grove of trees on the ridge top. After that we came down a gradual slope through a forest of ancient trees, over rock slides, losing 1000 feet, to Indian Camp – a flat with meadows, clumps of forest, a shelter and a more enclosed feeling than Yakbid Camp. There was a very pleasant mood about the place, restful after the high open expanse of White Pass. On one side of Indian Camp flows the north fork of the Sauk, on the other side Indian Creek flows down to Lake Wenatchee.

We ate lunch and Edith disappeared. I learned later she visited the small cabin built in the '20s by her brother Harry to serve as a shelter during his winter trapping. He would be away for months, living alone, not making contact until spring. I try to picture life for him during the lonely, cold months.

On the way back we paused to look over the meadows and to wonder how it was with the Indians encamped there hundreds of years ago; probably the same as now, even the trees – some hundreds of years old.

We got back to camp in time to build a fire, heat our lima beans and ham, and get our Jello out of the snow bank. We were in bed shortly after dinner, and I was wondering how the others are doing at Blue Lake.

Then, just after we got to bed, the wind began. I've never heard such wind – howling and whistling like a hurricane. It would start up and die down with an instantaneous effect as if someone was turning a switch on and off. The dogs cuddled close and shivered and finally got into my sleeping bag envelope, and we had a really nice night. Lightning and thunder flashed and banged, but far off to the east. Jean was at the shelter alone one time in a thunderstorm. She said it seemed like the lightning was below her.

Thursday morning we all thought for sure the Blue Lake gang would be back that night. Strong black clouds were thickest over Johnson Peak where Blue Lake is. We cooked a big dinner expecting them but when not here by six we knew they wouldn't be back until Friday.

Friday morning a man came over the ridge. Jean said, "there's Kenneth," but he just stood there, looking strange. Finally he came down the meadow. It turned out that he was a Mazama (a member of a Portland-based mountaineering organization). The man, named Earl Caldwell, was from Portland. He was expecting 19 other Mazamas to show up that day to climb Glacier Peak the next morning.

At about three, Kenneth and the boys arrived. A little later, Mrs. Tucker, the cook, preceded the trail crew around White Mountain. Mr. Hargrove, the foreman, Emil, Butler and old Tough arrived and said 'Dutch', the packer was supposedly on his way. He didn't get there by dinnertime, however, so we had a grand finale of our food and fed all. With Mazamas arriving over the ridge and camping a little way off in a clump of trees, the pass became very congested all of a sudden. Dutch and the horses and mules arrived just before dark. The trail crew pitched their tents over on the ridge near the outhouse. Kenneth and the boys bedded down just outside the shelter with the mules, and Jack was in their hair all night. Mrs. Tucker, the Bedals and I slept in the shelter.

We had a very pleasant evening with much laughter and congeniality between the trail crew and ourselves. There was considerable amusement over the alpine hats, knee britches, etc. of the Mazamas. We left for Sloan Creek with Dutch and the mules the next morning with rain threatening, after a large breakfast of bacon, eggs, Blue Lake trout and pancakes.

Mr. Hargrove left us with an appealing invitation: "We'll be up in the Suiattle country next," he said. "Mighty good country around there too." I hope we do meet them all again.

We started out at 8:30 and made it to Mackinaw Camp by 10:30 and were at Sloan Creek by about 1:00. It was fast going downhill with only a few brief stops. I was tired by Sloan Creek camp and sad to leave the girls and Jack. We must have another trip later.

A sad note of irony, we learned later that Edith's brother, who spent many long winters trapping that country alone as a young man without ever being sick, was drafted into the army in the '40s. Shortly after basic training, he caught pneumonia and died. Edith's solitary trip to his cabin at Indian Camp then took on deeper meaning.

44

I FIGHT WITH TOBE all the time lately because I hate his affair with Jo Mackenzie. It is another Bob Bundy-Helen Sutton deal, and she is such a little vulgarian and so persistent. She has a certain charm and cuteness and warm-heartedness, which makes it all the more difficult. I probably am wrong to harp on it so much, but I feel driven, probably much as old captain Ahab was driven in his relentless battle against the white whale. Well, Jo is my white whale, my Moby Dick, and her tender little hide resists all the harpoons I'm able to throw. It isn't that I'm resentful against the idea of Tobey having girls, because I really welcome the thought of girls around, and I did everything I could to be fair to Jo and to like her, but her commonness is just too much for me. She's vulgar, lacking in any comprehension, and sly and deceitful, too. When I think of how appealing the Lyons girls were at this age and how much fun he could be having with different kids, I get too damn depressed.

Kenneth is teaching tonight at Seattle U., and Tobe has gone to bed. There are storms along the mountains. It looks like a severe one around Glacier Peak. I love having a familiarity with this peak at last, for it was an aloof stranger for so long.

We went to Tacoma last night for the opening of Kenneth's show there with a supper party at the board president's beforehand. Everyone was so respectful and grateful to us for coming that we were quite bowled over. He has never had a wink of recognition at any Seattle showing. We liked the group, students at the College of Puget Sound and board members of the Art League. Burke Ormsby showed up, much to my surprise, sporting a very leonine head of hair. He is now teaching Television Communications at the college, and wants to broadcast art exhibitions of N.W. painters. I think he might be just the kid who could sell pictures, too.

Kenneth's teaching continues to expand, and he is now arranging exhibits for the History and Industry Museum, which adds about $25 a month. The yearly total if it keeps up as at present, should at least equal the museum salary, and allow him much more time to paint.

It's Monday evening, after a stormy winter weekend in the mountains. I called on the Ottoways and Susie Saturday afternoon. The Ottoways were about to eat dinner, so I sat on a box and talked with them while they ate. The baby girl, the twin that lived, is now four and very sweet, but I think of them all, Mike, the next to the youngest, also four (only eight months apart) and Butchie are my favorites. Stanley is now just sixteen and rather plump and shy. They are all nice kids. They were having goat, 'tame' goat they hastened to add (probably mountain goat shot without a permit)... I declined to partake, but was offered a piece of Dotty's pumpkin pie with fresh thick cream – delicious. She is a fine cook. The first thing Leonard said was, "say, is it true about Ken retiring to paint?" He was very concerned and sympathetic when I said he'd been fired. I asked about the garbage dump murders. Dorothy said the standard greeting among men now is to say, "why did you do it?" There are no theories, though, about who killed and then dragged the two men behind their car to the dump. Leonard told me about the latest shotgun weddings. "It happens all the time... a fellow gets to playing around too long in one place."

He took me out to show me his new root cellar, proud and pleased, quite a job, concrete poured about five feet high, then concrete blocks another three feet... the blocks cost more than all the poured concrete. It's full of canned fruits and vegetables, rutabagas and carrots from the garden.

Then I stopped at Susie's, and she was home this time. I've missed her the last couple of weeks at her little post office/home as she spends a lot of time at her mother's now. Ma Baker is more helpless all the time. Susie says she thinks after she has been asleep it is another day, so what with daily afternoon naps, every day is two days. "Remembers she doesn't like carrots, though. Bill Cool gave me an apple box of carrots and I like them so we had them for dinner two nights in succession. The second night mother said, 'how many of those carrots did Bill Cool give you?' 'Apple box full.' 'Well, I wish it had been a box of parsnips.'" Now Susie fixes her mother a parsnip and herself a carrot. Susie said, "I have a new boyfriend, you know." Surprise on my part. "Never did get a man amounted to anything. This one is a Frenchman, mother probably Indian and father French. His name's Johnny ViViere. Of course, being a Frenchman, he has to have two capital Vs. Him and an old Swede, perfectly nice old Swede but doesn't mean a thing to me, are cutting shakes up the valley. The Frenchman can't hardly see at all, couldn't see to dial a telephone number, so I had to do it for him. But he knows how to say nice things, being a Frenchman... even if he doesn't know what I look like. Drops by every evening, goes to see Mother, doesn't want me walking home along the highway after dark, so he sees me home. Earl was here and when Johnny left I went out on the porch with him and Earl said right away, 'Boyfriend?' I said 'I'm afraid so', and he said, 'Well why do you act so ornery about it? You're still a young enough woman to enjoy a man about the house.' I said, 'Well, if he had a car maybe I'd play around a little with him, but what good is he to me? All he's got is a pension.' Earl said, 'Well, if this post office cancellation goes through you may be glad enough to share his pension with him.'" Susie was obviously thrilled by it all.

What I hope is that the two old boys aren't reprobates who are sizing up the two old women with foul intent. After those garbage dump murders, all for some hundred dollars or so, I feel unsure of such customers.

Mrs. Barrett called Sunday afternoon with her youngest daughter, sons Herbert and Eugene, and some neighbors. They were looking for Christmas trees and wanted a permit from us, in case they were stopped by the Forest Service. Herbert was with the Air Force, Eugene with the Navy, both now discharged. It seems strange that such a short time ago they were kids, fishing the Robe pond. Herbert, the oldest, was younger than Tobe is now. He spent three years in Greenland, and Eugene was in the Far East. They're nice looking boys, both of them and quite intelligent. Ethel Barrett has done awfully well raising her family and always with the restlessness of her husband to cope with. Everett's working in Richland now. I'm glad they have their boys home.

I remember so clearly that conversation with Everett at Barlow Point, and he saying how terrible war was, how he feared it for his two sons. And two wars have come and gone since. And he is now working in Richland on the most dreaded weapon of all time. Strange how men are pushed around and their beliefs seemingly nullified.

1954 begins. Kenneth and Dave S. and Tobe went to the mountains for the day yesterday morning, but I stayed home because I have quite a lot to do. It was one of those enticingly beautiful full moon evenings with snow over everything, clouds making patterns in the luminous sky, not too cold, just at the borderline of freezing. I'd like to go out and walk and I wish Kenneth were here to go with me. I just returned from the Venetian theater where I saw that ridiculously romantic "Lili" movie, but the mood lasted on the walk home, so the snow and the moon and the moving clouds were especially beautiful.

Kenneth goes for his walk every morning after breakfast, a privilege he has enjoyed since he lost the Museum job. I'd like to go too, but don't like to return to dirty dishes. I've walked downtown and back twice, though, since the snow arrived. Fun. Everything looks so different you can pretend you're in another city, even Europe.

We went through the Museum yesterday, and on the way out to the car a tanager flew past, not more than six feet from our eyes; such a flash of color, with the snow heightening the brilliance!

I'm wondering what the snow is doing to the trees at the cabin. Some are sure to be pulled over. If it should be the clump of cedars overhanging the spring, we'll have to rebuild our flume and waterwheel. They come out of the bank at right angles and lean over the flume before they make a 45-degree bend and start their straight growth. They make a fine group, each about a foot in diameter, probably about three or four in the clump.

We lost two big hemlocks from the grove at the side of the house during a blow about three weeks ago. Their root mass is about twenty feet in diameter, but with no depth at all, just a shallow network. We're sorry to lose them, but they'll make good firewood, and now we have a chainsaw to make the job easier.

Yesterday we ate lunch in the market, the top floor of Mannings, where you have a view of the bay. In came the genial fish market man and a friend to sit at the next table. I asked whether the fishing boats were functioning in the icy weather. "Oh yes," he exclaimed. "They care nothing about this! The only thing they don't like is" – making great wavy motions with his arm. "You remember the famous blizzard, January 13th, about four years ago?" Of course we did. "Well, there wasn't any business, no customers. But we had more fish come in than we'd ever had. Those boats go out any time. Boy, that was one time I didn't envy them their job."

A slight, dark fisherman who always hails us, and whom we have encountered at the Museum several times, asked about art classes. He wants to study painting. "Well, some day I may get around to it. My wife," she says maybe sometime…"

And the Italian egg woman, my special one, the only food vendor in the whole flower growers' area, was so cold she had gone blue. Her face and hands were an indescribable color, like eggplant. I don't know how she stood it, all day with no moving about to get the circulation going. "You should have gloves," a customer said. "I do, but I can't a wear gloves," she said. "I breaka too many eggs. See, all the eggs I breaka today." I told her about hand warmers. "Yes, thata be fine, but I got no time to go look for such things." I suggested she have one of her kids get her one. "It's kinda hard," she said. "The kids they all leave home now." I resolved to look for a hand warmer.

I was in a bad mood yesterday morning, brought on by Kenneth and Tobey's complete indifference to household tasks. I asked Tobe to wash windows, which he did after a struggle (school is out because of snow). In prodding him I reminded him of the tasks I do, the unpleasant ones like scrubbing floors, washing dirty hankies and socks, constant washing and ironing, dishes, etc. "Well," he said in his most ornery tone, "that's your job. That's what you're here for."

This morning Kenneth and I walked downtown and back up the hill. We ran into Betty Willis near Howell Street and stopped at a little Swedish café (used to be the Tre Kroner years ago) for coffee and a chat. She was on her way in from a night with her daughter, Mary, near Edmonds. In the night some nearby oil tanks blew up, starting an enormous million-dollar fire, and they became so alarmed they left and spent the night at a tourist cabin. She was wondering whether Morris had been distressed, as he lives near the place where the fire happened. Those tremendous gasoline storage tanks could have caused a major disaster. As it was, just some smaller tanks blew up, but the big gas tanks nearby were spared.

Kenneth is painting animals. It all started with some trips to the zoo, where he sketched in pencil. These pencil sketches brought on a spell of pastel, then tempera, now oil. The work is very free and imaginative in color, vigorous, and possessing an untamed feeling. Color is applied freely and boldly and with a strong sense of beauty.\

Today I am fifty and I feel that I must make a statement. As I look back on what I can remember of five decades, I can find no one of them any better or any worse, in terms of enjoyment and trouble. My hope is that I shall continue to find this true of those remaining. I find the strong loves continue – and these are based principally upon nature and upon people. And the strong dislikes remain much the same, too: smugness, unreasoning conventionality, greed, sloth, waste, cruelty, vanity and unnecessary monotony. These things have always irked me and still do.

The only persistent discomfort for me is the way work I want to do doesn't get done. Kenneth doesn't have this, as he is always working.

Tobey was sixteen yesterday, and to celebrate we had Jo to dinner, and everything turned out awfully well. The chicken was delicious, the cake very good, the salad just right. Jo is appealing, and I don't feel as disturbed as I did about their relationship, but I still wish he would take out other girls occasionally.

He is dying to get his driver's license. I told him this morning he couldn't get it until he gets a sensible haircut. He goes from one ridiculous style to the next; just now it does a sort of forwards swoop, growing out from a crew cut. Like baldheaded men make their hair swoop to cover up the bare place. High style or no high style, it is revoltin'.

Only two art students have braved the weather today, as driving is still precarious. Glenn Trimble and Mrs. Keller are the two students of Kenneth that are most serious about painting. The two bakery daughters are terribly decadent, I'm afraid. Their Irish mother and stalwart Danish father should have produced hardier children. But both are always ailing, perhaps from the struggle to live a ree-fined life. So often in a case like this, the second-generation female born into new wealth takes to the boudoir sick bed and the male to high living and debauchery. These bakery daughters, living next door to each other in their splendid old castles on Queen Anne Hill with their dilapidated little husbands and pretty children, are typical of the dullness that often accompanies the nouveau riche. They're pretty mixed up and unhappy, too, I gather. Interestingly they both have talent, that is, in terms of being able to draw and paint, but they completely lack sensitivity.

Kay Perine and I are planning a party for Jack's 51st birthday at our house that includes the Codes, the Bakers, the Perines and us. Eight seems the most I want to cope with now, and I remember with vague horror the milling groups during the war, as many as twenty-four in an evening, and in our small house too. It never was fun, really. These were things Mary got me into. I have let myself be forced into various kinds of artificiality because of Mary's enthusiasms, yet I really don't regret those times because I have learned what Orthopedic guilds are, for instance, and know that I'm not missing anything by not striving for such a social stratum. Tomorrow night is the party for Jack, and by Sunday I will be as wrung out as a rag. Nevertheless, I do enjoy social events with old friends.

The evening with the Perines et al was strenuous for me, as I was tired anyway. The Bakers were kind of an unknown quantity, but the others seemed to have fun. They really soaked up the liquor, about four large bottles being the score. Kay and Jack didn't leave until 2:30. Jack was pretty lit and went into his fears about Dave. He is afraid David is missing out on the activities he should be having. He worries at his lack of initiative and poor grades in school. Jack's constant picking at him doesn't help, but I don't know whether there is any justification for his worries. I think Jack expects too much and takes out on Dave a lot of his own insecurities and fears.

Bill Baker is a psychiatrist. At the dinner table we got to talking about humor, which he insists is another form of hostility, that humor and hostility are characteristics of the highest state of civilization. Let's see now – man has progressed because of his hostility, then hostility turns into humor. For example, the cave man takes a look at the stinkin' hole he lives in, decides he can't stand those old bones and the smelly darkness another minute, so he moves on to something better, or maybe clears it out and cuts a hole for a window. And gradually we get civilization. Then when he is hostile to the mess civilization creates and can't do anything about it, he laughs about it; thus, we have humor (or some such line of reasoning). Both Kenneth and I would like to talk to him further about the whole thing, to find out just what psychiatrists base their theories on. I don't know whether Baker has learned these things, or whether he is trying to think independently, based on personal observation.

It seems to me much of psychiatry is negative in character. Why couldn't the cave man just like the smell of grass and the feeling of sunlight so much he decided to cut a window and enjoy it more? Anyway, I don't think everything comes from sex and hostility. Of course, I really don't know enough about it. But I think the philosophers and artists and writers of the world have expressed man's nature more beautifully.

Kenneth and I walked out around West Seattle this morning. It was a divine, sunny day, balmy in contrast to the recent freezing spell. Beach smells, wood fires, people stirring about, like insects just out of their larval wrappings.

I'm reconstituted today, having gone to bed at 9:30 last night, completely exhausted. I talked with Kay this morning and suggested she have Dave's metabolism checked. I was, in fact, surprised to find she hadn't done so already.

What Dave does have is a very special ability to be funny. He has a sense of the ludicrous and a natural sense of timing and control for story telling, but few know this. We saw it during summers when he would put on an act in the river, or impersonate Spike Jones, or give vent to his satirical take on people and their foibles. He is totally unselfconscious about it, but I worry that it may be beat out of him by Jack's criticisms.

I have just made an apple pie and find it a refreshing occupation to indulge in for a change. I think corny things like making apple pies are good for the soul. I still think all kids would be better off if parents still made apple pies and read aloud and weren't so damn restless and preoccupied. I do appreciate the danger of suffocating kids with too much hominess and momism and such. But I think if a home is comfortable and there are lots of things for each growing up period, whether it's roller skates, crayons, skis or jazz records, and there is a good kitchen and always books and music and art and contact with nature and laughter and a firm voice when needed, juveniles would not be so delinquent. It isn't really the 'juvs' who are delinquent; it is the life offered them. We need more simplicity and greater understanding. This won't steer us out of all the muddles, because youth is always going to have that terrible craving for it knows not what, but things would be a lot better.

Mary and I went out to the University library last evening to the Burns' Great Books group, the first time I've been this year. They were doing Machiavelli. When we did the same in the Queen Anne group six years ago, Machiavelli horrified everyone, and I took it upon myself to support him, alone. That is, I pointed out that his views were not so fantastic, that our government operated in this fashion a good deal of the time. And that Machiavelli at least was no hypocrite and recommended choosing your friends carefully, never double crossing them and always being consistent. *Everyone* in last night's group was an apologist for the arch schemer. An attractive young woman, about 30 I'd say, was the only one protesting. Timidly and hesitantly, she said she thought morality was important and should have a role in government.

What has brought about this mass disillusionment, if it can be regarded as that? Is it the toll of the post-Korean world, with its reliance on super-weapons? Or was this group just a not too representative segment of the population? I feel the attitude is pretty widespread and is dangerous. One typical supporter last night, a bleached blonde, chewing gum furiously, upheld the superiority of Machiavelli as compared with the vulgar masses. In her view, princes are above morals, can't afford morals in their political dealings. Morals are for the herd. She is of German descent, and I'll bet anything she is, or was, sympathetic to Hitler. I'll bet she's a Nietzscheite, too.

I puzzle and ponder over what is humankind? Are we an accidental outgrowth of some chemical process or just an evolved mammal with delusional thoughts? Or are we God's creatures with souls and wills and the knowledge of right and wrong and the freedom to make choices? Or are we a blight, a sort of disease on the earth's crust, like ringworm on skin? Is the final answer a supreme laugh, as the Zen Buddhists believe? Is there such a thing as a kindly and loving savior and a heaven for souls freed from mortal bodies? I don't see that it matters much.

Just now, I feel the best answer is making the most of what has been given and living in harmony with the big scheme of things and facing every situation courageously. But that's not easy with all this hydrogen bomb talk, which feeds on greed and blindness and could bring about ultimate destruction… and we are passing it on to the children we love so much.

45

DON MACDONALD CALLED AND came to borrow our power saw. We talked until noon, he telling me about their financial difficulties, as they are unable to sell their Vashon Island place and have to make huge payments on the California ranch. That's why Betty has dropped her novel for the time being and is doing an "I" book again. Don said rather wistfully that he didn't know whether or not he was willing to give up his privacy – that the first books dealt with subjects not particularly concerned with him, but that this one is closer to home, and "I don't know whether I want to give my all for the book." I know how he feels, but I don't think he has a prayer. Betty will put him through the mill, and he will come out a Bard figment, like hamburger from the grinder. But with Don's apparent lack of ability to make money and their extravagant life style, there seems to be no other solution. Listening to Betty's anecdotes, I think this may be a very funny book again, maybe as good as *The Egg and I*. Its tentative title is *The Plague and I* and will be about her episode with T.B.

This is one of those busy periods. I went to Mary's last night to have dinner with Betty and Don and Betty's mom Sidney. (Mary is in Mexico on a brief vacation.) Kenneth was teaching at Auburn. He came by to pick me up and we stayed until nearly one. Tonight Betty and Don are coming here, although Kenneth again has to be away – this time to Bellevue to take part in a dinner for the Art Festival.

I really had fun with Betty and Don. Betty seems more relaxed than she has for a long time, and we laughed a lot. Sidney, exactly as always, was walking with a spry step, cooking the dinner etc. Mary's girls were in their usual state of crisis; this time Sally was refusing to go to school the next day because she knew she'd flunk her French test. Among us all there seemed to be a real exchange, in a way more like old times. I feel we have moved on and are free of some of the constraints and affectations of the last ten years. I find that Kenneth's being out of the Museum improves our relations with many people; puts them on a more human and reciprocal level. I think Dick Fuller has never had a really free and unencumbered time in his life. It's ghastly to think about. He's like a walking mummy, insulated and hedged in with all the padding that comes with a bankroll and his introverted temperament.

Anyway, reconnecting with Betty reminded me of my first introduction to the amazing Bard family, who have played such an important role in my life, beginning when I was still at Lincoln High School. Several years ago I wrote the following story about that initial contact:

. . . . .One hot June afternoon in about 1922, I finally went out to the Bards for the first time. Mary drove their old air-cooled Franklin into our driveway just before noon and said to come on up to the Mandarin with her for lunch, after which we would go swimming. The Mandarin was Mrs. Bard's tearoom. It was in the University District, just across from the campus. Only Mrs. Bard would try to make a tearoom in the University District pay.

Mary looked pretty funny when driving. She would have been a poor driver even with good eyesight, and she was very nearsighted. She had to wear glasses when driving and their roundness accentuated the roundness of her face, as did her hair, which was pulled behind her ears. She concentrated so much on staying on the road that she didn't talk much on the way over.

The Mandarin was on the first floor of an old three-story house. I have always disliked tearooms, but Bard's was more comfortable than most. Mrs. Bard tended the cash register, which had recently replaced a small saucer full of change, and Mary was hostess. Mary's favorite role is being a hostess, unless maybe it is being a guest.

Lunch was a great, luscious crab salad with cheese crackers; dessert was deep dish apple pie with whipped cream. My brother, Bob, was impressed with the quantities of whipped cream they had once given him. He would tell about it with wide eyes – "and they gave me all that was left after the chocolate pudding was served – a half a bucket full."

It was about two o'clock when we left the Mandarin: Sidney, (as Mrs. Bard insisted she be called), Mary, and I. The lunch customers had cleared out, and the place was left in charge of Frankie, the very capable, brown-eyed waitress. In fact, had the place been left entirely under Frankie's direction, perhaps the grocery bills might have been paid, and the place might even have shown a profit.

A winding gravel road led up a small hill to the Bards' house in Laurelhurst. The house was a three-story frame affair, gray paint fading around big bay windows at the front and sides. It was spacious but unpretentious, as it perched on the top of the hill. Around it were fruit trees, grass and flowers. A horse grazed in the vacant lot at the rear of the house, and two dogs barked at us from the front yard as we drove up.

A girl of about nine was sitting on the front porch with a great many paper dolls scattered about her, and another girl of about four sat beside her absorbed with the process of dressing and undressing the dolls. The older, introduced as Dede, replied "How do you do" in a surprisingly deep voice, and continued unconcernedly playing with her dolls. The little one, I was told, was Allison. She gazed at us belligerently out of round, brown eyes through a fringe of long bangs.

Mary's other sister, Betty, came out of the house letting the screen door bang, holding in hand an aluminum kettle lined with the remains of chocolate candy and in the other a long-handled spoon. "Hello," she said to me. "You're too late to lick the pan," to Mary. "Has Mac called?" Mary asked. "He's in the house talking to Gammy. He's being an awful smart aleck today. I wouldn't speak to him if I were you." Betty's brown hair hung about her neck in a long bob, her green eyes were set wide apart, her nose was beautifully modeled, and her teeth were strong and white. While she still had a schoolgirl chubbiness about the middle, her legs were long and slim.

Betty took the younger girls upstairs to change for swimming, and Mary, Sidney and I went out to the kitchen. An old woman was washing a great many dishes and talking animatedly to a young man who sat a-straddle a chair. He got up to greet me, but paid no attention to Mary. His name was Duncan McConnell. The old woman was introduced as Gammy. The lines in her face bespoke a wealth of shrewd humor. "Go upstairs and get into your bathing suit, I want to talk to Mac."

Upstairs, Mary slid out of her clothes and plunged her skinny freckled legs into the tightness of a bright purple bathing suit. "We don't have to wear wraps, nobody does out here, but you'd better wear these sandals."

We ran down the curving street to the beach , the sun hot on our shoulders, with the Bards' two dogs, an ancient Airedale and a more ancient bulldog, scrambling about our feet. They barely tolerated each other, showing none of the devotion you might expect from two such old associates. Mary said they had terrible fights occasionally, the Airedale always the antagonist. "We've been on the verge of having Pat put down a half a dozen times," Mary said, "but he's always so apologetic after a brawl, we feel sorry for him. I could never stand to send him away anyway. He's too much like one of the family. Besides I guess his disposition isn't much worse than mine. We've both got lovely tempers, haven't we Pat," she said, patting the wiry head, "both jealous fools." The dog looked up out of bleary eyes and seemed to grimace a wry assent.

The smells of the trees and sandy marshes along the shore of Lake Washington reminded me of all the summers I'd spent sprawled out on the sand in a faded bathing suit, my hide getting black. We left our shoes behind a rock and ran into the water and hit out for a raft with a springboard on it. The water was the color of dill pickle juice and the coolness of it lapping about our chins was delicious. Mary swam a helter skelter sort of overhand, her thin freckled arms flashing in and out of the water. We scrambled dripping onto the raft and I barked my knee on an old spike. Every time after swimming, I was bruises and scratches all over.

Pretty soon Mac swam out to the raft to join us. "You going to be nice now?" Mary asked. "I'm always nice," Mac said. "It's you that's nasty." "No," said Mary. "It's you that's nasty. I'm nice." Feeling the sun burning my shoulders I dove from the springboards and swam a while before turning back toward the raft. On the southeast horizon, Mount Rainier was standing as tall as ever it did, wearing a flat, white cloud lopsided on her peak. I lay on my back and floated with eyes shut for a while, but the sun made purple spots through my eyelids, so I rolled over and swam back to the raft. Mary and Mac were in a fine humor when I clambered aboard. They had a better time together than any other couple I knew. Mac thought Mary terrifically funny in spite of the things she did that annoyed him, and Mary was the perfect foil for Mac's peculiar wit.

Mary said to me, "I bet you tan beautifully, don't you? I hate you, because I never do anything but burn and peel. I've tried olive oil and cocoa butter and everything I've ever heard of, but nothing helps." "You've got red hair," I said. "You can't have everything." "I don't want red hair. I'd give anything for long sleek black hair, straight as a licorice whip." Warming to the topic, Mary went on. "I always get everything I don't want and nothing I do. That Schlostein boy just loves me, for instance."

"I'm going to go in," Mac said, slipping off the raft. "See you at the house," he added over his shoulder, "If you aren't too long." "He'll be there," said Mary to me. "He's always just about to leave around meal time, but he generally ends up staying."

We talked for a while about the perversity of men, Mary being vehement on the subject. "There are so many small things some men could do to make a girl feel good, but do they ever want to? Some others want to do everything for you. That's the trouble. I hate men who treat me badly, but I can't stand men that are too nice to me." We decided that on the whole we would rather take insults from men that were fun to be around than get pretty things from the boring ones.

It was well past the middle of the afternoon when we left the raft. On shore we had to wait for our feet to dry before we could get our sandals on, but our tranquility was interrupted by wicked growls and snarls a short distance up the beach. Mary sprang to her feet and shouted, "Sam, Pat, stop it, do you hear, stop it." A group of boys watched the snarling mass with interest, one or two making half-hearted attempts to separate the combatants. Mary grabbed Pat's collar and tugged with all her might. "Stop it, you devils!" she shouted. Pat let go of Sam's throat just long enough to snap at Mary's arm, but she was too quick for him.

"One of you boys, get me a stick," she yelled, but they only stared stupidly, seemingly fascinated by the blood oozing from the two beasts.

I looked about for a club, but Mary was already tugging away at a half-buried branch of an alder that must have been six inches thick. Then, holding the heavy club with both hands over one shoulder she strode toward the battle scene. "Now, will you stop?" Wham, down came the log on the writhing dogs. Yelps of pain, but the snarling went on. Again Mary raised the club over her shoulder and let it fall on the dogs. I was aghast at her daring and fearful that the maddened fighters would turn on her. But the second blow of the stick had the desired effect and the dogs sprang apart, cowering and whimpering.

The picture of Mary standing with feet wide apart in the sand, club raised over her shoulder, red hair streaming wildly, is one that has always been vivid in my memory. Like a young goddess of fury she was, a goddess with freckled legs and arms and sand on the seat of her bathing suit. Most girls would have cringed and called for help in the face of the dogs' savagery. Most girls would have fluttered, wrung their hands and whimpered, but not Mary. Her decisiveness never failed her in a crisis. That decisiveness led her into all sorts of complications, but she never faltered. She enjoyed being decisive about other people's lives as well. She didn't hesitate to go about breaking up a love affair she felt to be harmful to one or both parties with the same gusto with which she broke up the dogfight.

We started up the hill towards the house in the yellow warmth of the late afternoon sun. "Filthy beasts!" Mary exploded. "Some day they'll kill each other and it'll serve Sid right." She *would* have both of them. If somebody gave her a cobra and a man-eating tiger, she'd say "oh, the dear little things," and keep them in her bedroom.

When we got to the house, Sidney and Mac were sitting on the canvas seat on the front porch drinking something fizzy and pale from tall glasses. "See," Mary said, plopping herself down on the top step. "I can't trust her for a minute. I'm just a drunkard's daughter." "Hey, I thought you were going to save that gin until Sunday. The Van Oersters are coming and you know how they'll be if they don't get cocktails." Mac said something in a low voice to Sidney and they both laughed. Mary watched them resentfully.

"Sam and Pat just tried to kill each other down at the beach," Mary said. "I had to break them up again. Next time I'll just let them chew each others' guts to ribbons." Eliciting little response, she turned to me. "Come on, Margaret, let's go pick some cherries." The cherries from the cherry tree in the backyard were the big black Bings that make your mouth purple and break crisply when your teeth crunch through the skin. "I like these better than gin anyway," Mary said as we leaned against the tight stretched bark of the tree. She bit savagely into a cherry. "Do men take you out?" she asked. "I mean to shows or dances." "Oh, sometimes," I said. " I guess I get to the Butler about once every three months or so. I'm not what you could call popular."

The Butler Hotel was an old madam of a Seattle hostelry with an elegant past, but she had fallen into pretty shady repute. When it was built, back in the pioneering days, it had been right in the center of things, but the city had moved up town, leaving the Butler just a few steps from skid road. Rapidly, the marble lobby, the brass spittoons, and the heavy black leather-upholstered chairs grew seedier and seedier. Politicians and travelling men continued to stop there, old timers, perhaps for old times sake, but more likely for the easy access to female companionship. But the Rose Room in the basement had a glory all its own. Dusty pink crepe paper was all over everything, dripping from the ceiling, twining up the pillars, creeping about the orchestra platform. At night dim lights cast a rosy glow through filters of pink crepe. Tables were crowded close together surrounding a small dance floor, and the orchestras were always Grade A. All during prohibition the Rose Room was in its glory. The proprietors paid good protection and you could take a bottle in safely most of the time. Raids were a rare occurrence. We college students found the Rose Room particularly alluring, partly because it was placed off limits by university authorities, but also because it exuded an atmosphere of 'life in the raw'. Of course, the reputation of any student, man or woman seen going *upstairs* at the Butler was ruined. Upstairs, anything might happen, and usually did.

"I wish I was more like Betty," Mary said. "She treats all men like they were repulsive and she's never in love. Sometimes I don't see how she can be my sister. We're so different... you and Bob are pretty different, too." I agreed. "He's more selfish than you are," Mary went on. "Of course we adore Bob and think he's the funniest thing in the world, but he *is* pretty selfish. He never takes Betty or me anywhere. The only time he's nice to us is when he's at our house. But I guess it's our own fault. We make both of those boys think they're so irresistible that you really can't blame them for being stinkers." Mary tucked a cherry into each cheek so she looked like she had mumps. "You and Bob look quite alike, except your eyes are much nicer. I'm glad Bob's going to a logging camp again this summer. He looks best when he gets lean and brown. He's looking pretty bad lately."

"Is he?" I questioned. "I hadn't noticed." "It's because of that Helen woman he's been spending so much time with. Every time Bob comes over here he's paler and has bigger circles under his eyes. She's a terrible necker, you know. She's seduced just about every man and boy in Laurelhurst." I could see that Mary's solicitude sprang not so much from regard for my brother's well being as from a resentment that his interests had strayed into fields outside the Bards' jurisdiction. There was a strong possessive, almost predatory quality in her attitude, and Sidney's, towards the males they chose to make their pets. Bob and Mac were theirs, and for other women to make claims upon them was an outrage.

I said I had never seen Bob's latest. "She's a good-looking woman," Mary said, "and intelligent, too. But she's way over-sexed. Every night you go for a walk down a path or on the beach you stumble over her necking with someone. Her family's tried putting her in private schools, convents, and what have you, but it doesn't do any good. She runs away. Bob's been crazy about her for three or four months, and he certainly looks it, too. I'm surprised your mother doesn't notice it."

"Nothing like that would ever occur to her," I said. "The worst she could imagine would be that he might be staying up too late at night." Looking surprised Mary said, "Sid's just the opposite. None of us could ever keep anything from her. Lots of people think she's crazy to let me smoke with her and drink cocktails, but she says she knows we'll smoke and drink anyway and she'd rather have us doing it at home where she can watch us. All the kids I know think I'm an idiot the way I tell her everything, but I always have. She's not like a mother a bit."

"Of course, it was the only philosophy for Sidney to adopt. She sought the company of her children and of her children's friends to ease the loneliness she felt when Mr. Darcey Bard died. More than anything, she wanted them to like her. "Daddy used to say Mother spoiled us. He used to discipline us and make us get good grades and wouldn't let me have tantrums or anything. My tantrums worked like a charm with Sid, but Daddy used to just lock me in my room until I got over them." "How long ago did he die?" I asked. "Four years ago.

Allison wasn't born yet and I was a junior at St. Nicholas and Betty was a sophomore. We left St. Nicholas then and went to Lincoln because St. Nicholas cost too much. At first I loathed it and went around being an awful snob and wouldn't speak to anybody. If I'd gone on at St. Nicholas I'd still be a perfectly repulsive snob. Betty was never as bad as I was. After a month at Lincoln I liked it better than I ever liked St. Nicholas."

I used to puzzle quite a lot over the death of Mr. Bard. I could never quite figure it out. My own life had been so peculiarly free from contact with either birth or death that both these fundamental realities were still mysteriously vague and unreal to me. My interest in the Bards was enhanced by the thought of the tragedy they had experienced. How strange it was to me that they should seem unmarked by calamity. It seemed that anyone who had embraced tragedy so intimately should bear some visible brand of the encounter. I didn't at that time recognize the invisible scars because there were no sackcloth and ashes strewn about the place.

It was time for us to get dressed. The warmth of the late sun bathed Mary's and Betty's bedroom as we peeled off the still slightly damp swim suits and brushed the clinging flecks of sand from our skin. Mary's complete indifference to being naked startled me a little. The girls I had known had always made an awning of their underslip and maneuvered into and out of bathing suits or pajamas beneath the modest covering. But Mary not only scorned such artifices, she deliberately chose to run about washing her face, powdering and combing her hair without any clothes on at all. It was obvious that she thoroughly enjoyed being nude. Her skin, where it had not been touched by the sun, was of a translucent whiteness. "We'll give you a ride to the tea room if you could walk home from there," Mary said as she pulled on her clothes.

Betty and the little girls came straggling up the hill from the lake just as we were all piling into the Franklin. "We can't wait for you," Sidney called. "I know it," Betty shouted back. "We don't want you to. We'll cook some spaghetti here." "Cleve may be here for dinner. If he is, either you or Gammy fix something for him," Sidney called as the car started away from the house. I hadn't seen brother Cleve yet, but I knew he was then about fourteen, a little younger than Betty. It seemed somehow incongruous for there to be a male child in that intensely feminine household.

On the way to town Mary commenced singing in a deep, throaty voice, strained slightly to make it sound like a Negro blues singer, a haunting song that I had never heard before. "Mountain Top Blues", she said it was. "Meet me at Ned Healey's music store on the Avenue tomorrow afternoon and we'll listen to records," she said. "I have to buy 'Mountain Top' and there are some others I want to hear. That's the way I learn to play things on the piano – listening to records and picking up the tunes by ear." "Will you be sure to ask Bob to call me this evening?" Sidney said, as I was leaving. As I walked home there was a comforting quality in the summer twilight and the rustling of the maple trees, content in their June fulsomeness that was somehow akin to the pleasantness that enveloped the Bards and their home.

When the phone rang later that night at the Bards' house, there was the usual race to answer its shrill beckoning. Mary usually got there first. Or else Sidney. This time it was Mary. "Ellaaow," came the voice, being silly British. "It's Bob." "Bob, you haven't been out here for so long." "I've been working pretty hard… no, honest I have." "Hey, Bob, I like your sister," Mary said. "Why?" he said in mild surprise. "Oh, everything I say, she knows what I mean. If I were to say I hated a man because he was the kind that read signboards out loud, I wouldn't have to go on explaining to her. She'd know."

So that is how began the friendship between Mary Bard Jensen and myself, a friendship that has, rather unaccountably, endured for three decades. I have never been much interested in paradoxes, yet Mary is surely a paradox if ever there was one. She is fundamentally so honest, yet with so much deception streaking her nature; at once so conventional and so scoffing at convention; so onto the imbecilities of the social world and so duped by them; so warm and giving in her responses to other human beings about her, yet at times so coldly selfish and cruel.

46

ON THE WAY TO the cabin last weekend we had Jack Webb at the Texaco station tune up the car. He is the only really honest mechanic we have discovered and a most agreeable individual to boot. I walked out to the Hills for lunch while waiting. The great news is Jean's pregnancy. She's about three months along and she and Vic are beside themselves with happiness. They had just about taken it for granted they would be childless because of Jean's operations for ileitis. We are really crossing our fingers for her. A disappointment now would have a serious effect on them, I'm afraid. She has always been so ramrod thin and frail looking but she does look better pregnant. There is lots of the usual joking about the situation: "Always knew we could do it if Vic stopped fooling around and got down to business." And from Vic: "We're going to have lots of kids now that Jean has figured out how," and so on and so on.

We talked about "the lack of law around here" and we agreed it really is like the early frontier days. The marshals are practically helpless, apparently, against criminals, both amateur and professional. According to Vic's and Jean's comments about one marshal, he is a bit of a delinquent himself. No further progress has been made regarding the garbage dump murders, and it's not only the relatives of the man who supposedly shot himself four times with a single shot 22 rifle who are convinced this was not a suicide, as the police have concluded.

From Granite I rode up to the cabin in Tobe's car with him and David Perine. We brought two cars so Kenneth could go down for a dinner at Seattle University. Dave and Tobey got to talking about school at the table during dinner. I always value these conversations about the idiosyncrasies of the teachers and such. Dave said the only straight A's he had were in Biology. "I was a terrible little kid in that class, always asking the bright little questions. The other kids hated me."

Tobe went to bed with his cold right after dinner. Dave and I had a pleasant evening playing some old jazz records from my 1920's and 30's collection. He is a most satisfactory listener to music; very perceptive, too, about styles, what is corny etc. His likes are narrower than mine. Mine are more on the hearty side; David leans toward "modern" jazz. Tobe's are definitely the popular things of the day, which Dave has no use for.

After a while we sat and talked, waiting for Kenneth to return. Dave very chatty and confidential. About his eyes: "Mother had me go to a woman who said she'd cure me with eye exercises and it nearly ruined my sight. Remember, at Robe Ranch, when I had to go stumbling around without glasses, and I had to do these exercises every few minutes? Well, it cost $350, and nearly wrecked me. But that's Mother and her gimmicks. Mother has lots of good qualities, bless her heart, but she does like gimmicks.

I walked alone to Robe Ranch Sunday morning, enjoying a sense of adventure, as large tracks had been made that morning. These tracks, I concluded, were those of a cougar hunting his breakfast and by a man and dog trailing the cougar. Small spots of blood occurred frequently in the dog's tracks, meaning either a hurt foot or a female in heat. The cougar's tracks were almost in a straight line, very deliberately placed, and between them was the line made in the snow by the tail as it dragged. The cat's tracks were wider than the dog's, the toes planted differently. The cat had entered from the highway over the new government road, and Mitzi and I intersected them where the little old road meets the logging road.

We walked the length of the road to the Robe Ranch entrance. The tracks went in toward the ranch. The man and dog, after a slight start into the ranch, had turned back. The cat's tracks, however, went on in and along the lower road at the foot of the old garden space. Then they made a circle into the woods and back, out to the logging road and on up toward Green Mountain. The cat had made his trip just about dawn, following the new fall of snow, but while the older snow was still freezing. The man and dog came a little later and had sunk in farther, the snow having softened up.

I walked on through Robe Ranch and up to the little cabin on the top of the hill, the lookout cabin, as I wanted to check on whether it had been broken into and possibly vandalized. A man's footprints showed that someone had been in and out again recently, possibly another cougar hunter. I felt an aching loneliness inside the little cabin, but also a sense of stepping back into another time, not a long ago time, but the recent past. I had an overwhelming feeling of nostalgia. I took out some of the supplies the Keens left. One mouse, kind of slow and dazed, slithered out of the cupboard and sort of groped its way across the floor, as when you're wakened from a sound sleep and stagger to the telephone. Only a few mice are around our cabin this year, and we don't see them or hear them at night as we have other years.

We have seen fewer tracks this year than in other years. Rabbits seem scarce, as well as the other small animals. Down near the millpond we did see some tracks that were probably a mink or an otter. The skunks are plentiful, however. We still smell traces of the one Mitzi got mixed up with a while back. We hope it has moved out from under the house. I can still see us all clustered about the garbage can, Kenneth about to pull off the lid, so we can see the "cute little gray animal" we didn't think could be a skunk. "Must be a weasel or something…" and our shocked surprise when it proved its identity by spraying strongly as it ran under the house with Mitzi in hot pursuit.

Most exciting, of course, were the wolf tracks we found awhile back on our first snowy week-end. They had apparently been made that morning, as they were very fresh. They were enormous. The old boy had done a thorough frisking of the place from the tool shed to the studio, across the orchard to the house, all around the house, out through the grove past the old outhouse, then down the road to the millpond. Instead of turning off toward Frank's, he kept on going toward Saunier's, then back up the hill and out to the highway. The boys tracked him the whole distance.

Wirt used to talk of hearing wolves in winter and said they were the only wildlife he found scary. When we told Frank about the tracks, he said right away, "That's a wolf. And they're dangerous!" It's interesting that so many of the old pioneers fear wolves more than cougars. The big cats seem to me to be more menacing.

The boys went down to Long Pool with the glint of the illegal hunter in their evil eyes, but the pond was still frozen. They did shoot a golden eye at the millpond, damn it. But it's the only duck of the whole year. They are such funny lawbreakers, and they have worked awfully hard for that one little carcass, through rain, sleet, mud, wet snow, everything. I guess they deserved it in the cosmic scheme of things, if not according to local game laws and my personal wishes.

When we got home from the cabin Sunday night we found a letter informing Kenneth he is one of seven selected to make mural sketches for the rotunda of the Nebraska State Capitol. He will be paid $750 for the sketches. The mural will be made up of panels 15 by 24 feet. Subject matter: works of man, hand, head and heart. It would be a big job, and a great opportunity to display his work on a large scale in something that will last.

As we thought about it, we decided there is no way of separating works of hand, head and heart, and that good and evil play a role in the results of all three. So he is doing the mural on that basis, with the outer edges reflecting the dark aspects of our history, shading into the good represented by a light central panel. I hope the judges are more astute than those that rejected all the finalists for the Olympia Washington Capital Dome project.

I'm just finishing Joseph Krutch's *Measure of Man*, and find it most agreeable, saying many things needing to be said. It is an affirmation of free will, denying convincingly that man is solely an instrument of conditioning. I recall my argument with those anthropologists, the Kings years ago, they insisting there are no innate abilities, no born artists, no born musicians; all individual characteristics are simply the result of environmental factors. I was furious with them, their self-assurance and immature, insensitive attitudes. But they were not to be moved an inch. No such thing, said they, as Latin temperament, no such thing as an innate love of anything, be it music, gardening, cooking, whatever.

I think Krutch is saying in his way what Kenneth has been saying through his painting, but it is far more difficult to convey such ideas through a visual medium. Krutch has reached his conclusions through reasoning and finds the words to reinforce his ideas. Kenneth has tried to portray his convictions through his art. Krutch should be the first to respect this process, but it is one which is being frowned upon by the general run of mainstream artists and teachers today. If, as Krutch states, the "new physics" accepts again the mystery of the universe, and this constitutes a new thinking, then Kenneth has been a most prophetic painter. I think my own fumbling thoughts about the importance of idea painting, the need to build anew on the razed foundations of Cubism, have been validated.

I know neither of us has ever ceased to believe in creativity beyond our understanding, and to have faith in the ultimate wisdom of this guidance, but at times my own faith has been weak and wavery. I tend to become blinded and confused by immediate problems and complexities far more easily than Kenneth. This is what deters me from the books I want so much to write. Actually I should go ahead and write out of my own experience, letting the exasperations enter, as they do into life, for only by such honest, if jumpy work, is any light shed on the nature of reality. The important thing is that each little cell of the whole, which we individuals are, records our reactions from the depths of our own nature and experiences.

47

JANUARY 9, 1955 – Tiger is my constant typing companion. He sits now on my desk, as my lap was too 'slidey,' and watches operations with intense interest. His whiskers are the most enormous I've ever seen on a domestic cat. Kenneth has gone for his walk, and I'm trying to get into a nine to one uninterrupted writing spell, daily. Oh god, what a struggle. With whom am I communicating? I'm sure I don't know, but I feel a connection somehow, somewhere.

We're hoping we can persuade Tobe to be satisfied without a job for one more summer, to just work for us or build his own cabin. He is really not eligible for anything until he's eighteen, but he is thinking about fudging his age and applying to the Forest Service. I would like all of us to do one more pack trip. How sad to think in terms of just one more summer together, but life is a constant breaking off. He said the other day, with a good deal of sadness, that he wouldn't have much more time in his life for pack trips. Soon he'd be in the army and then married and having to work all the time. I remember having the same appalling sensations when I was seventeen.

Now I ask only to be able to do the writing I want to do before it's too late. But still I can't throw out the living. But at this stage one faces a decline in physical energy, which means a jettisoning, and what to jettison? One's friends? Or frequent contact with them? Or trips to the country? No, this is impossible. What I should be able to do by now is to have help with the housework. But this I guess will never be possible, not with Tobe's college education coming up. I would be willing to cut some of our trees, but Kenneth doesn't want a solitary one to go. He has a good housekeeper, so what the hell. It seems to be impossible for me to live without the minimum of cleaning I do.

Yesterday morning the first song sparrow sang from the telephone wire over the alley. The roar of a chainsaw blotted out the song of the bird. The people two doors away are cutting down the three lovely trees on their parking strip. This follows the visit by the man from the engineer's office, leaving abrupt instructions to fix all sidewalks by such and such a date. I called him; he reappeared and said we would not have to do ours (as we had patched a crack in the cement last year to the inspector's satisfaction.) But it is part of a greater campaign to eliminate the big trees from parking strips. I am sure the trees all along the block between Prospect and Highland Drive will now go. For more than half a century these trees have grown, harbored the nests of birds, and given shade and beauty to a street otherwise ugly and dated by dull architecture.

I have just read in the *Saturday Review* a good article about the great new age of energy to be supplied by splitting atoms. There is little said about the danger of radiation, accident, or even more important, values. Why more energy? To produce what? Perhaps it is possible that we are heading for a golden era. But it will never come about until human beings have reckoned with beliefs, standards, morals, and a reverence for life itself, life which includes an infinite range of beautiful flowers, trees, grasses, insects, fish, reptiles, and birds. And how is this feeling, this reverence and understanding, to come about when we seem to see less and less beauty in these things. It is this I would like to get across in the book I want to write. God give me the capacities and the will at least to finish the attempt.

I read over the Russians' proposals on disarmament and to me they seem perfectly fair and feasible. Just to reach that first stage of no more testing would be encouraging. Our nation approaches the coming 'big four' conference like a dog with a spiky tail quivering aloft, stiffly advancing an inch at a time with its nose sniffing suspiciously. It really is just like the behavior of male dogs. Russia is the same.

With the possibility of self-destruction facing man will he succumb? Or will some latent will to survive come to the rescue? Has man simply come to the end of nature's tolerance? As other forms of life have disappeared, is it now his turn to vanish? With the scars man is making on the face of a good life-providing earth, has he now gone too far? This endless extracting of the juice of energy and unleashing it to pollute the air, water and soil – this may be the fatal mistake, the final impertinence.

I am driven to distraction by what I think and feel and what I have loved and hated. What I have loved is being destroyed with bigger and bigger bombs, mad scientists, the military, the moneygrubbers, the machines. It is waiting to grab Tobe, and I can't protect him from it.

It's Sunday evening, and we're just home from the country. Tobey and I walked into the Graces, a place east of our land, and down to the beaver pond beyond the house. It's the roughest going I've done in some time, and I was exhausted by the time we got there. The snow was hip deep in places in the thick woods, and we were always slipping down between blow-down trees, but it is wonderfully secluded and quiet back in there. A strong wild animal smell, almost like a zoo permeated the bank above the pond. It was probably from a bear, wolf, or coyote den nearby. There was snow all around the pond, but I found a mound to sit on where the snow had gone. I emptied my boots of an accumulation of snow as they act like a scoop every time I'd get in deep. My shoes and socks were soaked, but the air warm enough that it didn't matter. There were no fish biting at all, much to Tobe's disappointment.

Later in the day he did get six trout out of the millpond in a pre-season raid, which we don't feel guilty about because the public goes over our driveway to get there now. Last year for the first time they brought in outboard motors and every kind of gear and will again this year when the season opens. That ruins the pond for the kids. The fish tasted really divine for breakfast.

June 27, 1955 – I walked today past Frank's place and the millpond and on down to the entrance of the gorge. Such a jungle I've never seen. I took the glasses and the Audubon bird noise maker, but scared up nothing more than three large fishermen, who looked a bit surprised as they rounded the curve in the road and saw me and Mitzi instead of a thrush.

I picked some of Frank's rhubarb, looked at the noisy river, stared through the glasses at lots of leafy trees, from which issued songs of various birds, but without the visual evidence of same, noted that the raspberries growing on the original Robe town site near the gorge are still holding their own among the dense growth of salmon berries, thimble berries, nettles, snow berries, Indian plum and what have you.

Kenneth is working on the U.N. mural idea, and waiting to hear from the Jackson Hole Lodge about that mural commission. Tobe is three days gone on his first job with the United States Forest Service. His need to have a paying job won out over his desire to have one more free summer.

As he left the second morning, tin hat on head and lunch bucket in hand, Kenneth and I watched him stride to the car, and he looked to me like that young beaver I watched early this spring swimming slowly and persistently upstream until he was out of sight, bent on creating his own world, cut off from the family domicile for the first time. These milestones are hard at the time, but one must keep elastic and tough ("you've gotta be tough").

It seems long ago that we experienced that awful episode of Tobe's adolescence. During that stormy time we all held hands with the mountains, and that was what kept us friends and brought us through. Once we entered the lovely, cedary, firewood-and-ashes smell of the mountain cabin we were on common ground again: hustling kindling, starting fires, filling lamps, connecting the flume to make the water wheel begin turning, unpacking food, putting things in place. Whether the day was blithely sunny, sodden wet, frozen solid or tufted with snow, the chores were much the same. And always before they were done, the boys had disappeared either in the direction of the river, the millpond or Robe Ranch, in quest of whatever the season would allow in the way of a catch.

Kenneth and I were prepared to welcome 'teenagehood' with all its complications, awkwardness, girl trouble, expenses of social life, etc., but we didn't imagine the problems that were to come our way. Thank goodness, they seem to be over.

I have an extensive collection of jazz records dating from the '20's, a good record player, and an ardent willingness to teach Tobey to listen and dance. I had always been a marvelous dancer, but married a man who would rather sit it out with a cannibal than dance with Marilyn Monroe. So, thought I, it's going to be great fun, remembering rather wistfully the few homes that truly welcomed us when I was that age. Roll up the rugs any time, sodas in the refrigerator, cookies on the shelf. It would all be so simple. Give them free access to a good home environment, with a background however little used, of the world's best things – music, books, art – and juvenile delinquency will fade away. I was convinced of this, and actually I still am, but in a more chastened way.

I must record the wonderful early evening experience down at the millpond during Easter vacation. Tobe had been down the evening before, caught a lot of nice trout, and watched the beavers, two of them, that swam out to the raft, then played about in the water in a manner suggesting mating antics. Tobe wanted me to go with him and try to get a photograph of them, should they appear again. I've never been lucky about seeing the beavers down there. It was a quiet, gray afternoon, about five o'clock when we started out, no rain, but everything damp from the long wet winter. We took the short cut through the woods, sploshed through a bit of snow, but found none after we came out onto the clearing. The old hay field is a magical spot; now it's just tough marsh grass and cattails, ringed about with hemlock, spruce and alder. This is where the big bird used to be, the mysterious one we thought might be a California condor. It's very quiet there, very haunted. Then we picked our way silently through the brush between the clearing and the pond, using utmost stealth, because Tobe wanted to see some mallards he was sure would be there. They are such smart birds; it's almost impossible to sneak up on them. This time we did, though and were rewarded by seeing them swim about for a few minutes before they got the news and flew. Several other smaller ducks, black and white, were there. Two of them remained at the lower end of the pond until we poled the raft nearly to them, then they took off, circling about and flying directly over our heads.

The raft was moored against a moss-covered log that was sticking into the pond where we first came out of the trees. Tobe poled it into the smooth water, black as could be and perforated with trout rising. Patches of pale dead cattail rushes were reflected here and there along the shore. The elongated reflections of the bare alders and maples quivered gently on the belly of the pond. Early spring flies touched the waters. No frogs were in evidence, though. Occasionally there was a twittering of birds and once or twice a thrush whistled. But mostly it was silence that possessed the spot. Patches of dark blue sky showed through above and were also reflected in the black mirror of the water.

What a mood! This has been Tobe's haven since he was a very small lad. He loves it, and so do I. I hate to think of the desecration later when the fishing season opens and people bring every manner of craft here, even outboard motors, to raise general bedlam. There used to be lots of yellow lilies but the lily pads have been ruined. I wish we could buy it. It could be another sort of Walden Pond.

48

ILLNESS AND DEATH HAVE been playing a huge role in my life of late. In April my mother was again in hospital, her lungs filling with liquid. She has diabetes, muscular dystrophy and heart trouble, along with a few other complaints. How she manages to keep alive I don't know. She complains a great deal but has done so for many years. This sort of end causes one to wonder about the nature of things and the whys. She wails that perhaps she is being punished for her sins, and this I instinctively repudiate. I would like to have her know the Book of Job, but there would be no use in my introducing her to it, because she has no faith in the things I find helpful. She really doesn't understand me in the least. I sympathize with her for not having the kind of daughter she would have found congenial and simpatico.

The dramatic news of the summer and the thing I still can't adjust to and which haunts me to the point of nightmares, is Betty McDonald's illness. She was in Maynard Hospital for an operation, which proved too late, and Dr. Paul Rollins had to sew her up with ovarian cancer that had spread throughout the area. We went over to Mary's when we were in town, to see her, and stayed to dinner. The Bards are pretty thrown by it but keeping up in the same way, not allowing it to depress them. Betty herself is truly wonderful, and aside from wiping her eyes a few times, completely the same as usual. She is thin and showing the results of the surgery and the bad news, which they had told her only a few days before. Her girls, Allison and Ann came by after shopping, having had lunch and obviously cocktails at Rosselini's. Allison's hysterical laugh was pretty weird, and both of them called to Betty to hurry up with her enema and come out and see their "outfits," which in Allison's case was a terribly Cossacky hat, a dress from Magnin's, and a stole of imitation fur, and in Ann's case, just a stole.

The latter part of the summer we swam every day, first in the small pool by the log jam below the house, later in the main river, and a few times down at the old swimming hole which you can only reach now by walking on the rocks of the river bed. This is the most fun as the current is swift enough to play in and the water has that lovely green color from the overhanging trees on the opposite side. I swam across and stood awhile on the big smooth rocks with their carpet of black and green moss and brilliant small yellow and blue flowers and the soothing untouched quality of a spot where few human beings have been.

This year there are many deer close to the cabin and in the surrounding area, and how I love seeing them as they come into the open to graze or to drink from the river or frolic on the sands of the riverbank. The bear has been coming into our yard and eating green apples, leaving many piles of applesauce and breaking some of the high branches. It must look terribly funny flopping around up in the trees, reaching for apples far out on the limbs.

Our old Tiger cat disappeared just as the December cold spell was coming on, and I suppose has died in some hole under a garage down the alley. I've looked everywhere, but no sign of him. He was sick one night, wouldn't eat his dinner, and shortly afterward disappeared from the back porch. How odd that they know where to hide so they can't possibly be found. I've always had a special fondness for Tiger since the day about five years ago when Tobey rescued him from Edmond Meany Junior High and brought him home to face the challenge of making himself acceptable to two trigger-happy dogs and a coldly hostile cat. He made the grade by keeping at all times a superbly dismissive attitude. After all a kitten which simply faces his oppressors, purring blissfully and refusing on any provocation to run is poor fun, and after days of unsuccessful attempts to glare and pounce him into action the dogs gave up and Tiger was "in". We still have old Daffy, who is now seventeen. Since Tiger has gone he fancies himself the lord of the manor, and his personality has visibly expanded.

The memory of Molly, the black and white spaniel who died the summer of '54 when we were in Europe, is still vivid. She was 13 when she died. She was a strong- willed dog with an ingratiating manner that she exerted mostly by wagging her stump and stamping her front paws and bugging her eyes. Now we have only Mitzi and Daffy, both quite old and decrepit. Mitzi keeps herself denuded biting at fleas or eczema or whatever it is that plagues her skin. She is nearly blind I think, but still thinks she is a baby.

A tiny, frail, golden, almost transparent spider clung to the hard whiteness of our electric range this morning and, as I watched him, dropped a bit of invisible web and hung from it. I thought of the absolutely incomprehensible miracle of life there, like a gift, in the midst of the humdrum and mechanical fetishes among which we spend our days. Once I would have chilled and bristled and squashed it. But through deliberate use of will, I have come to the point where I want to rescue spiders. I transferred him to a piece of paper and escorted him to a safe landing on the dish of agates on the back porch. He scrambled quickly under a stone.

The wet cedar boards of our back fence with Kenneth's horses prancing over them are quite beautiful and luminous in the wetness and mist of this pearly day. The vine maple I transplanted from the cabin is festooned with droplets, silvery beads of water, like transparent pussy willows.

Everything has been happening so fast: the coming trip to Europe with the State Department show, the coming move from our house and the buying of another house in Madrona. But the death of Mabel, of course, was the major upheaval. This was something I had dreaded for so long. I can remember all the phases I have gone through from the days when I refused even to let my mind touch on the idea that someday my parents would die until recently when I knew that death would be a release. For a long time I wouldn't or couldn't believe this understanding could come, though I had heard it said many times.

We went to the ocean at Long Beach for the 1957 New Year's with Glenn Trimble and Ed Dunn, a lovely interlude with warmth, almost balminess in the air. At home New Year's night, I called my parents to say hello and that I would be down to see them the next day. She seemed well then, as well as ever, that is, for she had been failing in memory and enunciation and growing more confused.

The phone awakened us at 5:30 next morning. Don't answer it, said Kenneth, it's a wrong number. But I had to answer it. Dad's voice was choked. "It's Mother," He sobbed, "she's pretty bad." She was at Swedish Hospital, and Kenneth and I dressed hurriedly and drove over. Dad was in the entryway. He sobbed, "she's gone!" and put his head on my shoulder, and it was as though he were the little boy and I the parent.

The intern came in and we sat stricken in the empty lobby. He said, "She was very nauseated at first and having great pain but she lapsed into a coma before she went. The oxygen did no good, her arteries were in such bad shape."

Dad had been awake most of the night. He was exhausted, and I was worried about him. We had a sort of breakfast at our house and I took him home to rest. Brother Bob came over from Idaho, and we went out to the undertaker's that afternoon to arrange things. It was the unreality and strangeness and hollowness of everything that I remember most. I was there in the little business office with its hushed atmosphere and 'padded cell' feeling, talking with the mealy-mouthed man about what sort of words and music and flowers and prices, and yet I wasn't there at all. Bob was solid and imperturbable and it was easy to let him take charge. We agreed about everything, keeping things simple and not getting sentimental or emotional about these details, which seemed so removed from anything rational.

Mother became more of a living presence than she had been for years, and more like herself of younger days. It seemed she was there and understanding everything and trying to help us. But it was terrible to think of her pitifulness and her suffering and her strong, strong will letting go its hold. I had to take clothes to the undertaker for her – stockings, underwear, and a dress. This all seemed so unnecessary and her clothes, folded in her bureau drawer seemed to rebuke me.

The funeral was Friday – Bob's wife, Margaret, and son, Mike, came from Idaho, and Mike stayed overnight here. The funeral was at 11:00 in the morning, and the worst part was waiting in our good clothes for the moment of departure. Waiting again in the little anteroom of the funeral parlor, for we were early, was pretty awful, too. Dad's eyes were so dark with circles; it looked like he had been hit. He made a great effort and didn't break down, for which we were all grateful.

Nancy and Forrest, our cousins, came in first. I stepped out of the anteroom to greet them. "You aren't supposed to go out and speak to people," Bob said in the annoyed way he has with me when he feels I've been unbearably stupid. "They are our cousins," I told him and he felt better. We didn't shut the doors entirely and I saw the people as they came tiptoeing in, the way people do when trying to be reverent. Some of them peered curiously in toward us and others looked straight ahead. The chapel, I will say, was small and simple and the flowers were actually rather lovely. And the words of the Episcopalian service were soothing to hear. I listened intently to all the reading, and the meaning was very clear. If only more men could give such thought to all life's situations instead of only the milestones of birth, marriage, death.

The music of the organ was all right. There was no singing. The coffin was behind a partition. It seemed the most decent way. "Will you come and look at the flowers? There are some very lovely ones," the funeral man said when it was over, but none of us wanted to go and look more closely at the flowers. He gave me the cards and I wrote a note to each person in the days following. None of us wanted to look in the coffin. We were right in this I am sure.

At our house we had lunch with Nancy and Forrest and the family and Mikell Sherman, Tobey's new love who came up to be with him. She is a sweetheart and this made it easier for Tobe. We had drinks and Bob brought food from a delicatessen. Everyone was being rather jovial, or at least making a point of not being despondent. Dad was very controlled, but he had these strange black eyes. I felt sort of pulled apart. It is strange the way the shock affects you. I didn't think it actually was a shock at the time because heaven knows we had been expecting it long enough. But an acute physical exhaustion lasted for weeks.

Finally the mind takes it in and absorbs it and lives with it. There was something in the days following like a sweetness of companionship I sensed, and I knew and understood so many things about her struggles and the things she had wanted and worked for and her disappointments and fears.

I haven't written for months. Ed had another heart attack after Mabel's death. After a spell in a convalescent home, we decided the best solution would be to sell both houses and find one that would accommodate all of us. We found one in Madrona with a separate apartment for dad with a small room and bath for a nurse-caregiver.

We are moved in now to 740 35th Ave., but Kenneth is still fixing up his studio upstairs. Today he is plastering the cracks between the wallboard slabs. Tobey is studying for a plant physiology class, which involves a lot of chemistry and long dull passages that are about as far from the magic of plant life as it would be possible to get. But then, for me the magic is in hiding from everything, at present. I hope it is there for others.

My right shoulder is almost as painful as it was in Frankfurt during the State Department trip. I am working it too hard, perhaps. It is the decisions as to what one cuts out that makes this part of life so difficult. Mitzi has solved it nicely. She has eliminated all but sleeping and eating and following me about. She manages very well with her blindness and her coat is better than it has ever been. I love that little gray dog.

July 31, 1958 – I have a little room in which to type, but I have no time it seems. I am constantly torn by either resentment or guilt or pity or anger and of course the reason at the base of it is that there is love, the tyrant that traps us all and makes us slaves. There is no way but to have Ed live with us, and there is no way to make this feasible except to have this big house, and there is no one to cook and clean but me. Tobey is too busy with studies, and the small amount of amusement they demand at that age. Kenneth does a terrific amount in the yard considering the demands on his time with teaching and writing, and still he keeps painting, which is really a miracle.

Mark Tobey has won the grand prize at the Venice Biennale and has had his picture in Life magazine looking into a window so his reflection makes a dual image and both images are looking thinner, older and less happy than the face we knew in the years before success sprawled across the scene, sending reputations up and human relations down.

Tobe is at the U of W Forestry School experimental forest this summer and Kenneth and I are alone here at the cabin except for weekends and when Mikell stays with us. I am so happy that she and Tobe have found each other and thankful that we all seem to truly like each other and have fun together. She is beautiful and I believe not damned.

She and I climbed the Robe Ranch hill yesterday. Both of us love that place and would like to own it. She seems to feel the same strong pull toward it that I always have.

Kenneth said an old man drove in while we were out walking. He was looking for the site of the Robe Mill, where he worked 45 years ago. He used to put on black face and do an act with Wirt. Wirt had a big cardboard razor that he used to shave him with, removing the black make-up with each stroke. This brought down the house, he said. "Wirt was a great man. They don't make 'em like that no more."

We had one of the better hikes this fall – Neil Meitzler, Kenneth and I – to Mt. Dickerman. Neil bought Susie's old place and is planning a studio in the meadow near the river. The day began with a blurred sun behind a September haze. The temperature was favorable. Hot when climbing but jackety when we sat still. The first three miles over the switchbacks finally ended in the ever-beautiful meadows. The little rills were dried up, but the small pond was still holding water, rimmed by bright, yellow-green rushes. All flowers had gone to seed, but the huckleberries were at their prime. We picked two buckets full, from which I this morning made a batch of jam. We had huckleberry pancakes this a.m., and I still have enough for a pie. This has been a berry summer.

I went to the mountaintop while Neil and Kenneth stopped to draw. At one point in a glade of the gnarly old black hemlock and alpine firs, a large flock of what looked like hermit thrushes gathered about fluttering madly from branch to branch and doing little musical chirps. I've heard them do their lovely mating song, but never seen so many close by before. They seemed to want to stay near to me, and a moment or so later the reason became apparent. A young eagle flew directly toward me, passing about six feet over my head, so that I could look up and see the light coming through his banded wing feathers. He lit on a tree branch not more than eight feet from me and glared down for several minutes while I stared back, fascinated. His beak was strongly hooked and knife thin, his eyes fierce and his tawny chest splashed with dark, elongated spots. He was probably annoyed at me for inadvertently sheltering his prey. He continued to soar just over the meadows the rest of the day, but came that close only one more time, just shortly after the first visitation, when I traveled through a large colony of juncos. They accompanied me down the trail for a small distance.

Kenneth spotted two deer grazing in a meadow at the foot of a rock cliff, and also a mountain goat standing out on a projection of rock in the meadows that I call the Garden of the Gods. As I approached the place on the trail, where the cliff drops sheerly off to the left, I heard a whistle and thought I'd peer over the edge to see what caused it. I accidentally dislodged a rock and, as I watched the valley below, I saw a bushy gray and black animal with a wide tail running hell for breakfast over the meadow directly at the foot of the cliff. He kept scampering until he got to a large gray rock. When he stopped another became visible, also running at top speed toward the rocks. It too stopped when the gray rocks camouflaged it. They waited a few moments, almost invisible, then scampered a short distance further and disappearing into a rockslide. Considerably later, when Kenneth reached the spot, he had the very same experience: first the whistle, then these two animals, which had apparently gone back up to the meadow for grazing. I guess they were marmots.

We have talked a lot about the art situation in general and the museum with Neil, and both Kenneth and I find the museum subject exhausting, irritating and unrewarding. Hope we can keep off the subject now. How fruitless are the rivalries and jealousies. They mean nothing. The important things are effort and inspiration. But it's hard to keep that perspective at times. Old miseries and hurts return to smart all over again.

Tomorrow will mark a week since Father's death. I am slowly coming out of the grief, grief being a little different for each loss apparently - - very black, in this case, lots of regrets and lots of wishes.

I wish I had been able to be gayer, more communicative. He wanted more than anything to have everyone happy and to feel included and useful and wanted. I think for the most part he did feel that, but I could have done more. He knew we all loved him, but sometimes perhaps it could have been a less taken-for-granted love, and more unselfishness would probably have been desirable.

In keeping with our New Year's tradition, we were at Long Beach with Glenn Trimble and Ed Dunn. We left Seattle on the 31st. Father lingered on the porch after I kissed him good-bye. He didn't smile in farewell but seemed to peer at us with more than usual concentration. I shall always wonder if he knew or had some premonition. He had been in excellent spirits and feeling unusually well in the days prior. He had even waltzed with Beth Gottfredson, his caregiver, and visited at length with relatives.

We came home early Sunday the 4th, I assumed Ed would be up and we could tell him about the trip. Glen and Ed came in with us to have a drink before going home. Beth looked greenish in color. She smiled wanly and called Tobey, who appeared from upstairs. "We have bad news for you," he said. "Ed. He's gone." The house sort of reeled. I couldn't believe it. Another attack I could have believed, or more hospital trips. This would have been dismal, but it could have been expected. But the other – there was an element of relief, that it was over for him, and the on-going anxiety was over for all of us. But mostly there was a gaping hole of emptiness. I sat dazed. No tears came. I just sat trying to comprehend.

Waves of grief came later along with tears that just flowed. Then for days came depression and the recurrent sense of loss. The bitter regrets came, too, that we hadn't had more visits ; that I hadn't expressed the love and appreciation I felt so deeply. Kenneth says it was better to let things go along naturally, as we seem to have always been an undemonstrative family.

Dad's sharpness and ability to enjoy life continued until the very end. His definitions of conservative, liberal and reactionary, written for Beth's schoolwork, are definitive. Tom gave me the notes he had made his last day Friday at the law office. He had finished that day a case he had been working on for some time. He spent part of the morning on a ladder fishing down large books and his table was covered with great volumes. Beth said he enjoyed his supper, his drink and the usual chat from 8:30 to 9:00. He didn't take a pain pill, he didn't ring for Beth – he just died in his sleep. Tobe thought he was oversleeping the next morning and went in to investigate about 9 o'clock. He was lying just as though in sleep, with eyes closed. This is so much as he would have had it. I can't help but wonder whether he could have willed it so.

It's strange to have the house so quiet and empty, with only Kenneth and Mitzi and two cats in it. Rather luxurious in a way. Kenneth spends all his time in his studio room, after walking in the morning. If I didn't insist on Great Books meetings I don't know whether we would have any point of contact. This thought probably doesn't even occur to him. Perhaps this is customary in marriages at this stage, but I become very hungry for someone to talk ideas to. He oversimplifies everything – gets no relish out of discussion. Because of course, he gets everything he needs from painting. If I can begin to pour whatever I am into writing, maybe we can have a good partnership.

It does seem to be true that women generally want more social life from middle age on, and men more retirement. Mary has the same problem with Jens, and she finds other women friends on Vashon who are bitter over their shut-in status.

The artist, perhaps, must suffer from loneliness, which triggers the production of art. If true, real art is an attempt to communicate this loneliness. That's why so much of great art carries with it a quality of desperation, even when expressing serenity as in the work of Fra Angelico or Mondrian, for example. On the other hand our friend Millie Cummings said not to let Kenneth climb back into the womb, which is something men want very much to do, as they get older.

We discussed Voltaire at Great Books. Kenneth loves him because he oversimplifies the basics and is entertaining. He offers wonderful examples of the absurdities and extremes of human behavior. But his recommendations won't solve today's problems. The world continues to accelerate the pace of its follies with the resultant dire potentials.

I wonder whether it would ever be possible for men to live a planned existence, with populations regulated more or less by what the earth can support for a good life, by which I mean a life without violence, hunger, poverty and greed, a life where it is possible to get in touch with nature in her unspoiled beauty. It would be possible to have pure water, pure air, contact with the heritage of our past and a respect for the noble ideas of the human mind. I see no reason why, with populations kept at a decent figure, this couldn't be accomplished. It would call for a certain amount of self-denial, but this could be an enlightened self-denial. Religion would be defined in part by a reverence for life, but with tolerance for the mystical when felt sincerely. I suppose the profit system, ungoverned as it now is, wouldn't fit into this picture. Maybe human nature doesn't fit into it, I don't know. But, it seems to me, it has to be something like the above scenario or eventual annihilation.

49

DECEMBER 9, 1959 – Tobe and Mike seem very happy in the first year of married life, with Mike working for the welfare department and Tobe studying conscientiously and seeming to be more interested in what he's studying than previously. He has had a communication from the Yale Forestry School dean, following an interview, favoring Tobe's taking postgraduate work there. This I would love – it would be the sort of experience that would or could make a world of difference in their future. Tobe is going to need the sort of forestry work that will make sense to his conservationist nature. It probably won't happen until the fall of 1961 and there is always the draft and other potential hurdles offered by life that could interfere.

We are sort of trapped by this place, Kenneth willingly, I half willingly and half 'protestingly.' But what a hold it has on us! I rebel against the primitive living, yet after a few days in town I long for it.

Spring 1960 – Tobey brought home a baby bear with a broken leg about three weeks ago. He found it on a mountainside near Olympia where he was doing forestry school fieldwork. It was caught in the crotch of a tree branch, hanging by one leg and complaining loudly, apparently abandoned by its mother who in her efforts to free him had broken the imprisoned leg. Tobe took him to a vet to get the leg set and brought him home on the weekend, an adorable little black fellow about the size of a large teddy bear, still groggy from the anaesthetic with his lower leg in a metal splint.

We bedded him down in a packing crate in the spare bedroom and unsuccessfully coaxed him to eat warm milk and honey. After other futile experiments we tried applesauce, which he loved and lapped up greedily. Kenneth and I brought him to the cabin after a few days, packing box and all, and ensconced him in Kenneth's studio. We continued a diet of warm milk and applesauce, adding after the first few days Pablum to the mix. He was very messy and his box needed cleaning daily. We kept him supplied at night and during cold days with two hot water bottles, the filling of which added to the list of chores. A baby would have been no more trouble, and I don't think could have worried me more.

Our leaving him outside overnight in the new pen Kenneth built brought about a disastrous ending.. He escaped through an opening where the chicken wire overlapped on the roof of the pen. He tried furiously to break out when we first put him in, but after watching his lack of success and apparent resignation, we thought the cage secure. He ate his usual before bedtime supper, and seemed settled for the night in his little, shake-covered house, his head resting in the doorway and his small, beady eyes peering at us with no more than the usual resentment. He licked my hand when I offered it to him but my hunch was right – for I argued with Kenneth that he should not be left out overnight. He, however, was convinced it was better for him to get used to being outside, that he would be perfectly dry and comfortable in the little house. I suspect the morning's ordeal of washing the blankets from the packing box helped to convince him it was time for a change. Anyway, I went out in the morning with food only to find an empty pen, and no traces as to which direction he had gone.

We searched every inch of the surrounding country for days, but found no sign of the refugee. He may return if he gets hungry, but we have begun to give up. We hope he has been able to chew the tape from the splint and free his leg. And we hope the leg has healed and that he solved the problem of living in the wild, either by himself, or less likely, with some hospitable mother bear.

"He'll come back when he gets hungry," we were told by the old timers in the valley. "He'll be back when he gets bigger and will take your place apart looking for food." We learned recently that a highways employee saw a limping bear cub crossing the road in the direction of Robe Ranch and Green Mountain about the time he escaped.

It has been months since we had the little bear, but something happened that brought him to mind. I was walking along the Green Mountain road when a car coming my way stopped with a screech of brakes and three men all with guns jumped out. They leveled their guns into the trees and I shouted for them to stop. "This is our land," I said, hurrying toward them, "and we don't want it hunted."

They looked so furious I expected to see them level their rifles at me. Two of them lowered their guns, the third kept his aimed into the forest. "There's a bear in there. We just saw him take off. We could get him easy." They were excited, belligerent. "Besides, lady," said one, "if you don't want your property hunted you should post it."

"We had posted it, but the signs were knocked down," I said. This was true. Only then did I notice that over the hood of the car was draped a large dead and gutted carcass of a black bear. I stood there hating them, and they stood there hating me. Then, reluctantly, they got back into their car and roared away. I still choose to believe it was our little bear's life I saved that day.

Johnny ViVier was taken to hospital in Arlington about two weeks ago and the fears I had felt about the possibility of cancer were verified in a no-go operation. He died a few days ago, and Susie is now alone in the world again, more alone than ever before, as her mother is gone, too. She sits stolidly in her rocker; restlessly moving her arms on which the fat has gathered in such a way as to look almost like another arm. Each fatty accumulation forms a sort of appendage, which hangs from the bone and muscle of the arm. I think she gains weight when she is unhappy. Already she looks heavier than before Johnny's illness.

They were married for six years, and he said when they took him to the hospital they were the happiest years of his life. We had misgivings when she married him, as he was drinking heavily, and we thought it likely the worst could happen. Actually their marriage was perfect for both of them and is another of those curious arrangements life brings about, completely out of the blue. They were grandparents, she with her incongruously fat legs, and he with his lack of education, his health slipping and a history of alcoholism. But it turned into a beautiful human relationship surviving six of those long, wet, cold winters in their tiny cottage. It was of course her adamant faith that pulled both of them along. Always there, her faith, was like the mountain across the river, now snow covered, now bare rock. Sometimes stark and clear of outline; other times draped in mist and clouds, only to emerge again. Well, this may be overdoing Susie's Christian Science religion, but when I think of what it takes for a human being to live either alone or with another through the long days and nights of the mountain winters, I think it takes a tough philosophy to avoid complete disintegration. With Susie and Johnny there seemed to be no disintegration, mentally or emotionally.

I stopped in to see her and to buy some eggs. She gave us the handmade cowbell that the black cow wore on the long walk from Lewiston Idaho in 1907. The family was in a covered wagon. They had two cows and a horse and the four draught horses that pulled the wagon. She was born in Kansas – from there the family went to Texas, then to Colorado, then to Lewiston and finally to this valley. So now we have her mother's old rocking chair that came in the wagon, a chamber pot also via covered wagon and next week the smokehouse, the plough and the seeder. After receiving these honors I guess we'll have to remain in the valley and establish a little memorial museum to Susie's family.

On a beautiful clear evening we went to Gordon Creek to see a patch of forest that Tobey wanted to show us before it is logged. We followed new tractor tracks into an old woods that contained Douglas firs ten feet in diameter and enormous spruce. It's just a small area next to Gordon Creek and it should be preserved. Except for some of the big cedars remaining on Pilchuck, these are the only trees of this size in this part of the Cascades, possibly any part. The trees are so huge the underbrush is almost eliminated. Only deer fern and puppy-wood dot the moss of the forest floor. It was pure magic with thrushes singing and frogs croacking. I suppose the bad little boy mind-set that now seems to run things in this country can't feel veneration for anything like this forest. It's an inescapable feeling for me and Tobey feels it too.

The Seattle Symphony season opened October 17th with Benny Goodman as the guest artist. Kate Sherman, Mikell's mother, and I both elected to go to this one (the Shermans are sharing season tickets with us) and, as Kenneth's back was bothering him, the arrangement was fine with him. We met at the Camlin for dinner. The waiter overheard us mention the concert and asked if it was the Benny Goodman concert we were going to. "Yes" we said. Nodding to a nearby table he said, "He's eating dinner over there all alone." I craned my neck to look back at the table, and sure enough there sat a conservatively dressed man without glasses (probably so people wouldn't recognize him). I began a great struggle with myself to work up the gall to walk over to that table and say something, anything, even just to babble about getting an autograph, just to tell him how much, through all these years, his music had meant to me. And it would be something to tell Tobe about; because Tobe feels the same way I do about him.

Feeling utterly ridiculous, I summoned all my courage, and said my piece with a shaky voice, concluding lamely with a request for his autograph on my ticket. He reached in his pocket and said, "I haven't got a pencil." "I'll get one," I said, and sailed back to our table, couldn't find mine, finally got Kate's, and returned. I guess he must have asked me to sit down, because I did, and he said, "You said you came to town for the concert. Where do you live?" I told him, and he said, "Any fish in that river?" There had begun to be a warm, sort of twinkly and kindly look in his eyes, which are small and set rather deeply, so that you can't read the expression in them immediately. "I'd kind of like to catch a fish," he said. "A steelhead. Do you have steelhead?" "Hey," I said, "could you really take the time? We could take you up there tomorrow morning and bring you back whenever you say." I told him my son sometimes caught trout in the river. I had mentioned my husband being an artist, and he asked his name. "What sort of paintings does he do?" "He has a sort of personal style." I muttered. "Oh." He asked about galleries and said casually, "I have a few paintings," and added, "Well, I'd really like to get out. I tell you what, you call me about 8:30 or 9 o'clock in the morning. We'll see how it is then."

The concert had been arranged to open with a Berlioz, then Goodman's two numbers, concluding with the " New World Symphony". The director, Milton Katims, announced a change in the program, the Goodman things (a Weber and a Copeland) to come after the intermission. "Oh yes," he had said at the table, "we're going to have a little jam session after the concert. There's a fellow plays piano at that little place across from the theatre…" I had thought he meant the session would be in that place, maybe the Door or the Viceroy, and we were planning to try to locate it. But the session following the concert was on the stage, with piano, bass, drums and Goodman. It was very exciting and the audience was receptive to the point of foot stomping and whistling. The drummer got carried away and hogged the session, and Goodman was very courteous, a couple of times lifting the clarinet to play, assuming the drummer would retire, but the drummer was not about to give up the spotlight. It was annoying. The stupid *Seattle P.I.* said the next morning that the drummer was so good he nearly stole the show from Goodman. If he stole it, it was news to everybody that cared anything about Goodman.

Benny Goodman did go with us the next day, fished in the Stillaguamish unsuccessfully, and listened to himself on 78 vinyl records on our windup Victrola. At one point there was Benny Goodman, stretched out on Kenneth's hard bed in the cabin, arms behind his head listening to *After You've Gone, Sweet Sue, Sugar,* and other 78 records from the 30's. "You know," he said, "everyone is so worried about having the latest hi-fi equipment they forget to listen to the music. This sounds great." He created a small commotion when he walked into the Corner Tavern in Granite to get a fishing license.

When we got back to Seattle he invited us to come to Tacoma as his guests for his concert there. Our good friends Curt and Eve Green went with us, and Benny insisted we all accompany him to an obligatory cocktail party held in his honor. When I saw how adept he was at fending off his adoring public, I felt especially honored that he had allowed us in. He kept us all in stitches on the ride back to Seattle with tales from the evening's frivolities.

I think we have become real friends and I strongly suspect we will be taking him up on his invitation to visit at his home in Stanford, Connecticut when we are at Skowhegan for Kenneth's teaching job this summer.

April 19, 1961 – It is about 5 o'clock, and Tobe has just come in with the truck from his falling operations. Our tree farm is at last being tree farmed, in hopes Tobey will make enough out of it to help with his expenses at Yale next year. He had made a beautiful start at thinning the stand of hemlock on the east 40. The idea is to free the trees which are being held back, open the crown, hasten the growth and increase the value of the whole thing. We are for it completely and are more than willing to help any way we can, which has meant for Kenneth hours of work on the scene of action and, for both of us, financial aid.

Tobey looks like a born gyppo logger. His hair needs cutting. His clothes and boots are muddy. His hands black and a stubble over the cheeks and chin complete the picture. He and Mike are experiencing all the hard work of pioneer days, she with the baby, Sean, and only a wood stove and kerosene lamps. They use the spring for an icebox and the fireplace for heat. They like it though, I think, and are happy.

I'm about ready to settle for something plushier, like central heating and electricity, and to give up the country-city divided type of life. It takes too much just to keep up the necessities. The expense in both money and time are just too much. But I've been saying this for two years now, and we don't seem any closer to a settlement. Now I guess we'll wait another year until Tobey is out of Yale. Then the river question should be settled too; that is, what the country is going to do about saving the road from the encroaching river. We are purely incidental and would wash downstream in short order if they weren't going to have to do something about saving the Mountain Loop Highway. Whatever they do in that regard should give us protection, too.

Leonard stopped in one day last week, just for a visit apparently, but probably in hopes Tobey will be ready soon to take on a partner. He was telling us what a talented artist a seventeen-year-old neighbor girl is. He said she had made a painting of "an old 'abandent' wreck of a house, just like yours, only worse than yours – and it's sure good." Mike and Tobe and I bit our lips and carefully didn't look at each other, in order to keep from laughing.

June 16, 1961 – Thought last night between sleeping and waking of a possible solution for the valley book. I would write it with no one viewpoint, but rather a series of episodes tied together by the central theme of the valley with a strong sense of nature as the binding ingredient.

There would be a description of the great upheavals and cosmic thrashing about, followed by talk of the glaciers, the great melting, the lakes, the rivers beginning to flow, the great avalanches and rock slides, and the coming of the trees. The lives of the native Indians, sort of pre-dawn and misty, would play a part. Then the sharp introduction of modern times in the form of the pioneers, beginning with the blazing of the first trail, then the Robe family and the homesteading story with

Wirt introduced. Next would come the other settlers and happenings: the Ottos, the Bakers including Susie, the mining boom, the railroad, and the mills. Then the great financial crash, the Depression and then quiet again, after tumultuous floods and the destruction of the railroad. The small trees begin growing again, as they did in the beginning. Next would come the exodus, and the few who stayed on.

The valley slowly develops its magic and the artist comes to discover it. There is an interval of no activity during the war, other than an occasional Model-A chugging along the gravel roads. But this foreshadows still another era, which crashes into the forefront with the end of war, the coming of the bomb, the return of mobility, the beginning of tree cutting in the National Forest.

Animal episodes would include the finding of the young deer by the adolescent, the boys and their fishing, the frogs, the eagles and their young at Robe Ranch, the nighthawks, the scream of the cougar that day in the swamp, the whole bird thing, the waxwings taking strings from the garden for their nests, the violet green swallows teaching their young to fly, the varied thrushes, the olive backs, the tanagers, the flycatchers.

The weaving of it into some kind of meaningful pattern is the crux, of course, and always has been. But maybe I should just go ahead and do it, and then get at the pattern. Some of my former stuff could be used, but the ordeal of digging it out is staggering.

(Soon after the above journal entry, Margaret developed severe abdominal pain. Subsequent investigation led to a diagnosis of cancer. An exploratory operation revealed extensive involvement and she was given only weeks to live. At first she dealt with it as just another illness, trying not to lose hope. The following nearly unreadable comments were scrawled in a small notebook - BTC.)

Animal bodies help to create antibodies when you are in bed with the miseries and the world lonely – peopled only with 'I'm afraids' and 'what ifs' and all the other undesirables. There is sanity and comfort and unfretful warmth in an animal body crowding you out of your space, breathing against your legs or even sticking its cold wet nose right in your face.

The doctor is a voice at the other end of the wire – when the voice has spoken someone goes to the neighborhood pharmacy for the bottles and boxes of mysteries the voice has summoned to appear.

Being sick in winter is one thing – not altogether bad. But being sick in summer is like finding an oasis in a desert, only to discover that your mouth won't open.

I must write. I would still love to do a children's book on Tobey and Dave and the place in the mountains – Oh, I hope I will.

Gyppo is on my bed. Fortunately it is too warm for even Gyppo to be on me tonight. He sleeps with his front legs sprawled apart and his little white nose in between. He has selected a magazine – the *Atlantic Monthly* – to lie upon because it is cooler than the wool of the blanket.

A sort of miracle happened the night the sickness broke and I began to sweat and also to breathe. I prayed all night to the rhythm of my heart's pounding and there came a light like the little star on top of a Christmas tree, which said love was everything. It was the first time I had felt my own consciousness seared with these familiar yet unknown words. Do you love a lady like Mrs. Schnieder who called the dog pound to complain about Moses who never goes near her yard and who is loved universally in the neighborhood at least by all citizens up to the age of eleven? Yes, you even love a lady like Mrs. Schnieder who lives alone with no animal and votes for the dog leash law and against the school bonds. But you love her for her fears and loneliness and not the way they make her act.

Moses of the broad and candid brow, the gentle panting mouth, the steady brown eyes, rolling a bit on their white, white whites. But most of all Moses of the great tail – the plume all curled and coifed and reaching a length equal to the rest of his body – which with one sweep can wipe a tea table clean or topple a vase of flowers or wag a message of undying love and faithfulness.

I haven't got any guts. I can with one whiff of imagination turn my belly into goo and my heart into a maelstrom. The cries of children playing toss-about on the summer evening like toy boats on a breezy pond.

The writer who hurries to read what he has written is like the chicken who lays an egg only to peck it open and devour the inside.

(Margaret wrote nothing more except the following, which she penned in a faint scrawl on September 21. She died September 23, 1961 – BTC.)

Thoughts while dying…

Dislike hurting but so far feel no fear of the end, only a tranquility and welcoming. Big thoughts tend to melt into obscurity – the little day-to-days become huge, solving problems of growing weakness.

I need a routine even bedridden, so I make an arbitrary one.

Have I a soul? As the end comes nearer this question remains clouded. I am perfectly willing to settle for anything from complete oblivion eternally to something the equivalent of or better than what we have here – impossible for me to believe in the orthodox idea of Heaven and Hell.

I find the first four pages of John beautiful and sensible. The 23rd Psalm is (especially the part about the "table before thine enemies") helpful during wakeful nights. I've always loved the poetry of it, and there is a solace.

Important things in memory are the very simple and the sublime – walks with Kenneth, affection for pets, and the satisfaction of gardening…

Epilogue

MARGARET WAS CREMATED, AS was her wish, and we kept the urn containing her ashes in the Callahan cabin. One spring weekend in 1963, while my father was in Germany, Mikell and I invited two couples from Seattle to accompany us to the country. On Sunday morning, after washing the breakfast dishes, we took a drive up the valley to Barlow Pass. At the last minute, we decided to leave Moses behind to allow for more room in the car. The kitchen stove was cooling, but the cabin was warm enough for the dog.

I had just verified my upcoming job as a fire guard at Barlow and was interested in checking out the station and lookout. Coincidentally, Kenneth was the first Forest Service employee at that guard station after its construction in 1944. As it turned out, I was to be the last, as the station and lookout were intentionally burned by the U.S.F.S. on the grounds that the buildings were fire hazards.

Our group returned that afternoon to a horrifying scene. Our cabin was totally engulfed in flames. A neighbor, the only person present, had been unable to save anything, including Moses. After the initial shock, we realized that the best course was to let the fire burn as cleanly as possible. By evening, nothing remained in the smoking ruins but twisted metal, melted glass and the rock chimney. The hand-built cabin, the paintings, the books, the 78 records and so much more, were gone. Gone too was the urn containing Margaret's ashes.

I wired Kenneth the grim news. His initial reaction was to plan for another house and studio. Upon his return from Europe, however, one visit to the sad site changed his mind. He decided that the fire clearly symbolized the end of an era. After remarrying in 1964 he bought a place on the Long Beach peninsula near the oceanfront hotel where he and Margaret had spent their New Year's eves in recent years. The move was accompanied by a distinct change in his painting style. The natural world – the vital source that so infused his art – continued to be present, but his inspiration shifted from the mountains to the ocean.

Soon after the fire, I collected a small jar of ashes from the ruins of the cabin. I scattered some at Robe Ranch. I kept the rest for a long time before sprinkling them at the wilderness ranch where Mikell and I lived in northern British Columbia, a place Margaret would have loved.

B.T.C.

In 1971, Mikell and I built this barn on the foundation of the fire-destroyed cabin. Soon after its completion, Kenneth asked if he could paint on the end of the barn. Although he didn't express it in words, perhaps the resulting mural was a memorial to Margaret.

A Memory

THE FOLLOWING EXCERPT FROM an unsolicited letter
I received in 2005 from my old friend Dave Perine describes so clearly
the effect Margaret had on the people who knew and loved her.

"…I'm delighted to hear that you are doing a chronicle of the
journals of my Guru! If there was ever a Renaissance woman worthy of
the name, Margaret is it. You said she reminisces in her writings about
listening to music with me. As far as music is concerned, if Margaret
said it was good, then it was good enough for me. She loved trumpet
and cornet players, and I learned from her about Louis, Bix, Tommy
Ladnier, Muggsy Spanier, etc. I can still hear some of the old records
in what's left of my mind. She also introduced me to Bebop (Jazz at the
Philharmonic, the Groove Juice Special"). In the 40's and 50's. Bebop
was really avante-garde jazz, and Margaret was right there. I think her
heart was really with Benny Goodman and Count Basie, but she would
be up on all the "new" music. I can't imagine what my life would have
been like without her influence. I can't think of anyone else who could
talk us into eating cattail roots and make us like them as well. I used
to love watching her talk people into leaping into the South Fork at
the swimming hole, and watching them jump out again without even
touching the bottom because it was so cold. She created a wonderful
childhood for both of us. She let us do stupid stuff – like the ill-fated
diving helmet experiment in the river – even though she probably
thought it was dangerous. We were allowed to try things the kids don't

do much of today. I remember her teaching us about conservation. The time we caught 63 cutthroat trout out of the beaver ponds below Robe Ranch? (You caught 32, I caught 31 – oh the competition.) We then spent the next 3 days eating trout for breakfast, lunch and dinner. It definitely made me consider catch and release ever afterward. She would never have allowed us to throw them away. I know she wasn't thrilled with the time we shot the bear, but we ate the whole damn thing, even though each bite got bigger as we chewed it. I think she did all the right things to make us responsible human beings, and especially to be in tune with our environment. I hope when your children and theirs read her work, her ethic and her spirit will show through. She was always damn straight; I could look my mother in the eye and lie to her, but if I tried the same thing with Margaret, my goose was cooked. She had and still has my utmost admiration."

Acknowledgments

MY DEEP APPRECIATION TO all the friends who have encouraged me and helped bring this project to life. Special thanks to Mikell, Claire, Keith, Crystal, Corrine, Jean, David P. David M., Neil, Deirdre, and Rae.

Brief Identifications of Art World Personalities in the Order They Appear in the Book

Bill Cumming: youngest "old master" of the Northwest School.

Mark Tobey: senior member of the Northwest School. Winner of first prize at the Venice Biennale in 1958.

Tom Toomey: worked for Dr. Richard Fuller at the Seattle Art Institute.

Rufino Tomayo: a Zapotecan Indian from Oaxaca. Now one of the best-known Latin American artists. Died in 1955.

Maria Izquierdo: an art student who lived with Tamayo as a wife in the 1930s. Known today for her folk art .

Martha Graham: American dancer and choreographer regarded as one of the foremost pioneers of modern dance. She died in 1991 at age 97.

Diego Rivera: Preeminent Mexican painter and muralist. Married to Frieda Kahlo, who is now recognized as a very important Mexican painter.

Juan O'Gorman: best known as one of the first "modern" architects. He designed and built a house and studio for Rivera and Kahlo in 1931-32 Also a muralist.

C.S. Price: moved to Portland in 1929 from California. His paintings of landscapes and animals bordered on abstract. expressionism.

Barney Nestor: a somewhat successful portrait painter.He and wife, Marge, were active in leftist politics.

Charles Heaney: Portland watercolorist and printmaker.

Louis Bunce: helped establish modern art in Portland. Has been called an artistic genius. Died in 1983.

Earl Field: modestly successful painter. worked many years with Callahan at the Seattle Art Museum. A long time close friend of the Callahans.

Kamekichi Tokita: perhaps the most successful of a group of young Seattle Japanese Artists in the 1920s and 1930s. He was a member of the Group of Twelve, as were Callahan and Nomura.

Takuichi Fujii and Kenjiro Nomura: two other young Japanese painter friends of the Callahans.

Malcolm Roberts: surrealist landscape painter and printmaker.

George Mantor: accomplished photographer and classical music lover. Influenced Mary Randlett, a well-known Washington state photographer.

Morris Graves: usually ranked number two of the top four Northwest Masters. Died in 2001.

Guy Anderson: one of the four "Northwest Mystic" painters featured in a 1953 Life Magazine article. His middle and later works were strongly influenced by Northwest Native art.

Viola Patterson: painter and friend of the Callahans over many years.

Ted Abrams: lived in a hand built cabin in West Seattle on a lot next door to his friend, Ivar Haglund. He was a restaurateur and collector of art, writings, and antiques. He lost his nest egg in the crash of 1929 but remained a friend and supporter of the artists in the Callahan circle.

Margaret Camfferman: and her husband, Peter, were moderately successful landscape and still life modernists. She died in 1964.

Ambrose Patterson: established the University of Washington School of Painting and Design. He married one of his students, Viola, in 1922. He died in 1966.

Richard Bennett: a writer and illustrator of children's books including Jim Stevens' Paul Bunyon stories.

Leuben Petric: a modest artistic talent connected romantically in the 1930s with Morris Graves' sister, Celia. He was a good friend of Bill Cumming.

Bill and Celia Graves Leary: Celia married Bill at the start of WWII. They remained friends of the Callahans for many years and visited them at Robe on a number of occasions.

Emily McIntyre: a minor painter in Seattle during the 1930s and 1940s.

Louise Gilbert: an accomplished figure and cityscape painter and good friend of Emily. She died in 1987.

Walter Isaacs: early director of the University of Washington School of Art and Design. He was a recognized figure and portrait painter.

Neil Meitzler: a well-known northwest figurative and abstract painter. He studied with Callahan, Graves, and others. He spent considerable time in the Robe Valley in the late 50s and early 60s and was a good friend of the Callahans.